lonely pl[anet]

USA

TOP SIGHTS, AUTHENTIC EXPERIENCES

D0711528

Karla Zimmerman,
Kate Armstrong, Amy C Balfour, Robert Balkovich, Ray
Bartlett, Andrew Bender, Alison Bing, Cristian Bonetto,
Gregor Clark, Bridget Gleeson, Michael Grosberg, Mark
Johanson, Adam Karlin, Ali Lemer, Hugh McNaughtan, Becky
Ohlsen, Regis St Louis, John A Vlahides, Benedict Walker

Contents

Plan Your Trip

▼

USA's Top 12 4
Need to Know 16
Hot Spots for... 18

▼

Local Life 20
Month by Month 22
Get Inspired 25

▼

Itineraries 26
Family Travel 32

New York City   34

at a Glance...   36
Central Park 38
Statue of Liberty
& Ellis Island 42
Museum of
Modern Art 46
High Line 48
Broadway 52
National September 11
Memorial & Museum.. 56
Empire State
Building 58
Sights 62
Activities 70
Tours 70
Shopping 71
Eating 75
Drinking & Nightlife 81
Entertainment 84
Information 86
Getting There
& Around 86
Where to Stay 87

Washington, DC 88

at a Glance...   90
National Mall 92
Capitol Hill 98
Sights 100
Tours 105
Shopping 105
Eating 106

Drinking & Nightlife.... 112
Entertainment 116
Information 116
Getting There
& Around 117

Chicago   118

at a Glance...   120
Millennium Park 122
Art Institute
of Chicago 124
Wrigley Field 126
Sights 130
Activities 135
Tours 136
Shopping 136
Eating 137
Drinking & Nightlife.... 139
Entertainment 141
Information 143
Getting There
& Around 143

Miami   144

at a Glance...   146
Art Deco Historic
District 148
Key Biscayne 152
Sights 154
Activities 160
Tours 160
Shopping 161
Eating 162

Drinking & Nightlife... 167
Entertainment 168
Information 169
Getting There
& Away 169
Getting Around 170

Orlando & Walt
Disney World®
Resort   176

at a Glance...   178
Walt Disney
World® Resort 180
Universal Orlando
Resort 186
Orlando 192
Winter Park 196

New Orleans   198

at a Glance...   200
Mardi Gras 202
St Charles
Avenue Streetcar ... 206
Sights 208
Tours 212
Shopping 212
Eating 213
Drinking & Nightlife....216
Entertainment 216
Information 217
Getting There
& Around 217

Austin	**218**
at a Glance...	220
Congress Avenue Bridge Bat Colony	**222**
Bob Bullock Texas State History Museum	**224**
Sights	228
Activities	229
Tours	229
Shopping	231
Eating	232
Drinking & Nightlife	235
Entertainment	236
Information	237
Getting There & Around	237

Las Vegas	**238**
at a Glance...	240
Cruising the Strip	**242**
Vegas Shows	**246**
Sights & Activities	248
Eating	249
Drinking & Nightlife	250

Entertainment	251
Information	251
Getting There & Around	251

Grand Canyon National Park	**252**
at a Glance...	254
South Rim Overlooks	**256**
South Rim	258
North Rim	260
Flagstaff	262

Los Angeles	**264**
at a Glance...	266
Santa Monica Pier	**268**
Hollywood	**270**
Griffith Park	**274**
Sights	278
Eating	281
Drinking & Nightlife	285
Entertainment	286
Information	287
Getting There & Away	287
Getting Around	287

San Francisco	**288**
at a Glance...	290
Golden Gate Bridge	**292**
Historic Cable Cars	**294**
Alcatraz	**296**
Ferry Building	**300**
Chinatown	**302**
Sights	306
Eating	312
Drinking & Nightlife	315
Entertainment	318
Information	319
Getting There & Away	319
Getting Around	319

Yosemite National Park	**320**
at a Glance...	322
Glacier Point	**324**
Half Dome	**326**
Yosemite Valley Waterfalls	**328**
Groveland	333
Mariposa	334

In Focus	**336**
USA Today	338
History	340
Food & Drink	350
Sports	354
Arts & Culture	357

Survival Guide	**360**
Directory A–Z	361
Transportation	371
Index	377
Symbols & Map Key	382

Maggie Daley Park (p131), Chicago
F11PHOTO / SHUTTERSTOCK ©

USA's Top 12

LUCIANO MORTULA / SHUTTERSTOCK ©

New York City

The USA's dynamic mega city

Home to striving artists, hedge-fund moguls and immigrants from every corner of the globe, New York City (p34) is constantly re-inventing itself. A staggering number of museums, parks and ethnic neighborhoods are scattered through the five boroughs. Do as locals do and hit the streets. Every block reflects the character and history of this dizzying kaleidoscope, and on even a short walk you can cross continents. Left: Times Square (p67); Right: High Line (p48)

Date: 8/23/18

917.3 DIS 2018
Discover USA : top sights,
authentic experiences /

MATT MUNRO / LONELY PLANET ©

Grand Canyon National Park

Jaw-dropping, red-rock chasm

The sheer immensity of the Grand Canyon (p252) is what grabs you at first – a two-billion-year-old rip across the landscape that reveals the earth's geologic secrets with commanding authority. But it's Mother Nature's artistic touches, from sun-dappled ridges and crimson buttes to lush oases and a ribbon-like river, that hold your attention and demand your return. To explore the canyon, take your pick of adventures: hiking, biking, rafting or mule riding.

ANTON_IVANOV / SHUTTERSTOCK ©

Washington, DC

The nation's monument-laden capital

No matter what your politics, it's hard to not fall for the nation's capital (p88). A buzz percolates among the city's grand boulevards, iconic monuments and power-broking buildings. There's no better place for exploring American history, whether tracing your hand along the Vietnam Veterans Memorial, checking out the parchment-scrawled Constitution at the National Archives, or gaping at Abe Lincoln's hat at the Smithsonian Institution. Kennedy Center (p116)

New Orleans

Southern charmer where the good times roll

Caribbean-colonial architecture, Creole cuisine and a riotous air of celebration beckon in New Orleans (p198). Nights are spent catching Dixieland jazz, blues and rock amid bouncing live-music joints, and the city's annual festivals (such as Mardi Gras) are famous the world over. The Big Easy is also a food-loving town that celebrates its myriad culinary influences. Feast on lip-smacking jambalaya (pictured), soft-shelled crab and Louisiana *cochon* (pulled pork) before hitting the good-time bar scene.

San Francisco

Hilly beauty with a beatnik soul

Change is afoot in this boom-and-bust city (p288), currently enjoying a very high-profile boom. Amid the fog and the clatter of old-fashioned trams, San Francisco's diverse neighborhoods invite long days of wandering, with fabulous restaurants and bohemian nightlife. Highlights include exploring Alcatraz, strolling the Golden Gate, and taking at least one ride on the cable car. How cool is San Francisco? Trust us – crest that hill to your first stunning waterfront view, and you'll be hooked. Lombard Street (p307)

Yosemite National Park

Gorgeous landscape of peaks and waterfalls

Meander through wildflower-strewn meadows in valleys carved by rivers and glaciers, the hard, endless work of which makes everything look simply colossal. Here in Yosemite (p320), thunderous waterfalls tumble over sheer cliffs, ant-sized climbers scale the enormous granite domes of El Capitan (pictured) and Half Dome, and hikers walk beneath ancient groves of giant trees. Even the subalpine meadows of Tuolumne are magnificently vast.

Los Angeles

Art, beaches and movie stars

A perpetual influx of dreamers, go-getters and hustlers gives this sprawling coastal city (p264) an energetic buzz. Learn the tricks of movie-making during a studio tour. Wander gardens and galleries at the hilltop Getty Center. And stargazing? Take in the big picture at the Griffith Observatory or look for stylish, earthbound 'stars' at Bar Marmont. Ready for your close-up? You will be – an hour on the beach guarantees that sun-kissed LA glow. Santa Monica Pier (p268)

Miami

Beachy Latin–art deco mash-up

Most cities content themselves with one or two highlights, but Miami (p144) seems to have it all. Beyond the stunning beaches and Art Deco Historic District (pictured; p148), there's culture at every turn. In cigar-filled dance halls, Havana expats dance to *son* and boleros; in nightclubs, stiletto-heeled Brazilian models shake to Latin hip-hop; and in the parks, old men clack dominoes. To top it off, restaurants dish out zippy flavors from the Caribbean, Cuba, Argentina and Spain.

FILPHOTO / SHUTTERSTOCK ©

KAMIRA / SHUTTERSTOCK ©

CHEN LIU / EYEEM / GETTY IMAGES ©

9

Chicago

Low-key culture amid skyscrapers

The Windy City (p118) will blow you away with its architecture, lakefront beaches and world-class museums. But its real lure is its blend of high culture and earthy pleasures. Is there another metropolis that dresses its Picasso sculpture in local sports team gear? Where residents queue just as long for hot dogs as for some of North America's top restaurants? Winters are brutal, but come summer, Chicago fetes the warm days with festivals and outdoor cafes galore.

Left: Jay Pritzker Pavilion, designed by Gehry Partners LLP (p123); Right: Nature Boardwalk, Lincoln Park Zoo (p134)

FOTO5593 / SHUTTERSTOCK ©

CHRIS HEPBURN / GETTY IMAGES ©

Las Vegas

Garish oasis of indulgence

Just when you think you've got a handle on the West – majestic, sublime, soul-nourishing – here comes Vegas (p238) shaking her thing. Beneath the neon lights of the Strip, she puts on a dazzling show: dancing fountains, a spewing volcano, the Eiffel Tower. But she saves her most dangerous charms for the gambling dens – seductive lairs where the fresh-pumped air and bright colors share one goal: separating you from your money. Top: Fremont Street Experience (p248)

Austin

Texas' capital keeps it weird

With its bohemian vibe and renegade subculture, Austin (p218) rocks great dining, drinking and shopping scenes. It's one of America's music capitals, where a variety of sounds blast on stages nightly. And it's an outdoor playground, where kayakers skim across local lakes, swimmers soak in spring-fed pools, and cyclists hit the urban trails. It's easy to see why this funky city is one of America's fastest-growing hot spots.

Orlando & Walt Disney World® Resort

Fantastical theme parks, and their escape

Walt Disney World® Resort (p176) calls itself the 'Happiest Place on Earth' and then delivers the sensation that you are the most important character in the show. Exhilarating rides, eye-popping entertainment and nostalgia are all part of the magical package. Host city Orlando (pictured; p192) makes for a lovely, leafy refuge.

Plan Your Trip
Need to Know

When to Go

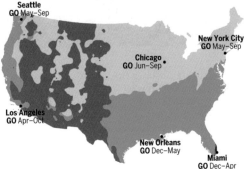

Tropical climate
Dry climate
Warm to hot summers, mild winters
Mild to hot summers, cold winters

Seattle
GO May–Sep

New York City
GO May–Sep

Chicago
GO Jun–Sep

Los Angeles
GO Apr–Oct

New Orleans
GO Dec–May

Miami
GO Dec–Apr

High Season (Jun–Aug)

o Warm days across the country, with generally high temperatures.

o Busiest season, with big crowds and higher prices.

o In ski resort areas, January to March is high season.

Shoulder Season (Apr–May & Sep–Oct)

o Milder temperatures, fewer crowds.

o Spring flowers (April) and fiery autumn colors (October) in many parts of the country.

Low Season (Nov–Mar)

o Wintery days, with snowfall in the north, and heavier rains in some regions.

o Lowest prices for accommodations (aside from ski resorts and warmer getaway destinations).

Currency
US dollar ($)

Language
English

Visas
Visitors from Canada, the UK, Australia, New Zealand, Japan and many EU countries don't need visas for stays of less than 90 days. Other nations see http://travel.state.gov.

Money
ATMs widely available. Credit cards accepted at most hotels, restaurants and shops.

Cell Phones
Foreign phones that operate on tri- or quad-band frequencies will work in the USA. Or purchase inexpensive cell phones with a pay-as-you-go plan here.

Time
The continental USA has four time zones: EST Eastern (GMT/UTC minus five hours), CST Central (GMT/UTC minus six hours), MST Mountain (GMT/UTC minus seven hours), PST Pacific (GMT/UTC minus eight hours).

Daily Costs

Budget: Less than $150

○ Dorm bed: $25–40; double room in a budget motel: $45–80

○ Lunch from a cafe or food truck: $6–12

○ Local bus, subway or train tickets: $2–4

Midrange: $150–250

○ Double room in midrange hotel: $100–250

○ Popular restaurant dinner for two: $30–60

○ Car hire per day: from $30

Top End: More than $250

○ Double room in a resort or top-end hotel: from $200

○ Dinner in a top restaurant: $60–100

○ Concert or theater tickets: $60–200

Useful Websites

Lonely Planet (www.lonelyplanet.com/usa) Destination information, hotel bookings, traveler forum and more.

National Park Service (NPS; www.nps.gov) Gateway to America's greatest natural treasures, its national parks.

Eater (www.eater.com) Foodie insight into two-dozen American cities.

Punch (www.punchdrink.com) Quirky guides and helpful insights on how to drink well in America's cities.

New York Times Travel (www.nytimes.com/travel) Travel news, practical advice and engaging features.

Roadside America (www.roadsideamerica.com) For all things weird and wacky.

Arriving in the USA

John F Kennedy International Airport, New York AirTrain ($5) to subway ($2.75) takes one hour to Manhattan. Taxis $52 plus tolls and tip (45 to 60 minutes).

Los Angeles International Airport Door-to-door shuttles cost $17 to $30 (35 minutes to 1½ hours). Taxis have flat rates (eg $47 to downtown LA, $35 to Santa Monica). LAX Flyaway bus to Union Station costs $9.75 (45 minutes).

Miami International Airport Taxis ($35) and shared SuperShuttle vans (about $22) run to South Beach (40 minutes). The Miami Beach Airport Express (bus 150) costs $2.65 and makes stops all along Miami Beach.

Getting Around

Air Flying is usually more expensive than traveling by train or car, but it's the way to go when you're in a hurry. The domestic air system is extensive and reliable.

Car For maximum flexibility and convenience, and to explore rural America and its wide, open spaces, a car is essential. Although gas prices are high, you can often score fairly inexpensive rentals (NYC excluded), with rates as low as $20 per day.

Train Amtrak has an extensive rail system throughout the USA. Trains are rarely the quickest, cheapest, timeliest or most convenient option, but they're relaxing and scenic.

For more on **getting around**, see p372 ➡

Plan Your Trip
Hot Spots for...

PHOTO.UA / SHUTTERSTOCK ©

Fabulous Food

Feasts await, from fresh-shucked oysters and bourbon-soaked bread pudding to fried chicken and duck-fat biscuits. Pack your stretchy pants.

San Francisco At a transit hub turned gourmet emporium, foodies taste-test artisan cheeses, organic breads and local wines.

Ferry Building Sustainable food producers and a farmers market (pictured; p300).

Chicago The boisterous taverns and small storefronts in Logan Square dish out inventive fare along tree-shaded boulevards.

Longman & Eagle Comfort foods and whiskey (p136).

New Orleans A bohemian vibe and good cheap restaurants percolate in Faubourg Marigny & Bywater, a colorful part of town.

Bacchanal Whatever hits the table will blow your mind (p213).

NAGEL PHOTOGRAPHY / SHUTTERSTOCK ©

Public Art

Ambitious, open-air 'galleries' pop up in town plazas, leafy parks and derelict industrial districts across the country. The groovy eye candy is always free to see.

Miami A psychedelic collection of murals brightens warehouses in the gallery-packed Wynwood district.

Wynwood Walls Get the scoop on the latest murals with a walking tour (p158).

Austin Graffiti artists have beautified the concrete ruins of an abandoned construction project.

HOPE Outdoor Gallery Spray paint your own work (pictured; p229).

Chicago Whimsical sculptures dot Chicago's main green space, including the silvery Bean and Crown Fountain's video gargoyles.

Millennium Park Look for the Bean reflecting the city's skyline (p122).

Outdoor Adventures

The landscape's soaring mountains, raging rivers, emerald coves and craggy clifftops send out their siren song to hikers, paddlers and nature appreciators of all types.

KERI OBERLY / GETTY IMAGES ©

Grand Canyon National Park The ancient, red-orange chasm is prime for hiking, biking, rafting and sunset gawping.

Mule Riding Saddle up with Canyon Vistas Mule Rides (p258).

Yosemite National Park (pictured) Hard-core hikers, climbers and campers will find their bliss amid the park's glaciated valleys and earth-shaking waterfalls.

Hiking Standing atop America's tallest cascade on Yosemite Falls Trail (p328).

Los Angeles After taking in the arcades and carnival rides of Santa Monica Pier, stroll the oceanside path to the beach.

Bicycling Take a spin on the South Bay Bicycle Trail (p269).

Eye-Popping Spectacles

If you build it – and razzle-dazzle it with flashing lights and lots of hype – they will come. Some places really pull out all the stops.

MARIAKRAYNOVA / SHUTTERSTOCK ©

Las Vegas The Eiffel Tower, an erupting volcano and the Statue of Liberty on the same street? Anything goes, as long as it's over-the-top.

Venetian Take a gondola ride – a highlight of a visit to the Venetian (pictured; p245).

New York City There's enough neon to sear your retinas, plus cabs, skyscrapers and crowds of people creating a hustle-bustle like no other.

Broadway Where's there's no business like show business (p52).

Walt Disney World® Resort Princesses, pirates, sorcerers, spaceships and a giant talking mouse fill the fairy-tale world of the Happiest Place on Earth.

Magic Kingdom Cinderella's Castle is one of the most iconic sights (p181).

Plan Your Trip
Local Life

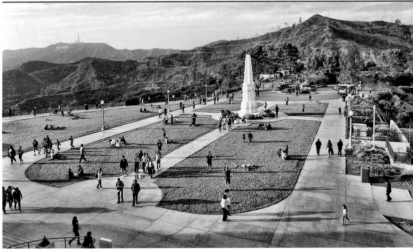

JOSEPH BRODERICK / EYEEM / GETTY IMAGES ©

Activities

The USA has no shortage of spectacular settings for a bit of adventure. No matter your weakness – hiking, biking, kayaking, rafting, surfing, horseback riding – you'll find world-class places to commune with the great outdoors. Take the national parks. They're gigantic outdoor playgrounds designed for everyone to enjoy, from tots toddling down nature trails to grungy rock-climbing champions scaling high-flying domes. Big cities let you get a move on, too, via urban paths such as New York City's High Line and wild, trail-striped green spaces like Los Angeles' Griffith Park.

Shopping

Streets such as Rodeo Drive in Los Angeles and the Magnificent Mile (aka Michigan Ave) in Chicago are America's retail meccas, with plenty of high-end shops. For something more authentically American, check out the many markets that have work from local potters, jewelry makers and other artists. The nation's major museums often have terrific gift shops with quality, locally inspired products.

Eating

In a country of such size and regional variation, you could spend a lifetime eating your way across America and barely scratch the surface. Owing to such scope, dining American-style could mean many things: from munching on pulled-pork sandwiches at an old roadhouse to feasting on sustainably sourced seafood in a waterfront dining room. Waves of immigrants have added great variety to American gastronomy by adapting foreign ideas to home soil, from Italian pizza and German hamburgers to Mexican huevos rancheros and Japanese sushi. Classic comfort foods such as mac 'n' cheese, pot roast, grilled cheese sandwiches, biscuits and gravy and fried chicken are also common on local menus.

BRENT HOFACKER / SHUTTERSTOCK ©

Drinking & Nightlife

Americans have a staggering range of choices when it comes to beverages. A booming microbrewery industry has brought finely crafted beers to every corner of the country. The US wine industry continues to produce first-rate vintages – and it's not just Californian vineyards garnering all the awards. Cocktail bars abound, where mixologists blend small-batch liqueurs, whipped egg whites, hand-chipped ice and fresh fruits into snazzy elixirs. Meanwhile, coffee culture continues to prevail, with cafes and roasteries elevating the once humble cup of coffee to high art.

Entertainment

Live music venues are thick on the ground, with tunes spilling out of sticky clubs, sunny outdoor amphitheaters, DIY dive bars and everyplace in between. Austin, Chicago and New Orleans host particularly rich gigs, where blues, rock and jazz waft

★ Best Live Music

Carnegie Hall (p84), New York City

Preservation Hall (p216), New Orleans

Broken Spoke (p236), Austin

Hideout (p141), Chicago

Black Cat (p116), Washington, DC

from atmospheric local halls. Many large cities have polished theater scenes that export their musicals and dramas to Broadway in New York City, the theater world's epicenter. Then there's sports, the most popular entertainment of all. Americans are devoted to their favorite team, whether it's baseball, football, basketball or hockey. Watching a game live alongside 40,000 screaming fans at a stadium makes a mighty impression.

From left: Griffith Park (p274), Los Angeles; Memorial Day picnic

Plan Your Trip
Month by Month

STUART MONK / SHUTTERSTOCK ©

January
Snowfall blankets large swaths of the country. Ski resorts kick into high gear, while sun lovers seek refuge in warmer climes (especially Florida).

✤ Chinese New Year
In late January or early February, you'll find colorful celebrations and feasting anywhere there's a Chinatown. NYC throws a festive parade, though San Francisco's is the best, with floats, firecrackers, bands and plenty of merriment.

February
Aside from mountain getaways, many Americans dread February with its long dark nights and frozen days. For foreign visitors, this can be the cheapest time to travel, with discounted rates for flights and hotels.

✤ Mardi Gras
Held in late February or early March, on the day before Ash Wednesday, Mardi Gras (Fat Tuesday) is the finale of Carnival. New

Orleans' celebrations (www.mardigras neworleans.com) are legendary as colorful parades, masquerade balls, feasting and plenty of hedonism rule the day.

March
The first blossoms of spring arrive (at least in the south – the north still shivers in the chill). Meanwhile, drunken spring-breakers descend on Florida.

✤ St Patrick's Day
On the 17th, the patron saint of Ireland is honored with brass bands and ever-flowing pints of Guinness; huge parades occur in New York and Chicago (which goes all-out by dyeing the Chicago River green).

☆ South by Southwest
Each year Austin, TX, becomes ground zero for one of the biggest music festivals in North America. More than 2000 performers play at nearly 100 venues. SXSW (www.sxsw.com) is also a major film festival and interactive fest – a platform for groundbreaking ideas.

KIT LEONG / SHUTTERSTOCK ©

✿ National Cherry Blossom Festival

The brilliant blooms of Japanese cherry blossoms around DC's Tidal Basin are celebrated with concerts, parades, taiko drumming, kite-flying and 90 other events during the four-week fest (www.national cherryblossomfestival.org). More than one million go each year, so don't forget to book ahead.

April

The weather is warming up, though up north April can still be unpredictable, bringing chilly weather mixed with a few, teasingly warm days. Down south, it's a fine time to travel.

☆ Jazz Fest

Beginning the last weekend in April, New Orleans hosts the country's best jazz jam (www.nojazzfest.com), with top-notch acts (local resident Harry Connick Jr sometimes plays) and plenty of good cheer. In addition to world-class jazz, there's also great food and crafts.

★ Best Festivals

Mardi Gras, February

South by Southwest, March

National Cherry Blossom Festival, March

Chicago Blues Festival, June

Art Basel, December

May

May is true spring and one of the loveliest times to travel, with blooming wildflowers and generally mild sunny weather.

✿ Cinco de Mayo

Celebrate Mexico's victory over the French with salsa music and pitchers of margaritas across the country. LA and San Francisco throw some of the biggest bashes.

From left: St Patrick's Day parade; Cinco de Mayo celebrations

June

Summer is here. School is out; vacationers fill the highways and resorts, bringing higher prices.

✤ Gay Pride

In some cities, gay pride celebrations last a week, but in San Francisco, it's a month-long party (www.sfpride.org), where the last weekend in June sees giant parades. You'll find other great pride events at major cities across the country.

☆ Chicago Blues Festival

It's the globe's biggest free blues fest (www.chicagobluesfestival.us), with three days of the music that made Chicago famous. More than 500,000 people unfurl blankets by the multiple stages in Grant Park in early June.

July

Summer is in full swing. The prices are high and the crowds can be fierce, but it's one of the liveliest times to visit.

✤ Independence Day

On July 4, the nation celebrates its birthday with a bang, as nearly every town and city stages a massive fireworks show.

☆ Pageant of the Masters

This eight-week arts fest (www.foapom.com) brings a touch of the surreal to Laguna Beach, CA. On stage, meticulously costumed actors create living pictures – imitations of famous works of art – accompanied by narration and an orchestra.

August

Expect blasting heat, with temperatures and humidity less bearable the further south you go. You'll find people-packed beaches, high prices and empty cities on weekends, when residents escape to the nearest waterfront.

☆ Lollapalooza

This mondo rock fest (www.lollapalooza.com) sees more than 100 bands spilling off eight stages in Chicago's Grant Park on the first Thursday-to-Sunday in August.

October

Temperatures are falling, as autumn brings fiery colors to northern climes.

☆ New York Film Festival

Just one of many big film fests in NYC – Tribeca Film Festival in late April is another goodie; this one features world premieres from across the globe (www.filmlinc.com).

✤ Halloween

In NYC, you can don a costume and join the Halloween parade up Sixth Ave. West Hollywood in Los Angeles and San Francisco's Castro district are also great places to see outrageous outfits.

November

No matter where you go, this is generally low season, with cold winds discouraging visitors despite lower prices (although airfares skyrocket around Thanksgiving).

✤ Thanksgiving

On the fourth Thursday of November, Americans gather with family and friends over day-long feasts – roast turkey, sweet potatoes and loads of other dishes. NYC hosts a huge parade, and there's pro football on TV.

December

Aside from winter sports, December means heading inside and curling up by the fire.

✤ Art Basel

This massive arts fest (www.artbaselmiamibeach.com) offers four days of cutting-edge art, film, architecture and design. More than 200 major galleries from across the globe come to the event, with works by some 4000 artists, plus much hobnobbing with a glitterati crowd in Miami Beach.

✤ New Year's Eve

Americans are of two minds when it comes to ringing in the New Year. Some join festive crowds to celebrate, others plot a getaway to escape the mayhem. Whichever you choose, plan well in advance. Expect high prices (especially in NYC).

Plan Your Trip
Get Inspired

Read

On the Road (Jack Kerouac; 1957) A journey through post–WWII America.

The Great Gatsby (F Scott Fitzgerald; 1925) A powerful Jazz Age novel.

Beloved (Toni Morrison; 1987) A Pulitzer Prize–winning novel set during the post–Civil War years.

The Adventures of Huckleberry Finn (Mark Twain; 1884) A moving tale of journey and self-discovery.

Blue Highways (William Least Heat-Moon; 1982) A classic of American travel writing.

The Underground Rail-road (Colson Whitehead; 2016) Pulitzer Prize–winning novel chronicling a young slave's bid for freedom.

Watch

Singin' in the Rain (1952) Among the best in the era of musicals, with an exuberant Gene Kelly and a timeless score.

Annie Hall (1977) Woody Allen's brilliant romantic comedy, with New York City playing a starring role.

North by Northwest (1959) Alfred Hitchcock thriller with Cary Grant on the run across America.

The Godfather (1972–90) Famed trilogy looking at American society through immigrants and organized crime.

Boyhood (2014) Richard Linklater's coming-of-age tale, shot over the course of 12 years.

Listen

America (Simon & Garfunkel; 1968) Young lovers hitchhiking in search of America.

Cowboy Take Me Away (Dixie Chicks; 1999) Classic country music at its best.

Smells Like Teen Spirit (Nirvana; 1991) *The* Gen-X grunge-rock anthem.

Gangsta's Paradise (Coolio; 1995) A hip-hop classic lamenting the cyclical nature of violence.

Born This Way (Lady Gaga; 2011) A gay anthem for a new era in LGBTIQ rights.

Alright (Kendrick Lamar; 2015) The song against injustice chanted at Black Lives Matter protests.

Above: Times Square (p67)

Plan Your Trip
Five-Day Itineraries

Mighty Metropolises

The bright lights beckon in the country's largest and third-largest cities. New York is the one that never sleeps, the great dynamo of art, fashion and culture. Big-shouldered Chicago is the Midwest's mecca, a marvel of steely skyscrapers and enormous pizzas.

FROM LEFT: ANNA ANGRES / GETTY IMAGES ©, LUKE1138 / GETTY IMAGES / ISTOCKPHOTO ©

New York City (p34) Wander in Central Park, get lost in world-class museums, and dive into the city's dizzying nightlife.

Chicago (p118) Wallow in the food scene and gape at eye-popping art and architecture for two days.
✈ 2 hrs to New York City

Southern Roots

For southern hospitality with a dose of cool-cat style, Austin and New Orleans deliver. Two things are certain when you visit these hot spots: you'll stuff your face and you'll hear great live music. Mural-splashed neighborhoods, funky shops and sociable bars add to the fun.

1

Austin (p218) Soak up the honky-tonks, backyard bars and wildly creative food trucks for two days.

✈ 1½ hrs to New Orleans

2

New Orleans (p198) The antebellum mansions, gumbo, hot jazz and Mardi Gras vibe are hard to resist; three days'll do it.

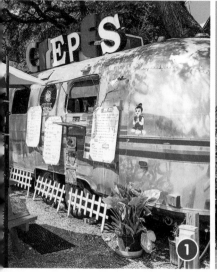

1

2

10-Day Itinerary

Big Apple to Big Easy

Delve into NYC and Washington, DC for world-class museums, iconic buildings and top-notch food. Then head south for sparkling beaches, Disney magic and Cajun cooking on a ramble through Miami, Orlando and New Orleans.

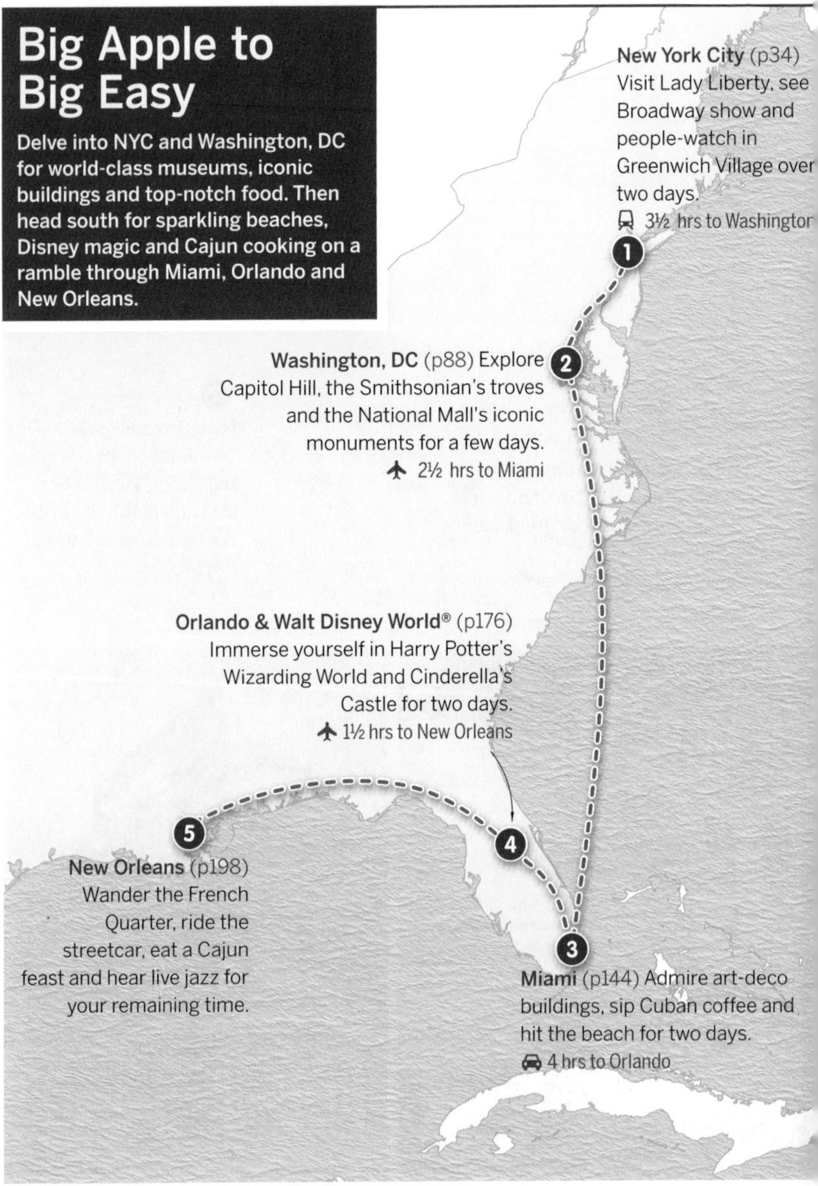

New York City (p34) Visit Lady Liberty, see Broadway show and people-watch in Greenwich Village over two days.
🚌 3½ hrs to Washington

①

② **Washington, DC** (p88) Explore Capitol Hill, the Smithsonian's troves and the National Mall's iconic monuments for a few days.
✈ 2½ hrs to Miami

Orlando & Walt Disney World® (p176) Immerse yourself in Harry Potter's Wizarding World and Cinderella's Castle for two days.
✈ 1½ hrs to New Orleans

⑤

④

New Orleans (p198) Wander the French Quarter, ride the streetcar, eat a Cajun feast and hear live jazz for your remaining time.

③

Miami (p144) Admire art-deco buildings, sip Cuban coffee and hit the beach for two days.
🚗 4 hrs to Orlando

Plan Your Trip
Two-Week Itinerary

The Wild West

This journey takes in the best of the west, road-tripping through neon-lit Las Vegas, movie-star-rich Los Angeles and freewheeling San Francisco. Yosemite, a national park with mammoth mountains and raging waterfalls, pops up, as does another national park with an awe-inspiring canyon.

San Francisco (p288) Take three days to check out Alcatraz, Chinatown and the fog-clad Golden Gate Bridge.
🚗 4 hrs to Yosemite National Park

Yosemite National Park (p320) End your trip in this dreamy landscape of dizzying granite peaks, thunderous waterfalls and gemstone lakes.

Las Vegas (p238) Spend three days gawking at the Strip's mind-blowing oddities and riotous nightlife.
🚗 5 hrs to Grand Canyon

Los Angeles (p264) Wander around Hollywood and get beachy in Santa Monica for three days.
🚗 6 hrs to San Francisco

Grand Canyon (p252) Allocate two days to hike, view sunsets and experience one of the earth's great wonders.
🚗 7½ hrs to Los Angeles

Plan Your Trip
Family Travel

© 2016 LOCK + LAND, CHIP LITHERLAND

Planning

Weather and crowds are all-important considerations when planning a US family getaway. The peak travel season across the country is from June to August, when schools are out and the weather is warmest. Expect high prices and abundant crowds, meaning long lines at amusement and water parks, fully booked resort areas and heavy traffic on the roads – you'll need to reserve well in advance for popular destinations. The same holds true for winter resorts during their high season of late December to March.

Accommodations

Motels and hotels typically have rooms with two beds, which are ideal for families. Some also have rollaway beds or cribs that can be brought into the room for an extra charge – but keep in mind these are usually Pack 'n' Plays (portable cots), which not all children sleep well in. Some hotels offer 'kids stay free' programs for children up to

12 or sometimes 18 years of age. Be wary of B&Bs, as many don't allow children; check before reserving.

Eating Out

The US restaurant industry seems built on family-style service: children are not just accepted almost everywhere, but usually are encouraged by special children's menus with smaller portions and lower prices. In some restaurants children under a certain age even eat for free. Restaurants usually provide high chairs and booster seats. Some restaurants may also offer children crayons and puzzles, and occasionally live performances by cartoon-like characters.

Restaurants without children's menus don't necessarily discourage kids, though higher-end restaurants might. Even at the nicer places, however, if you show up early enough (right on dinnertime opening hours, often 5pm or 6pm), you can usually eat without too much stress – and you'll likely be joined by other foodies with kids. You

can ask if the kitchen will make a smaller order of a dish (also ask how much it will cost), or if it will split a normal-size main dish between two plates for the kids.

Planes, Trains & Automobiles

Every car-rental agency should be able to provide an appropriate child seat, since these are required in every state, but you need to request it when booking and expect to pay $10 to $14 more per day.

Domestic airlines don't charge for children under two years. Children aged two and older must have a seat, and discounts are unlikely. Rarely, some resorts (eg Disneyland) offer a 'kids fly free' promotion. Amtrak, America's national train service, offers half-price fares for children 12 years and under.

Useful Websites

Baby's Away (www.babysaway.com) Rents cribs, high chairs, car seats, strollers and even toys at locations across the country.

★ Best Theme Parks & Zoos

Walt Disney World® Resort (p180)

Universal Orlando Resort (p186)

Legoland® Florida Resort (p193)

National Zoo (p109)

Audubon Zoological Gardens (p209)

Family Travel Files (www.thefamilytravelfiles. com) Ready-made vacation ideas, destination profiles and travel tips.

Kids.gov (www.kids.usa.gov) Eclectic, enormous national resource. Download songs and activities, or even link to the CIA Kids' Page.

Travel BaBees (www.travelbabees.com) A reputable baby-gear rental outfit, with locations nationwide.

From left: Legoland® Florida Resort (p193); Audubon Zoological Gardens (p209)

One World Trade Center

Whitehall Building

The Battery

NEW YORK CITY

One New York Plaza

Brooklyn Bridge

South Ferry
Termininal

N 0 — 4 km
0 — 2 miles

North Hudson Park

Riverside Park

Hudson River

Upper West Side & Central Park
Walking past brownstones on quiet side streets still makes you feel like you've stepped out of a New York movie.

Upper East Side
Home to the so-called 'Museum Mile' – one of the most cultured strips in New York (and possibly the world).

MU
MO

BROADWAY

West Village, Chelsea & the Meatpacking District
Mellow and raucous, quaint and sleekly contemporary, it's a 'hood to call your own.

Pennsylvania (Penn) Station

Grand Central Terminal

EM
F

East River

SoHo & Chinatown
Offering a delicious, contradictory jumble of cast-iron architecture, strutting fashionistas, temples and hook-hung salami.

HIGH LINE

Financial District & Lower Manhattan
Bold, architectural icons, eateries and a booming residential population; it's no longer strictly business here.

NATIONAL SEPTEMBER 11 MEMORIAL & MUSEUM

Upper New York Bay

ELLIS ISLAND

Governors Island

STATUE OF LIBERTY

Grand Central Terminal (p68)

Arriving in New York City

John F Kennedy International Airport
AirTrain ($5) to subway ($2.75) takes
one hour to Manhattan. Taxis $52 plus
tolls and tip (45 to 60 minutes).

LaGuardia Airport Express bus to
Midtown costs $15. Taxis $34 to $53
plus tolls and tip (30 minutes).

Newark Liberty International Airport
AirTrain to Newark Airport train station
to any train bound for NYC's Penn
Station ($13, 25 minutes).

Sleeping

NYC room prices are high. Weekdays are
often cheaper than weekends. No Manhattan neighborhood has a monopoly
on a single style and you'll find better-
value hotels in Brooklyn and Queens.
A few B&Bs and hostels are scattered
throughout. See Where to Stay (p87) for
details on lodgings by neighborhood.

Central Park

Lush lawns, cool forests, flowering gardens, glassy bodies of water and meandering, wooded paths provide a dose of serene nature amid the urban rush of New York City. Today, this 'people's park' is still one of the city's most popular attractions, beckoning throngs of New Yorkers with concerts, events and wildlife.

Great For...

ℹ Need to Know

Map p78; www.centralparknyc.org; 59th to 110th Sts, btwn Central Park West & Fifth Ave; ⏱6am-1am;

★ **Top Tip**

To escape the crowds, try the North Meadow (north of 97th St) or the Harlem Meer.

Like the city's subway system, the vast and majestic Central Park, an 843-acre rectangle of open space in the middle of Manhattan, is a great class leveler – which is exactly what it was envisioned to be. Created in the 1860s and '70s by Frederick Law Olmsted and Calvert Vaux on the marshy northern fringe of the city, the immense park was designed as a leisure space for all New Yorkers, regardless of color, class or creed.

Olmsted and Vaux (who also created Prospect Park in Brooklyn) were determined to keep foot and road traffic separate and cleverly designed the crosstown transverses under elevated roads to do so.

Throughout the year, visitors find free outdoor concerts at the Great Lawn, precious animals at the Central Park Wildlife Center and top-notch drama at the annual Shakespeare in the Park productions, held each summer at the open-air Delacorte Theater. Some other recommended stops include the ornate Bethesda Fountain, which edges the Lake, and its Loeb Boathouse, where you can rent rowboats or enjoy lunch at an outdoor cafe; the Shakespeare Garden (west side between 79th and 80th Sts), which has lush plantings and excellent skyline views; and the Ramble (mid-park from 73rd to 79th Sts), a wooded thicket that's popular with bird-watchers. While parts of the park swarm with joggers, in-line skaters, musicians and tourists on warm weekends, it's quieter on weekday afternoons – but especially in less well-trodden spots above 72nd St such as the Harlem Meer and the North Meadow (north of 97th St).

Folks flock to the park even in winter, when snowstorms can inspire cross-country skiing and sledding or a simple stroll through

Bethesda Fountain

the white wonderland, and crowds turn out every New Year's Eve for a midnight run. The **Central Park Conservancy** (📞212-310-6600; www.centralparknyc.org/tours; 14 E 60th St, btwn Madison & Fifth Aves; §N/R/W to 5th Ave-59th St) offers ever-changing guided tours of the park, including those that focus on public art, wildlife and places of interest to kids.

Strawberry Fields

This tear-shaped garden serves as a memorial to former Beatle John Lennon. It is composed of a grove of stately elms and a tiled mosaic that reads, simply, 'Imagine.' Find it at the level of 72nd St on the park's west side.

> ☑ **Don't Miss**
>
> Tours with the Central Park Conservancy; many are free, others cost $15.

ALESSIO CATELLI / SHUTTERSTOCK ©

Bethesda Terrace & Mall

The arched walkways of Bethesda Terrace, crowned by the magnificent Bethesda Fountain, have long been a gathering area for New Yorkers of all flavors. To the south is the Mall (featured in countless movies), a promenade shrouded in mature North American elms. The southern stretch, known as Literary Walk, is flanked by statues of famous authors.

Conservatory Water & Around

North of the zoo at the level of 74th St is the Conservatory Water, where model sailboats drift lazily and kids scramble about on a toadstool-studded statue of Alice in Wonderland. There are Saturday story hours at the Hans Christian Andersen statue to the west of the water (at 11am from June to September).

Great Lawn & Around

The Great Lawn is a massive emerald carpet at the center of the park – between 79th and 86th Sts – and is surrounded by ball fields and London plane trees. Immediately to the southeast is the Delacorte Theater, home to the annual Shakespeare in the Park festival, as well as Belvedere Castle, a lookout. Further south, between 72nd and 79th Sts, is the leafy Ramble, a popular birding destination. On the southeastern end is the Loeb Boathouse, home to a waterside restaurant that offers rowboat and bicycle rentals.

✕ Take a Break

Class things up with an afternoon martini at the **Loeb Boathouse** (📞212-517-2233; www.thecentralparkboathouse. com; Central Park Lake, near E 74th St; mains lunch $27-38, dinner $27-45; ⊙restaurant noon-4pm Mon-Fri, 9:30am-4pm Sat & Sun year-round, 5:30-9:30pm Mon-Fri, from 6pm Sat & Sun Apr-Nov; §B, C to 72nd St; 6 to 77th St).

Ellis Island

Statue of Liberty & Ellis Island

Stellar skyline views, a scenic ferry ride, a lookout from Lady Liberty's crown, and a moving tribute to America's immigrants at Ellis Island – unmissable is an understatement.

Great For...

☑ **Don't Miss**

The breathtaking views from Lady Liberty's crown (remember to reserve tickets well in advance).

Statue of Liberty

A Powerful Symbol

Lady Liberty has been gazing sternly toward 'unenlightened Europe' since 1886. Dubbed the 'Mother of Exiles,' the statue symbolically admonishes the rigid social structures of the old world. 'Give me your tired, your poor, your huddled masses yearning to breathe free, the wretched refuse of your teeming shore' she declares in Emma Lazarus' famous 1883 poem 'The New Colossus.'

History of the Statue

Conceived as early as 1865 by French intellectual Édouard Laboulaye as a monument to the republican principles shared by France and the USA, the Statue of Liberty is still generally recognized as a symbol for at least the ideals of opportunity and freedom

Statue of Liberty

ROBERT PADOVANI / 500PX ©

ⓘ Need to Know

☎212-363-3200, tickets 877-523-9849; www.nps.gov/stli; Liberty Island; adult/child incl Ellis Island $18.50/9, incl crown $21.50/12; ⊙8:30am-5:30pm, hours vary by season; ⑤1 to South Ferry or 4/5 to Bowling Green, then ⛴to Liberty Island

✕ Take a Break

Pack a picnic or chow beforehand at the Hudson Eats (p75) food hall.

★ Top Tip

Pick up a free audioguide when you reach Liberty Island; there's even a kids' version.

to many. French sculptor Frédéric-Auguste Bartholdi traveled to New York in 1871 to select the site, then spent more than 10 years in Paris designing and making the 151ft-tall figure *Liberty Enlightening the World*. It was then shipped to New York, erected on a small island in the harbor and unveiled in 1886. Structurally, it consists of an iron skeleton (designed by Gustave Eiffel) with a copper skin attached to it by stiff but flexible metal bars.

Visiting the Statue

Access to the crown is limited, so reservations are required. Book as far in advance as possible (additional $3). Pedestal access is also limited, so reserve in advance (no additional fee). Keep in mind, there's no elevator and the climb from the base is equal to a 22-story building. Otherwise, a

visit means you can wander the grounds and enjoy the view of Lady Liberty from all sides (plus the great views of Manhattan). A free audioguide (available upon arrival to the island) provides historical details and little-known facts about the statue.

The trip to Liberty Island, via ferry, is usually made in conjunction with nearby Ellis Island. Ferries leave from **Battery Park** (Map p64; www.nycgovparks.org; Broadway, at Battery Pl; ⊙sunrise-1am; ⑤4/5 to Bowling Green; R/W to Whitehall St; 1 to South Ferry) and tickets include admission to both sights. Reserve in advance to cut down on long wait times.

Ellis Island

America's most famous and historically important gateway, **Ellis Island** (☎212-363-3200, tickets 877-523-9849; www.nps.gov/elis; Ellis Island; ferry incl Statue of Liberty adult/child $18.50/9; ⊙8:30am-6pm, hours vary by season; ⑤1 to South Ferry or 4/5 to Bowling

Green, then  to Ellis Island) is the very spot where old-world despair met new-world promise. Between 1892 and 1924, more than 12 million immigrants passed through this processing station, their dreams in tow. An estimated 40% of Americans today have at least one ancestor who was processed here, confirming the major role this tiny harbor island has played in the making of modern America.

Main Building Architecture

With their Main Building, architects Edward Lippincott Tilton and William A Boring created a suitably impressive and imposing 'prologue' to America. The designing duo won the contract after the original wooden building burnt down in 1897. Having attended the École des Beaux Arts in Paris, it's not surprising that they opted for a beaux-arts

aesthetic for the project. The building evokes a grand train station, with majestic triple-arched entrances, decorative Flemish bond brickwork, and granite quoins (cornerstones) and belvederes.

Inside, it's the 2nd-floor, 338ft-long Registry Room (also known as the Great Hall) that takes the breath away. It was under its beautiful vaulted ceiling that the newly arrived lined up to have their documents checked, and that the polygamists, paupers, criminals and anarchists were turned back. The original plaster ceiling was severely damaged by an explosion of munition barges at nearby Black Tom Wharf. It was a blessing in disguise; the rebuilt version was adorned with striking, herringbone-patterned tiles by Rafael Guastavino. The Catalan-born engineer is also behind the beautiful tiled ceiling at the Grand Central

Ellis Island Immigration Museum

Oyster Bar & Restaurant at Grand Central Terminal.

Main Building Restoration

After a $160 million restoration, the Main Building was reopened to the public as the Ellis Island Immigration Museum in 1990. Now anybody who rides the ferry to the island can experience a cleaned-up, modern version of the historic new-arrival experience, the museum's interactive exhibits paying homage to the hope, jubilation and sometimes bitter disappointment of the millions who came here in search of a new beginning. Among them were Hungarian Erik Weisz (Harry Houdini), Italian Rodolfo Guglielmi (Rudolph Valentino) and Brit Archibald Alexander Leach (Cary Grant).

Immigration Museum Exhibits

The museum's exhibits are spread over three levels. To get the most out of your visit, opt for the 50-minute self-guided audio tour (free with ferry ticket, available from the museum lobby). Featuring narratives from a number of sources, including historians, architects and the immigrants themselves, the tour brings to life the museum's hefty collection of personal objects, official documents, photographs and film footage. It's an evocative experience to relive personal memories – both good and bad – in the very halls and corridors in which they occurred.

The collection itself is divided into a number of permanent and temporary exhibitions. If you're very short on time, skip the 'Journeys: The Peopling of America 1550–1890' exhibit on the 1st floor and focus on the 2nd floor. It's here that you'll find the two most fascinating exhibitions. The first, 'Through America's Gate,' examines the step-by-step process faced by the newly arrived, including the chalk-marking of those suspected of illness, a wince-inducing eye examination, and 29 questions in the beautiful, vaulted Registry Room. The second, 'Peak Immigration Years,' explores the motives behind the immigrants' journeys and the challenges they faced once free to begin their new American lives. Particularly interesting is the collection of old photographs, which offers intimate glimpses into the daily lives of these courageous new Americans.

PISAPHOTOGRAPHY / SHUTTERSTOCK ©

☑ Quick Facts

The robed statue represents Libertas, the Roman goddess of freedom. The tablet she holds is inscribed with the date of America's declaration of independence (July 4, 1776).

★ Did You Know?

One of NYC's most famous mayors worked at Ellis Island before going into politics. Fluent in Italian, Croatian and Yiddish, Fiorello LaGuardia worked as a translator while attending NYU law school at night.

ANTON_IVANOV / SHUTTERSTOCK ©

Museum of Modern Art

The Museum of Modern Art is a cultural promised land. With a vast collection, a scenic sculptural garden, and some of the best temporary shows in New York City, the MoMA is a thrilling crash course in all that is beautiful and addictive about art.

Great For...

☑ Don't Miss

The outdoor sculpture garden makes a fine retreat when you have gallery fatigue.

Since its founding in 1929, the Museum of Modern Art (MoMA) has amassed over 150,000 artworks, documenting the emerging creative ideas and movements of the late 19th century through to those that dominate today. For art buffs, it's Valhalla.

Visiting MoMA

It's easy to get lost in MoMA's vast collection. To maximize your time; download the museum's free smartphone app from the website beforehand. MoMA's permanent collection spans four levels, with prints, illustrated books and the unmissable Contemporary Galleries on level two; architecture, design, drawings and photography on level three; and painting and sculpture on levels four and five. Many of the big hitters are on these last two levels, so tackle the museum from the top down before the fatigue sets in. Must-sees include Van Gogh's *Starry Night,* Cézanne's *The Bather* and Henri Rousseau's

Museum of Modern Art ◎

W 53rd St

🛇 Fifth Ave-
53rd St

Sixth Ave

Fifth Ave

❶ Need to Know

MoMA; Map p72; ☎212-708-9400; www.
moma.org; 11 W 53rd St, btwn Fifth & Sixth
Aves; adult/child 16yr and under $25/free,
4-9pm Fri free; ⏱10:30am-5:30pm Sat-Thu,
to 9pm Fri; ♿; ⑤E, M to 5th Ave-53rd St

✖ Take a Break

For a casual vibe, try Italian-inspired fare
at MoMA's **Cafe 2** (☎212-333-1299; www.
momacafes.com; 2nd fl; sandwiches & salads
$8-14, mains $12-18; ⏱11am-5pm, to 7:30pm
Fri; 🛜).

★ Top Tip

Keep your museum ticket handy,
as it also provides free entry to film
screenings and MoMA PS1 (p63) in
Queen's.

The Sleeping Gypsy, not to mention iconic
American works such as Warhol's *Camp-
bell's Soup Cans* and *Gold Marilyn Monroe,*
Lichtenstein's equally poptastic *Girl With Ball*
and Hopper's haunting *House by the Rail-
road.* Another 50,000 sq ft of gallery space
will be added in an expansion and redesign
to be completed in 2019.

Abstract Expressionism

One of the greatest strengths of MoMA's
collections is abstract expressionism, a
radical movement that emerged in New
York in the 1940s and boomed a decade
later. Defined by its penchant for irreverent
individualism and monumentally scaled
works, this so-called 'New York School'
helped turn the metropolis into the epicenter of Western contemporary art. Among
the stars are Rothko's *Magenta, Black, Green
on Orange,* Pollock's *One: Number 31, 1950*
and de Kooning's *Painting.*

Lunchtime Talks

Delve a little deeper into MoMA's collection:
join one of the museum's daily lunchtime
talks and readings (⏱11:30am & 1:30pm)
where writers, artists, curators and
designers offer expert insight into specific works and
exhibitions. Click the 'Exhibitions & Events'
link on the MoMA website for more.

Film Screenings

Not only a palace of visual art, MoMA
screens an incredibly well-rounded selection
of celluloid gems from its collection of over
22,000 films, including the works of the
Maysles brothers and every Pixar animation
film ever produced. Expect anything from
Academy Award–nominated documentary
shorts and Hollywood classics, to experimental works and international retrospec-
tives. Best of all, your museum ticket will get
you in for free.

High Line

A resounding triumph of urban renewal, the High Line is a remarkable linear public park built along a disused elevated rail line. Each year, this aerial greenway attracts millions of visitors who come for stunning vistas of the Hudson River, public art installations, willowy stretches of native-inspired landscaping and a thoroughly unique perspective on the neighborhood streets below.

Great For...

❶ Need to Know

Map p64; ☎212-500-6035; www.thehigh line.org; Gansevoort St; ⏱7am-11pm Jun-Sep, to 10pm Apr, May, Oct & Nov, to 7pm Dec-Mar; 🚌M11 to Washington St; M11, M14 to 9th Ave; M23, M34 to 10th Ave, 🚇A/C/E, L to 14th St-8th Ave; C/E to 23rd St-8th Ave

★ **Top Tip**

Entrances are at Gansevoort, 14th, 16th, 18th, 20th, 23rd, 26th, 30th and 34th Sts.

History

It's hard to believe that the High Line was once a disused railway that anchored a rather unsavory district of ramshackle domestic dwellings and slaughterhouses. The tracks that would one day become the High Line were commissioned in the 1930s when the municipal government decided to raise the street-level tracks after years of deadly accidents.

By the 1980s, the rails became obsolete (thanks to a rise in truck transportation). Petitions were signed by local residents to remove the eyesores, but in 1999 a committee called the Friends of the High Line was formed to save the tracks and to transform them into a public open space.

Community support grew and, on June 9, 2009, part one of the celebrated project opened with much ado.

Along the Way

The main things to do on the High Line are stroll, sit and picnic in a park 30ft above the city. Along the park's length you'll pass by lush native plants, lounge chairs for soaking up the view and some surprising vantage points over the bustling streets – especially at the cool Gansevoort Overlook, where bleacher-like seating faces a huge pane of glass that allows you to view the traffic, buildings and pedestrians beyond as living works of urban art.

Information, Tours, Events & Eats

As you walk along the High Line you'll find staffers wearing shirts with the signature double-H logo; they can point you in the right direction or offer additional information about the converted rails. There are also myriad staffers behind the scenes organizing public art exhibitions and activity sessions, including warm-weather family events such as story time, science and craft projects.

Free tours take place periodically and explore a variety of topics: history, horticulture, design, art and food. Check the event schedule on the website for the latest details.

> ☑ **Don't Miss**
>
> The third and final part of the High Line, which bends by the Hudson River at 34th St.

To top it all off, the High Line also invites various gastronomic establishments from around the city to set up vending carts and stalls so that strollers can enjoy to-go items on the green. Expect a showing of the finest coffee and ice-cream establishments during the warmer months.

What's Nearby?

○ Whitney Museum of American Art
(Map p64; ☎212-570-3600; www.whitney.org; 99 Gansevoort St, at Washington St; adult/child $25/free; ☺10:30am-6pm Mon, Wed, Thu & Sun, to 10pm Fri & Sat) After years of construction, the Whitney's new downtown location opened to much fanfare in 2015. Perched near the foot of the High Line, this architecturally stunning building – designed by Renzo Piano – makes a suitable introduction to the museum's superb collection. Inside the spacious, light-filled galleries, you'll find works by all the great American artists, including Edward Hopper, Jasper Johns, Georgia O'Keeffe and Mark Rothko.

○ Hudson River Park (Map p64; www. hudsonriverpark.org; 👣) The High Line may be all the rage these days, but one block away from that famous elevated green space, there stretches a 5-mile-long ribbon of green that has dramatically transformed the city over the past decade. Covering 550 acres, and running from Battery Park at Manhattan's southern tip to 59th St in Midtown, the Hudson River Park is Manhattan's wondrous backyard. The long riverside path is a great spot for cycling, running and strolling. Several boathouses (including one in Chelsea near W 26th, and another in the West Village near Houston) offer kayak hire and longer excursions for the more experienced.

✕ **Take a Break**

A cache of eateries is stashed within Chelsea Market (p76) at the 14th St exit.

Times Square

ALLEN.G / SHUTTERSTOCK ©

Broadway

Broadway is NYC's dream factory – a place where romance, betrayal, murder and triumph come with dazzling costumes, toe-tapping tunes and stirring scores. Reserve well ahead for top shows, which sell out months in advance.

Great For...

☑ **Don't Miss**

The **Brill Building** (Map p72; 1619 Broadway, at W 49th St; Ⓢ N/R/W to 49th St; 1, C/E to 50th St); Carole King and Burt Bacharach both started out here.

Broadway Beginnings

The neighborhood's first playhouse was the long-gone Empire, opened in 1893 and located on Broadway between 40th and 41st Sts. Two years later, cigar manufacturer and part-time comedy scribe Oscar Hammerstein opened the Olympia, also on Broadway, before opening the Republic, now children's theater **New Victory** (Map p72; ☏ 646-223-3010; www.newvictory.org; 209 W 42nd St, btwn Seventh & Eighth Aves; 👶; Ⓢ N/Q/R/W, S, 1/2/3, 7 to Times Sq-42nd St; A/C/E to 42nd St-Port Authority Bus Terminal), in 1900. This led to a string of new venues, among them the still-beating **New Amsterdam Theatre** (Aladdin; Map p72; ☏ 844-483-9008; www.new-amsterdam-theatre. com; 214 W 42nd St, btwn Seventh & Eighth Aves; 👶; Ⓢ N/Q/R/W, S, 1/2/3, 7 to Times Sq-42nd St; A/C/E to 42nd St-Port Authority Bus Terminal)

New Amsterdam Theatre

SHELDON LEVIS / GETTY IMAGES ©

❶ Need to Know

Theatermania (www.theatermania.com) provides listings, reviews and ticketing for any form of theater.

✕ Take a Break

Stiff drinks and a whiff of nostalgia await at no-bull **Jimmy's Corner** (Map p72; 🌙212-221-9510; 140 W 44th St, btwn Sixth & Seventh Aves; ⊙11:30am-2:30am Mon-Thu, to 4am Fri, 12:30pm-4am Sat, 3pm-2:30am Sun; ⑤N/Q/R/W, 1/2/3, 7 to 42nd St-Times Sq; B/D/F/M to 42nd St-Bryant Park).

★ Top Tip

Check show websites for cheap-ticket digital lotteries, entered the day of or day prior to a performance.

and **Lyceum Theatre** (Map p72; www.shubert.nyc/theatres/lyceum; 149 W 45th St, btwn Sixth & Seventh Aves; ⑤N/R/W to 49th St).

The Broadway of the 1920s was well known for its lighthearted musicals, commonly fusing vaudeville and music-hall traditions, and producing classic tunes like Cole Porter's 'Let's Misbehave'. At the same time, Midtown's theater district was evolving as a platform for new American dramatists. One of the greatest was Eugene O'Neill. Born in Times Square at the long-gone Barrett Hotel (1500 Broadway) in 1888, the playwright debuted many of his works here, including Pulitzer Prize–winners *Beyond the Horizon* and *Anna Christie*. O'Neill's success on Broadway paved the way for other American greats like Tennessee Williams, Arthur Miller and Edward Albee – a surge of serious talent

that led to the establishment of the annual Tony Awards in 1947.

These days, New York's Theater District covers an area stretching roughly from 40th St to 54th St between Sixth and Eighth Aves, with dozens of Broadway and off-Broadway theaters ranging from block-buster musicals to new and classic drama.

Getting a Ticket

Unless there's a specific show you're after, the best – and cheapest – way to score tickets in the area is at the **TKTS Booth** (Map p72; www.tdf.org/tkts; Broadway, at W 47th St; ⊙3-8pm Mon & Fri, 2-8pm Tue, 10am-2pm & 3-8pm Wed & Sat, 10am-2pm Thu, 11am-7pm Sun; ⑤N/Q/R/W, S, 1/2/3, 7 to Times Sq-42nd St), where you can line up and get same-day discounted tickets for top Broadway and off-Broadway shows. Smartphone users can download the free TKTS app, which offers rundowns of both

Broadway and off-Broadway shows, as well as real-time updates of what's available on that day. Always have a back-up choice in case your first preference sells out, and never buy from scalpers on the street.

The TKTS Booth is an attraction in its own right, with its illuminated roof of 27 ruby-red steps rising a panoramic 16ft 1in above the 47th St sidewalk.

What's On?

Musicals rule the marquees on Broadway, with the hottest shows of the day blending song and dance in lavish, star-studded productions.

Hamilton

Broadway's hottest ticket, Lin-Manuel Miranda's acclaimed musical *Hamilton*, uses contemporary hip-hop beats to recount the story of America's first Secretary of the Treasury, Alexander Hamilton. Inspired by Ron Chernow's biography *Alexander Hamilton*, the show has won a flock of awards, with 11 Tony Awards (including Best Musical), a Grammy for its triple-platinum cast album and the Pulitzer Prize for Drama.

Book of Mormon

Subversive, obscene and ridiculously hilarious, this cutting musical satire is the work of *South Park* creators Trey Parker and Matt Stone and *Avenue Q* composer Robert Lopez. Winner of nine Tony Awards, it tells the story of two naive Mormons on a mission to 'save' a Ugandan village.

Kinky Boots

Adapted from a 2005 British indie film, Harvey Fierstein and Cyndi Lauper's smash hit tells the story of a doomed English shoe factory unexpectedly saved by Lola, a business-savvy drag queen. Its solid characters and electrifying energy have not been lost on critics, and the musical has won six Tony Awards, including Best Musical in 2013.

Lion King

A top choice for families with kids, Disney's blockbuster musical tells the tale of a lion cub's journey to adulthood and the throne of the animal kingdom. The spectacular sets, costumes and African chants are worth the ticket alone.

Chicago

A little easier to score tickets to than some of the newer Broadway musicals, this beloved Bob Fosse–directed, Kander and Ebb classic tells the story of showgirl Velma Kelly, wannabe Roxie Hart, lawyer Billy Flynn and the fabulously sordid goings-on of the Chicago underworld. Revived by director Walter Bobbie, its sassy, infectious energy more than makes up for the theater's tight-squeeze seating.

Wicked

An extravagant prequel to *The Wizard of Oz*, this long-running, pop-rock musical gives the story's witches a turn to tell the tale. The musical is based on Gregory Maguire's 1995 novel.

Aladdin

This witty dervish of a musical recounts the tale of a street urchin who falls in love with the daughter of a sultan. Based on the 1992 Disney animation, the stage version includes songs from the film, numerous numbers that didn't make the final cut, as well as new material written specifically for the live production.

> ### ★ Did You Know?
> The term 'off Broadway' is not a geographical one – it simply refers to theaters that are smaller in size (200 to 500 seats).

PITR / SHUTTERSTOCK ©

☑ Quick Facts

The annual Tony Awards are the Oscars of the theater world, bestowing awards across a host of categories. Check out the latest winners on www.tony awards.com.

Reflecting pools

National September 11 Memorial & Museum

An evocative museum and North America's largest artificial waterfalls are as much a symbol of hope and renewal as they are a tribute to the victims of terrorism.

Great For...

☑ Don't Miss

Look for the so-called 'Angel of 9/11,' the eerie outline of a woman's anguished face on a twisted girder.

The National September 11 Memorial and Museum is a dignified tribute to the victims of the worst terrorist attack on American soil. Titled *Reflecting Absence,* the memorial's two massive reflecting pools are a symbol of renewal and commemorate the thousands who lost their lives. Beside them stands the Memorial Museum, a striking, solemn space documenting that horrific fall day in 2001.

Reflecting Pools

Surrounded by a plaza planted with more than 400 swamp white oak trees, the 9/11 Memorial's reflecting pools occupy the very footprints of the ill-fated twin towers. From their rim, a steady cascade of water pours 30ft down toward a central void. The flow of the water is richly symbolic, beginning as thousands of smaller streams, merging into a massive torrent of collective confusion, and ending with a slow journey toward an abyss. Bronze panels frame the pools, inscribed

National September 11 Memorial

IMAGE PROVIDED BY FELIPE MULE / GETTY IMAGES ©

ⓘ Need to Know

Map p64; www.911memorial.org; 180 Greenwich St; ⊙7:30am-9pm; ⑤E to World Trade Center; R/W to Cortlandt St; 2/3 to Park Pl FREE

✕ Take a Break

Head up to Tribeca for great dining options such as Locanda Verde (p75).

★ Top Tip

To minimize queuing, purchase tickets online or at one of the vending machines outside the museum building.

with the names of those who died in the terrorist attacks of September 11, 2001, and in the World Trade Center car bombing on February 26, 1993. Designed by Michael Arad and Peter Walker, the pools are both striking and deeply poignant.

Memorial Museum

The contemplative energy of the memorial is further enhanced by the National September 11 Memorial Museum. Standing between the reflective pools, the museum's glass entrance pavilion eerily evokes a toppled tower. Inside the entrance, an escalator leads down to the museum's main subterranean lobby. On the descent, visitors stand in the shadow of two steel tridents, originally embedded in the bedrock at the base of the North Tower. Each standing over 70ft tall and weighing 50 tons, they once provided the structural support that allowed the towers to soar over 1360ft into the sky. In the subsequent sea of

rubble, they remained standing, becoming immediate symbols of resilience.

Also among the collection is the Vesey Street Stairs; dubbed the 'Survivors' Stairs,' they allowed hundreds of workers to flee the WTC site. At the bottom of these stairs is the moving In Memoriam gallery, its walls lined with the photographs and names of those who perished. Interactive touch screens and a central reflection room shed light on the victims' lives.

Around the corner from the In Memoriam gallery is the New York City Fire Department's Engine Company 21. One of the largest artifacts on display, its burnt-out cab is testament to the inferno faced by those at the scene. The fire engine stands at the entrance to the museum's main Historical Exhibition. Divided into three sections – Events of the Day, Before 9/11 and After 9/11 – its collection of videos, real-time audio recordings, images, objects and testimonies provide a rich, meditative exploration of the tragedy, the events that preceded it (including the WTC bombing of 1993), and the stories of grief, resilience and hope that followed.

Empire State Building

The striking art-deco skyscraper has appeared in dozens of films and still provides one of the best views in town – particularly around sunset when the lights of the city switch on. Although the crowds are substantial, no one regrets making the journey to the top.

The Chrysler Building may be prettier, and One World Trade Center and 432 Park Avenue may be taller, but the Queen Bee of the New York skyline remains the Empire State Building. NYC's biggest star, it has enjoyed close-ups in around 100 films, from *King Kong* to *Independence Day*. Heading up to the top is a quintessential NYC experience.

Observation Decks

There are two observation decks. The open-air 86th-floor deck offers an alfresco experience, with coin-operated telescopes for close-up glimpses of the metropolis in action. Further up, the enclosed 102nd-floor deck is New York's second-highest observation deck, trumped only by the observation deck at One World Trade Center. Needless to say, the views over the city's five boroughs (and five neighboring

Great For...

☑ **Don't Miss**

Live jazz held on Thursday to Saturday nights from 9pm to 1am.

Entrance foyer

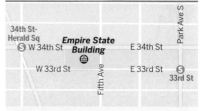

❶ Need to Know

Map p72; www.esbnyc.com; 350 Fifth Ave, at W 34th St; 86th-fl observation deck adult/child $34/27, incl 102nd-fl observation deck $54/47; ⏱8am-2am, last elevators up 1:15am; Ⓢ B/D/F/M, N/Q/R/W to 34th St-Herald Sq

✕ Take a Break

Feast on dumplings, barbecue and kimchi in nearby **Koreatown** (32nd St, btwn Fifth & Sixth Aves).

★ Top Tip

To beat the crowds, buy tickets online (worth the $2 convenience fee).

states, weather permitting) are spectacular. Particularly memorable are the views at sunset, when the city dons its nighttime cloak in dusk's afterglow. For a little of that 'Arthur's Theme' magic, head to the 86th floor between 9pm and 1am from Thursday to Saturday, when the twinkling sea of lights is accompanied by a soundtrack of live sax (yes, requests are taken). Alas, the passage to heaven will involve a trip through purgatory: the queues to the top are notorious. Getting here very early or very late will help you avoid delays – as will buying your tickets online, ahead of time.

By the Numbers

The statistics are astonishing: 10 million bricks, 60,000 tons of steel, 6400 windows and 328,000 sq ft of marble. Built on the original site of the Waldorf-Astoria,

construction took a record-setting 410 days, using seven million hours of labor and costing a mere $41 million. It might sound like a lot, but it fell well below its $50 million budget (just as well, given it went up during the Great Depression). Coming in at 102 stories and 1454ft from bottom to top, the limestone monolith opened for business on May 1, 1931.

Language of Light

Since 1976, the building's top 30 floors have been floodlit in a spectrum of colors each night, reflecting seasonal and holiday hues. Famous combos include orange, white and green for St Patrick's Day; blue and white for Chanukah; white, red and green for Christmas; and the rainbow colors for Gay Pride weekend in June. For a full rundown of the color schemes, check the website.

Iconic Architecture Walk

Head for Midtown for New York City's most iconic architecture, spanning the 20th and 21st centuries.
Start Grand Central Terminal
Finish Rockefeller Center
Distance 1.8 miles
Duration 3½ hours

6 Admire the splendor of **St Patrick's Cathedral** (☎212-753-2261; www.saintpatrickscathedral.org; ⏰6:30am-8:45pm), its impressive rose window the work of American artist Charles Connick.

W 53rd St   Fifth Ave-53rd St Ⓢ

W 52nd St

W 51st St

FINISH

W 50th St

W 49th St

W 48th St

47th-50thSts-Rockefeller Center

Rockefeller Plaza

Sixth Ave (Avenue of the Americas)

Fifth Ave

DIAMOND DISTRICT

W 45th St

W 44th St

42nd St-Bryant Park

5th Ave

Bryant Park

W 40th St

Take a Break... Cocktail bar Sixty-Five (p83)

5 The unique **Diamond District** (www.diamonddistrict.org; btwn Fifth & Sixth Aves) has more than 2600 businesses selling diamonds, gold, pearls and watches.

4 The soaring **Bank of America Tower** (Sixth Ave, btwn W 42nd & 43rd Sts), NYC's fourth-tallest building, is one of its most ecofriendly.

Classic Photo Top of the Rock (p67) observation deck.

7 The **Rockefeller Center** (p67) is a magnificent complex of art-deco skyscrapers and sculptures.

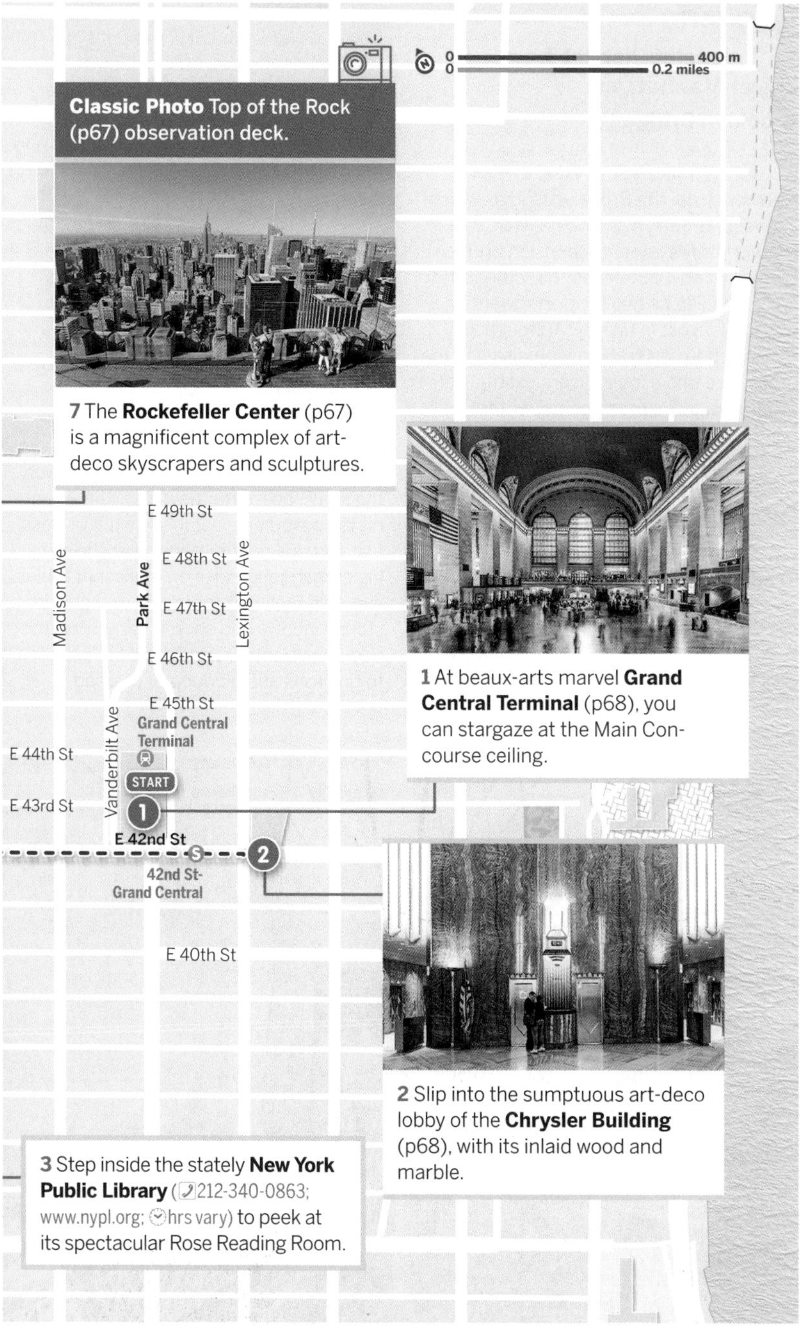

1 At beaux-arts marvel **Grand Central Terminal** (p68), you can stargaze at the Main Concourse ceiling.

2 Slip into the sumptuous art-deco lobby of the **Chrysler Building** (p68), with its inlaid wood and marble.

3 Step inside the stately **New York Public Library** (☎212-340-0863; www.nypl.org; ⏲hrs vary) to peek at its spectacular Rose Reading Room.

Madison Ave
Park Ave
Lexington Ave
Vanderbilt Ave

E 49th St
E 48th St
E 47th St
E 46th St
E 45th St
E 44th St
E 43rd St
E 42nd St
E 40th St

Grand Central Terminal

START

42nd St-Grand Central

400 m
0.2 miles

◎ SIGHTS

◎ Financial District & Lower Manhattan

Brooklyn Bridge   Bridge

(Map p64; S 4/5/6 to Brooklyn Bridge-City Hall; J/Z to Chambers St; R/W to City Hall) A New York icon, the Brooklyn Bridge, which connects Brooklyn and Manhattan, was the world's first steel suspension bridge. Indeed, when it opened in 1883, the 1596ft span between its two support towers was the longest in history. Although its construction was fraught with disaster, the bridge became a magnificent example of urban design, inspiring poets, writers and painters. Its pedestrian walkway delivers soul-stirring views of lower Manhattan, the East River and the rapidly developing Brooklyn waterfront.

One World Trade Center   Notable Building

(One WTC; Map p64; cnr West & Vesey Sts; S E to World Trade Center; 2/3 to Park Pl; A/C, J/Z, 4/5 to Fulton St; R/W to Cortlandt St) Home to **One World Observatory** (📞844-696-1776; www.oneworldobservatory.com; adult/child $34/28; ☺9am-8pm, last ticket sold at 7:15pm) – New York's highest observation deck – the 104-floor One World Trade Center is architect David M Childs' redesign of Daniel Libeskind's original 2002 concept. Not only the loftiest building in America, this tapered giant is currently the tallest building in the Western Hemisphere, not to mention the fourth tallest in the world by pinnacle height.

◎ SoHo & Chinatown

Chinatown   Area

(Map p64; www.explorechinatown.com; south of Broome St & east of Broadway; S N/Q/R/W, J/Z, 6 to Canal St; B/D to Grand St; F to East Broadway) A walk through Manhattan's most colorful, cramped neighborhood is never the same, no matter how many times you hit the pavement. Catch the whiff of fresh fish and ripe persimmons, hear the clacking of mah-jongg tiles on makeshift tables, eye-up dangling duck roasts swinging in store windows and shop for anything from rice-paper lanterns and 'faux-lex' watches to tire irons and a pound of pressed

Brooklyn Bridge

nutmeg. America's largest congregation of Chinese immigrants is your oyster – dipped in soy sauce, of course.

Little Italy
Area

(Map p64; $\boxed{S}$N/Q/R/W, J/Z, 6 to Canal St; B/D to Grand St) This once-strong Italian neighborhood (film director Martin Scorsese grew up on Elizabeth St) saw an exodus in the mid-20th century when many of its residents moved to more suburban neighborhoods in Brooklyn and beyond. Today, it's mostly concentrated on Mulberry St between Broome and Canal Sts, a stretch packed with checkerboard tablecloths and (mainly mediocre) Italian fare. If you're visiting in late September, be sure to check out the raucous **San Gennaro Festival** (www.sangennaro.org), which honors the patron saint of Naples.

◎ East Village & Lower East Side

Lower East Side Tenement Museum
Museum

(Map p64; $\boxed{J}$877-975-3786; www.tenement. org; 103 Orchard St, btwn Broome & Delancey Sts, Lower East Side; tours adult/student & senior $25/20; ⊗10am-6:30pm Fri-Wed, to 8:30pm Thu; $\boxed{S}$B/D to Grand St; J/M/Z to Essex St; F to Delancey St) This museum puts the neighborhood's heartbreaking but inspiring heritage on full display in three re-created turn-of-the-20th-century tenement apartments, including the late-19th-century home and garment shop of the Levine family from Poland, and two immigrant dwellings from the Great Depressions of 1873 and 1929. Visits to the tenement building are available only as part of scheduled guided tours, with many departures each day.

New Museum of Contemporary Art
Museum

(Map p64; $\boxed{J}$212-219-1222; www.newmuseum. org; 235 Bowery, btwn Stanton & Rivington Sts; adult/child $18/free, 7-9pm Thu by donation; ⊗11am-6pm Tue, Wed & Fri-Sun, to 9pm Thu; $\boxed{S}$R/W to Prince St; F to 2nd Ave; J/Z to Bowery; 6 to Spring St) Rising above the neighborhood, the New Museum of Contemporary Art is

🏳️ Detour: Queens

Of the city's five boroughs, Queens is biggest, and runner-up in head count.

If it's not Tuesday or Wednesday (when many galleries close), start with a day in Long Island City, home to contemporary art hubs **MoMA PS1** ($\boxed{J}$718-784-2084; www.momaps1.org; 22-25 Jackson Ave, Long Island City; suggested donation adult/child $10/free, free with MoMA ticket, Warm Up party online/at venue $18/22; ⊗noon-6pm Thu-Mon, Warm Up parties noon-9pm Sat Jul-Aug; $\boxed{S}$E, M to Court Sq-23rd St; G, 7 to Court Sq), **SculptureCenter** (www.sculpture-center.org) and the **Fisher Landau Center for Art** (www.flcart.org). Watch the sun set from **Gantry Plaza State Park** (www.parks.ny.gov/parks/149), and sip-and-sup on neighborly Vernon Blvd.

Spend a day exploring neighboring Astoria, taste-testing a variety of eateries, sipping local brews and checking out the **Museum of the Moving Image** (www.movingimage.us). In summer, catch an alfresco film at **Socrates Sculpture Park** (www.socratessculpturepark.org).

Further east, Flushing (home to NYC's biggest Chinatown) also merits a full-day adventure with its jumble of street foods, Asian groceries and kitschy malls. Time poor? Spend the morning on Main St and Roosevelt Ave, then hit neighboring Corona for the **Queens Museum** (www.queensmuseum. org) and **Louis Armstrong House** (www. louisarmstronghouse.org).

If it's hot, tackle the surf at Rockaway Beach, home to NYC's coolest beach scene (take your board on the A train).

The new NYC Ferry service connects a few spots along the waterfront in Queens with Manhattan, and the Rockaways.

a sight to behold: a seven-story stack of off-kilter, white, ethereal boxes designed by Tokyo-based architects Kazuyo Sejima

West & East Villages, Chinatown & Lower Manhattan

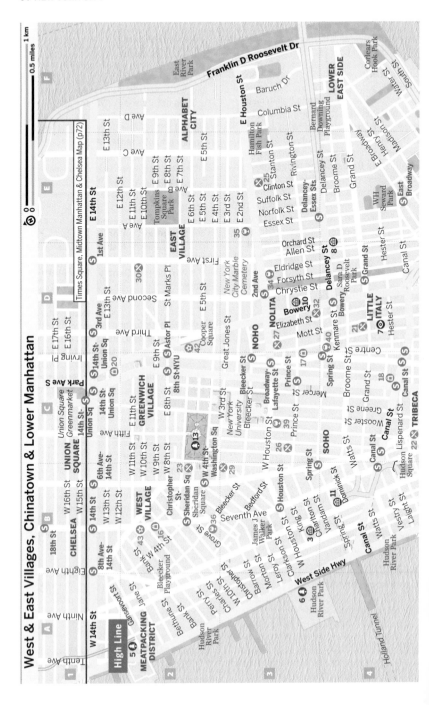

0.5 miles
1 km

Times Square, Midtown Manhattan & Chelsea Map (p72)

High Line

MEATPACKING DISTRICT

CHELSEA

UNION SQUARE

Union Square Greenmarket

GREENWICH VILLAGE

WEST VILLAGE

Sheridan Sq
Sheridan Square

NOHO

NOLITA

Bowery

LITTLE ITALY

SOHO

TRIBECA

EAST VILLAGE

ALPHABET CITY

Tompkins Square Park

New York City Marble Cemetery

LOWER EAST SIDE

Franklin D Roosevelt Dr

East River Park

Corlears Hook Park

WH Seward Park

East River Park

Baruch Dr

E Houston St

Columbia St

Hamilton Fish Park

Bernard Downing Playground

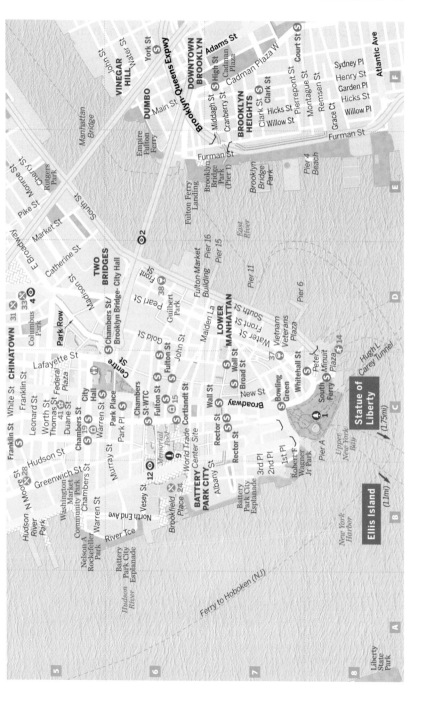

West & East Villages, Chinatown & Lower Manhattan

⊚ **Sights**
1 Battery Park..C8
2 Brooklyn Bridge.................................E6
3 Children's Museum of the Arts.................B3
4 Chinatown..D5
5 High Line..A2
6 Hudson River Park A3
7 Little Italy...D4
8 Lower East Side Tenement
   Museum...D4
9 National September 11 Memorial..............C6
10 New Museum of Contemporary
   Art...D3
11 New York City Fire Museum B4
   One World Observatory....................(see 12)
12 One World Trade Center B6
13 Washington Square Park C2
   Whitney Museum of
   American Art..............................(see 5)

⊕ **Activities, Courses & Tours**
14 Staten Island Ferry.............................D8

⊕ **Shopping**
15 Century 21...C6
16 Idlewild Books....................................B2
17 McNally Jackson C3
18 Opening Ceremony..............................C4
19 Philip Williams Posters........................C5
20 Strand Book Store C1

⊗ **Eating**
21 Bánh Mì Saigon Bakery.......................D4
22 Bâtard...C4
23 Blue Hill..B2
24 Brookfield Place..................................B6
25 Clinton Street Baking Company...............E3
26 Dutch..C3
27 Estela..D3
   Hudson Eats............................(see 24)
28 Locanda Verde....................................B5
29 Mamoun's...B3
30 Momofuku Noodle Bar..........................D2
31 Nice Green Bo.....................................D5
32 Uncle Boons D3
33 Xi'an Famous Foods.............................D5

⊕ **Drinking & Nightlife**
34 Bar Goto...D3
35 Berlin...E3
36 Buvette...B2
37 Dead Rabbit..C7
38 Keg No 229...D6
39 Pegu Club C3
40 Spring Lounge.....................................D4

⊕ **Entertainment**
41 Flea Theater C5
42 Joe's Pub..D2
43 Village Vanguard.................................B2

and Ryue Nishizawa of SANAA and the New York–based firm Gensler. It was a long-awaited breath of fresh air along what was a completely gritty Bowery strip when it arrived back in 2007 – though since its opening, many glossy new constructions have joined it, quickly transforming this once down-and-out avenue.

◎ West Village, Chelsea & the Meatpacking District

Washington Square Park   Park

(Map p64; Fifth Ave at Washington Sq N; ⊕; §A/C/E, B/D/F/M to W 4th St-Washington Sq; R/W to 8th St-NYU) What was once a potter's field and a square for public executions is now the unofficial town square of Greenwich Village, and plays host to lounging NYU students, tuba-playing street performers, curious canines and their owners, speed-chess pros and bare-footed children who splash about in the fountain on warm days.

Rubin Museum of Art   Gallery

(Map p72; ☑212-620-5000; www.rmanyc.org; 150 W 17th St, btwn Sixth & Seventh Aves; adult/child $15/free, 6-10pm Fri free; ⊗11am-5pm Mon & Thu, to 9pm Wed, to 10pm Fri, to 6pm Sat & Sun; §1 to 18th St) The Rubin is the first museum in the Western world to dedicate itself to the art of the Himalayas and surrounding regions. Its impressive collections include embroidered textiles from China, metal sculptures from Tibet, Pakistani stone sculptures and intricate Bhutanese paintings, as well as ritual objects and dance masks from various Tibetan regions, spanning from the 2nd to the 19th centuries.

◎ Union Square, Flatiron District & Gramercy

Union Square   Square

(Map p72; www.unionsquarenyc.org; 17th St, btwn Broadway & Park Ave S; §4/5/6, N/Q/R, L to 14th St-Union Sq) Union Sq is like the

Noah's Ark of New York, rescuing at least two of every kind from the curling seas of concrete. In fact, one would be hard pressed to find a more eclectic cross-section of locals gathered in one public place: suited businessfolk gulping fresh air during their lunch breaks, dreadlocked loiterers tapping beats on their tabla, skateboarders flipping tricks on the southeastern stairs, rowdy college kids guzzling student-priced eats, and throngs of protesting masses chanting fervently for various causes.

Flatiron Building   Historic Building
(Map p72; Broadway, cnr Fifth Ave & 23rd St; ⑤N/R, F/M, 6 to 23rd St) Designed by Daniel Burnham and built in 1920, the 20-story Flatiron Building has a uniquely narrow triangular footprint that resembles the prow of a massive ship. It also features a traditional beaux-arts limestone and terra-cotta facade, built over a steel frame, that gets more complex and beautiful the longer you stare at it. Best viewed from the traffic island north of 23rd St between Broadway and Fifth Ave, this unique structure dominated the plaza back in the dawning skyscraper era of the early 1900s.

◎ **Midtown**

Times Square   Area
(Map p72; www.timessquarenyc.org; Broadway, at Seventh Ave; ⑤N/Q/R/W, S, 1/2/3, 7 to Times Sq-42nd St) Love it or hate it, the intersection of Broadway and Seventh Ave (aka: Times Square) pumps out the NYC of the global imagination – yellow cabs, golden arches, soaring skyscrapers and razzle-dazzle Broadway marquees. It's right here that Al Jolson 'made it' in the 1927 film *The Jazz Singer,* that photojournalist Alfred Eisenstaedt famously captured a lip-locked sailor and nurse on V-J Day in 1945, and that Alicia Keys and Jay-Z waxed lyrically about this 'concrete jungle where dreams are made.'

**Radio City
Music Hall**   Historic Building
(Map p72; www.radiocity.com; 1260 Sixth Ave, at W 51st St; tours adult/child $27/20; ◷tours

9:30am-5pm; ⓚ; ⑤B/D/F/M to 47th-50th Sts-Rockefeller Center) This spectacular Moderne movie palace was the brainchild of vaudeville producer Samuel Lionel 'Roxy' Rothafel. Never one for understatement, Roxy launched his venue on December 23, 1932 with an over-the-top extravaganza that included camp dance troupe the Roxy-ettes (mercifully renamed the Rockettes). Guided tours (75 minutes) of the sumptuous interiors include the glorious auditorium, Witold Gordon's classically inspired mural *History of Cosmetics* in the Women's Downstairs Lounge, and the *très* exclusive VIP Roxy Suite.

Rockefeller Center   Historic Building
(Map p72; ☎212-332-6868; www.rockefeller center.com; Fifth to Sixth Aves, btwn W 48th & 51st Sts; ⑤B/D/F/M to 47th-50th Sts-Rockefeller Center) This 22-acre 'city within a city' debuted at the height of the Great Depression, with developer John D Rockefeller Jr footing the $100 million price tag. Taking nine years to build, it was America's first multiuse retail, entertainment and office space – a sprawl of 19 buildings (14 of which are the original Moderne structures). The center was declared a National Landmark in 1987. Highlights include the Top of the Rock observation deck and **NBC Studio Tours** (☎212-664-3700; www.thetouratnbcstudios. com; 30 Rockefeller Plaza, entrance at 1250 Sixth Ave; tours adult/child $33/29, children under 6yr not admitted; ◷8:20am-2pm Mon-Fri, to 5pm Sat & Sun).

Top of the Rock   Viewpoint
(Map p72; ☎212-698-2000, toll free 877-692-7625; www.topoftherocknyc.com; 30 Rockefeller Plaza, entrance on W 50th St, btwn Fifth & Sixth Aves; adult/child $37/31, sunrise/sunset combo $54/43; ◷8am-midnight, last elevator at 11pm; ⑤B/D/F/M to 47th-50th Sts-Rockefeller Center) Designed in homage to ocean liners and opened in 1933, this 70th-floor open-air observation deck sits atop the GE Building, the tallest skyscraper at the Rockefeller Center. Top of the Rock beats the Empire State Building (p59) on several levels: it's less crowded, has wider observation

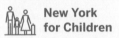

New York for Children

While the American Museum of Natural History (p70) and Central Park (p38) and its zoo reign as favorites, other good options include:

New York City Fire Museum (Map p64; ☑212-691-1303; www.nycfiremuseum.org; 278 Spring St, btwn Varick & Hudson Sts, SoHo; adult/child $8/5; ⊙10am-5pm; ⑤C/E to Spring St) In a grand old firehouse dating from 1904, this ode to firefighters includes a fantastic collection of historic equipment and artifacts. Eye up everything from horse-drawn firefighting carriages and early stovepipe firefighter hats, to Chief, a four-legged firefighting hero from Brooklyn. Exhibits trace the development of the NYC firefighting system, and the museum's heavy equipment and friendly staff make this a great spot for kids.

Children's Museum of the Arts (Map p64; ☑212-274-0986; www.cmany.org; 103 Charlton St, btwn Greenwich & Hudson Sts, SoHo; admission $12, 4-6pm Thu by donation; ⊙noon-5pm Mon, noon-6pm Thu & Fri, 10am-5pm Sat & Sun; ⊕; ⑤1 to Houston St; C/E to Spring St) This small but worthy stop encourages kids aged 10 months to 15 years to view, make and share art. Rotating exhibitions aside, the center offers a vast program of daily activities for fledgling artists, from sculpture and collaborative mural painting, to songwriting and children's book design. It also runs movie nights and other special treats. See the website for upcoming offerings.

decks (both outdoor and indoor) and offers a view of the Empire State Building itself.

Grand Central Terminal
Historic Building

(Map p72; www.grandcentralterminal.com; 89 E 42nd St, at Park Ave; ⊙5:30am-2am; ⑤S, 4/5/6, 7 to Grand Central-42nd St) Completed in 1913, Grand Central Terminal – more commonly, if technically incorrectly, called Grand Central Station – is one of New York's beaux-arts beauties. Adorned with Tennessee-marble floors and Italian-marble ticket counters, its glorious main concourse is capped by a vaulted ceiling depicting the constellations, designed by French painter Paul César Helleu. When commuters complained that the sky is backwards – painted as if looking down from above, not up – it was asserted as intentional (possibly to avoid having to admit an error).

Chrysler Building
Historic Building

(Map p72; 405 Lexington Ave, at E 42nd St; ⊙lobby 8am-6pm Mon-Fri; ⑤S, 4/5/6, 7 to Grand Central-42nd St) Designed by William Van Alen in 1930, the 77-floor Chrysler Building is prime-time architecture: a fusion of Moderne and Gothic aesthetics, adorned with steel eagles and topped by a spire that screams *Bride of Frankenstein.* The building was constructed as sthe headquarters for Walter P Chrysler and his automobile empire; unable to compete on the production line with bigger rivals Ford and General Motors, Chrysler trumped them on the skyline, and with one of Gotham's most beautiful lobbies.

◉ Upper East Side

Metropolitan Museum of Art
Museum

(Map p78; ☑212-535-7710; www.metmuseum.org; 1000 Fifth Ave, at 82nd St; suggested admission adult/student/child $25/12/free; ⊙10am-5:30pm Sun-Thu, to 9pm Fri & Sat; ⊕; ⑤4/5/6, Q to 86th St) This sprawling encyclopedic museum, founded in 1870, houses one of the largest art collections in the world. Its permanent collection has more than two million individual objects, from Egyptian temples to American paintings. Known colloquially as 'The Met,' the museum attracts over six million visitors a year to its 17 acres of galleries – making it the largest single-site attraction in New York City. In other words, plan on spending some time here – it is B-I-G.

Metropolitan Opera House

Guggenheim Museum   Museum

(Map p78; ☑212-423-3500; www.guggenheim.
org; 1071 Fifth Ave, at 89th St; adult/child $25/
free, pay-what-you-wish 5:45-7:45pm Sat;
☺10am-5:45pm Sun-Wed & Fri, to 7:45pm Sat,
closed Thu; ☝; ⑤4/5/6 to 86th St) A sculpture in its own right, architect Frank Lloyd
Wright's building almost overshadows the
collection of 20th-century art it houses.
The museum's holdings include works by
Kandinsky, Picasso and Jackson Pollock.
Over time, other key additions have been
made, including paintings by Monet, Van
Gogh and Degas, photographs by Robert
Mapplethorpe, and key surrealist works.
Temporary exhibitions are the real draw,
the best of which are stunning site-specific
installations by some of the great visionary
artists of today.

Frick Collection   Gallery

(Map p78; ☑212-288-0700; www.frick.org; 1 E
70th St, cnr Fifth Ave; adult/student $22/12,
pay-what-you-wish 2-6pm Fri; ☺10am-6pm
Tue-Sat, 11am-5pm Sun; ⑤6 to 68th St-Hunter
College) This spectacular art collection sits
in a mansion built by prickly steel magnate

Henry Clay Frick, one of the many such
residences that made up what was once
called Millionaires' Row. The museum has
over a dozen splendid rooms displaying
masterpieces by Titian, Vermeer, Gilbert
Stuart, El Greco and Goya.

◉ Upper West Side & Central Park

Lincoln Center   Arts Center

(Map p78; ☑212-875-5456, tours 212-875-5350;
www.lincolncenter.org; Columbus Ave, btwn W
62nd & 66th Sts; tours adult/student $25/20;
☺tours 11:30am & 1:30pm Mon-Sat, 3pm Sun;
☝; ⑤1 to 66th St-Lincoln Center) **FREE** This
stark arrangement of gleaming modernist
temples houses some of Manhattan's most
important performance companies: the
New York Philharmonic (☑212-875-5656;
www.nyphil.org), the **New York City Ballet**
(☑212-496-0600; www.nycballet.com) and the
iconic **Metropolitan Opera House**
(☑tickets 212-362-6000, tours 212-769-7028;
www.metopera.org), whose lobby's interior
walls are dressed with brightly saturated
murals by painter Marc Chagall. Various

Iconic
Sports Venues

Yankee Stadium (☎718-293-4300, tours 646-977-8687; www.mlb.com/yankees; E 161st St, at River Ave; tours $25; ⑤B/D, 4 to 161st St-Yankee Stadium) The Boston Red Sox like to talk about their record of eight World Series championships in the last 90 years...well, the Yankees have won a mere 27 in that period. The team's magic appeared to have moved with them across 161st St to the new Yankee Stadium, where they played their first season in 2009 – winning the World Series there in a six-game slug-fest against the Phillies. The Yankees play from April to October.

Madison Square Garden (MSG, 'the Garden'; Map p72; www.thegarden.com; 4 Pennsylvania Plaza, Seventh Ave, btwn 31st & 33rd Sts; ⑤A/C/E, 1/2/3 to 34th St-Penn Station) NYC's major performance venue – part of the massive complex housing **Penn Station** (W 33rd St, btwn Seventh & Eighth Aves; ⑤1/2/3, A/C/E to 34th St-Penn Station) – hosts big-arena performers, from Kanye West to Madonna. It's also a sports arena, with **New York Knicks** (www.nba.com/knicks) and **New York Liberty** (www.liberty.wnba.com) basketball games and **New York Rangers** (www.nhl.com/rangers) hockey games, as well as boxing and events like the Annual Westminster Kennel Club Dog Show.

Madison Square Garden
LITTLENYSTOCK / SHUTTERSTOCK ©

other venues are tucked in and around the 16-acre campus, including a theater, two film-screening centers and the renowned Juilliard School.

American Museum
of Natural History   Museum
(Map p78; ☎212-769-5100; www.amnh.org; Central Park West, at W 79th St; suggested admission adult/child $23/13; ⊙10am-5:45pm; ⑭; ⑤B, C to 81st St-Museum of Natural History; 1 to 79th St) Founded in 1869, this classic museum contains a veritable wonderland of more than 30 million artifacts – including lots of menacing dinosaur skeletons – as well as the Rose Center for Earth & Space, with its cutting-edge planetarium. From September through May, the museum is home to the Butterfly Conservatory, a glasshouse featuring 500-plus butterflies from all over the world.

⊕ ACTIVITIES
Staten Island Ferry   Cruise
(Map p64; www.siferry.com; Whitehall Terminal, 4 South St, at Whitehall St; ⊙24hr; ⑤1 to South Ferry; R/W to Whitehall St; 4/5 to Bowling Green) **FREE** Staten Islanders know these hulking, dirty-orange ferryboats as commuter vehicles, while Manhattanites like to think of them as their secret, romantic vessels for a spring-day escape. Yet many a tourist (at last count, two million a year) is clued into the charms of the Staten Island Ferry, whose 5.2-mile journey between Lower Manhattan and the Staten Island neighborhood of St George is one of NYC's finest free adventures.

☞ TOURS
Municipal Art Society   Walking
(☎212-935-3960; www.mas.org; tours adult/child from $25/20) The Municipal Art Society offers various scheduled tours focusing on architecture and history. Among them is a 75-minute tour of Grand Central Terminal (p68), departing daily at 12:30pm from the station's Main Concourse.

Big Onion Walking Tours   Walking

(☎888-606-9255; www.bigonion.com; tours $25) Choose from nearly 30 tours, including Brooklyn Bridge and Brooklyn Heights, the 'Official' Gangs of New York Tour, a Gay and Lesbian History Tour – Before Stonewall, and Chelsea and the High Line.

🔒 SHOPPING

🔒 Financial District & Lower Manhattan

Century 21   Fashion & Accessories

(Map p64; ☎212-227-9092; www.c21stores. com; 22 Cortlandt St, btwn Church St & Broadway; ⊗7:45am-9pm Mon-Wed, to 9:30pm Thu & Fri, 10am-9pm Sat, 11am-8pm Sun; ⓢA/C, J/Z, 2/3, 4/5 to Fulton St; R/W to Cortlandt St) For penny-pinching fashionistas, this giant cut-price department store is dangerously addictive. Physically dangerous as well, considering the elbows you might have to throw to ward off the competition bee-lining for the same rack. Not everything is a knockout or a bargain, but persistence pays off. You'll also find accessories, shoes, cosmetics, homewares and toys.

Philip Williams Posters   Vintage

(Map p64; ☎212-513-0313; www.poster museum.com; 122 Chambers St, btwn Church St & W Broadway; ⊗10am-7pm Mon-Sat; ⓢA/C, 1/2/3 to Chambers St) You'll find nearly a half million posters in this cavernous treasure trove, from oversized French advertise-ments for perfume and cognac to Soviet film posters and retro-fab promos for TWA. Prices range from $15 for small reproduc-tions to $500,000 for rare, showpiece originals like an AM Cassandre Toulouse-Lautrec. There's a second entrance at 52 Warren St.

🔒 SoHo & Chinatown

McNally Jackson   Books

(Map p64; ☎212-274-1160; www.mcnally jackson.com; 52 Prince St, btwn Lafayette & Mulberry Sts, Nolita; ⊗store 10am-10pm Mon-Fri, to 9pm Sun, cafe 9am-9pm Mon-Fri, from 10am Sat, 10am-8pm Sun; ⓢN/R to Prince St; 6 to

Spring St) Bustling indie MJ stocks an excellent selection of magazines and books, covering contemporary fiction, food writing, architecture and design, art and history. If you can score a seat, the in-store cafe is a fine spot to settle in with some reading material or to catch one of the frequent readings and book signings held here.

Opening   Fashion & Ceremony   Accessories, Shoes

(Map p64; ☎212-219-2688; www.opening ceremony.com; 35 Howard St, btwn Broadway & Lafayette St, SoHo; ⊗11am-8pm Mon-Sat, noon-7pm Sun; ⓢN/Q/R/W, J/Z, 6 to Canal St) Unisex Opening Ceremony is famed for its

---

✨ NYC's Best Fests

Tribeca Film Festival (☎212-941-2400; www.tribecafilm.com; ⊗Apr) Founded in 2003 by Robert De Niro and Jane Rosenthal, the Tribeca Film Festival is now a major star of the indie movie circuit. Gaggles of celebs come to walk the red carpets each spring.

July Fourth Fireworks (www.macys. com; ⊗Jul 4) America's Independence Day is celebrated with fireworks over the East River, starting at 9pm. Good viewing spots include the waterfronts of the Lower East Side and Williams-burg, Brooklyn, or any high rooftop or east-facing Manhattan apartment.

Village Halloween Parade (www. halloween-nyc.com; Sixth Ave, from Spring St to 16th St; ⊗7-11pm Oct 31) This is not your average suburban Halloween parade. The largest in the country, with 60,000 participants and millions more spectators, this is an all-out bacchanal, a mix of Mardi Gras and art project, with marchers decked out in spectacular costumes. It begins at 7pm at Sixth Ave and Spring St and continues up Sixth until 16th St.

Times Square, Midtown Manhattan & Chelsea

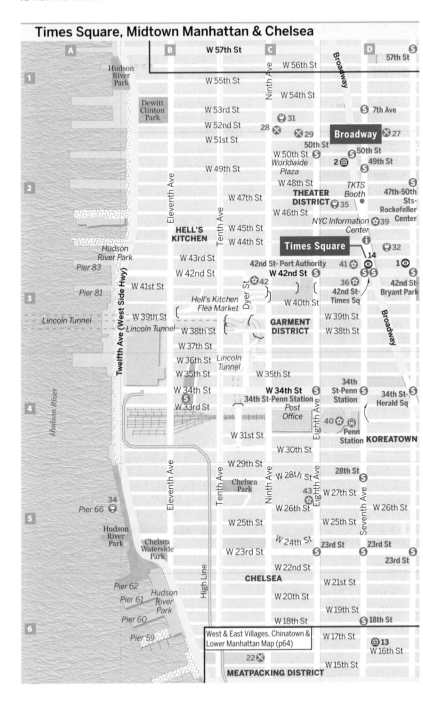

0   1 km
0   0.5 miles

E E 57th St

E 56th St

Museum of   Central Park & Uptown Map (p78)   G
Modern Art

E 55th St

🏛 9   E 54th St   H

S E 53rd St   Lexington Ave-   1
Fifth Ave-   53rd St
53rd St   E 52nd St   Roosevelt
Island

E 51st St   S 51st St   Southpoint
🏛 11   Park

St Patrick's   E 50th St
Cathedral

🏛 18
7 15 12   E 49th St   Franklin D
E 48th St   Roosevelt Four
Freedoms Park

5   E 47th St
◎
DIAMOND   2
DISTRICT   E 46th St

E 45th St   Grand
Central   E 44th St
Terminal

21   United
🏛 8   Nations
E 43rd St   🔒

25   E 42nd St

Bryant   42nd St-   Queens-Midtown Tunnel   3
Park   5th Ave   Grand Central
10   S   E 41st St   MoMA PS1
3   🏛   E 40th St   (1mi)

E 39th St

E 38th St

E 37th St

E 36th St   Tunnel   St Vartan
Entrance St   Park

E 35th St

6 🏛   E 34th St   Franklin D Roosevelt Dr

S   E 33rd St

26   E 32nd St   MURRAY   4
HILL   East River
E 31st St

E 30th St

28th St   28th St   LITTLE   E 29th St
S   INDIA   E 28th St   Bellevue
Hospital
38   Center
🌸   E 26th St

FLATIRON   Madison   E 25th St   5
DISTRICT   Square Park   24th St
Park
23 ⊗   E 24th St

7 🏛 23rd St   23rd St   E 23rd St
E 22nd St   GRAMERCY

E 21st St

24   E 20th St
30   19 ⊗   GRAMERCY   STUYVESANT
PARK   E 19th St   TOWN   6
33   20   E 18th St

E 17th St

UNION   14th St-   16   E 16th St
SQUARE   Union Sq   37   Stuyvesant   E 15th St
S   Irving Pl   Square   EAST VILLAGE

Times Square, Midtown Manhattan & Chelsea

⊚ **Sights**
1 Bank of America Tower D3
2 Brill Building D2
3 Bryant Park E3
4 Chrysler Building F3
5 Diamond District E2
6 Empire State Building E4
7 Flatiron Building E5
8 Grand Central Terminal F3
9 Museum of Modern Art E1
10 New York Public Library E3
11 Radio City Music Hall E2
12 Rockefeller Center E2
13 Rubin Museum of Art D6
14 Times Square D3
15 Top of the Rock E2
16 Union Square E6

⊕ **Activities, Courses & Tours**
17 NBC Studio Tours E2
18 Rink at Rockefeller Center E2

⊜ **Shopping**
19 ABC Carpet & Home E6
20 Bedford Cheese Shop F6
21 Grand Central Market F3
MoMA Design & Book Store .... (see 9)

⊗ **Eating**
Cafe 2 .... (see 9)
22 Chelsea Market C6

23 Eataly E5
24 Gramercy Tavern E6
25 Grand Central Oyster Bar &
Restaurant F3
26 Hangawi E4
27 Le Bernardin D2
28 Totto Ramen C1
29 ViceVersa C2

⊜ **Drinking & Nightlife**
Bar SixtyFive .... (see 15)
Birreria .... (see 23)
30 Flatiron Lounge E6
31 Industry C1
32 Jimmy's Corner D3
33 Old Town Bar & Restaurant E6
34 Pier 66 Maritime A5
35 Rum House D2

⊛ **Entertainment**
36 Aladdin D3
37 Irving Plaza F6
38 Jazz Standard F5
39 Lyceum Theatre D2
40 Madison Square Garden D4
41 New Victory Theater D3
42 Playwrights Horizons C3
43 Upright Citizens Brigade Theatre C5

never-boring edit of A-list indie labels. The place showcases a changing roster of names from across the globe, both established and emerging; complementing them are Opening Ceremony's own avant-garde creations. No matter who's hanging on the racks, you can always expect showstopping, 'where-did-you-get-that?!' threads that are street-smart, bold and refreshingly unexpected.

🅰 West Village, Chelsea & the Meatpacking District

Strand Book Store   Books

(Map p64; ☑212-473-1452; www.strandbooks.com; 828 Broadway, at E 12th St; ⊙9:30am-10:30pm Mon-Sat, from 11am Sun; ⑤L, N/Q/R/W, 4/5/6 to 14th St-Union Sq) Beloved and legendary, the iconic Strand embodies downtown NYC's intellectual *bona fides* – a bibliophile's Oz, where generations of book

lovers carrying the store's trademark tote bags happily lose themselves for hours. In operation since 1927, the Strand sells new, used and rare titles, spreading an incredible 18 miles of books (over 2.5 million of them) among three labyrinthine floors.

Idlewild Books   Books

(Map p64; ☑212-414-8888; www.idlewildbooks.com; 170 Seventh Ave S, at Perry St; ⊙noon-8pm Mon-Thu, to 6pm Fri-Sun; ⑤1 to Christopher St-Sheridan Sq; 2/3 to 14th St-7th Ave) Named after JFK Airport's original moniker, this indie travel bookshop gets feet seriously itchy. Books are divided by region and cover guidebooks as well as fiction, travelogues, history, cookbooks and other stimulating fare for delving into different corners of the world. The store also runs popular language classes in French, Italian, Spanish and German; see the website for details.

🅐 Union Square, Flatiron District & Gramercy

ABC Carpet & Home   Homewares

(Map p72; 📞212-473-3000; www.abchome. com; 888 Broadway, at E 19th St; ⏰10am-7pm Mon-Wed, Fri & Sat, to 8pm Thu, 11am-6:30pm Sun; Ⓢ4/5/6, N/Q/R/W, L to 14th St-Union Sq) A mecca for home designers and decorators brainstorming ideas, this beautifully curated, seven-level temple to good taste heaves with all sorts of furnishings, small and large. Shop for easy-to-pack knickknacks, textiles and jewelry, as well as statement furniture, designer lighting, ceramics and antique carpets. Come Christmas season the shop is a joy to behold.

Bedford Cheese Shop   Food

(Map p72; 📞718-599-7588; www.bedford cheeseshop.com; 67 Irving Pl, btwn E 18th & 19th Sts; ⏰8am-9pm Mon-Sat, to 8pm Sun; Ⓢ4/5/6, N/Q/R/W, L to 14th St-Union Sq) Whether you're after local, raw cow's-milk cheese washed in absinthe or garlic-infused goat's-milk cheese from Australia, chances are you'll find it among the 200-strong selection at this outpost of Brooklyn's most celebrated cheese vendor. Pair the cheesy goodness with artisanal charcuterie, deli treats and ready-to-eat sandwiches ($8 to $11), as well as a proud array of Made-in-Brooklyn edibles.

🅐 Midtown

MoMA Design & Book Store   Gifts, Books

(Map p72; 📞212-708-9700; www.moma store.org; 11 W 53rd St, btwn Fifth & Sixth Aves; ⏰9:30am-6:30pm Sat-Thu, to 9pm Fri; Ⓢ E, M to 5th Ave-53rd St) The flagship store at the Museum of Modern Art (p46) is a fab space for souvenir shopping. Besides gorgeous books (from art and architecture tomes to pop-culture readers and kids' picture books), you'll find art prints and posters and one-of-a-kind knickknacks. For furniture, lighting, homewares, jewelry, bags and MUJI merchandise, head to the MoMA Design Store across the street.

✴ EATING

✴ Financial District & Lower Manhattan

Hudson Eats   Food Hall $

(Map p64; 📞212-417-2445; www.brookfield placeny.com/directory/food; Brookfield Place, 230 Vesey St, at West St; dishes from $7; ⏰10am-9pm Mon-Sat, noon-7pm Sun; 📶; Ⓢ E to World Trade Center; 2/3 to Park Place; R/W to Cortlandt St; 4/5 to Fulton St; A/C to Chambers St) Renovated office and retail complex **Brookfield Place** (📞212-978-1698; www.brookfieldplaceny. com) is home to Hudson Eats, a sleek, fashionable, new-school food hall. Decked out in terrazzo floors, marble counter tops and floor-to-ceiling windows with views of Jersey City and the Hudson River, its string of respected, chef-driven eateries includes Blue Ribbon Sushi, Umami Burger and Dos Toros Taqueria.

Locanda Verde   Italian $$$

(Map p64; 📞212-925-3797; www.locandaverde nyc.com; 377 Greenwich St, at N Moore St; mains lunch $23-34, dinner $25-38; ⏰7am-11pm Mon-Thu, to 11:30pm Fri, 8am-11:30pm Sat, to 11pm Sun; Ⓢ A/C/E to Canal St; 1 to Franklin St) Step through the velvet curtains into a scene of loosened button-downs, black dresses and slick barmen behind a long, crowded bar. This celebrated brasserie showcases modern, Italo-inspired fare like housemade pappardelle with lamb Bolognese, mint-and-sheep's-milk ricotta and Sicilian-style halibut with heirloom squash and almonds. Weekend brunch is no less creative: try scampi and grits or lemon ricotta pancakes with blueberries.

Bâtard   Modern American $$$

(Map p64; 📞212-219-2777; www.batard tribeca.com; 239 W Broadway, btwn Walker & White Sts; 2/3/4 courses $58/75/85; ⏰5:30-10:30pm Mon-Sat, plus noon-2:30pm Fri; Ⓢ 1 to Franklin St; A/C/E to Canal St) Austrian chef Markus Glocker heads this warm, Michelin-starred hot spot, where a pared-back interior puts the focus squarely on the food. It's attention well deserved. Glocker's dishes are beautifully balanced and textured, whether it's Icelandic cod with lentil *gulasch, n'duja* (spicy, spreadable pork *salumi)* and brussels sprouts, or grilled venison with sweet potato, roasted mushrooms and bitter chocolate.

⊗ SoHo & Chinatown

Uncle Boons   Thai $$

(Map p64; ☎646-370-6650; www.uncleboons. com; 7 Spring St, btwn Elizabeth St & Bowery, Nolita; small plates $12-16, large plates $21-29; ⊙5:30-11pm Mon-Thu, to midnight Fri & Sat, to 10pm Sun; ☎; ⑤J/Z to Bowery; 6 to Spring St) Michelin-star Thai served up in a fun, tongue-in-cheek combo of retro wood-paneled dining room with Thai film posters and old family snaps. Spanning the old and the new, zesty, tangy dishes include fantastically crunchy *mieng kum* (betel-leaf wrap with ginger, lime, toasted coconut, dried shrimp, peanuts and chili), *kao pat puu* (crab fried rice) and banana blossom salad.

Estela   Modern American $$$

(Map p64; ☎212-219-7693; www.estelanyc. com; 47 E Houston St, btwn Mulberry & Mott Sts, Nolita; lunch mains $13-30, dinner mains $17-39; ⊙5:30-11pm Sun-Thu, to 11:30pm Fri & Sat; ⑤B/ D/F/M to Broadway-Lafayette St; 6 to Bleecker St) Estela might be hopeless at hide-and-seek (its location up some nondescript stairs hardly tricks savvy gourmands), but this busy, skinny wine bar slays on the food and vino front. Graze from market-driven sharing plates, from phenomenal beef tartare (spiked with beef heart for added complexity) to moreish mussels *escabeche* on toast, or an impossibly sexy endive salad with walnuts and anchovy.

Dutch   Modern American $$$

(Map p64; ☎212-677-6200; www.thedutchnyc. com; 131 Sullivan St, at Prince St, SoHo; mains lunch $18-37, dinner $28-66; ⊙11:30am-11pm Mon-Thu, from 10am Sun, to 11:30pm Fri-Sat; ⑤C/E to Spring St; R/W to Prince St; 1 to Houston St) Whether perched at the bar or dining snugly in the back room, you can always expect smart, farm-to-table comfort grub at this see-and-be-seen stalwart. Flavors traverse the globe, from sweet potato

tempura with Thai basil and fermented chili sauce to ricotta ravioli with Swiss chard and walnut pesto. Reservations are recommended, especially for dinner and all day on weekends.

⊗ East Village & Lower East Side

Momofuku Noodle Bar   Noodles $$

(Map p64; ☎212-777-7773; www.noodlebar-ny. momofuku.com; 171 First Ave, btwn E 10th & 11th Sts; mains $16; ⊙noon-11pm Sun-Thu, to 1am Fri & Sat; ⑤L to 1st Ave; 6 to Astor Pl) With just 30 stools and a no-reservations policy, you'll always have to wait to cram into this bustling phenomenon. Queue up for the namesake special: homemade ramen noodles in broth, served with poached egg and pork belly or some interesting combos. The menu changes daily and includes buns (such as brisket and horseradish), snacks (smoked chicken wings) and desserts.

Clinton Street Baking Company   American $$

(Map p64; ☎646-602-6263; www.clinton streetbaking.com; 4 Clinton St, btwn Stanton & Houston Sts; mains $12-20; ⊙8am-4pm & 5:30-11pm Mon-Sat, 9am-5pm Sun; ⑤J/M/Z to Essex St; F to Delancey St; F to 2nd Ave) Mom-and-pop shop extraordinaire, Clinton Street Baking Company gets the blue ribbon in so many categories – best pancakes (blueberry!), best muffins, best po'boys (Southern-style sandwiches), best biscuits etc – that you're pretty much guaranteed a stellar meal no matter what time you stop by. In the evenings, you can opt for 'breakfast for dinner' (pancakes, eggs Benedict), fish tacos or the excellent buttermilk fried chicken.

⊗ West Village, Chelsea & the Meatpacking District

Chelsea Market   Market $

(Map p72; www.chelseamarket.com; 75 Ninth Ave, btwn 15th & 16th Sts; ⊙7am-9pm Mon-Sat, 8am-8pm Sun; ⑤A/C/E to 14th St) In a shining example of redevelopment and preservation, the Chelsea Market has taken a factory formerly owned by cookie giant

Nabisco (creator of Oreo) and turned it into an 800ft-long shopping concourse that caters to foodies. Taking the place of the old factory ovens that churned out massive numbers of biscuits are eclectic eateries that fill the renovated hallways of this food haven.

Mamoun's
Middle Eastern $

(Map p64; www.mamouns.com; 119 Macdougal St; sandwiches from $3, plates from $6; ⏰11am–5am; ⓈF, M, B, D, A, C, or E train to West 4th St) Need a quick meal that is filling, cheap and overloaded with flavor? This falafel and schwarma restaurant in lower Manhattan specializes in big, dripping platters and wraps that come at you quick and don't cost much. A NYC favorite, Mamoun's even has their own branded hot sauce. Be warned: it's not for anyone with a sensitive tongue!

Blue Hill
American $$$

(Map p64; ☎212-539-1776; www.bluehillfarm. com; 75 Washington Pl, btwn Sixth Ave & Washington Sq W; prix-fixe menu $95-108; ⏰5-11pm Mon-Sat, to 10pm Sun; ⓈA/C/E, B/D/F/M to W 4th St-Washington Sq) A place for slow-food junkies with deep pockets, Blue Hill was an early crusader in the 'Local is Better' movement. Gifted chef Dan Barber, who hails from a farm family in the Berkshires, Massachusetts, uses harvests from that land and from farms in upstate New York to create his widely praised fare.

⊗ Union Square, Flatiron District & Gramercy

Gramercy Tavern
Modern American $$$

(Map p72; ☎212-477-0777; www.gramercy tavern.com; 42 E 20th St, btwn Broadway & Park Ave S; tavern mains $29-36, dining room 3-course menu $125, tasting menus $149-179; ⏰tavern noon-11pm Sun-Thu, to midnight Fri & Sat, dining room noon-2pm & 5:30-10pm Mon-Thu, to 11pm Fri, noon-1:30pm & 5:30-11pm Sat, 5:30-10pm Sun; 🛜🍴; ⓈR/W, 6 to 23rd St) ✿ Seasonal, local ingredients drive this perennial favorite, a vibrant, country-chic institution aglow with copper sconces, murals and

⑩ Best Cheap Eats in Chinatown

Xi'an Famous Foods (Map p64; www. xianfoods.com; 45 Bayard St, btwn Elizabeth St & Bowey; dishes $3-12; ⏰11:30am-9pm Sun-Thu, to 9:30pm Fri & Sat; ⓈN/Q/R/W, J/Z, 6 to Canal St, B/D to Grand St) Food bloggers hyperventilate at the mere mention of this small chain's hand-pulled noodles. Another star menu item is the spicy cumin lambburger – tender lamb sautéed with ground cumin, toasted chili seeds, peppers, red onions and scallions.

Bánh Mì Saigon Bakery (☎212-941-1541; www.banhmisaigonnyc.com; 198 Grand St, btwn Mulberry & Mott Sts; sandwiches $3.50-6; ⏰8am-6pm) This no-frills storefront doles out some of the best banh mi in town – we're talking crisp, toasted baguettes generously stuffed with hot peppers, pickled carrots, daikon, cucumber, cilantro and your choice of meat. Top billing goes to the classic BBQ pork version. Head in by 3pm: if the banh mi sell out, the place closes early. Cash only.

Deluxe Green Bo (Nice Green Bow; ☎212-625-2359; www.deluxegreenbo.com; 66 Bayard St, btwn Elizabeth & Mott Sts; mains $5.95-19.95; ⏰11am-midnight) Not a shred of effort – not even a new sign! – has been made to spruce up Nice Green Bo, and that's the way we like it. It's all about the food here: gorgeous *xiao long bao* served in steaming drums, heaping portions of noodles and gleaming plates of salubrious, sautéed spinach. Cash only.

Dumplings

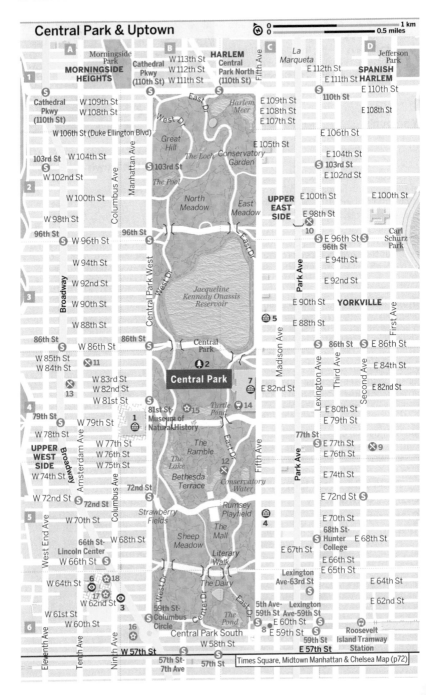

Central Park & Uptown

◎ **Sights**
  1 American Museum of Natural
      History B4
  2 Central Park B4
  3 David Rubenstein Atrium B6
  4 Frick Collection..................................... C5
  5 Guggenheim Museum C3
  6 Lincoln Center A6
  7 Metropolitan Museum of Art C4

◉ **Activities, Courses & Tours**
  8 Central Park Conservancy C6

🍴 **Eating**
  9 Boqueria D4
     Cafe 3..(see 5)
 10 Earl's Beer & Cheese C2

 11 Jacob's Pickles..A4
 12 Lakeside Restaurant at Loeb
      Boathouse C5
 13 Peacefood Cafe A4
     Wright.. (see 5)

🍸 **Drinking & Nightlife**
 14 Cantor Roof Garden Bar.........................C4

🎭 **Entertainment**
 15 Delacorte Theater B4
     Frick Collection Concerts .... (see 4)
 16 Jazz at Lincoln Center B6
     Metropolitan Opera House................. (see 6)
 17 New York City Ballet..................................A6
 18 New York Philharmonic A6

dramatic floral arrangements. Choose from two spaces: the walk-in-only tavern and its à la carte menu, or the swankier dining room and its fancier prix-fixe and degustation feasts. Tavern highlights include a showstopping duck meatloaf with mushrooms, chestnuts and brussels sprouts.

🍴 Midtown

Totto Ramen   Japanese $

(Map p72; ☑212-582-0052; www.tottoramen. com; 366 W 52nd St, btwn Eighth & Ninth Aves; ramen $11-18; ◷noon-4:30pm & 5:30pm-midnight Mon-Sat, 4-11pm Sun; Ⓢ C/E to 50th St) There might be another two branches in Midtown, but purists know that neither beats the tiny, 20-seat original. Write your name and number of guests on the clipboard and wait your turn. Your reward: extraordinary ramen. Go for the pork, which sings in dishes like miso ramen (with fermented soybean paste, egg, scallion, bean sprouts, onion and homemade chili paste).

Burger Joint   Burgers $

(☑212-708-7414; www.burgerjointny.com; Le Parker Meridien, 119 W 56th St, btwn Sixth & Seventh Aves; burgers $9-16; ◷11am-11:30pm Sun-Thu, to midnight Fri & Sat; Ⓢ F to 57th St) With only a small neon burger as your clue, this speakeasy-style burger hut lurks behind the lobby curtain in the Le Parker Meridien hotel. Though it might not be as 'hip' or as

'secret' as it once was, it still delivers the same winning formula of graffiti-strewn walls, retro booths and attitude-loaded staff slapping up beef 'n' patty brilliance.

Hangawi   Korean, Vegan $$

(Map p72; ☑212-213-0077; www.hangawi restaurant.com; 12 E 32nd St, btwn Fifth & Madison Aves; mains lunch $11-30, dinner $19-30; ◷noon-2:30pm & 5:30-10:15pm Mon-Thu, to 10:30pm Fri, 1-10:30pm Sat, 5-9:30pm Sun; ☑; Ⓢ B/D/F/M, N/Q/R/W to 34th St-Herald Sq) Meat-free Korean is the draw at high-achieving Hangawi. Leave your shoes at the entrance and slip into a soothing, Zen-like space of meditative music, soft low seating and clean, complex dishes. Showstoppers include the leek pancakes and a seductively smooth tofu claypot in ginger sauce.

ViceVersa   Italian $$$

(Map p72; ☑212-399-9291; www.viceversanyc. com; 325 W 51st St, btwn Eighth & Ninth Aves; 3-course lunch $29, dinner mains $24-33; ◷noon-2:30pm & 5-11pm Mon-Fri, 4:30-11pm Sat, 11:30am-3pm & 5-10pm Sun; Ⓢ C/E to 50th St) ViceVersa is quintessential Italian: suave and sophisticated, affable and scrumptious. The menu features refined, cross-regional dishes like arancini with black truffle and fontina cheese. For a celebrated classic, order the *casoncelli alla bergamasca* (ravioli-like pasta filled with minced veal, raisins and amaretto cookies and seasoned with sage, butter, pancetta and Grana Padano), a nod to chef Stefano Terzi's Lombard heritage.

Le Bernardin   Seafood $$$

(Map p72; ☎212-554-1515; www.le-bernardin. com; 155 W 51st St, btwn Sixth & Seventh Aves; prix fixe lunch/dinner $88/157, tasting menus $185-225; ☺noon-2:30pm & 5:15-10:30pm Mon-Thu, to 11pm Fri, 5:15-11pm Sat; Ⓢ1 to 50th St; B/D, E to 7th Ave) The interiors may have been subtly sexed-up for a 'younger clientele' (the stunning storm-themed triptych is by Brooklyn artist Ran Ortner), but triple-Michelin-starred Le Bernardin remains a luxe, fine-dining holy grail. At the helm is French-born celebrity chef Éric Ripert, whose deceptively simple-looking seafood often borders on the transcendental.

⊗ Upper East Side

Earl's Beer & Cheese   American $

(Map p78; ☎212-289-1581; www.earlsny.com; 1259 Park Ave, btwn 97th & 98th Sts; grilled cheese $8; ☺11am-midnight Sun-Thu, to 2am Fri & Sat; Ⓢ6 to 96th St) This sibling-run, tiny comfort-food outpost channels a hipster hunting vibe, complete with a giant deer-in-the-woods mural and a mounted buck's head. Basic grilled cheese is a paradigm shifter, served with pork belly, fried egg and kimchi. There is also mac 'n' cheese (with goat's cheese and crispy rosemary) and tacos (featuring braised pork shoulder and *queso fresco*).

Boqueria   Spanish $$

(Map p78; ☎212-343-2227; www.boquerianyc. com; 1460 Second Ave, btwn 76th & 77th Sts; tapas $6-18, paella for 2 $38-46; ☺noon-10:30pm Sun-Thu, 11am-11:30pm Fri & Sat; ☝; Ⓢ6 to 77th St; Q to 72nd St) This lively, much-loved tapas place brings a bit of downtown cool to the Upper East Side, with nicely spiced *patatas bravas,* tender slices of *jamon ibérico* and rich *pulpo a gallega* (grilled octopus). Head chef Marc Vidal, who hails from Barcelona, also creates an exquisite seafood paella. Wash it all down with a pitcher of excellent sangria.

⊗ Upper West Side & Central Park

Peacefood Cafe
Vegan $

(Map p78; ☎212-362-2266; www.peace foodcafe.com; 460 Amsterdam Ave, at 82nd St; mains $12-18; ⊙10am-10pm; ☑; Ⓢ1 to 79th St) This bright and airy vegan haven dishes up a popular fried seitan panino (served on homemade focaccia and topped with cashew cheese, arugula, tomatoes and pesto), as well as pizzas, roasted vegetable plates and an excellent quinoa salad. There are daily raw specials, energy-fueling juices and rich desserts. Healthy and good – for you, the animals and the environment.

Jacob's Pickles
American $$

(Map p78; ☎212-470-5566; www.jacobs pickles.com; 509 Amsterdam Ave, btwn 84th & 85th; mains $16-24; ⊙10am-2am Mon-Thu, to 4am Fri, 9am-4am Sat, to 2am Sun; Ⓢ1 to 86th St) Jacob's elevates the humble pickle to exalted status at this inviting and warmly lit eatery. Aside from briny cukes and other preserves you'll find heaping portions of upscale comfort food, such as catfish tacos, wine-braised turkey-leg dinner, and

mushroom mac 'n' cheese. The biscuits are top-notch.

🍷 DRINKING & NIGHTLIFE

🍸 Financial District & Lower Manhattan

Dead Rabbit
Cocktail Bar

(Map p64; ☎646-422-7906; www.deadrabbit nyc.com; 30 Water St, btwn Broad St & Coenties Slip; ⊙taproom 11am-4am, parlor 5pm-2am Mon-Sat, to midnight Sun; ⓈR/W to Whitehall St; 1 to South Ferry) Named in honor of a dreaded Irish-American gang, this most-wanted rabbit is regularly voted one of the world's best bars. Hit the sawdust-sprinkled Tap-room for specialty beers, historic punches and pop-inns (lightly hopped ale spiked with different flavors). Come evening, scurry upstairs to the cozy Parlor for meticulously researched cocktails. The Wall Street crowd packs the place after work.

Keg No 229
Beer Hall

(Map p64; ☎212-566-2337; www.kegno229. com; 229 Front St, btwn Beekman St & Peck Slip; ⊙11am-midnight; ⓈA/C, J/Z, 2/3, 4/5 to Fulton

Top Five for Foodies

Uncle Boons (p76)

Chelsea Market (p76)

Totto Ramen (p79)

Bâtard (p75)

Blue Hill (p77)

From left: Chelsea Market (p76); Lower East Side bar; miso ramen, Totto Ramen (p79)

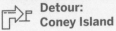

Detour: Coney Island

About 50 minutes by subway from Mid-town, this popular beach neighborhood makes for a great day trip. The wide sandy beach of Coney Island has retained its nostalgic, kitschy and slightly sleazy charms, wood-plank boardwalk and famous 1927 Cyclone roller coaster amid a modern amusement-park area.

Nathan's Famous (☑718-333-2202; www.nathansfamous.com; 1310 Surf Ave, cnr Stillwell Ave; hot dog from $4; ⊙10am-midnight; ☜; ⑤D/F to Coney Island-Stillwell Ave) churns out hot dogs, and the **New York Aquarium** (www.nyaquarium.com; 602 Surf Ave, at W 8th St; $12; ⊙10am-6pm Jun-Aug, to 4:30pm Sep-May, last entry 1hr before closing; ☙; ⑤F, Q to W 8th St-NY Aquarium) is a big hit with kids, as is taking in an early evening baseball game at **MCU Park** (☑718-372-5596; www.brooklyncyclones.com; 1904 Surf Ave, at 17th St; tickets $10-20, all tickets on Wed $10; ⑤D/F, N/Q to Coney Island-Stillwell Ave), the waterfront stadium for the minor league Brooklyn Cyclones.

Nathan's Famous
ELZBIETA SEKOWSKA / SHUTTERSTOCK ©

St; R/W to Cortlandt St) From Butternuts Pork Slap to New Belgium Fat Tire, this bar's battalion of drafts, bottles and cans are a Who's Who of boutique American brews. One fun, potentially costly twist: if you lose count, some drafts are available for 'self-pour.'

○ SoHo & Chinatown

Spring Lounge   Bar

(Map p64; ☑212-965-1774; www.thespringlounge.com; 48 Spring St, at Mulberry St, Nolita; ⊙8am-4am Mon-Fri, from noon Sat-Sun; ⑤6 to Spring St; R/W to Prince St) This neon-red rebel has never let anything get in the way of a good time. In Prohibition days, it peddled buckets of beer. In the '60s its basement was a gambling den. These days, it's best known for its kooky stuffed sharks, early-start regulars and come-one, come-all late-night revelry. Perfect last stop on a bar-hopping tour of the neighborhood.

Pegu Club   Cocktail Bar

(Map p64; ☑212-473-7348; www.peguclub.com; 77 W Houston St, btwn W Broadway & Wooster St, SoHo; ⊙5pm-2am Sun-Wed, to 4am Thu-Sat; ⑤B/D/F/M to Broadway-Lafayette St; C/E to Spring St) Dark, elegant Pegu Club (named after a legendary gentleman's club in colonial-era Rangoon) is an obligatory stop for cocktail connoisseurs. Sink into a velvet lounge and savor seamless libations such as the silky-smooth Earl Grey MarTEAni (tea-infused gin, lemon juice and raw egg white). Grazing options are suitably Asian-esque, among them duck wontons and Mandalay coconut shrimp.

○ East Village & Lower East Side

Bar Goto   Bar

(Map p64; ☑212-475-4411; www.bargoto.com; 245 Eldridge St, btwn E Houston & Stanton Sts; ⊙5pm-midnight Tue-Thu & Sun, to 2am Fri & Sat; ⑤F to 2nd Ave) Maverick mixologist Kenta Goto has cocktail connoisseurs spellbound at his eponymous hot spot. Expect meticulous, elegant drinks that revel in Koto's Japanese heritage (the sake-spiked Sakura Martini is utterly smashing), paired with authentic, Japanese comfort bites such as *okonomiyaki* (savory pancakes).

Berlin   Club

(Map p64; ☑646-827-3689; 25 Ave A, btwn First & Second Aves; ⊙8pm-4am; ⑤F to 2nd Ave) Like a secret bunker hidden beneath the ever-gentrifying streets of the East Village, Berlin is a throwback to the neighborhood's more riotous days of wildness and dancing. Once you find the unmarked entrance, head downstairs to the grotto-like space with vaulted brick ceilings, a long bar and tiny dancefloor, with funk and rare grooves spilling all around.

🍷 West Village, Chelsea & the Meatpacking District

Buvette   Wine Bar

(Map p64; ☎212-255-3590; www.ilovebuvette. com; 42 Grove St, btwn Bedford & Bleecker Sts; ☺7am-2am Mon-Fri, from 8am Sat & Sun; ⑤1 to Christopher St-Sheridan Sq; A/C/E, B/D/F/M to W 4th St-Washington Sq) The rustic-chic decor here (think delicate tin tiles and a swooshing marble counter) makes it the perfect place for a glass of wine – no matter the time of day. For the full experience at this self-proclaimed *gastrotèque*, grab a seat at one of the surrounding tables and nibble on small plates while enjoying old-world wines (mostly from France and Italy).

Pier 66 Maritime   Bar

(Map p72; ☎212-989-6363; www.pier66 maritime.com; Pier 66, at W 26th St; ☺noon-midnight May-Oct; ⑤C/E to 23rd St) Salvaged from the bottom of the sea (or at least the Chesapeake Bay), the Lightship *Frying Pan* and the two-tiered dockside bar where it's moored are fine go-to spots for a sundowner. On warm days, the rustic open-air space brings in the crowds, who laze on deck chairs and drink ice-cold beers ($7 for a microbrew, $25 for a pitcher).

🍸 Union Square, Flatiron District & Gramercy

Flatiron Lounge   Cocktail Bar

(Map p72; ☎212-727-7741; www.flatiron lounge.com; 37 W 19th St, btwn Fifth & Sixth Aves; ☺4pm-2am Mon-Wed, to 3am Thu, to 4am Fri, 5pm-4am Sat; ☎; ⑤F/M, R/W, 6 to 23rd St) Head through a dramatic archway and into a dark, swinging, deco-inspired fantasy of lipstick-red booths, racy jazz tunes and sassy grown-ups downing seasonal drinks.

The Lincoln Tunnel (dark rum, applejack, maple syrup and bitters) is scrumptious. Happy-hour cocktails go for $10 a pop (4pm to 6pm weekdays).

Old Town Bar & Restaurant   Bar

(Map p72; ☎212-529-6732; www.oldtownbar. com; 45 E 18th St, btwn Broadway & Park Ave S; ☺11:30am-11:30pm Mon-Fri, noon-11:30pm Sat, to 10pm Sun; ⑤4/5/6, N/Q/R/W, L to 14th St-Union Sq) It still looks like 1892 in here, with the mahogany bar, original tile floors and tin ceilings – the Old Town is an old-world drinking-man's classic (and -woman's: Madonna lit up at the bar here – when lighting up in bars was still legal – in her 'Bad Girl' video). There are cocktails around, but most come for beers and a burger (from $11.50).

Birreria   Beer Hall

(Map p72; ☎212-937-8910; www.eataly.com; 200 Fifth Ave, at W 23rd St; ☺11:30am-11pm; ⑤F/M, R/W, 6 to 23rd St) The crown jewel of Italian food emporium **Eataly** (☎212-229-2560; www.eataly.com; ☺7am-11pm; ☑) is this rooftop beer garden tucked betwixt the Flatiron's corporate towers. An encyclopedic beer menu offers drinkers some of the best suds on the planet. If you're hungry, the signature beer-braised pork shoulder will pair nicely, or check out the seasonally changing menu of the on-site pop-up restaurant (mains $17 to $37).

🍸 Midtown

Bar SixtyFive   Cocktail Bar

(Map p72; ☎212-632-5000; www.rainbow room.com/bar-sixty-five; 30 Rockefeller Plaza, entrance on W 49th St; ☺5pm-midnight Mon-Fri, 4-9pm Sun; ⑤B/D/F/M to 47th-50th Sts-Rockefeller Center) Not to be missed, sophisticated SixtyFive sits on level 65 of the GE Building at Rockefeller Center (p67). Dress well (no sportswear or guests under 21) and arrive by 5pm for a seat with a multi-million-dollar view. Even if you don't score a table on the balcony or by the window, head outside to soak up that sweeping New York panorama.

Jazz Hot Spots

Jazz Standard (Map p72; ☎212-576-2232; www.jazzstandard.com; 116 E 27th St, btwn Lexington & Park Aves; cover $25-40; ⑤6 to 28th St) Jazz luminaries like Ravi Coltrane, Roy Haynes and Ron Carter have played at this sophisticated club. Service is impeccable, and the food is great. There's no minimum and it's programmed by Seth Abramson, a guy who really knows his jazz.

Village Vanguard (Map p64; ☎212-255-4037; www.villagevanguard.com; 178 Seventh Ave South, at W 11th St; cover around $33; ☺7:30pm-12:30am; ⑤1/2/3 to 14th St) Possibly the city's most prestigious jazz club, the Vanguard has hosted literally every major star of the past 50 years. It started as a home to spoken-word performances and occasionally returns to its roots, but most of the time it's just big, bold jazz all night long.

Rum House   Cocktail Bar
(Map p72; ☎646-490-6924; www.therumhousenyc.com; 228 W 47th St, btwn Broadway & Eighth Ave; ☺noon-4am; ⑤N/R/W to 49th St) This sultry, revamped slice of old New York is revered for its cognoscenti rums and whiskeys. Savor them straight up or mixed in impeccable cocktails like a classic Dark & Stormy (rum, ginger beer and lime). Adding to the magic is nightly live music, spanning solo piano tunes to jaunty jazz trios and sentimental torch divas.

Industry   Gay
(Map p72; ☎646-476-2747; www.industry-bar.com; 355 W 52nd St, btwn Eighth & Ninth Aves; ☺5pm-4am; ⑤C/E, 1 to 50th St) What was once a parking garage is now one of the hottest gay bars in Hell's Kitchen – a slick, 4000-sq-ft watering hole with handsome lounge areas, a pool table and a stage for top-notch drag divas. Head in between 4pm and 9pm for the two-for-one drinks

special or squeeze in later to party with the eye-candy party hordes. Cash only.

⭐ ENTERTAINMENT

For current listings, check out *New York Magazine*, the *Village Voice* and *Time Out*.

Carnegie Hall   Live Music
(☎212-247-7800; www.carnegiehall.org; 881 Seventh Ave, at W 57th St; ☺tours 11:30am, 12:30pm, 2pm & 3pm Mon-Fri, 11:30am & 12:30pm Sat Oct-Jun; ⑤N/R/W to 57th St-7th Ave) This legendary music hall may not be the world's biggest, nor grandest, but it's definitely one of the most acoustically blessed venues around. Opera, jazz and folk greats feature in the Isaac Stern Auditorium, with edgier jazz, pop, classical and world music in the popular Zankel Hall. The intimate Weill Recital Hall hosts chamber-music concerts, debut performances and panel discussions.

Upright Citizens Brigade Theatre   Comedy
(UCB; Map p72; ☎212-366-9176; www.ucbtheatre.com; 307 W 26th St, btwn Eighth & Ninth Aves; free-$10; ☺7pm-midnight; ⑤C/E to 23rd St) Comedy sketch shows and improv reign at this below-ground 74-seat venue, which gets drop-ins from casting directors and often features well-known figures from TV. Getting in is cheap, and so are the beer and wine. You'll find quality shows happening nightly, from about 7:30pm, though the Sunday night Asssscat Improv session is always a riot.

Playwrights Horizons   Theater
(Map p72; ☎212-564-1235; www.playwrightshorizons.org; 416 W 42nd St, btwn Ninth & Tenth Aves, Midtown West; ⑤A/C/E to 42nd St-Port Authority Bus Terminal) An excellent place to catch what could be the next big thing, this veteran 'writers' theater' is dedicated to fostering contemporary American works. Notable past productions include Kenneth Lonergan's *Lobby Hero*, Bruce Norris' Tony Award–winning *Clybourne Park*, as well as Doug Wright's *I Am My Own Wife* and *Grey Gardens*.

Irving Plaza
Live Music

(Map p72; ☎212-777-6817; www.irvingplaza.
com; 17 Irving Pl, at 15th St; ⑤4/5/6, N/Q/R, L to
14th St-Union Sq) Rocking since 1978, Irving
Plaza has seen them all: the Ramones, Bob
Dylan, U2, Pearl Jam, you name it. These
days it's a great in-between stage for quirk-
ier rock and pop acts – from indie chicks
Sleater-Kinney to hard rockers Disturbed.
There's a cozy floor around the stage, and
good views from the mezzanine.

Joe's Pub
Live Music

(Map p64; ☎212-539-8778, tickets 212-967-
7555; www.joespub.com; Public Theater, 425
Lafayette St, btwn Astor Pl & 4th St, Nolita; ⑤6
to Astor Pl; R/W to 8th St-NYU) Part bar, part
cabaret and performance venue, intimate
Joe's serves up both emerging acts and
top-shelf performers. Past entertainers
have included Patti LuPone, Amy Schumer,
Leonard Cohen and British songstress
Adele (in fact, it was right here that Adele
gave her very first American performance,
back in 2008).

Delacorte Theater
Theater

(Map p78; www.publictheater.org; Central Park,
enter at W 81st St; ⑤B, C to 81st St) Every
summer the Joseph Papp Public Theater
presents its fabulous free productions
of Shakespeare in the Park at Delacorte
Theater, which Papp began back in 1954,
before the lovely, leafy, open-air theater
was even built. Productions are usually
superb, but regardless of their quality, it's
a magical experience and waiting in line for
tickets is a rite of passage for newcomers
to the city.

Flea Theater
Theater

(Map p64; ☎tickets 212-226-0051; www.the
flea.org; 20 Thomas St, btwn Church St & Broadway; 🚇; ⑤A/C, 1/2/3 to Chambers St; R/W to
City Hall) One of NYC's top off-off-Broadway
companies, Flea is famous for performing
innovative and timely new works. Spring
2017 is the inaugural season in its new
space (four blocks south of the old one).
Luminaries including Sigourney Weaver
and John Lithgow have trod the boards
here, and the year-round program also
includes music and dance performances.

Carnegie Hall

KEITH LEVIT / GETTY IMAGES ©

ℹ INFORMATION

NYC Information Center (Map p72; ☎212-484-1222; www.nycgo.com; Broadway Plaza, btwn W 43rd & 44th Sts; ⊘9am-6pm Dec-Apr, 8am-8pm May-Nov; ⑤N/Q/R/W, S, 1/2/3, 7, A/C/E to Times Sq-42nd St) There are official NYC Visitor Information Centers throughout the city. The main office is in Midtown.

ℹ GETTING THERE & AROUND

TO/FROM THE AIRPORT

John F Kennedy International Airport (JFK; ☎718-244-4444; www.kennedyairport.com) It's located 15 miles from Midtown in southeastern Queens. The AirTrain ($5) links to the Metropolitan Transportation Authority's (MTA's) subway ($2.75), which makes the one-hour journey into Manhattan. Express bus to Grand Central or Port Authority costs $18. Shared vans to Manhattan hotels run from $20 to $25 per person. Taxis cost a flat rate of $52 excluding tolls, tip and rush hour surcharge.

LaGuardia Airport (LGA; ☎718-533-3400; www.panynj.gov; ᾌM60, Q70) Used mainly for domestic flights, this is the closest airport to Manhattan but least accessible by public transit: take the Q70 express bus from the airport to the 74th St–Broadway subway station (7 line, or the E, F, M and R lines at the connecting Jackson Heights Roosevelt Ave station). Express bus to Midtown costs $15. Taxis range from $34 to $53 (excluding tolls and tip) depending on traffic.

Newark Liberty International Airport (EWR; ☎973-961-6000; www.panynj.gov) It is about the same distance from Midtown as JFK (16 miles). Take the AirTrain to Newark Airport train station, and board any train bound for New York's Penn Station ($13). Express bus to Port Authority or Grand Central costs $16. Shared shuttle to Midtown costs $20 to $26. Taxis range from $60 to $80 (excluding the unavoidable $15 toll and tip). Allow 45 minutes to one hour of travel time.

BICYCLE

The city's popular bike share program Citi Bike (www.citibikenyc.com) provides excellent access to most parts of Manhattan, with growing service elsewhere. To use a Citi Bike, purchase a 24-hour or three-day access pass (around $12 or $24 including tax) at any Citi Bike kiosk.

PUBLIC TRANSPORTATION

Check the Metropolitan Transportation Authority website (www.mta.info) for public transportation information (buses and subway), including a handy travel planner and regular notifications of delays and alternate travel routes during frequent maintenance. Unfortunately, the frequency and length of delays has only increased as ridership has expanded.

Subway Inexpensive, somewhat efficient and operates around the clock, though can be confusing to the uninitiated. Color-coded subway lines are named by a letter or number. Each line is shared by local trains and express trains; the latter make only select stops in Manhattan (indicated by a white circle on subway maps). Single ride is $2.75 with a MetroCard. A 7-Day Unlimited Pass costs $32.

Buses Convenient during off hours – especially when transferring between the city's eastern and western sides. Uses the MetroCard; same price as the subway.

Inter-borough ferries Spots along the East River in Manhattan, Brooklyn, Queens (and soon the Bronx), including the Rockaway beaches in Queens, are now connected by the new New York City Ferry (www.ferry.nyc); the New York Water Taxi (www.nywatertaxi.com) hits a few piers with regular services. Journey across New York Harbor on the free, commuter Staten Island Ferry (p70).

TAXI & RIDE SHARE

⊙ Taxi meters start at $2.50 and increase roughly $5 for every 20 blocks. See www.nyc.gov/taxi for more information.

⊙ App-based car-hailing services have taken over the streets of the five boroughs. Now, with nearly five times as many cars as yellow cabs and growing, they're both convenient, indispensable for some, and of course adding to the already terrible traffic problem.

Where to Stay

Expect high prices and small spaces. Rates waver by availability, not by high-season or low-season rules, and accommodations fill up quickly.

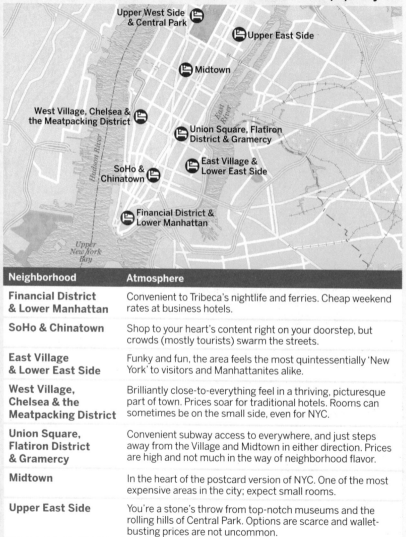

Neighborhood	Atmosphere
Financial District & Lower Manhattan	Convenient to Tribeca's nightlife and ferries. Cheap weekend rates at business hotels.
SoHo & Chinatown	Shop to your heart's content right on your doorstep, but crowds (mostly tourists) swarm the streets.
East Village & Lower East Side	Funky and fun, the area feels the most quintessentially 'New York' to visitors and Manhattanites alike.
West Village, Chelsea & the Meatpacking District	Brilliantly close-to-everything feel in a thriving, picturesque part of town. Prices soar for traditional hotels. Rooms can sometimes be on the small side, even for NYC.
Union Square, Flatiron District & Gramercy	Convenient subway access to everywhere, and just steps away from the Village and Midtown in either direction. Prices are high and not much in the way of neighborhood flavor.
Midtown	In the heart of the postcard version of NYC. One of the most expensive areas in the city; expect small rooms.
Upper East Side	You're a stone's throw from top-notch museums and the rolling hills of Central Park. Options are scarce and wallet-busting prices are not uncommon.
Upper West Side & Central Park	Convenient access to Central Park and the Museum of Natural History. Tends to swing in the familial direction.

WASHINGTON, DC

In this Chapter

National Mall	92
Capitol Hill	98
Sights	100
Tours	105
Shopping	105
Eating	106
Drinking & Nightlife	112
Entertainment	116

Washington, DC at a Glance...

The USA's capital teems with iconic monuments, vast museums and the corridors of power where visionaries and demagogues roam. Seeing the White House and soaring Capitol will thrill, but it's the cobblestoned neighborhoods, global cafes and buzzy quarters popping with live music and beer gardens that really make you fall for DC, no matter what your politics. The city can be a bargain, thanks to the slew of free Smithsonian museums and other gratis institutions. Plan on jam-packed days sightseeing and nights spent with locals sipping DC-made brews and chowing in cozy restaurants.

Two Days in Washington, DC

Start at the National Mall. Check out the **Air and Space Museum** (p94) and **Museum of African American History and Culture** (p94). Continue to the **Washington Monument** (p92), **Vietnam Veterans Memorial** (p93) and **Lincoln Memorial** (p92). Have dinner Downtown. Next day, tour Capitol Hill, visit the **National Archives** (p101) and saunter by the **White House** (p100). At night go to U Street or Shaw for eats and drinks.

Four Days in Washington, DC

On day three, explore Georgetown and have lunch there. In the evening, catch a show at the **Kennedy Center** (p116). Start day four at Dupont Circle and gape at mansions along **Embassy Row** (p104). Visit the **National Gallery of Art** (p95), **Newseum** (p101) and other sights you might have missed. For dinner, browse 14th St in Logan Circle.

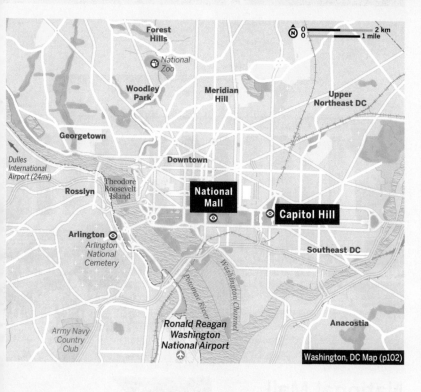

Washington, DC Map (p102)

Arriving in Washington, DC

Ronald Reagan Washington National Airport Metro trains (around $2.60) depart every 10 minutes from 5am and midnight (to 3am Friday and Saturday); 20 minutes to center. Taxis $15 to $22.

Dulles International Airport Silver Line Express bus runs every 15 to 20 minutes to Wiehle-Reston East Metro between 6am and 10:40pm (from 7:45am weekends); 60 to 75 minutes to center, around $11 total. Taxis $62 to $73.

Where to Stay

Washington has loads of posh properties for all the dignitaries who come to town. Chain hotels, guesthouses and apartments blanket the cityscape, too. But nothing comes cheap, especially in popular areas around the White House, Downtown and Dupont Circle.

KAMIRA / SHUTTERSTOCK ©

National Mall

This 2-mile-long lawn is anchored at one end by the Lincoln Memorial, at the other by Capitol Hill, intersected by the Reflecting Pool and WWII memorial, and centered by the Washington Monument.

Great For...

☑ **Don't Miss**

The Lincoln Memorial step where Martin Luther King Jr gave his 'I Have a Dream' speech.

Memorials & Monuments

Lincoln Memorial (www.nps.gov/linc; 2 Lincoln Memorial Circle NW; ⊙24hr; ⊒Circulator, ⓂOrange, Silver, Blue Lines to Foggy Bottom-GWU) FREE Anchoring the Mall's west end is the hallowed shrine to Abraham Lincoln, who gazes peacefully across the Reflecting Pool beneath his neoclassical, Doric-columned abode. The words of his Gettysburg Address and Second Inaugural speech flank the statue on the north and south walls. On the steps, Martin Luther King Jr delivered his famed 'I Have a Dream' speech; look for the engraving that marks the spot (it's on the landing 18 stairs from the top).

Washington Monument (www.nps.gov/wamo; 2 15th St NW; ⊙9am-5pm, to 10pm Jun-Aug; ⊒Circulator, ⓂOrange, Silver, Blue Lines to Smithsonian) FREE Peaking at 555ft (and 5in)

MARTIN CHILD / GETTY IMAGES ©

🛈 Need to Know

The DC Circulator National Mall bus route stops by many of the museum and monument hot spots.

🍴 Take a Break

In the National Museum of the American Indian, **Mitsitam Native Foods Cafe** (www.mitsitamcafe.com; cnr 4th St & Independence Ave SW; mains $12-22; ⊗11am-5pm, reduced hours in winter, Ⓜ Orange, Silver, Blue, Green, Yellow Lines to L'Enfant Plaza) serves unique, indigenous dishes.

★ Top Tip

Dining options are thin on the Mall, so bring snacks. Museums typically allow you to bring in food.

and comprised of 36,000 blocks of stone, this is the tallest building in the district. It took so long to build that the original quarry ran out; note the delineation in color where the old and new marble meet about a third of the way up. Alas, the monument is closed until spring 2019 for repairs, so you'll have to wait until then for stellar views from the observation deck.

Martin Luther King Jr Memorial (www.nps.gov/ mlkm; 1850 W Basin Dr SW; ⊗24hr; 🚌Circulator, Ⓜ Orange, Silver, Blue Lines to Smithsonian) FREE Opened in 2011, this is the Mall's newest memorial and the first one to honor an African American. Sculptor Lei Yixin carved the piece. Besides Dr King's striking, 30ft-tall image, known as the Stone of Hope, there are two blocks of granite behind him that represent the Mountain of Despair. A wall inscribed with King's moving quotes about democracy, justice and peace flanks the piece.

Vietnam Veterans Memorial (www.nps.gov/ vive; 5 Henry Bacon Dr NW; ⊗24hr; 🚌Circulator, Ⓜ Orange, Silver, Blue Lines to Foggy Bottom-GWU) FREE The opposite of DC's white, gleaming marble is this black, low-lying 'V,' an expression of the psychic scar wrought by the Vietnam War. The monument descends into the earth, with the names of the war's 58,300-plus casualties – listed in the order they died – chiseled into it. A subtle but profound monument, it was designed by 21-year-old undergraduate student Maya Lin in 1981.

National WWII Memorial (www.nps.gov/wwii; 17th St; ⊗24hr; 🚌Circulator, Ⓜ Orange, Silver, Blue Lines to Smithsonian) FREE Dedicated in 2004, the WWII memorial honors the 400,000 Americans who died in the conflict, along with the 16 million US soldiers who served between 1941 and 1945. The plaza's dual arches symbolize victory in the Atlantic and Pacific theaters.

The 56 surrounding pillars represent each US state and territory.

Smithsonian Museums

You could spend your entire trip here. Of the Smithsonian Institution's 19 vast museums, 10 are on the Mall, offering everything from dinosaur skeletons to lunar modules to exquisite artworks. All of the sights are free.

National Air & Space Museum (☎202-633-2214; www.airandspace.si.edu; cnr 6th St & Independence Ave SW; ◷10am-5:30pm, to 7:30pm some days; ⛟; ⬚Circulator, ⓜOrange, Silver, Blue, Green, Yellow Lines to L'Enfant Plaza) **FREE** One of the most popular Smithsonian museums. Everyone flocks to see the Wright brothers' flyer, Chuck Yeager's *Bell X-1*, Charles Lindbergh's *Spirit of St Louis*, Amelia Earhart's natty red plane and the Apollo Lunar Module. An Imax theater, a planetarium and flight simulators are all here ($8 to $10 each).

National Museum of Natural History (☎20 2-663-1000; www.naturalhistory.si.edu; cnr 10th St & Constitution Ave NW; ◷10am-5:30pm, to 7:30pm some days; ⛟; ⬚Circulator, ⓜOrange, Silver, Blue Lines to Smithsonian or Federal Triangle) **FREE** It's another Smithsonian top draw. The beloved dinosaur hall is under renovation until 2019, but the giant squid (1st floor, Ocean Hall) and tarantula feedings (2nd floor, Insect Zoo) fill in the thrills.

National Air & Space Museum

National Museum of African American History & Culture (☎844-750-3012; www.nmaahc.si.edu; 1400 Constitution Ave NW; ⊙10am-5:30pm; 🚹; 🚋Circulator, MOrange, Silver, Blue Lines to Smithsonian or Federal Triangle) FREE Opened in 2016, the Smithsonian's newest museum covers the diverse African American experience and how it helped shape the nation. The museum is so wildly popular you need a timed entry pass to get in. Your best bet to obtain one is via the same-day online release, when tickets are made available at 6:30am on the museum's website. Be ready, because they're snapped up within minutes.

> ☑ **Don't Miss**
>
> An atmospheric nighttime walk along Constitution Ave past the dramatically lit monuments.

National Museum of American History (☎202-663-1000; www.americanhistory.si.edu; cnr 14th St & Constitution Ave NW; ⊙10am-5:30pm, to 7:30pm some days; 🚹; 🚋Circulator, MOrange, Silver, Blue Lines to Smithsonian or Federal Triangle) FREE The centerpiece is the flag that flew over Fort McHenry in Baltimore during the War of 1812 – the same flag that inspired Francis Scott Key to pen 'The Star-Spangled Banner.' Other highlights include Julia Child's kitchen (1st floor, Food exhibition), George Washington's sword (3rd floor, Price of Freedom exhibition) and Dorothy's ruby slippers (2nd floor, American Stories exhibition).

National Gallery of Art

The staggering collection at the **National Gallery of Art** (☎202-737-4215; www.nga.gov; Constitution Ave NW, btwn 3rd & 7th Sts; ⊙10am-5pm Mon-Sat, 11am-6pm Sun; 🚋Circulator, MGreen, Yellow Lines to Archives) FREE spans art from the Middle Ages to the present. The neoclassical west building showcases European art through the early 1900s. The IM Pei–designed east building displays modern art. Recently renovated and expanded, this new wing really dazzles. A trippy underground walkway connects the two buildings.

SEAN PAVONE / SHUTTERSTOCK ©

★ Did You Know?

The Smithsonian Institution holds approximately 156 million artworks, scientific specimens and artifacts, of which less than 2% are on display at any given time.

National Mall

A DAY TOUR

Folks often call the Mall 'America's Front Yard,' and that's a pretty good analogy. It is indeed a lawn, unfurling scrubby green grass from the Capitol west to the Lincoln Memorial. It's also America's great public space, where citizens come to protest their government, go for scenic runs and connect with the nation's most cherished ideals writ large in stone, landscaping, monuments and memorials.

You can sample quite a bit in a day, but it'll be a full one that requires roughly 4 miles of walking.

Start at the ❶ **Vietnam Veterans Memorial**, then head counterclockwise around the Mall, swooping in on the ❷ **Lincoln Memorial**, ❸ **Martin Luther King Jr Memorial** and ❹ **Washington Monument**. You can also pause for the cause of the Korean War and

FLIPHOTO / SHUTTERSTOCK ©

Smithsonian Castle

Seek out the tomb of James Smithson, the eccentric Englishman whose 1826 financial gift launched the Smithsonian Institution. His crypt is in a room by the Mall entrance.

DAVE NEWMAN / SHUTTERSTOCK ©

Martin Luther King Jr Memorial

Walk all the way around the towering statue of Dr King by Lei Yixin and read the quotes. His likeness, incidentally, is 11ft taller than Lincoln and Jefferson in their memorials.

Tidal Basin

Department of Agriculture

FSTOCKFOTO / SHUTTERSTOCK ©

National Air & Space Museum

Simply step inside and look up, and you'll be impressed. Lindbergh's *Spirit of St Louis* and Chuck Yeager's sound barrier–breaking Bell X-1 are among the machines hanging from the ceiling.

National Museum of the American Indian

US Capitol

West Building

East Building

❺

❻

❼

WWII, among other monuments that dot the Mall's western portion.

Then it's onward to the museums, all fabulous and all free. Begin at the **❺ Smithsonian Castle** to get your bearings – and to say thanks to the guy making all this awesomeness possible – and commence browsing through the **❻ National Air & Space Museum**, **❼ National Gallery of Art & National Sculpture Garden** and **❽ National Museum of Natural History**.

Lincoln Memorial

Commune with Abe in his chair, then head down the steps to the marker where Martin Luther King Jr gave his 'Dream' speech. The view of the Reflecting Pool and Washington Monument is one of DC's best.

ADAM PARENT / SHUTTERSTOCK ©

Korean War Veterans Memorial

National WWII Memorial

National Museum of African American History & Culture

National Museum of American History

National Sculpture Garden

Vietnam Veterans Memorial

Check the symbol that's beside each name. A diamond indicates 'killed, body recovered.' A plus sign indicates 'missing and unaccounted for.' There are approximately 1200 of the latter.

Washington Monument

As you approach the obelisk, look a third of the way up. See how it's slightly lighter in color at the bottom? Builders had to use different marble after the first source dried up.

National Museum of Natural History

Wave to Henry, the elephant who guards the rotunda, then zip to the 2nd floor's Hope Diamond. The 45.52-carat bauble has cursed its owners, including Marie Antoinette, or so the story goes.

National Gallery of Art & National Sculpture Garden

Beeline to Gallery 6 (West Building) and ogle the Western Hemisphere's only Leonardo da Vinci painting. Outdoors, amble amid whimsical sculptures by Miró, Calder and Lichtenstein. Also check out IM Pei's design of the East Building.

KAMIRA / SHUTTERSTOCK ©

Capitol Hill

First-time visitors will be forgiven for assuming Capitol Hill, the city's geographic and legislative heart, is all about power-broking and politics. Truth is, it's pretty much a traditional neighborhood, but there's no denying that the big-domed building grabs all the attention.

Great For

☑ Don't Miss

The 1507 Waldseemuller World Map (the first to show America) at the Library of Congress.

The Capitol

Since 1800, the **Capitol** (☏202-226-8000; www.visitthecapitol.gov; 1st St NE & E Capitol St; ◷8:30am-4:30pm Mon-Sat; MOrange, Silver, Blue Lines to Capitol South) FREE is where Congress, the legislative branch of American government, has met to write the country's laws. The lower House of Representatives (435 members) and upper Senate (100) meet respectively in the south and north wings of the building. Enter via the underground visitor center below the East Plaza. Guided tours of the building are free, but you need a ticket. Get one at the information desk, or reserve online in advance (there's no fee).

To watch Congress in session, you need a separate visitor pass. US citizens must get one from their representative or senator; foreign visitors should take their passports

ORHAN CAM / SHUTTERSTOCK ©

Constitution Ave NW

Supreme Court ◎
Capitol ◎
E Capitol St NE
◎ **Library of Congress**

Independence Ave SW

Capitol South Ⓜ

❶ Need to Know

Groovy underground tunnels connect the Capitol, Supreme Court and Library of Congress, making for easy, weather-proof access.

✖ Take a Break

Eastern Market (p113) is a short stroll away for butchers, bakers and blue-crab makers.

★ Top Tip

Military bands perform on the Capitol steps weekdays (except Thursday) at 8pm June through August.

o the House and Senate Appointment Desks on the upper level. Congressional committee hearings are actually more interesting (and substantive) if you care bout what's being debated; check for a schedule, locations and to see if they're pen to the public (they often are) at www. ouse.gov and www.senate.gov.

Supreme Court

he highest court in the USA, the **Supreme Court** (☎202-479-3030; www.supremecourt. ov; 1 1st St NE; ◎9am-4:30pm Mon-Fri; ꓵOrange, Silver, Blue Lines to Capitol South) ꞟꞟꞟ sits in a pseudo-Greek temple that ou enter through 13,000lb bronze doors. rrive early to watch arguments (periodic 1onday through Wednesday October to pril). You can visit the permanent exhibits

and the building's five-story, marble-and-bronze, spiral staircase year-round. On days when court is not in session you also can hear lectures (every hour on the half-hour) in the courtroom.

Library of Congress

The world's largest **library** (☎202-707-8000; www.loc.gov; 1st St SE; ◎8:30am-4:30pm Mon-Sat; ꓵOrange, Silver, Blue Lines to Capitol South) ꞟꞟꞟ – with 164 million books, manuscripts, maps, photos, films and other items – awes in both scope and design. The centerpiece is the 1897 Jefferson Building. Gawk at the Great Hall, done up in stained glass, marble and mosaics of mythical characters, then seek out the Gutenberg Bible (c 1455), Thomas Jefferson's round library and the reading-room viewing area. Free tours take place between 10:30am and 3:30pm on the half-hour.

◎ SIGHTS

◎ White House Area

White House   Landmark

(📞202-456-7041; www.whitehouse.gov; 1600 Pennsylvania Ave NW; ⊘tours 7:30-11:30am Tue-Thu, to 1:30pm Fri & Sat; Ⓜ Orange, Silver, Blue Lines to Federal Triangle or McPherson Sq) **FREE** The 'President's House' was built between 1792 and 1800. If you're lucky enough to get inside on a public tour, you'll see several rooms in the main residence, each rich in presidential lore. Tours must be arranged in advance. Americans must apply via one of their state's members of Congress, and non-Americans must apply through their country's embassy in DC. Applications are taken from 21 days to three months in advance; the earlier you request during this time frame the better.

White House Visitor Center   Museum

(📞202-208-1631; www.nps.gov/whho; 1450 Pennsylvania Ave NW; ⊘7:30am-4pm; Ⓜ Orange, Silver, Blue Lines to Federal Triangle) **FREE** Getting

Smithsonian Institution

The **Smithsonian Institution** (www.si.edu) is not a single place, as commonly thought; rather, it consists of 19 museums, the National Zoo and nine research facilities. Most are in DC, but others are further flung in the US and abroad. Together they comprise the world's largest museum and research complex – and it's all free to visitors. Thanks go to the curious Englishman James Smithson, who never visited the USA, but willed the fledgling nation $508,318 to found an 'establishment for the increase and diffusion of knowledge' after he died in 1829.

Most Smithsonian museums are open daily (except Christmas Day). Some have extended hours in summer. Be prepared for lines and bag checks.

inside the White House can be tough, so here is your backup plan. Browse artifacts such as Roosevelt's desk for his fireside chats and Lincoln's cabinet chair. Multimedia exhibits give a 360-degree view into the White House's rooms. It's obviously not the same as seeing the real deal firsthand, but the center does do its job very well, giving good history sprinkled with great anecdotes on presidential spouses, kids, pets and dinner preferences.

Renwick Gallery   Museum

(📞202-633-7970; http://renwick.americanart.si.edu; 1661 Pennsylvania Ave NW; ⊘10am-5:30pm; Ⓜ Orange, Silver, Blue Lines to Farragut West) **FREE** Part of the Smithsonian diaspora, the Renwick Gallery is set in a stately 1859 mansion and exhibits a playful collection of contemporary American craft and decorative-art pieces.

◎ Georgetown

Georgetown Waterfront Park   Park

(www.georgetownwaterfrontpark.org; Water St NW, btwn 30th St & Key Bridge; 👫; ⌨Circulator) The park is a favorite with couples on first dates, families on an evening stroll and power players showing off their big yachts. Benches dot the way, where you can sit and watch the rowing teams out on the Potomac River. Alfresco restaurants cluster near the harbor at 31st St NW. They ring a terraced plaza filled with fountains (which become an ice rink in winter). The docks are also here for sightseeing boats that ply the Potomac to Alexandria, VA.

Dumbarton Oaks   Gardens, Museum

(📞202-339-6401; www.doaks.org; 1703 32nd St NW; museum free, gardens adult/child $10/5; ⊘museum 11:30am-5:30pm Tue-Sun, gardens 2-6pm; ⌨Circulator) The mansion's 10 acres of enchanting formal gardens are straight out of a storybook. In springtime, the blooms – including heaps of cherry blossoms – are stunning. The mansion itself is worth a walk-through to see exquisite Byzantine and pre-Columbian art (including El Greco's *The Visitation*) and the fascinating library of rare books.

◎ Capitol Hill

United States Holocaust Memorial Museum   Museum

(📞202-488-0400; www.ushmm.org; 100 Raoul Wallenberg Pl SW; ◷10am-5:20pm, extended hours Apr–mid-Jun; 🚇Circulator, MOrange, Silver, Blue Lines to Smithsonian) **FREE** For a deep understanding of the Holocaust – its victims, perpetrators and bystanders – this harrowing museum is a must-see. The main exhibit gives visitors the identity card of a single Holocaust victim, whose story is revealed as you take a winding route into a hellish past marked by ghettos, rail cars and death camps. It also shows the flip side of human nature, documenting the risks many citizens took to help the persecuted.

National Postal Museum   Museum

(📞202-633-5555; www.postalmuseum.si.edu; 2 Massachusetts Ave NE; ◷10am-5:30pm; ♿; MRed Line to Union Station) **FREE** The Smithsonian-run Postal Museum is way cooler than you might think. Level 1 has exhibits on postal history from the Pony Express to modern times, where you'll see antique mail planes and touching old letters from soldiers and pioneers. Level 2 holds the world's largest stamp collection. Join the stamp geeks pulling out drawers and snapping photos of the world's rarest stamps (the Ben Franklin Z Grill!), or start your own collection, choosing from among thousands of free international stamps (Guyana, Congo, Cambodia...).

◎ Downtown

National Archives   Landmark

(📞866-272-6272; www.archives.gov/museum; 700 Pennsylvania Ave NW; ◷10am-5:30pm; MGreen, Yellow Lines to Archives) **FREE** It's hard not to feel a little in awe of the big three documents in the National Archives: the Declaration of Independence, the Constitution and the Bill of Rights, plus one of four copies of the Magna Carta. Taken together, it becomes clear just how radical the American experiment was for its time. The Public Vaults, a bare scratching of archival bric-a-brac, make a flashy rejoinder to the main exhibit.

Reynolds Center for American Art & Portraiture   Museum

(📞202-633-1000; www.americanart.si.edu; cnr 8th & F Sts NW; ◷11:30am-7pm; MRed, Yellow, Green Lines to Gallery Pl-Chinatown) **FREE** If you only visit one art museum in DC, make it the Reynolds Center, which combines the National Portrait Gallery and the American Art Museum. There is, simply put, no better collection of American art in the world than at these two Smithsonian museums. Famed works by Edward Hopper, Georgia O'Keeffe, Andy Warhol, Winslow Homer and loads more celebrated artists fill the galleries.

Newseum   Museum

(📞202-292-6100; www.newseum.org; 555 Pennsylvania Ave NW; adult/child $25/15; ◷9am-5pm; ♿; MGreen, Yellow Lines to Archives) This six-story, interactive museum is worth its admission. You can delve into the major events of recent years (the fall of the Berlin Wall, September 11, Hurricane Katrina), and spend hours watching moving film footage and perusing Pulitzer Prize–winning photographs. The concourse level displays FBI artifacts from prominent news stories, such as the Unabomber's cabin and gangster Whitey Bulger's fishing hat.

Ford's Theatre   Historic Site

(📞202-347-4833; www.fords.org; 511 10th St NW; ◷9am-4:30pm; MRed, Orange, Silver, Blue Lines to Metro Center) **FREE** On April 14, 1865, John Wilkes Booth assassinated Abraham Lincoln in his box seat here. Timed-entry tickets let you see the flag-draped site. They also provide entry to the basement museum (displaying Booth's .44-caliber pistol, his muddy boot etc) and to Petersen House (across the street), where Lincoln died. Arrive early (by 8:30am) because tickets do run out. Better yet, reserve online ($3 fee) to ensure admittance.

Chinatown   Area

(7th & H Sts NW; MRed, Yellow, Green Lines to Gallery Pl-Chinatown) DC's dinky Chinatown was once a major Asian entrepôt, but today most Asians in the Washington area live in the Maryland or Virginia suburbs. That said, Chinatown is still an intriguing browse. Enter through **Friendship Arch** (7th & H Sts NW), the largest single-span arch in the world.

Washington, DC

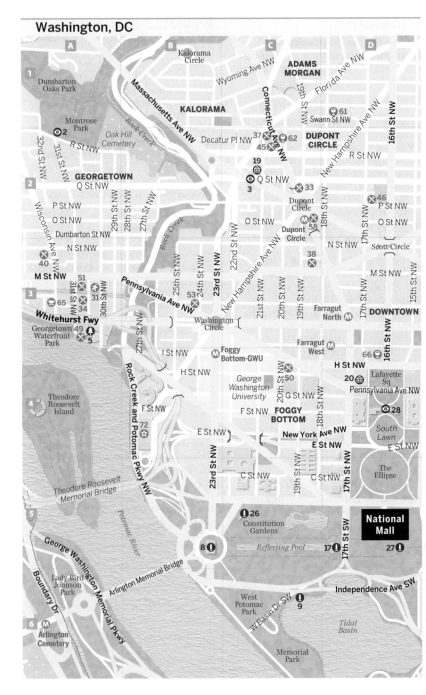

A
B
C
D

1

Dumbarton
Oaks Park

Kalorama
Circle

Wyoming Ave NW

**ADAMS
MORGAN**

Florida Ave NW

Massachusetts Ave NW

Rock Creek

KALORAMA

Connecticut Ave NW

19th St NW

🅟61
Swann St NW

16th St NW

Montrose
Park

Oak Hill
Cemetery

Decatur Pl NW

37

45

🅟62

**DUPONT
CIRCLE**

New Hampshire Ave NW

R St NW

32nd St NW

31st St NW

R St NW

2

GEORGETOWN
Q St NW

29th St NW

28th St NW

27th St NW

19
🅞 Q St NW
3

🅧33

Dupont
Circle

🅟46
P St NW

17th St NW

16th St NW

Wisconsin Ave NW

P St NW

O St NW

Dumbarton St NW

N St NW

25th St NW

24th St NW

23rd St NW

22nd St NW

New Hampshire Ave NW

O St NW

🅜
🅧58

Dupont
Circle

O St NW

N St NW

Scott Circle

🅧40

M St NW

51

🅧

🅟

31

30th St NW

31st St NW

Pennsylvania Ave NW

53

21st St NW

20th St NW

19th St NW

38
🅧

M St NW

15th St NW

3

🅟65

🅧34

Whitehurst Fwy

Washington
Circle

Farragut
North 🅜

DOWNTOWN

16th St NW

Georgetown
Waterfront
Park

49
🅧
5

27th St NW

I St NW

🅜
**Foggy
Bottom-GWU**

**Farragut
West** 🅜

66🅟

17th St NW

4

Theodore
Roosevelt
Island

Rock Creek and Potomac Pkwy NW

H St NW

F St NW

72
🅣

*George
Washington
University*

20th St NW

50
🅧

G St NW

18th St NW

H St NW

20🏛

Lafayette
Sq

Pennsylvania Ave NW

F St NW

**FOGGY
BOTTOM**

🅟28

*South
Lawn*

E St NW

E St NW

23rd St NW

E St NW

New York Ave NW

19th St NW

18th St NW

17th St NW

*The
Ellipse*

C St NW

C St NW

**National
Mall**

5

Theodore Roosevelt
Memorial Bridge

Potomac River

🅟26
Constitution
Gardens

8🅟

Reflecting Pool

17🅟

17th St SW

27🅟

George Washington Memorial Pkwy

Boundary Dr

Lady Bird
Johnson
Park

Arlington Memorial Bridge

West
Potomac
Park

W Basin Dr SW

🅟
9

Independence Ave SW

*Tidal
Basin*

6

🅜

**Arlington
Cemetery**

*Memorial
Park*

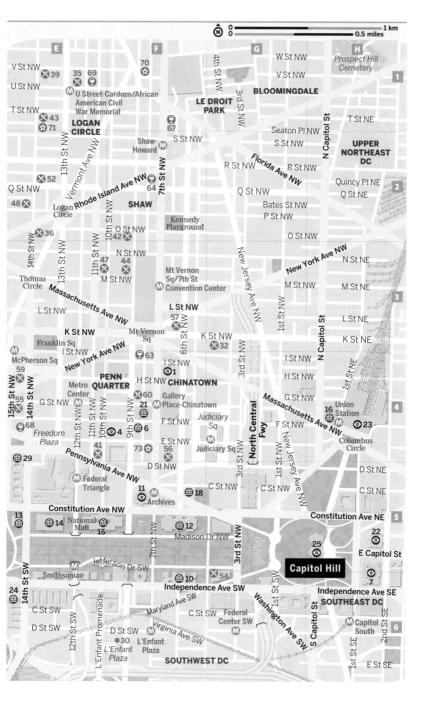

0 1 km
0 0.5 miles

E **F** **G** **H**

V St NW ⊗39
35 69
U St NW Ⓜ U Street-Cardozo/African *Prospect Hill*
American Civil *Cemetery*
War Memorial W St NW **1**
V St NW
T St NW ⊗43 **BLOOMINGDALE**
71 **LOGAN** **LE DROIT**
CIRCLE **PARK**
Shaw- Ⓟ Seaton Pl NW T St NE
Howard 67 S St NW
S St NW **UPPER**
NORTHEAST
R St NW Florida Ave NW R St NW **DC**
⊗52 R St NW
64 **SHAW** Q St NW Quincy Pl NE
Q St NW Ⓜ Q St NE
48⊗ Logan Bates St NW **2**
Circle P St NW
Kennedy
Playground O St NW
36 O St NW
42
Mt Vernon N St NE
N St NW Sq/7th St New York Ave NW
47 44 Ⓜ Convention Center M St NE
M St NW N St NE
3
Thomas L St NW M St NW M St NE
Circle Massachusetts Ave NW
57
L St NW L St NE
K St NW Mt Vernon K St NE
Sq K St NW
Franklin Sq I St NW 63 ⊗32 K St NE
Ⓜ New York Ave NW
McPherson Sq I St NW I St NW
59 **PENN** H St NW H St NE
QUARTER ⊙1
Metro **CHINATOWN** Union **4**
Center Ⓜ⊗60 Gallery 16 Station
68 G St NW 21 Place-Chinatown G St NW ⊙23
⊙ ⊙4 ⊙6 F St NW *Judiciary* F St NW Columbus
29 41 *Sq* Ⓜ Circle
73 56 Judiciary Sq
Pennsylvania Ave NW E St NW D St NE
Ⓜ Federal D St NW Massachusetts Ave NW
Triangle 11 Ⓜ C St NE
Constitution Ave NW Archives 18 Constitution Ave NE **5**
13 14 12 22
National ⊙
Mall 15 25
Madison Dr NW E Capitol St
Capitol Hill
Ⓜ Jefferson Dr SW ⊙
Smithsonian 10 54 7
24 Independence Ave SW Independence Ave SE
C St SW **SOUTHEAST DC**
C St SW Federal
D St SW Center SW Ⓜ Capitol **6**
Maryland Ave SW South
Virginia Ave SW
30 L'Enfant
L'Enfant Plaza E St SE
L'Enfant Plaza **SOUTHWEST DC**
Promenade

Washington, DC

◎ Sights
1	Chinatown	F4
2	Dumbarton Oaks	A2
3	Embassy Row	C2
4	Ford's Theatre	F4
	Friendship Arch	(see 1)
5	Georgetown Waterfront Park	A3
6	International Spy Museum	F4
7	Library of Congress	H6
8	Lincoln Memorial	B5
9	Martin Luther King Jr Memorial	C6
10	National Air and Space Museum	F6
11	National Archives	F5
12	National Gallery of Art	F5
13	National Museum of African American History and Culture	E5
14	National Museum of American History	E5
15	National Museum of Natural History	E5
16	National Postal Museum	H4
17	National WWII Memorial	D5
18	Newseum	F5
19	Phillips Collection	C2
20	Renwick Gallery	D4
21	Reynolds Center for American Art & Portraiture	F4
22	Supreme Court	H5
23	Union Station	H4
24	United States Holocaust Memorial Museum	E6
25	US Capitol	H5
26	Vietnam Veterans Memorial	C5
27	Washington Monument	D5
28	White House	D4
29	White House Visitor Center	E4

⊕ Activities, Courses & Tours
30	Bike & Roll – L'Enfant Plaza	F6
31	C&O Canal Towpath	A3
	DC Brew Tours	(see 21)

ⓐ Shopping
	Kramerbooks	(see 33)
	White House Historical Association Museum Shop	(see 29)

⊗ Eating
32	A Baked Joint	G3
33	Afterwords Cafe	C2

34	Baked & Wired	A3
35	Ben's Chili Bowl	E1
36	Birch & Barley	E2
37	Bistrot du Coin	C2
38	Bub & Pop's	C3
39	Busboys & Poets	E1
40	Cafe Milano	A3
41	Central Michel Richard	E4
42	Chercher	F2
43	Compass Rose	E1
44	Dabney	F3
45	Dolcezza	C2
46	Duke's Grocery	D2
47	El Sol	E3
48	Estadio	E2
49	Fiola Mare	A3
50	Founding Farmers	C4
51	Il Canale	A3
52	Le Diplomate	E2
	Little Serow	(see 46)
53	Marcel's	B3
54	Mitsitam Native Foods Cafe	G6
55	Old Ebbitt Grill	E4
56	Rasika	F4
57	Shouk	F3
58	Un Je Ne Sais Quoi	C2
59	Woodward Takeout Food	E4
60	Zaytinya	F4

⊜ Drinking & Nightlife
61	Bar Charley	D1
62	Board Room	C2
	Churchkey	(see 36)
63	City Tap House	F4
	Columbia Room	(see 44)
64	Dacha Beer Garden	F2
65	Grace Street Coffee	A3
66	Off The Record	D4
67	Right Proper Brewing Co	F1
68	Round Robin	E4
69	U Street Music Hall	E1

⊛ Entertainment
70	9:30 Club	F1
71	Black Cat	E1
	Howard Theatre	(see 67)
72	Kennedy Center	B4
73	Shakespeare Theatre Company	F4
	Woolly Mammoth Theatre Company	(see 56)

◎ Dupont Circle

Embassy Row Architecture

(www.embassy.org; Massachusetts Ave NW, btwn Observatory & Dupont Circles NW; Ⓜ Red Line to Dupont Circle) Want to take a trip around the world? Stroll northwest along Massachu-setts Ave from Dupont Circle (the actual traffic circle) and you pass more than 40 embassies housed in mansions that range from elegant to imposing to discreet. Tunisia, Chile, Turkmenistan, Togo, Haiti – flags flutter above heavy doors and mark the nations inside, while dark-windowed sedans ease out of driveways ferrying dip-lomats to and fro. The district has another 130 embassies sprinkled throughout, but this is the main vein.

Phillips Collection   Museum

(☎202-387-2151; www.phillipscollection.org; 1600 21st St NW; Tue-Fri free, Sat & Sun $10, ticketed exhibitions per day $12; ⓧ10am-5pm Tue, Wed, Fri & Sat, to 8:30pm Thu, noon-7pm Sun; ⓂRed Line to Dupont Circle) The first modern-art museum in the country (opened in 1921) houses a small but exquisite collection of European and American works. Renoir's *Luncheon of the Boating Party* is a highlight, along with pieces by Gauguin, Van Gogh, Matisse, Picasso and many other greats. The intimate rooms, set in a restored mansion, put you unusually close to the artworks. The permanent collection is free on weekdays. Download the free app or dial ☎202-595-1839 for audio tours through the works.

⊙ TOURS

DC by Foot   Walking

(☎202-370-1830; www.freetoursbyfoot.com/washington-dc-tours) Guides for this pay-what-you-want walking tour offer engaging stories and historical details on different jaunts covering the Lincoln's assassination, National Mall, Dupont Circle's ghosts and many more. Most takers pay around $10 per person. Reserve in advance to guarantee a spot.

Bike & Roll – L'Enfant Plaza   Cycling

(☎202-842-2453; www.bikeandrolldc.com; 955 L'Enfant Plaza SW; tours adult/child $45/35; ⓧmid-Mar–early Dec; ⓂOrange, Silver, Blue, Yellow, Green Lines to L'Enfant Plaza) This branch of the bike-rental company (from $16 per two hours) is the one closest to the Mall. In addition to bike rental, it also provides tours. Three-hour jaunts wheel by the main sights of Capitol Hill and the National Mall. The evening rides to the monuments are particularly good.

Key Bridge Boathouse   Kayaking

(☎202-337-9642; www.boatingindc.com/boat-houses/key-bridge-boathouse; 3500 Water St NW; ⓧhours vary mid-Apr–Oct; ⓠCirculator) Located beneath the Key Bridge, the boathouse rents canoes, kayaks and stand up paddle boards (prices start at $16 per hour). In summer, it also offers guided, 90-minute kayak trips ($45 per person) that glide past the Lincoln Memorial as the sun sets. If you have a bike, the boathouse is a mere few steps from the Capital Crescent Trail.

DC Brew Tours   Bus

(☎202-759-8687; www.dcbrewtours.com; 801 F St NW; tours $65-90; ⓂRed, Yellow, Green Lines to Gallery Pl-Chinatown) Visit three to four breweries by van. Routes vary but could include DC Brau, Bardo, Capital City and Port City, among others. Five-hour jaunts feature tastings of 15-plus beers and a beer-focused meal. The 3½-hour Sips and Sights tour forgoes the meal and adds stops at the Lincoln Memorial, Pentagon and more. Departure is from downtown by the Reynolds Center.

⛒ SHOPPING

White House Historical Association Museum Shop   Gifts & Souvenirs

(shop.whitehousehistory.org; 1450 Pennsylvania Ave NW; ⓧ7:30am-4pm; ⓂFederal Triangle) Located inside the White House Visitor Center, this is the spot to get official White House–branded mementos, like the official Bo Obama Christmas ornament, or the official Blue Room necklace with glass beads, or the official Burning of the White House 1814 puzzle. The selection shocks and awes.

Capitol Hill Books   Books

(☎202-544-1621; www.capitolhillbooks-dc.com; 657 C St SE; ⓧ11:30am-6pm Mon-Fri, from 9am Sat & Sun; ⓂOrange, Silver, Blue Lines to Eastern Market) A trove of secondhand awesomeness, this shop has so many books staff have to double-stack them on the shelves. Superb notes by the cantankerous clerks help guide your selection. Categories are, er, unconventional, including 'Hinduism and Bobby Knight' and 'Sideshows and Carnivals.' The section on US presidents is huge (Chester Arthur books! An entire shelf of Truman books!).

📖 Arlington National Cemetery

Arlington National Cemetery (☎877-907-8585; www.arlingtoncemetery.mil; ⊙8am-7pm Apr-Sep, to 5pm Oct-Mar; MBlue Line to Arlington Cemetery) FREE is the somber final resting place for more than 400,000 military personnel and their dependents. The 624-acre grounds contain the dead of every war the US has fought since the Revolution. Highlights include the Tomb of the Unknown Soldier, with its elaborate changing of the guard ceremony (every hour on the hour October through March, every half-hour April through September), and the grave of John F Kennedy and his family, marked by an eternal flame. Departing from the visitor center, hop-on, hop-off bus tours are an easy way to visit the cemetery's main sights. Though Arlington is in Virginia, it's only a few Metro stops southwest of the National Mall.

Kramerbooks   Books

(☎202-387-1400; www.kramers.com; 1517 Connecticut Ave NW; ⊙7:30am-1am Sun-Thu, to 3am Fri & Sat; MRed Line to Dupont Circle) This flagship independent – which leapt into First Amendment history when it refused to release Monica Lewinsky's book-buying list to Ken Starr's snoops – features first-rate literature, travel and politics sections. The bookstore attaches to the fun-loving **Afterwords Cafe** (☎202-387-3825; mains $17-21), which brings in a frisky crowd that flirts over drinks and pages into the wee hours.

✸ EATING

✸ White House Area

Woodward Takeout Food   American $

(☎202-347-5355; http://woodwardtable.com; 1426 H St NW; mains $7-11; ⊙7:30am-4:30pm Mon-Fri; MOrange, Silver, Blue Lines to McPherson Sq) Woodward Takeout is the small, mostly carryout adjunct to Woodward Table, a

sharp, sit-down restaurant. Go ahead: jump in the line with all the office workers angling for the duck Reuben sandwich, housemade pastrami on sourdough rye or butternut squash flatbread. It'll move fast. Breakfast is busy, too, with egg-laden sandwiches on crumbly biscuits and salted chocolate croissants flying from the kitchen.

Founding Farmers   American $$

(☎202-822-8783; www.wearefoundingfarmers.com; 1924 Pennsylvania Ave NW; mains $15-28; ⊙7am-10pm Mon, 7am-11pm Tue-Thu, 7am-midnight Fri, 9am-midnight Sat, 9am-10pm Sun; ✐; MOrange, Silver, Blue Lines to Foggy Bottom-GWU or Farragut West) ✐ A frosty decor of pickled goods in jars adorns this buzzy dining space. The look is a combination of rustic-cool and modern art that reflects the nature of the food: locally sourced, New American fare. Buttermilk fried chicken and waffles, and butternut squash mascarpone ravioli, are a few of the favorites that hit the wood tables. The restaurant is located in the IMF building.

Old Ebbitt Grill   American $$

(☎202-347-4800; www.ebbitt.com; 675 15th St NW; mains $18-28; ⊙7:30am-1am Mon-Fri, from 8:30am Sat & Sun; MRed, Orange, Silver, Blue Lines to Metro Center) This legendary tavern, opened in 1856, has occupied prime real estate near the White House since 1983. Political players and tourists pack into the Victorian-style, brass and wood interior, where thick burgers, crab cakes and fish and chips are rotated out almost as quickly as the clientele. Pop in for a cocktail and oysters during happy hour.

Marcel's   French $$$

(☎202-296-1166; www.marcelsdc.com; 2401 Pennsylvania Ave NW; 4-/5-/7-course menus $95/115/155; ⊙5-10pm Mon-Thu, to 11pm Fri & Sat, to 9:30pm Sun; MOrange, Silver, Blue Lines to Foggy Bottom-GWU) Marcel's keeps true to classic French cuisine while adding modern embellishments. Old school, fill-you-up-by-a-fire fare such as pork belly and turbot with peas is hearty and thick. But the sprucing on the side – quail egg and cornichons, or the miso that accompanies the Alaskan cod – is just understated enough to ratchet the experience to greatness. The menu changes daily.

🏵 Georgetown

Baked & Wired   Bakery $

(📞202-333-2500; www.bakedandwired.com; 1052 Thomas Jefferson St NW; baked goods $3-6; ⏰7am-8pm Mon-Thu, 7am-9pm Fri, 8am-9pm Sat, 8am-8pm Sun; 🚌Circulator) Sniff out Baked & Wired, a cheery cafe that whips up beautifully made coffees, bacon cheddar buttermilk biscuits and enormous cupcakes (like the banana and peanut-butter-frosted Elvis). It's a fine spot to join university students and cyclists coming off the nearby trails. When the weather permits, patrons take their treats outside to the adjacent grassy area by the C&O Canal.

Simply Banh Mi   Vietnamese $

(📞202-333-5726; www.simplybanhmidc.com; 1624 Wisconsin Ave NW; mains $7-10; ⏰11am-7pm Tue-Sun; 🍴; 🚌Circulator) There's nothing fancy about the small, below-street-level space, and the compact menu sticks mostly to sandwiches and bubble tea. But the brother-sister owners know how to take a crusty baguette, stuff it with delicious lemongrass pork or other meat (or tofu), and make your day. They're super attentive to quality and to customer needs (vegan, gluten free etc).

Il Canale   Italian $$

(📞202-337-4444; www.ilcanale.com; 1063 31st St NW; mains $19-25; ⏰11:30am-10:30pm Mon-Thu, 11am-11pm Fri & Sat, 11am-10pm Sun; 🚌Circulator) Real-deal Neapolitan pizza emerges from the real-deal, Italian wood-fired oven in Il Canale's bouncy townhouse digs. It's casual and low-cost for Georgetown, which is why families, couples and groups of friends pile in at all hours. The calamari, lasagna, pastas and cannoli are all crowd pleasers.

Fiola Mare   Seafood $$$

(📞202-628-0065; www.fiolamaredc.com; 3050 K St NW; mains $28-50; ⏰5-10pm Mon, 11:30am-2:30pm & 5-10pm Tue-Fri, 11:30am-2pm & 5-10:30pm Sat, 11am-2pm & 5-10pm Sun; 🚌Circulator) Fiola Mare delivers the chi-chi Georgetown experience. It flies in fresh fish and crustaceans from Maine to Tasmania daily. The yacht-bobbling river view rocks.

Chinatown (p101)

The see-and-be-seen multitudes are here. It's DC at its luxe best. Try it at lunchtime on a weekday, when $24 gets you an Italian-style seafood main and a drink in the bar area. Make reservations.

Cafe Milano   Italian $$$

(☏202-333-6183; www.cafemilano.com; 3251 Prospect St NW; mains $25-45; ☺11:30am-11pm Mon & Tue, to midnight Wed-Sat, 11am-11pm Sun; 🚌Circulator) Milano has been reeling in the political glitterati and besotted Georgetown couples for years with its executions of northern Italian favorites. Be prepared to pay for the European-chic ambience and celebrity-spotting. The pastas get the biggest praise, especially the ones prepared tableside.

⊗ Capitol Hill

Toki Underground   Asian $

(☏202-388-3086; www.tokiunderground.com; 1234 H St NE; mains $13-15; ☺11:30am-2:30pm & 5-10pm Mon-Thu, to midnight Fri & Sat; Ⓜ Red Line to Union Station then streetcar) Spicy ramen noodles and dumplings sum up wee Toki's menu. Steaming pots obscure the busy chefs, while diners slurp and sigh contentedly. The eatery takes limited reservations, so there's typically a wait. Use the opportunity to explore the surrounding bars; Toki will text when your table is ready. The restaurant isn't signposted; look for the Pug bar, and Toki is above it.

Ambar   Balkan $$

(☏202-813-3039; www.ambarrestaurant.com; 523 8th St SE; small plates $7-13; ☺11am-2pm & 4-10pm Mon-Thu, to 11pm Fri, 10am-11pm Sat, 10am-10pm Sun; Ⓜ Orange, Silver, Blue Lines to Eastern Market) Ambar buzzes, especially at happy hour, when the convivial, European-style restaurant slings heaps of small plates. Roasted pepper and eggplant, smoked trout and pickled peppers, braised cabbage, lamb salami, brandy-soaked mussels – intriguing Balkan dishes hit the table one after the other to be shared between friends. Serbian beer, Moldovan whites and Bulgarian reds flow in copious quantities alongside.

Ethiopic   Ethiopian $$

(☏202-675-2066; www.ethiopicrestaurant.com; 401 H St NE; mains $13-19; ☺5-10pm Tue-Thu, from noon Fri-Sun; 🖊; Ⓜ Red Line to Union Station) In a city with no shortage of Ethiopian joints, Ethiopic stands above the rest. Top marks go to the various *wats* (stews) and the signature *tibs* (sautéed meat and veg), derived from tender lamb that has sat in a bath of herbs and hot spices. Vegans get lots of love here.

Ted's Bulletin   American $$

(☏202-544-8337; www.tedsbulletincapitolhill. com; 505 8th St SE; mains $11-19; ☺7am-10:30pm Sun-Thu, to 11:30pm Fri & Sat; 🚼; Ⓜ Orange, Silver, Blue Lines to Eastern Market) Plop into a booth in the art-deco-meets-diner ambience, and loosen the belt. Beer biscuits and sausage gravy for breakfast, meatloaf with ketchup glaze for dinner and other hipster spins on comfort foods hit the table. You've got to admire a place that lets you substitute pop tarts for toast. Breakfast is available all day.

Rose's Luxury   American $$$

(☏202-580-8889; www.rosesluxury.com; 717 8th St SE; small plates $13-16, family-style plates $28-33; ☺5-10pm Mon-Sat; Ⓜ Orange, Silver, Blue Lines to Eastern Market) Michelin-starred Rose's is one of DC's most buzzed-about eateries. Crowds fork into worldly Southern comfort food as twinkling lights glow overhead and candles flicker around the industrial, half-finished room. Rose's doesn't take reservations, but ordering your meal at the upstairs bar can save time (and the cocktails are delicious).

⊗ Downtown

A Baked Joint   Cafe $

(☏202-408-6985; www.abakedjoint.com; 440 K St NW; mains $5-11; ☺7am-8pm Mon-Thu, 7am-9pm Fri, 8am-8pm Sat & Sun; Ⓜ Red, Yellow, Green Lines to Gallery Pl-Chinatown) Order at the counter then take your luscious, heaped-on-housemade-bread sandwich – perhaps the roasted sweet potato and goat cheese on focaccia, or the Nutella and banana on whole-wheat sourdough – to a bench or table in the big, open room.

Natural light streams in the floor-to-ceiling windows. Not hungry? It's also a great place for a well-made latte.

El Sol   Mexican $

([📞]202-815-4789; www.elsol-dc.com; 1227 11th St NW; tacos $2.50-3, mains $10-16; [🕐]10am-1am Sun-Thu, to 2am Fri & Sat; [M]Green, Yellow Lines to Mt Vernon Sq/7th St-Convention Center) El Sol feels like a sunny neighborhood taqueria, but the food goes way beyond. Thin, crisp corn tortillas cradle juicy chicken, slow-braised pork, cactus paddles and other fillings, with almost all ingredients made in-house (the mole sauce comes from the chef's mom in Mexico). Besides tacos, the *pambazo* (a chorizo-and-potato-stuffed sandwich) and fiery guacamole rock the palate.

Shouk   Israeli $

([📞]202-652-1464; www.shouk.com; 655 K St NW; mains $10; [🕐]11am-10pm; [🥬]; [M]Green, Yellow Lines to Mt Vernon Sq/7th St-Convention Center) Small, fast-casual Shouk creates big flavor in its vegan menu of Israeli street food. A crazy-good burger made of chickpeas, black beans, lentils and mushrooms gets stuffed into a toasty pita with pickled turnips, arugula and charred onions. The mushroom-and-cauliflower pita and sweet-potato fries with cashew *labneh* (creamy 'cheese') are other lip smackers. Craft beer and tap wine add to the pleasure.

Rasika   Indian $$

([📞]202-637-1222; www.rasikarestaurant.com; 633 D St NW; mains $14-28; [🕐]11:30am-2:30pm Mon-Fri, 5:30-10:30pm Mon-Thu, 5-11pm Fri & Sat; [🥬]; [M]Green, Yellow Lines to Archives) Rasika is as cutting-edge as Indian food gets. The room resembles a Jaipur palace decorated by a flock of modernist art-gallery curators. Top marks go to the *murgh mussalam*, a plate of juicy tandoori chicken with cashews and quail eggs; and to the deceptively simple *dal* (lentils), which have just the right kiss of sharp fenugreek. Vegetarians will feel a lot of love here.

👪 DC for Children

DC Cool Kids (www.washington.org/dc-cool-kids) features activity guides, insider tips from local youngsters on things to do, and museum info. Top draws beyond the Natural History Museum (p94) and Air and Space Museum (p94):

National Zoo ([📞]202-633-4888; www.nationalzoo.si.edu; 3001 Connecticut Ave NW; [🕐]9am-6pm mid-Mar–Sep, to 4pm Oct–mid-Mar, grounds 8am-7pm mid-Mar–Sep, to 5pm Oct–mid-Mar; [M]Red Line to Cleveland Park or Woodley Park-Zoo/Adams Morgan) Home to more than 1800 individual animals (300-plus different species) in natural habitats, the National Zoo is famed for its giant pandas Mei Xiang and Tian Tian. Other highlights include the African lion pride, Asian elephants, and dangling orangutans swinging 50ft overhead from steel cables and inter-connected towers (aka the 'O Line').

International Spy Museum ([📞]202-393-7798; www.spymuseum.org; 800 F St NW; adult/child $22/15; [🕐]9am-7pm mid-Apr–mid-Aug, 10am-6pm rest of year; [♿]; [M]Red, Yellow, Green Lines to Gallery Pl-Chinatown) One of DC's most popular museums is flashy, over the top, and probably guilty of overtly glamming up a life of intelligence-gathering. But who cares? You basically want to see Q's lab, and that's what the Spy Museum feels like. Check out James Bond's tricked-out Aston Martin, the KGB's lipstick-concealed pistol and more. It's hugely popular; reserve online to avoid the queues ($2 surcharge).

Zaytinya   Mediterranean $$

([📞]202-638-0800; www.zaytinya.com; 701 9th St NW; mezze $8-14; [🕐]11am-10pm Sun & Mon, to 11pm Tue-Thu, to midnight Fri & Sat; [🥬]; [M]Red, Yellow, Green Lines to Gallery Pl-Chinatown) One of the culinary crown jewels of chef José Andrés, ever-popular Zaytinya serves superb Greek, Turkish and Lebanese mezze (small plates) in a long, noisy dining room with soaring ceilings and all-glass walls. It's a favorite after-work meet-up spot.

Dabney American $$$

(☎202-450-1015; www.thedabney.com; 122 Blagden Alley NW; small plates $14-22; ⏲5:30-10pm Tue-Thu, 5:30-11pm Fri & Sat, 5-10pm Sun; ⓜGreen, Yellow Line to Mt Vernon Sq/7th St-Convention Center) Chef Jeremiah Langhorne studied historic cookbooks, discovering recipes that used local ingredients and lesser-explored flavors in his quest to resuscitate mid-Atlantic cuisine lost to the ages. Most of the dishes are even cooked over a wood-burning hearth. But this isn't George Washington's resto. Chef Langhorne has given it all a modern twist – enough to earn him a Michelin star.

Central Michel Richard American $$$

(☎202-626-0015; www.centralmichelrichard. com; 1001 Pennsylvania Ave NW; mains $25-35; ⏲11:30am-2:30pm Mon-Fri, 5-10pm Mon-Thu, 5-10:30pm Fri & Sat, 11am-2:30pm Sun; ⓜOrange, Silver, Blue Lines to Federal Triangle) Michel Richard was one of Washington's first star chefs. He died in 2016, but his namesake Central blazes onward. It's a special dining experience, eating in a four-star bistro where the food is old-school, comfort-food favorites with a twist: perhaps lobster burgers, or a sinfully complex meatloaf, or fried chicken that redefines what fried chicken can be.

✖ Dupont Circle

Bub & Pop's Sandwiches $

(☎202-457-1111; www.bubandpops.com; 1815 M St NW; sandwiches half/whole $10/18; ⏲11am-4pm Mon-Sat; ⓜRed Line to Dupont Circle) A chef tired of the fine-dining rat race opened this gourmet sandwich shop with his parents. Ingredients are made from scratch in-house – the meatballs, pickles, mayonnaise, roasted pork. Congenial mom Arlene rules the counter and can answer questions about any of it. The sandwiches are enormous, and best consumed hot off the press in the bright aqua and red room.

Un Je Ne Sais Quoi Bakery $

(☎202-721-0099; www.facebook.com/unjene-saisquoipastry; 1361 Connecticut Ave NW; pastries $2.50-5; ⏲7:30am-7:30pm Mon-Thu, to 8pm Fri, 10am-8pm Sat; ⓜRed Line to Dupont Circle) The smell of rich coffee envelops you when you enter this little bakery, where a couple of French expats bake *merveilleux*, their signature pastry plumped with layers of meringue and ganache. It's like biting into a glorious cloud. Tarts, eclairs and other sweets are equally exquisite, served on china plates amid vintage Parisian decor.

Dolcezza Gelato $

(☎202-299-9116; www.dolcezzagelato.com; 1704 Connecticut Ave NW; gelato $5-8; ⏲7am-10pm Mon-Thu, 7am-11pm Fri, 8am-11pm Sat, 8am-10pm Sun; ⏶; ⓜRed Line to Dupont Circle) The local mini-chain Dolcezza whips up the District's best gelati. Some flavors are unusual, such as sweet-potato pecan and Thai coconut milk, and change with the seasons. Traditionalists can always get their licks with chocolate, salted caramel and peppermint. Good coffee, vintage-chic decor and free wi-fi add to the pleasure.

Bistrot du Coin French $$

(☎202-234-6969; www.bistrotducoin.com; 1738 Connecticut Ave NW; mains $16-29; ⏲11:30am-midnight Mon-Wed, 11:30am-1am Thu & Fri, noon-1am Sat, noon-midnight Sun; ⓜRed Line to Dupont Circle) The lively and much-loved Bistrot du Coin is a neighborhood favorite for roll-up-your sleeves, working-class French fare. The kitchen sends out consistently good onion soup, classic *steak-frites* (grilled steak and French fries), cassoulet, open-face sandwiches and nine varieties of its famous *moules* (mussels). Regional wines from around the motherland accompany the food by the glass, carafe and bottle.

Duke's Grocery Cafe $$

(☎202-733-5623; www.dukesgrocery.com; 1513 17th St NW; mains $12-16; ⏲11am-10pm Mon & Tue, 11am-1am Wed & Thu, 11am-2am Fri, 10am-2am Sat, 10am-10pm Sun; ⏶; ⓜRed Line to Dupont Circle) 'The taste of East London in East Dupont' is Duke's tagline, and that means black pudding and baked beans in the morning, veggie tikka masala in the afternoon and Brick Lane salt-beef sandwiches late night. Couples on low-maintenance dates and groups of chit-chatty friends angle for tables by the bay windows to people-watch. The genial vibe invites all-day lingering.

Little Serow   Thai $$$

(www.littleserow.com; 1511 17th St NW; set menu $49; ⏰5:30-10pm Tue-Thu, to 10:30pm Fri & Sat; Ⓜ Red Line to Dupont Circle) Little Serow has no phone, no reservations and no sign on the door. It only seats groups of four or fewer (larger parties will be separated), but despite all this, people line up around the block. And what for? Superlative Northern Thai cuisine. The single-option menu – which consists of six or so hot-spiced courses – changes by the week.

🌀 Adams Morgan

Donburi   Japanese $

(📞202-629-1047; www.facebook.com/donburidc; 2438 18th St NW; mains $10-15; ⏰11am-10pm; Ⓜ Red Line to Woodley Park-Zoo/Adams Morgan) Hole-in-the-wall Donburi has 15 seats at a wooden counter where you get a front-row view of the slicing, dicing chefs. *Donburi* means 'bowl' in Japanese, and that's what arrives steaming hot and filled with, say, panko-coated shrimp atop rice and blended with the house's sweet-and-savory sauce. It's a simple, authentic meal. There's often a line, but it moves quickly. No reservations.

Tail Up Goat   Mediterranean $$

(📞202-986-9600; www.tailupgoat.com; 1827 Adams Mill Rd NW; mains $18-27; ⏰5:30-10pm Mon-Thu, 5-10pm Fri-Sun; Ⓜ Red Line to Woodley Park-Zoo/Adams Morgan) With its pale-blue walls, light wood decor and lantern-like lights dangling overhead, Tail Up Goat wafts a warm, island-y vibe. The lamb ribs are the specialty – crispy and lusciously fatty, with grilled lemon, figs and spices. The house-made breads and spreads star on the menu too – say, flaxseed sourdough with beets. No wonder Michelin gave it a star.

Mintwood Place   American $$

(📞202-234-6732; www.mintwoodplace.com; 1813 Columbia Rd NW; mains $18-30; ⏰5:30-10pm Tue-Thu, to 10:30pm Fri & Sat, to 9pm Sun, plus 10:30am-2:30pm Sat & Sun; Ⓜ Red Line to Woodley Park-Zoo/Adams Morgan) In a neighborhood known for jumbo pizza slices and Jell-o shots, Mintwood Place is a romantic anomaly. Take a seat in a brown-leather booth or at a reclaimed-wood table under twinkling lights. Then sniff the French-American fusion dishes that emerge from the wood-burning oven. The *flammekueche* (onion and bacon tart), chicken-liver mousse and escargot hush puppies show how it's done.

🌀 Logan Circle, U Street & Shaw

Ben's Chili Bowl   American $

(📞202-667-0909; www.benschilibowl.com; 1213 U St; mains $6-10; ⏰6am-2am Mon-Thu, 6am-4am Fri, 7am-4am Sat, 11am-midnight Sun; Ⓜ Green, Yellow Lines to U St) Ben's is a DC institution. The main stock in trade is half-smokes, DC's meatier, smokier version of the hot dog, usually slathered in mustard, onions and the namesake chili. For nearly 60 years presidents, rock stars and Supreme Court justices have come in to indulge in the humble diner, but despite the hype, Ben's remains a true neighborhood establishment. Cash only.

Chercher   Ethiopian $

(📞202-299-9703; www.chercherrestaurant. com; 1334 9th St NW; mains $11-17; ⏰11am-11pm Mon-Sat, noon-10pm Sun; 🥢; Ⓜ Green, Yellow Lines to Mt Vernon Sq/7th St-Convention Center) Ethiopian expats have been known to compare Chercher's food to their grandma's home cooking. It prepares terrific *injera* (spongy bread) for dipping into hot spiced *wats* (stews). Vegetarians will find lots to devour. There's beer and honey wine from the motherland, and spices you can buy to go. The restaurant spreads over two floors in an intimate townhouse with brightly painted walls and artwork.

Compass Rose   International $$

(☏202-506-4765; www.compassrosedc.com; 1346 T St NW; small plates $10-15; ☺5pm-2am Mon-Thu, 5pm-3am Fri & Sat, 11am-2am Sun; Ⓜ Green, Yellow Lines to U St) Compass Rose feels like a secret garden, set in a discreet townhouse a whisker from 14th St's buzz. The exposed brick walls, rustic wood decor and sky-blue ceiling give it a casually romantic air. The menu is a mash-up of global comfort foods, so dinner might entail, say, a Chilean *lomito* (pork sandwich), Lebanese *kefta* (ground lamb and spices) and Georgian *khachapuri* (buttery, cheese-filled bread).

Busboys & Poets   Cafe $$

(☏202-387-7638; www.busboysandpoets.com; 2021 14th St NW; mains $11-21; ☺8am-midnight Mon-Thu, 8am-2am Fri, from 9am Sat & Sun; ☏; Ⓜ Green, Yellow Lines to U St) Busboys & Poets is one of U St's linchpins. Locals pack the place for coffee, wi-fi and a progressive vibe (and attached bookstore) that make San Francisco feel conservative. The hearty menu spans sandwiches, pizzas and Southern fare like shrimp and grits. Tuesday night's open-mic poetry reading ($5 admission, from 9pm to 11pm) draws big crowds.

Estadio   Spanish $$

(☏202-319-1404; www.estadio-dc.com; 1520 14th St NW; tapas $6-17; ☺5-10pm Mon-Thu, to 11pm Fri & Sat, to 9pm Sun, 11:30am-2pm Fri-Sun; Ⓜ Green, Yellow Lines to U St) Estadio buzzes with a low-lit, date-night vibe. The tapas menu (which is the focus) is as deep as an ocean trench. There are three variations of *Ibérico* ham and a delicious foie gras, scrambled egg and truffle open-faced sandwich. Wash it down with some traditional *calimocho* (red wine and Coke). No reservations after 6pm, which usually means a wait at the bar.

Le Diplomate   French $$$

(☏202-332-3333; www.lediplomatedc.com; 1601 14th St NW; mains $23-35; ☺5-11pm Mon-Thu, 5pm-midnight Fri, 9:30am-midnight Sat, 9:30am-11pm Sun; Ⓜ Green, Yellow Lines to U St) This charming French bistro is one of the hottest tables in town. DC celebrities galore cozy up in the leather banquettes and at the sidewalk tables. They come for an authentic slice of Paris, from the *coq au vin* (wine-braised chicken) and aromatic baguettes to the vintage curios and nudie photos decorating the bathrooms. Make reservations.

🍸 DRINKING & NIGHTLIFE
🍷 White House Area
Off The Record   Bar

(☏202-638-6600; 800 16th St NW, Hay-Adams Hotel; ☺11:30am-midnight Sun-Thu, to 12:30am Fri & Sat; Ⓜ Orange, Silver, Blue Lines to McPherson Sq) Intimate red booths, a hidden basement location in one of the city's most prestigious hotels, right across from the White House – no wonder DC's important people submerge to be seen and not heard (as the tagline goes) at Off The Record. Experienced bartenders swirl martinis and Manhattans for the suit-wearing crowd. Groovy framed political caricatures hang on the walls.

Round Robin   Bar

(☏202-628-9100; 1401 Pennsylvania Ave NW, Willard InterContinental Hotel; ☺noon-1am Mon-Sat, to midnight Sun; Ⓜ Red, Orange, Silver, Blue Lines to Metro Center) Dispensing drinks since 1850, the bar at the Willard hotel is one of DC's most storied watering holes. The small, circular space is done up in Gilded Age accents, all dark wood and velvet green walls, and while it's touristy, you'll still see officials here likely determining your latest tax hike over a mint julep or single malt Scotch.

🍷 Georgetown
Grace Street Coffee   Coffee

(☏202-470-1331; www.gracestcoffee.com; 3210 Grace St NW; ☺7am-5pm Mon-Thu, 7am-6pm Fri, 9am-6pm Sat & Sun; � Circulator) The little shop roasts its own beans and makes its own syrups, and then morphs them into exquisite coffee drinks. It's in a mini food hall that shares space with a juice bar and top-notch sandwich shop (called Sundevich, which specializes in creations named after global cities, like the chicken-and-avocado

Lima and the Gruyère-and-ham Paris). Lots of hip locals relax over a cup here.

Tombs   Pub

([202-337-6668](tel:202-337-6668); www.tombs.com; 1226 36th St NW; ☺11:30am-1:30am Mon-Thu, to 2:30am Fri & Sat, 9:30am-1:30am Sun; [Circulator) Every college of a certain pedigree has 'that' bar – the one where faculty and students alike sip pints under athletic regalia of the old school. The Tombs is Georgetown's contribution to the genre. If it looks familiar, think back to the '80s: the subterranean pub was one of the settings for the film *St Elmo's Fire*.

🍸 Capitol Hill

Copycat Co   Cocktail Bar

([202-241-1952](tel:202-241-1952); www.copycatcompany.com; 1110 H St NE; ☺5pm-2am Sun-Thu, to 3am Fri & Sat; MRed Line to Union Station then DC Streetcar) When you walk into Copycat it feels like a Chinese fast-food restaurant. That's because it is (sort of) on the 1st floor, where Chinese-street-food nibbles are available. The fizzy drinks and egg-white-topped cocktails fill glasses upstairs, in the dimly lit, speakeasy-meets-opium-den-vibed bar. Staff are unassuming and gracious in helping newbies figure out what they want from the lengthy menu.

Granville Moore's   Pub

([202-399-2546](tel:202-399-2546); www.granvillemoores.com; 1238 H St NE; ☺5pm-midnight Mon-Thu, 5pm-3am Fri, 11am-3am Sat, 11am-midnight Sun; MRed Line to Union Station then streetcar) Besides being one of DC's best places to grab frites and a steak sandwich, Granville Moore's has an extensive Belgian beer menu that should satisfy any fan of low-country boozing. With its raw, wooden fixtures and walls that look as if they were made from daub and mud, the interior resembles a medieval barracks. The fireside setting is ideal on a winter's eve.

Bluejacket Brewery   Brewery

([202-524-4862](tel:202-524-4862); www.bluejacketdc.com; 300 Tingey St SE; ☺11am-2am Sun-Thu, to 2am Fri & Sat; MGreen Line to Navy Yard) Beer-lovers' heads will explode in Bluejacket. Pull up a stool at the mod-industrial bar, gaze at the

🛍 To Market, to Market

Eastern Market ([202-698-5253](tel:202-698-5253); www.easternmarket-dc.org; 225 7th St SE; ☺7am-7pm Tue-Fri, to 6pm Sat, 9am-5pm Sun; MOrange, Silver, Blue Lines to Eastern Market) One of the icons of Capitol Hill, this roofed bazaar sprawls with delectable chow and good cheer, especially on the weekends. Built in 1873, it is the last of the 19th-century covered markets that once supplied DC's food. The South Hall has a bakery, a dairy, a fishmonger, butchers, flower vendors, and fruit and vegetable sellers.

Flea Market (www.easternmarket.net; 7th St SE, btwn C St and Penn Ave; ☺10am-5pm Sat & Sun; MOrange, Silver, Blue Lines to Eastern Market) On weekends an outdoor flea market sets up on a two-block stretch of 7th St SE, adjacent to Eastern Market. Vendors sell all kinds of cool art, antiques, furniture, maps, prints, global wares, clothing, crafts and curios. Sunday is the bigger day, with more stalls setting up.

Union Market (www.unionmarketdc.com; 1309 5th St NE; mains $6-11; ☺11am-8pm Tue-Fri, 8am-8pm Sat & Sun; MRed Line to NoMa) The cool crowd hobnobs at this sunlit warehouse-turned-food-hall where culinary entrepreneurs sell their herbed goat cheeses and smoked meats. Among the stalls featuring prepared foods, everything from Burmese milkshakes to Korean tacos boggle taste buds. It's located a mile northeast of Union Station.

Eastern Market

Hit the Trail in Georgetown

Leafy Georgetown offers some great opportunities for actives types:

C&O Canal Towpath (www.nps.gov/choh; 1057 Thomas Jefferson St NW; Circulator) This shaded hiking-cycling path – part of a larger national historic park – runs alongside a waterway constructed in the mid-1800s to transport goods all the way to West Virginia. The canal and environs are being restored and enhanced into mid-2018, but once the work is finished, you can step on at Jefferson St for a lovely green escape from the crowd.

Big Wheel Bikes (202-337-0254; www.bigwheelbikes.com; 1034 33rd St NW; per 3hr/day $21/35; 11am-7pm Tue-Fri, 10am-6pm Sat & Sun; Circulator) Big Wheel has a wide variety of two-wheelers to rent, and you can spin onto the C&O Canal Towpath practically from the front door. Staff members also provide the lowdown on the nearby Capital Crescent Trail and Mount Vernon Trail. There's a three-hour minimum with rentals. For an extra $10 you can keep your bike overnight.

silvery tanks bubbling up the ambitious brews, then make the hard decision about which of the 25 tap beers you want to try. A dry-hopped kolsch? Sweet-spiced stout? A cask-aged farmhouse ale? Four-ounce tasting pours help with decision-making.

Little Miss Whiskey's Golden Dollar
Bar

(www.littlemisswhiskeys.com; 1104 H St NE; 5pm-2am Sun-Thu, to 3am Fri & Sat; Red Line to Union Station then streetcar) If Alice had returned from Wonderland so traumatized by her near beheading that she needed a stiff drink, we imagine she'd pop down to Little Miss Whiskey's. She'd love the whimsical-meets-dark-nightmares decor. And she'd probably have fun with the club

kids partying on the upstairs dancefloor on weekends. She'd also adore the weirdly fantastic back patio.

Downtown

Columbia Room
Cocktail Bar

(202-316-9396; www.columbiaroomdc.com; 124 Blagden Alley NW; 5pm-12:30am Tue-Thu, to 1:30am Fri & Sat; Green, Yellow Lines to Mt Vernon Sq/7th St-Convention Center) Serious mixology goes on at Columbia Room, the kind of place that sources spring water from Kentucky to Scotland, and uses pickled cherry blossom and barley tea among its ingredients. But it's done in a refreshingly non-snooty environment. Choose from three distinct areas: the festive Punch Garden on the outdoor roof deck, the comfy, leather-chair-dotted Spirits Library or the 14-seat, prix-fixe Tasting Room.

City Tap House
Pub

(202-733-5333; www.citytaphousedc.com; 901 9th St NW; 11:30am-midnight Sun-Wed, to 1:30am Thu, to 2:30am Fri & Sat; Red, Yellow, Green Lines to Gallery Pl-Chinatown) What's not to like about a wood-paneled, lodge-like gastropub with craft beers flowing from 40 taps? The vintage photos of folks boozing set the good-time mood. Settle in and make your own four-beer flight (4.5oz each) for $16. The brick-oven pizzas, Korean-short-rib tacos and other upscale bar food help soak it up.

Dupont Circle

Bar Charley
Bar

(202-627-2183; www.barcharley.com; 1825 18th St NW; 5pm-12:30am Mon-Thu, 4pm-1:30am Fri, 10am-1:30am Sat, 10am-12:30am Sun; Red Line to Dupont Circle) Bar Charley draws a mixed crowd from the neighborhood – young, old, gay and straight. They come for groovy cocktails sloshing in vintage glassware and ceramic tiki mugs, served at very reasonable prices by DC standards. Try the gin and gingery Suffering Bastard. The beer list isn't huge, but it is thoughtfully chosen with some wild ales. Around 60 wines are available, too.

Board Room   Bar

(☎202-518-7666; www.boardroomdc.com; 1737 Connecticut Ave NW; ☺4pm-2am Mon-Thu, 4pm-3am Fri, noon-3am Sat, noon-2am Sun; MRed Line to Dupont Circle) Grab a table, pull up a stool and crush your opponent at Hungry Hungry Hippos. Or summon spirits with a Ouija board. Board Room lets you flash back to childhood via its stacks of board games. Battleship, Risk, Operation – name it, and it's available to rent for $2.

🍸 Adams Morgan

Dan's Cafe   Bar

(☎202-265-0299; 2315 18th St NW; ☺7pm-2am Tue-Thu, to 3am Fri & Sat; MRed Line to Woodley Park-Zoo/Adams Morgan) This is one of DC's great dive bars. The interior looks sort of like an old Elks Club, all unironically old-school 'art,' cheap paneling and dim lights barely illuminating the unapologetic slumminess. It's famed for its whopping, mix-it-yourself drinks, where you get a ketchup-type squirt bottle of booze, a can of soda and bucket of ice for barely $20. Cash only.

Songbyrd Record Cafe & Music House   Cafe

(☎202-450-2917; www.songbyrddc.com; 2477 18th St NW; ☺8am-2am Sun-Thu, to 3am Fri & Sat; ☞; MRed Line to Woodley Park-Zoo/Adams Morgan) By day hang out in the retro cafe, drinking excellent coffee, munching delicious sandwiches and browsing the small selection of soul and indie LPs for sale. You can even cut your own record in the vintage recording booth ($15). By night the party moves to the bar, where beer and cocktails flow alongside burgers and tacos, and indie bands rock the basement club.

🍸 Logan Circle, U Street & Shaw

Right Proper Brewing Co   Brewery

(☎202-607-2337; www.rightproperbrewery.com; 624 T St NW; ☺5pm-midnight Mon-Thu, 11:30am-1am Fri & Sat, 11:30am-11pm Sun; MGreen, Yellow Lines to Shaw-Howard U) As if the artwork – a chalked mural of the National Zoo's giant pandas with laser eyes destroying downtown DC – wasn't enough, Right Proper Brewing Co makes sublime ales in a building where Duke Ellington used to play pool. It's the Shaw district's neighborhood clubhouse, a big, sunny space filled with folks gabbing at reclaimed wood tables.

Dacha Beer Garden   Beer Garden

(☎202-350-9888; www.dachadc.com; 1600 7th St NW; ☺4-10:30pm Mon-Thu, noon-midnight Fri & Sat, 11am-10:30pm Sun; MGreen, Yellow Lines to Shaw-Howard U) Happiness reigns in Dacha's freewheeling beer garden. Kids and dogs bound around the picnic tables, while adults hoist glass boots filled with German brews. When the weather gets nippy, staff bring heaters and blankets and stoke the fire pit. And it all takes place under the sultry gaze of Elizabeth Taylor (or a mural of her, which sprawls across the back wall).

U Street Music Hall   Club

(☎202-588-1889; www.ustreetmusichall.com; 1115 U St NW; ☺hours vary; MGreen, Yellow Lines to U St) This is the spot to get your groove on sans the VIP/bottle service crowd. Two local DJs own and operate the basement club. It looks like a no-frills rock bar, but it has a pro sound system, a cork-cushioned dancefloor and other accoutrements of a serious dance club. Alternative bands also thrash a couple of nights per week to keep it fresh.

Churchkey   Bar

(☎202-567-2576; www.churchkeydc.com; 1337 14th St NW; ☺4pm-1am Mon-Thu, 4pm-2am Fri, 11:30am-2am Sat, 11:30am-1am Sun; MOrange, Silver, Blue Lines to McPherson Sq) Coppery, mod-industrial Churchkey glows with hipness. Fifty beers flow from the taps, including five brain-walloping, cask-aged ales. If none of those please you, another 500 types of brew are available by bottle (including gluten-free suds). Churchkey is the upstairs counterpart to **Birch & Barley** (www.birchandbarley.com; mains $16-29; ☺5:30-10pm Tue-Thu, 5:30-11pm Fri & Sat, 11am-8pm Sun), a popular nouveau comfort-food restaurant, and you can order much of its menu at the bar.

⭐ ENTERTAINMENT

Kennedy Center — Performing Arts
(☎202-467-4600; www.kennedy-center.org; 2700 F St NW; MOrange, Silver, Blue Lines to Foggy Bottom-GWU) Sprawled on 17 acres along the Potomac River, the magnificent Kennedy Center hosts a staggering array of performances – more than 2000 each year among its multiple venues including the Concert Hall (home to the National Symphony) and Opera House (home to the National Opera). A free shuttle bus runs to and from the Metro station every 15 minutes from 9:45am (noon on Sunday) to midnight.

Black Cat — Live Music
(☎202-667-4490; www.blackcatdc.com; 1811 14th St NW; MGreen, Yellow Lines to U St) A pillar of DC's rock and indie scene since the 1990s, the battered Black Cat has hosted all the greats of years past (White Stripes, the Strokes, Arcade Fire among others). If you don't want to pony up for $20-a-ticket bands on the upstairs main stage (or the smaller Backstage below), head to the Red Room for the jukebox, billiards, pinball and strong cocktails.

Nationals Park — Stadium
(☎202-675-6287; www.mlb.com/nationals; 1500 S Capitol St SE; 🛜; MGreen Line to Navy Yard) The major-league Washington Nationals play baseball at this spiffy stadium beside the Anacostia River. Don't miss the mid-fourth-inning 'Racing Presidents' – an odd foot race between giant-headed caricatures of George Washington, Abraham Lincoln, Thomas Jefferson, Teddy Roosevelt and William Taft. Hip bars and eateries and playful green spaces surround the ballpark, and more keep coming as the area gentrifies.

Shakespeare Theatre Company — Theater
(☎202-547-1122; www.shakespearetheatre.org; 450 7th St NW; MGreen, Yellow Lines to Archives) The nation's foremost Shakespeare company presents masterful works by the bard, as well as plays by George Bernard Shaw, Oscar Wilde, Eugene O'Neill and other greats. The season spans about a half-dozen productions annually, plus a free summer Shakespeare series on-site for two weeks in late August.

Woolly Mammoth Theatre Company — Theater
(☎202-393-3939; www.woollymammoth.net; 641 D St NW; MGreen, Yellow Lines to Archives) Woolly Mammoth is the edgiest of DC's experimental groups. For most shows, $20 'stampede' seats are available at the box office two hours before performances. They're limited in number, and sold first-come, first-served, so get there early.

9:30 Club — Live Music
(☎202-265-0930; www.930.com; 815 V St NW; MGreen, Yellow Lines to U St) The 9:30, which can pack 1200 people into a surprisingly compact venue, is the granddaddy of the live-music scene in DC. Pretty much every big name that comes through town ends up on this stage, and a concert here is the first-gig memory of many a DC-area teenager. Headliners usually take the stage between 10:30pm and 11:30pm. Tickets range from $20 to $35.

Howard Theatre — Theater
(☎202-803-2899; www.thehowardtheatre.com; 620 T St NW; MGreen, Yellow Lines to Shaw-Howard U) Built in 1910, Howard Theatre was the top address when U St was known as 'Black Broadway.' Duke Ellington, Ella Fitzgerald and other famed names lit the marquee. Now big-name comedians, blues and jazz acts fill the house, as does the monthly Sunday gospel brunch. There's a photo op out front with the steel-and-granite statue of Ellington pounding the keys of a swirling treble clef.

ℹ️ INFORMATION

Destination DC (☎202-789-7000; www.washington.org) DC's official tourism site, with the mother lode of online information.

ⓘ GETTING THERE & AROUND

TO/FROM THE AIRPORT

Ronald Reagan Washington National Airport
(DCA; www.flyreagan.com) Just 4.5 miles south of downtown in Arlington, VA.

○ **Metro** The airport has its own Metro station on the Blue and Yellow Lines. Trains (around $2.60) depart every 10 minutes or so between 5am and midnight (to 3am Friday and Saturday); they reach the city center in 20 minutes.

○ **Shuttle van** The **Supershuttle** (www.super shuttle.com) door-to-door shared van service goes downtown for $16. It takes 10 to 30 minutes and runs from 5:30am to 12:30am.

○ **Taxi** Rides to the city center take 10 to 30 minutes (depending on traffic) and cost $15 to $22.

Dulles International Airport (IAD; www.flydulles.com) In the Virginia suburbs 26 miles west of DC.

○ **Bus & Metro** The **Washington Flyer** (www.washfly.com) Silver Line Express bus runs every 15 to 20 minutes from Dulles (main terminal, arrivals level door 4) to the Wiehle-Reston East Metro station between 6am and 10:40pm (from 7:45am weekends). Total time to DC's center is 60 to 75 minutes, total bus-Metro cost around $11.

○ **Shuttle van** The **Supershuttle** (www.super shuttle.com) door-to-door shared van service goes downtown for $30. It takes 30 to 60 minutes and runs from 5:30am to 12:30am.

○ **Taxi** Rides to the city center take 30 to 60 minutes (depending on traffic) and cost $62 to $73.

BICYCLE

Capital Bikeshare (www.capitalbikeshare.com) has stations all over the city. Kiosks issue passes (one day for $8 or three days for $17) on the spot. There's also an option for a 'single trip' ($2), ie a one-off ride of under 30 minutes.

PUBLIC TRANSPORTATION

METRO

○ DC's modern subway network is the **Metrorail** (www.wmata.com), commonly called Metro.

○ There are six color-coded lines: Red, Orange, Blue, Green, Yellow and Silver.

○ Trains start running at 5am Monday through Friday (from 7am on weekends); the last service is around midnight Sunday through Thursday and 3am on Friday and Saturday.

○ Fare cards are called SmarTrip cards. Machines inside all stations sell them. The plastic, rechargeable card costs $10, with $8 of that stored for fares. You then add value as needed.

○ Fares cost $1.85 to $6, depending on distance traveled and time of day. Fares increase slightly during morning and evening rush hour.

○ Use the card to enter *and* exit station turnstiles.

DC CIRCULATOR BUS

DC Circulator (www.dccirculator.com) buses run along handy local routes, including Union Station to/from the Mall (looping by all major museums and memorials), Union Station to/from Georgetown (via K St), Dupont Circle to/from Georgetown (via M St), and the White House area to/from Adams Morgan (via 14th St).

○ Circulator buses operate from roughly 7am to 9pm weekdays (midnight or so on weekends).

○ Fare is $1. Pay with exact change, or use a SmarTrip card.

TAXI & RIDE SHARE

○ Fares are meter-based. The meter starts at $3.25, then it's $2.16 per mile thereafter.

○ There's a $2 surcharge for telephone dispatches. Try DC Yellow Cab (☎202-544-1212) if you need a pick-up.

○ Ride-hailing companies Uber, Lyft and **Via** (www.ridewithvia.com) are popular in the District.

TRAIN

Magnificent, beaux-arts **Union Station** (www.unionstationdc.com; 50 Massachusetts Ave NE; Ⓜ Union Station) is the city's rail hub. There's a handy Metro station (Red Line) here for transport onward in the city. **Amtrak** (www.amtrak.com) arrives at least once per hour from major east-coast cities. Many bus lines (Megabus, Greyhound etc) also use the station.

CHICAGO

In this Chapter

Millennium Park 122
Art Institute of Chicago 124
Wrigley Field 126
Sights 130
Activities 135
Tours 136
Shopping 136
Eating 137
Drinking & Nightlife 139
Entertainment 141

Chicago at a Glance...

Take cloud-scraping architecture, lakefront beaches and world-class museums, stir in wild comedy, fret-bending guitars and very hefty pizza, and you've got a town that won't let you down.

The city center is a steely wonder, but it's Chicago's mural-splashed neighborhoods – with their inventive storefront restaurants, corner rock clubs and sociable dive bars – that really blow you away. The food scene, in particular, has gotten its groove on. Chicago is now a chowhound's hot spot, where Michelin-starred eateries pop up throughout, serving masterful food in come-as-you-are environs. Get ready to loosen the belt.

Two Days in Chicago

Explore the art and greenery of **Millennium Park** (p122) then stop for a deep-dish pizza at **Giordano's** (p138). Take a tour with the **Chicago Architecture Foundation** (p136) to get the lowdown on the city's skyscrapers. On day two explore the **Art Institute of Chicago** (p125). Grab a stylish dinner in the West Loop, then listen to blues at **Buddy Guy's Legends** (p141).

Four Days in Chicago

On your third day, rent a bicycle, visit **North Avenue Beach** (p135) and cruise through **Lincoln Park** (p134). If it's baseball season, go watch the Cubs at **Wrigley Field** (p127). In the evening yuck it up at **Second City** (p141). Pick a neighborhood for day four: record shops in Wicker Park or brainy museums in Hyde Park.

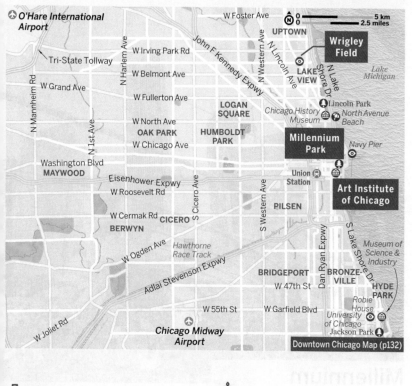

O'Hare International Airport

W Foster Ave

0 ——— 5 km
0 ——— 2.5 miles

UPTOWN

Wrigley Field

Tri-State Tollway

W Irving Park Rd

N Harlem Ave

John F Kennedy Expwy

N Western Ave

N Lincoln Ave

LAKE VIEW

N Lake Shore Dr

Lake Michigan

W Belmont Ave

N Mannheim Rd

W Grand Ave

N 1st Ave

W Fullerton Ave

LOGAN SQUARE

Chicago History Museum

Lincoln Park

North Avenue Beach

W North Ave

OAK PARK

HUMBOLDT PARK

Millennium Park

Navy Pier

W Chicago Ave

Washington Blvd

MAYWOOD

Eisenhower Expwy

W Roosevelt Rd

S Cicero Ave

S Western Ave

Union Station

Art Institute of Chicago

W Cermak Rd CICERO

BERWYN

PILSEN

W Ogden Ave

Hawthorne Race Track

Adlai Stevenson Expwy

Dan Ryan Expwy

S Lake Shore Dr

Museum of Science & Industry

BRIDGEPORT

BRONZE-VILLE

HYDE PARK

W 47th St

W Joliet Rd

Chicago Midway Airport

W 55th St

W Garfield Blvd

Robie House

University of Chicago

Jackson Park

Downtown Chicago Map (p132)

Arriving in Chicago

O'Hare International Airport The Blue Line El train ($5) runs 24/7 and departs every 10 minutes and reaches downtown in 40 minutes. Shuttle vans cost $35, taxis around $50.

Chicago Midway Airport The Orange Line El train ($3) runs between 4am and 1am every 10 minutes and reaches downtown in 30 minutes. Shuttle vans cost $30, taxis $35 to $40.

Where to Stay

The Loop and Near North are the most lodging-filled neighborhoods, offering a mix of cool design hotels and chain properties. Trendy brands such as Ace Hotel are starting to pop up in the West Loop. Posh hostels are popular, with several in fun, outlying neighborhoods such as Wicker Park and Wrigleyville.

AMADEUSTX / SHUTTERSTOCK ©

Millennium Park

This stunning art-filled green space sits in the heart of the Loop. Lovely views, daring works of sculpture, high-tech fountains, hidden gardens, free summer concerts and a winter skating rink are all part of the allure.

Great For...

☑ **Don't Miss**

The Lurie Garden, filled with prairie flowers and a little river to dip your toes.

The Bean

The park's biggest draw is the 'Bean' – officially titled *Cloud Gate* – Anish Kapoor's 110-ton, silver-drop sculpture. It reflects both the sky and the skyline, and everyone clamors around to take a picture and touch its silvery smoothness. Good vantage points for photos are at the sculpture's north and south ends. For great people-watching, go up the stairs on Washington St, on the Park Grill's north side, where there are shady benches.

Crown Fountain

Jaume Plensa's *Crown Fountain* is another crowd-pleaser. Its two, 50ft-high, glass-block towers contain video displays that flash a thousand different faces. The people shown are all native Chicagoans who agreed to strap into Plensa's special dental

Jay Pritzker Pavilion, designed by Gehry Partners

❶ Need to Know

📞312-742-1168; www.millenniumpark.
org; 201 E Randolph St; ⊗6am-11pm; 🚻;
Ⓜ Brown, Orange, Green, Purple, Pink Line to
Washington/Wabash

✕ Take a Break

Grab a sandwich and bottle of wine at
Pastoral (p137) for a picnic in the
park.

★ Top Tip

Free walking tours take place at
11:30am and 1pm daily from late
May to mid-October.

chair, where he immobilized their heads
for filming. Each mug puckers up and
spurts water, just like the gargoyles atop
Notre Dame Cathedral. A fresh set of non-
puckering faces appears in winter, when
the fountain is dry. On hot days the fountain
crowds with locals splashing around to cool
off. Kids especially love it.

Jay Pritzker Pavilion

The Pritzker Pavilion is Millennium Park's
acoustically awesome band shell. Architect
Frank Gehry designed it and gave it his
trademark swooping silver exterior. The
pavilion hosts free concerts at 6:30pm
most nights June to August. There's indie
rock, world music and jazz on Monday and
Thursday, and classical music on Wednesday, Friday and Saturday. On Tuesday
there's usually a movie beamed onto the

huge screen on stage. Seats are available
up close in the pavilion, or you can sit on
the grassy Great Lawn.

For all shows – but especially the classical ones, which the top-notch Grant Park
Orchestra performs – folks bring blankets,
picnics, wine and beer. There is nothing
quite like sitting on the lawn, looking up
through Gehry's wild grid and seeing all the
skyscraping architecture that forms the
backdrop while hearing the music. If you
want a seat up close, arrive early.

The pavilion also hosts daytime action.
Concert rehearsals take place Tuesday to
Friday, usually from 11am to 1pm, offering
a taste of music if you can't catch the
evening show.

BARRY WINIKER / GETTY IMAGES ©

Art Institute of Chicago

The second-largest art museum in the country, the Art Institute has the kind of celebrity-heavy collection that routinely draws gasps from patrons.

Great For...

☑ Don't Miss

Grant Wood's *American Gothic* (Gallery 263), one of America's most famous paintings.

Must-See Works: Floor 2

First up is *A Sunday Afternoon on the Island of La Grande Jatte* by Georges Seurat (Gallery 240). Get close enough for the painting to break down into its component dots and you'll understand why it took Seurat two long years to complete his pointillist masterpiece. Next seek out *Nighthawks* by Edward Hopper (Gallery 262). His lonely, poignant snapshot of four solitary souls at a neon-lit diner was inspired by a Greenwich Ave restaurant in Manhattan. In the next room you'll find *American Gothic* by Grant Wood (Gallery 263). The artist, a lifelong resident of Iowa, used his sister and his dentist as models for the two stern-faced farmers.

STEVE CUKROV / SHUTTERSTOCK ©

ℹ️ Need to Know

☎312-443-3600; www.artic.edu; 111 S Michigan Ave; adult/child $25/free; ⏱10:30am-5pm Fri-Wed, to 8pm Thu; 👪; Ⓜ️Brown, Orange, Green, Purple, Pink Line to Adams

✕ Take a Break

The nearby Berghoff (p139), dating from 1898, is tops for a beer and a dose of Chicago history.

★ Top Tip

Ask at the information desk about free talks and tours once you're inside.

Must-See Works: Other Floors

Stop by Marc Chagaall's *America Windows* (Gallery 144). He created the huge, blue stained-glass pieces to celebrate the USA's bicentennial. Another favorite is *The Old Guitarist* by Pablo Picasso (Gallery 391). The elongated figure is from the artist's Blue Period. Not far away is Salvador Dalí's *Inventions of the Monsters* (Gallery 396). He painted it in Austria before the Nazi annexation. The title refers to a Nostradamus prediction that the apparition of monsters presages the outbreak of war.

More Intriguing Sights

The Thorne Miniature Rooms (Lower Level, Gallery 11) and Paperweight Collection (Lower Level, Gallery 15) are awesome, overlooked galleries. In the light-drenched Modern Wing, the ongoing exhibition 'The New Contemporary' (Galleries 288 and 290–99) bursts with iconic works by Andy Warhol, Roy Lichtenstein and Jasper Johns.

Visiting the Museum

Download the museum's free app, either at home or using the on-site wi-fi. It offers several audio tours through the collection. Highlights, architecture and pop art are among the themes.

Allow two hours to browse the museum's highlights; art buffs should allocate much longer. The museum's main entrance is on Michigan Ave, but you can also enter via the Modern Wing on Monroe St. Advance tickets are available (surcharge $2), but unless there's a blockbuster exhibit going on they're usually not necessary. The entrance queue moves fast.

SUSAN MONTGOMERY / SHUTTERSTOCK ©

Wrigley Field

Built in 1914, Wrigley Field is the second-oldest baseball park in the major leagues. It's filled with legendary traditions and curses, including a team that didn't win a championship for 108 years.

Great For...

☑ **Don't Miss**

Ninety-minute stadium tours ($25) are available most days April through September.

Environs

The ballpark provides an old-school slice of Americana, with a hand-turned scoreboard, ivy-covered outfield walls and an iconic neon sign over the front entrance. The field is uniquely situated smack in the middle of a neighborhood, surrounded on all sides by houses, bars and restaurants. The grassy plaza just north of the main entrance – aka The Park – has tables, chairs, a coffee shop and a huge video screen. On non-game days it's open to the public and hosts free movie nights, concerts and a Thursday farmers market; on game days it's a beer garden for ticket holders.

The Curse & Its Reverse

It started with Billy Sianis, owner of the Billy Goat Tavern. The year was 1945 and the

❶ Need to Know

www.cubs.com; 1060 W Addison St; Ⓜ Red Line to Addison

✘ Take a Break

It's a pre-game ritual to beer up at **Murphy's Bleachers** (☏773-281-5356; www.murphysbleachers.com; 3655 N Sheffield Ave; ⏱11am-2am), steps away from the ballpark.

★ Top Tip

Buy tickets at the Cubs' website or Wrigley box office. Online ticket broker StubHub (www.stubhub.com) is also reliable.

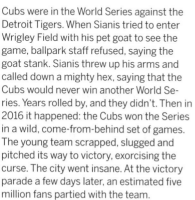

Cubs were in the World Series against the Detroit Tigers. When Sianis tried to enter Wrigley Field with his pet goat to see the game, ballpark staff refused, saying the goat stank. Sianis threw up his arms and called down a mighty hex, saying that the Cubs would never win another World Series. Years rolled by, and they didn't. Then in 2016 it happened: the Cubs won the Series in a wild, come-from-behind set of games. The young team scrapped, slugged and pitched its way to victory, exorcising the curse. The city went insane. At the victory parade a few days later, an estimated five million fans partied with the team.

The Traditions

When the middle of the seventh inning arrives, it's time for the seventh inning stretch.

You then stand up for the group sing-along of 'Take Me Out to the Ballgame,' typically led by a guest celebrity along the lines of Mr T, Ozzy Osbourne or the local weather reporter. Here's another tradition: if you catch a home run slugged by the competition, you're honor-bound to throw it back onto the field. After every game the ballpark hoists a flag atop the scoreboard. A white flag with a blue 'W' indicates a victory; a blue flag with a white 'L' means a loss.

Art of the City Walking Tour

This tour swoops through the Loop, highlighting Chicago's revered art and architecture, with a visit to Al Capone's dentist thrown in for good measure.
Start Chicago Board of Trade
Finish Chicago Cultural Center
Distance 2.5 miles
Duration Two hours

Chicago River

6 Picasso's abstract *Untitled* sculpture is ensconced in **Daley Plaza** (p131). Baboon, dog, woman? You decide.

W Randolph St

Daley Plaza
6

Washington
5

5 Al Capone's dentist drilled teeth in what's now Room 809 of the **Alise** (www.staypineapple.com; 1 W Washington St) hotel.

W Madison St
THE LOOP
N State St
S LaSalle St
S Clark St
Monroe
M   M

W Adams St

2

Quincy
M

Jackson
M   M

W Jackson Blvd

START   1

2 Step into the nearby **Rookery** (p130) to see Frank Lloyd Wright's handiwork in the atrium.

CHICAGO BOARD OF TRADE

1 Start at the **Chicago Board of Trade** (141 W Jackson Blvd) with its art-deco building and rooftop statue of Ceres.

Take a Break... Gage (p137) – for lunch or a drink in classy surroundings.

7 Pop into the **Chicago Cultural Center** (p130) to see what free art exhibits or concerts are on.

Chicago - Millennium
Station (Metra)

7

FINISH

E Washington St

S Michigan Ave

E Monroe St

4

Adams/Wabash

3

4 Walk around **Millennium Park** (p122) to ogle the famous 'Bean' sculpture and human gargoyle fountains.

E Jackson Blvd

Classic Photo Art Institute of Chicago lions

3 The **Art Institute** (p125) always draws crowds. Snap a photo with the lion statues out front.

◉ SIGHTS
◉ The Loop
Willis Tower   Tower

(☎312-875-9696; www.theskydeck.com; 233 S Wacker Dr; adult/child $23/15; ⊙9am-10pm Mar-Sep, 10am-8pm Oct-Feb; Ⓜ Brown, Orange, Purple, Pink Line to Quincy) It's Chicago's tallest building, and the 103rd-floor Skydeck puts you high into the heavens. Take the ear-popping, 70-second elevator ride to the top and then step onto one of the glass-floored ledges jutting out in mid-air for a knee-buckling perspective straight down. On clear days the view sweeps over four states. The entrance is on Jackson Blvd. Queues can take up to an hour on busy days (peak times are in summer, between 11am and 4pm Friday through Sunday).

Chicago Cultural
Center   Notable Building

(☎312-744-6630; www.chicagoculturalcenter.org; 78 E Washington St; ⊙9am-7pm Mon-Thu, to 6pm Fri & Sat, 10am-6pm Sun; Ⓜ Brown, Orange, Green, Purple, Pink Line to Washington/Wabash) FREE This exquisite, beaux-arts building

began its life as the Chicago Public Library in 1897. Today the block-long building houses terrific art exhibitions (especially the 4th-floor Yates Gallery), as well as jazz and classical concerts at lunchtime (12:15pm most Mondays and every Wednesday). It also contains the world's largest Tiffany stained-glass dome, on the 3rd floor where the library circulation desk used to be.

InstaGreeter (www.chicagogreeter.com/instagreeter; ⊙10am-3pm Fri & Sat, 11am-2pm Sun) tours of the Loop depart from the Randolph St lobby (77 E Randolph St), as do Millennium Park tours. And it's all free!

Rookery   Architecture

(☎312-994-4000; www.flwright.org; 209 S La-Salle St; ⊙9am-5pm Mon-Fri; Ⓜ Brown, Orange, Purple, Pink Line to Quincy) The famed firm of Burnham and Root built the Rookery in 1888 and Frank Lloyd Wright remodeled the atrium 19 years later. It's renowned because while it looks hulking and fortress-like outside, it's light and airy inside. You can walk in and look around for free. Tours ($10 to $15) are available weekdays at 11am, noon and 1pm.

Navy Pier

Daley Plaza   Plaza

(50 W Washington St; ⓂBlue Line to Washington)
Picasso's eye-popping untitled sculpture
marks the heart of Daley Plaza, which is the
place to be come lunchtime, particularly
when the weather warms up. You never
know what will be going on – dance performances, bands, ethnic festivals, holiday
celebrations – but you do know it'll be free.
A farmers market sets up on Thursday
(7am to 3pm) and food trucks add to the
action once a week (11am to 3pm, often on
Friday) from April through October.

◎ Near North

Navy Pier   Waterfront

(☏312-595-7437; www.navypier.com; 600 E
Grand Ave; ◎10am-10pm Sun-Thu, to midnight
Fri & Sat Jun-Aug, 10am-8pm Sun-Thu, to 10pm
Fri & Sat Sep-May; ⓘ; ⓂRed Line to Grand) **FREE**
Half-mile-long Navy Pier is one of Chicago's
most-visited attractions, sporting a 196ft
Ferris wheel (adult/child $15/12) and other
carnival rides ($6 to $15 each), an **IMAX
theater** (☏312-595-5629; www.imax.com; tickets $15-22), a beer garden and lots of chain
restaurants. Locals groan over its com-
mercialization, but its lakefront view and
cool breezes can't be beat. The fireworks
displays on summer Wednesdays (9:30pm)
and Saturdays (10:15pm) are a treat too.

Magnificent Mile   Area

(www.themagnificentmile.com; N Michigan Ave;
ⓂRed Line to Grand) Spanning Michigan Ave
between the river and Oak St, the Mag Mile
is Chicago's much-touted upscale shopping
strip, where Bloomingdale's, Apple, Burber-
ry and many more will lighten your wallet.
The retailers are mostly high-end chains
that have stores nationwide.

◎ Gold Coast

360° Chicago   Observatory

(☏888-875-8439; www.360chicago.com; 875 N
Michigan Ave, John Hancock Center, 94th fl; adult/
child $20.50/13.50; ◎9am-11pm; ⓂRed Line to
Chicago) This is the new name for the John
Hancock Center Observatory. In many ways
the view here surpasses the one at Willis

Chicago for Children

Chicago is a kid's kind of town. For
child-friendly happenings around
the city, see **Chicago Kids** (www.
chicagokids.com). Top attractions:

Chicago Children's Museum (☏312-
527-1000; www.chicagochildrensmuseum.org;
700 E Grand Ave; $14; ◎10am-5pm, to 8pm
Thu; ⓘ; ⓂRed Line to Grand) Designed to
challenge the imaginations of toddlers
to 10-year-olds, this colorful museum near Navy Pier's main entrance
gives young visitors enough hands-on
exhibits to keep them climbing and
creating for hours. Among the favorites,
Dinosaur Expedition explores the world
of paleontology and lets kids excavate
'bones.' They can also climb a ropey
schooner; bowl in a faux alley; get wet
in the waterways (and learn about
hydroelectric power); and use real tools
to build things in the Tinkering Lab.

Maggie Daley Park (www.maggiedaley
park.com; 337 E Randolph St; ◎6am-11pm;
ⓘ; ⓂBrown, Orange, Green, Purple, Pink
Line to Washington/Wabash) Families love
this park's fanciful free playgrounds
in all their enchanted-forest and
pirate-themed glory. There's also a
rock-climbing wall, 18-hole mini-golf
course, in-line skating ribbon (which
becomes an ice-skating ribbon in winter) and tennis courts; these features
have fees. Multiple picnic tables make
the park an excellent spot to relax. It
connects to Millennium Park via the
pedestrian BP Bridge.

Tower. The 94th-floor lookout has informa-
tive displays and the TILT feature (floor-to-
ceiling windows that you stand in as they tip
out over the ground; it costs $7 extra and is
less exciting than it sounds). Not interested
in such frivolities? Shoot straight up to
the 96th-floor **Signature Lounge** (www.
signatureroom.com; ◎11am-12:30am Sun-Thu, to

Downtown Chicago

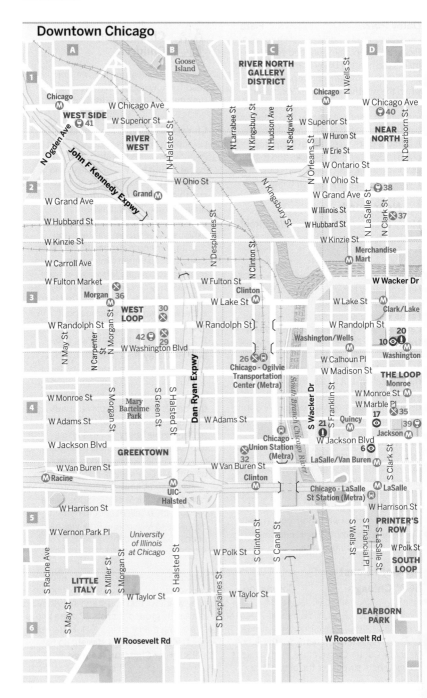

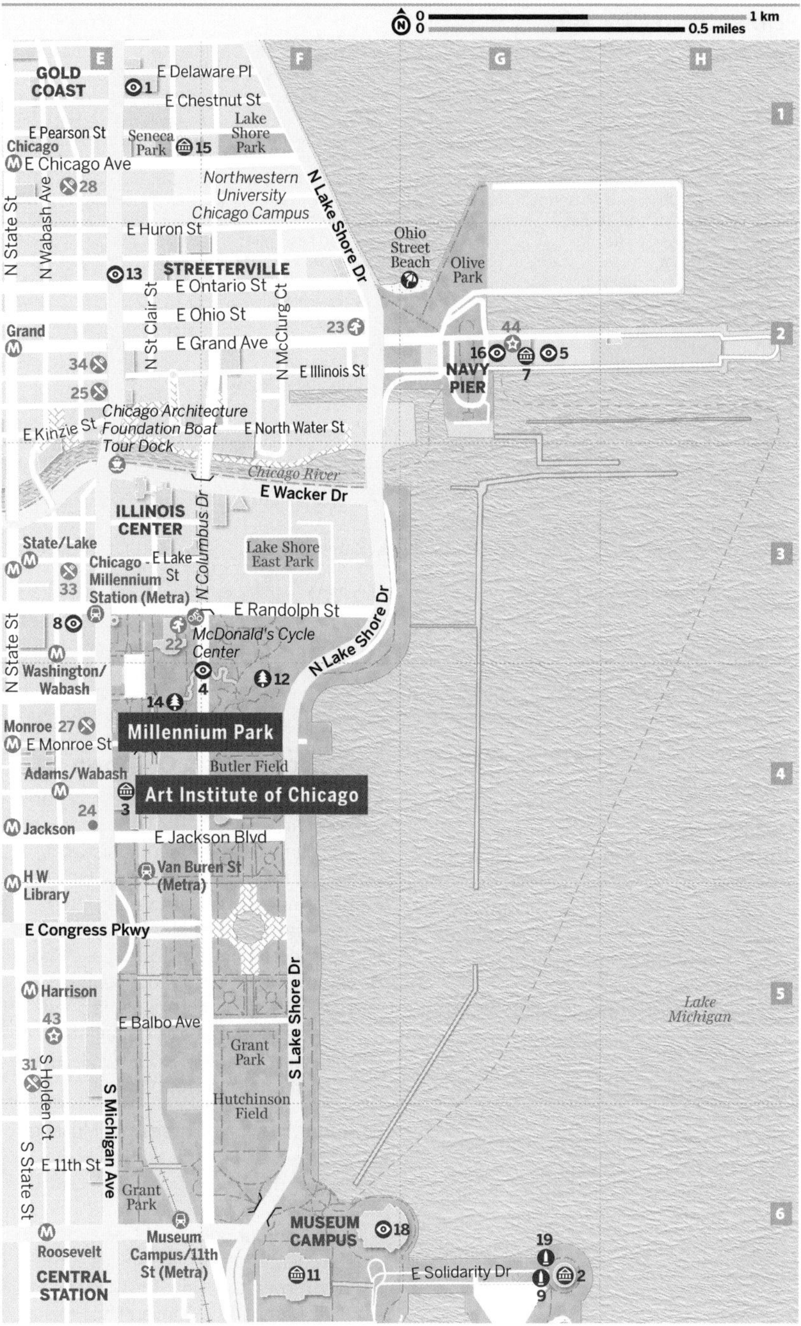
0 1 km
0 0.5 miles
GOLD COAST
E Delaware Pl
E Chestnut St
Lake Shore Park
E Pearson St
Chicago
Seneca Park
15
E Chicago Ave
28
Northwestern University Chicago Campus
N Lake Shore Dr
N State St
N Wabash Ave
E Huron St
Ohio Street Beach
Olive Park
13
STREETERVILLE
E Ontario St
E Ohio St
N St Clair St
N McClurg Ct
23
Grand
E Grand Ave
44
16
5
7
NAVY PIER
34
E Illinois St
25
Chicago Architecture Foundation Boat Tour Dock
E Kinzie St
E North Water St
Chicago River
E Wacker Dr
ILLINOIS CENTER
N Columbus Dr
State/Lake
Lake Shore East Park
Chicago - Millennium Station (Metra)
E Lake St
33
E Randolph St
8
McDonald's Cycle Center
22
Washington/Wabash
4
12
14
Monroe
27
E Monroe St
Millennium Park
Butler Field
Adams/Wabash
Art Institute of Chicago
3
24
Jackson
E Jackson Blvd
Van Buren St (Metra)
H W Library
E Congress Pkwy
Harrison
43
E Balbo Ave
S Lake Shore Dr
Grant Park
Lake Michigan
31
S Holden Ct
S Michigan Ave
Hutchinson Field
S State St
E 11th St
Grant Park
MUSEUM CAMPUS
18
19
Roosevelt
Museum Campus/11th St (Metra)
11
E Solidarity Dr
2
9
CENTRAL STATION

Downtown Chicago

⊙ Sights
1 360° Chicago E1
2 Adler Planetarium G6
3 Art Institute of Chicago E4
4 BP Bridge F4
5 Centennial Wheel G2
6 Chicago Board of Trade D4
7 Chicago Children's Museum.................. G2
8 Chicago Cultural Center....................... E3
9 Copernicus Statue G6
10 Daley Plaza... D3
11 Field Museum of Natural History F6
12 Maggie Daley Park F4
13 Magnificent Mile E2
14 Millennium Park.................................. E4
15 Museum of Contemporary Art E1
16 Navy Pier G2
17 Rookery D4
18 Shedd Aquarium F6
19 Sundial G6
20 Untitled D3
21 Willis Tower.. D4

⊘ Activities, Courses & Tours
22 Bike Chicago....................................... E3
23 Bobby's Bike Hike F2
24 Chicago Architecture Foundation............ E4
    InstaGreeter...(see 8)

⊟ Shopping
   Chicago Architecture
    Foundation Shop........................... (see 24)

⊗ Eating
25 Billy Goat Tavern E2
26 French Market..................................... C4
27 Gage E4
28 Giordano's...E1
    Giordano's Navy Pier .... (see 7)
29 Girl & the Goat..................................... B3
30 Little Goat.. B3
31 Lou Malnati's....................................... E5
32 Lou Mitchell's..................................... C4
33 Pastoral.. E3
34 Purple Pig E2
35 Revival Food Hall D4
36 Roister.. A3
37 Xoco.. D2

⊖ Drinking & Nightlife
38 Arbella... D2
39 Berghoff... D4
40 Clark Street Ale House D1
41 Matchbox... A1
42 RM Champagne Salon B3
    Signature Lounge ....(see 1)

⊗ Entertainment
43 Buddy Guy's Legends E5
44 IMAX Theater G2

1:30am Fri & Sat), where the view is free if you buy a drink ($8 to $16).

Museum of Contemporary Art Museum

(MCA; ☑312-280-2660; www.mcachicago. org; 220 E Chicago Ave; adult/child $15/free; ⊙10am-8pm Tue, to 5pm Wed-Sun; ⓜRed Line to Chicago) Consider it the Art Institute's brash, rebellious sibling, with especially strong minimalist, surrealist and conceptual photography collections, and permanent works by René Magritte, Cindy Sherman and Andy Warhol. Covering art from the 1920s onward, the MCA's collection spans the gamut, with displays arranged to blur the boundaries between painting, sculpture, video and other media. Exhibits change regularly so you never know what you'll see, but count on it being offbeat and provocative.

◉ Lincoln Park & Old Town

Lincoln Park Park

(⊙6am-11pm; ⓟ; ⊒151) The neighborhood gets its name from this park, Chicago's largest. Its 1200 acres stretch for 6 miles, from North Ave north to Diversey Pkwy, where it narrows along the lake and continues on north until the end of Lake Shore Dr. On sunny days locals come out to play in droves, taking advantage of the ponds, paths and playing fields or visiting the zoo and beaches. It's a fine spot to while away a morning or afternoon (or both).

Chicago History Museum Museum

(☑312-642-4600; www.chicagohistory.org; 1601 N Clark St; adult/child $16/free; ⊙9:30am-4:30pm Mon & Wed-Sat, to 7:30pm Tue, noon-5pm Sun; ⓟ; ⊒22) Curious about Chicago's storied past? Multimedia displays at this museum cover it all, from the Great Fire to the 1968 Democratic Convention. President

Lincoln's deathbed is here, as is the bell worn by Mrs O'Leary's cow. So is the chance to 'become' a Chicago hot dog covered in condiments (in the kids' area, but adults are welcome for the photo op).

North Avenue Beach   Beach

(www.cpdbeaches.com; 1600 N Lake Shore Dr; [icon]; [icon]151) Chicago's most popular strand of sand wafts a southern California vibe. Buff teams spike volleyballs, kids build sand-castles and everyone jumps in for a swim when the weather heats up. Bands and DJs rock the steamboat-shaped beach house, which serves ice cream and margaritas in equal measure. Kayaks, jet-skis, stand up paddle boards, bicycles and lounge chairs are available to rent, and there are daily beach yoga classes.

◎ South Loop

Field Museum of Natural History   Museum

([icon]312-922-9410; www.fieldmuseum.org; 1400 S Lake Shore Dr; adult/child $22/15; ◎9am-5pm; [icon]; [icon]146, 130) The Field Museum houses some 30 million artifacts and includes everything but the kitchen sink – beetles, mummies, gemstones, Bushman the stuffed ape – all tended by a slew of PhD–wielding scientists, as the Field remains an active research institution. The collection's rock star is Sue, the largest *Tyrannosaurus rex* yet discovered. She even gets her own gift shop. Special exhibits, such as the 3-D movie, cost extra.

Shedd Aquarium   Aquarium

([icon]312-939-2438; www.sheddaquarium.org; 1200 S Lake Shore Dr; adult/child $40/30; ◎9am-6pm Jun-Aug, 9am-5pm Mon-Fri, to 6pm Sat & Sun Sep-May; [icon]; [icon]146, 130) Top draws at the kiddie-mobbed Shedd Aquarium include the Wild Reef exhibit, where there's just 5in of Plexiglas between you and two-dozen fierce-looking sharks, and the Oceanari-um, with its rescued sea otters. Note the Oceanarium also keeps beluga whales and Pacific white-sided dolphins, a practice that has become increasingly controversial in recent years.

Adler Planetarium   Museum

([icon]312-922-7827; www.adlerplanetarium. org; 1300 S Lake Shore Dr; adult/child $12/8; ◎9:30am-4pm; [icon]; [icon]146, 130) Space enthu-siasts will get a big bang (pun!) out of the Adler. There are public telescopes to view the stars (10am to 1pm daily, by the Galileo Cafe), 3-D lectures to learn about super-novas (in the Space Visualization Lab), and the Planet Explorers exhibit where kids can 'launch' a rocket. The immersive digital films cost extra (from $13 per ticket). The Adler's front steps offer Chicago's best skyline view, so get your camera ready.

◉ ACTIVITIES

The flat, 18-mile Lakefront Trail is a beautiful route along the water, though on nice days it's jam-packed with runners and cyclists. It also connects the city's 26 beaches.

Bike Chicago   Cycling

([icon]312-729-1000; www.bikechicago.com; 239 E Randolph St; bikes per hr/day from $9/30; ◎6:30am-10pm Mon-Fri, from 8am Sat & Sun Jun-Aug, reduced hours rest of year; [M]Brown, Orange, Green, Purple, Pink Line to Washington/Wabash) Rent a bike to explore DIY-style, or go on a guided tour. Tours cover themes such as lakefront parks and attractions, breweries and historic neighborhoods, or downtown's sights and fireworks at night (highly recom-mended). Prices include lock, helmet and map. This main branch operates out of the **McDonald's Cycle Center** (◎6:30am-10pm Mon-Fri, 8am-8pm Sat & Sun Jun-Aug, shorter hours Sep-May) in Millennium Park; there's another branch on Navy Pier (p131).

Bobby's Bike Hike   Cycling

([icon]312-245-9300; www.bobbysbikehike.com; 540 N Lake Shore Dr; per hr/day from $10/34; ◎8:30am-8pm Mon-Fri, 8am-8pm Sat & Sun Jun-Aug, 9am-7pm Mar-May & Sep-Nov; [M]Red Line to Grand) Locally based Bobby's earns rave reviews from riders. It rents bikes and has easy access to the Lakefront Trail. It also offers cool tours ($35 to $66) of South Side gangster sites, the lakefront, nighttime vis-tas, and venues to indulge in pizza and beer.

Foodie Trip to Logan Square

Logan Square has become Chicago's 'it' neighborhood for gastronomes, the place to go for creative fare in casual digs. It's a 20-minute ride from downtown via the Blue Line El train. Hot spots:

Revolution Brewing (773-227-2739; www.revbrew.com; 2323 N Milwaukee Ave; 11am-1am Mon-Fri, 10am-1am Sat, 10am-11pm Sun; Blue Line to California) Raise your fist to Revolution, a big, buzzy, industrial-chic brewpub that fills glasses with heady beers such as the Eugene porter and hopped-up Anti-Hero IPA. The brewmaster here led the way for Chicago's huge craft beer scene, and his suds are top notch. The haute pub grub includes a pork belly and egg sandwich and bacon-fat popcorn with fried sage.

Longman & Eagle (773-276-7110; www.longmanandeagle.com; 2657 N Kedzie Ave; mains $16-30; 9am-2am Sun-Fri, to 3am Sat; Blue Line to Logan Square) Hard to say whether this shabby-chic tavern is best for eating or drinking. Let's say eating, since it earned a Michelin star for its beautifully cooked comfort foods such as duck egg hash for breakfast, wild-boar sloppy joes for lunch, and fried chicken and duck-fat biscuits for dinner. There's a whole menu of juicy small plates and whiskeys too. No reservations.

The Tike Hike caters to kids. Enter through the covered driveway to reach the shop.

TOURS

Chicago Architecture Foundation

Tours

(CAF; 312-922-3432; www.architecture.org; 224 S Michigan Ave; tours $15-50; Brown, Orange, Green, Purple, Pink Line to Adams) The gold-standard boat tours ($46) sail from the **river dock** (Brown, Orange, Green, Purple, Pink Line to State/Lake) on the southeast side of the Michigan Ave Bridge. The popular Historic Skyscrapers walking tours ($20) leave from the main downtown address. Weekday lunchtime tours ($15) explore individual landmark buildings and meet on-site. CAF sponsors bus, bike and El train tours, too. Buy tickets online or at CAF; boat tickets can also be purchased at the dock.

Chicago by Foot

Walking

(312-612-0826; www.freetoursbyfoot.com/chicago-tours) Guides for this pay-what-you-want walking tour offer engaging stories and historical details on different jaunts covering the Loop, Gold Coast, Lincoln Park's gangster sites and much more. Most takers pay around $10 per person. Reserve in advance to guarantee a spot; walk-up guests are welcome if space is available (chancy).

SHOPPING

The main shopping bonanza is on N Michigan Ave, along the Magnificent Mile (p131).

Reckless Records

Music

(773-235-3727; www.reckless.com; 1379 N Milwaukee Ave; 10am-10pm Mon-Sat, to 8pm Sun; Blue Line to Damen) Chicago's best indie-rock record and CD emporium allows you to listen to everything before you buy. It's certainly the place to get your finger on the pulse of the local, au courant underground scene. There's plenty of elbow room in the big, sunny space, which makes for happy hunting through the new and used bins. Reasonable prices too.

Chicago Architecture Foundation Shop

Gifts & Souvenirs

(312-322-1132; www.architecture.org/shop; 224 S Michigan Ave; 9am-9pm, shorter hours in winter; Brown, Orange, Green, Purple, Pink Line to Adams) Skyline posters, Frank Lloyd Wright note cards, skyscraper models and heaps of books celebrate local architecture at this haven for anyone with an edifice complex. The items make excellent only-in-Chicago-type souvenirs.

🍴 EATING

🍴 The Loop

Revival Food Hall   American $

(☎773-999-9411; www.revivalfoodhall.com; 125 S Clark St; mains $7-12; ☺7am-7pm Mon-Fri; MBlue Line to Monroe) The Loop has craved a forward-thinking food court for ages. Which is why, come lunchtime, hipster office workers pack the blond wood tables at Revival Food Hall, the modern, lantern-adorned marketplace on the ground floor of the historic National building. The all-local dining concept brings some of Chicago's best fast-casual food to the masses, from Antique Taco and Smoque BBQ to Furious Spoon ramen.

Pastoral   Deli $

(☎312-658-1250; www.pastoralartisan.com; 53 E Lake St; sandwiches $8-12; ☺10:30am-8pm Mon-Fri, 11am-6pm Sat & Sun; ☑; MBrown, Orange, Green, Purple, Pink Line to Randolph or State/Lake) Pastoral makes a mean sandwich. Fresh-shaved serrano ham, Basque salami and other carnivorous fixings meet smoky mozzarella, Gruyère and piquant spreads slathered on crusty baguettes. Vegetarians also have options. There's limited seating; most folks take away for picnics in Millennium Park (call in your order a few hours in advance to avoid a queue). The shop sells bottles of beer and wine too.

Gage   Gastropub $$$

(☎312-372-4243; www.thegagechicago.com; 24 S Michigan Ave; mains $18-36; ☺11am-9pm Mon, to 11pm Tue-Thu, to midnight Fri, 10am-midnight Sat, 10am-10pm Sun; MBrown, Orange, Green, Purple, Pink Line to Washington/Wabash) This always-hopping gastropub dishes up fanciful grub, from Gouda-topped venison burgers to mussels vindaloo or Guinness-battered fish and chips. The booze rocks too, including a solid whiskey list and small-batch beers that pair with the food.

Deep-dish pizza

SHINYSHOT / SHUTTERSTOCK ©

🍽 Deep-Dish Pizza Icons

Giordano's (☎312-951-0747; www.
giordanos.com; 730 N Rush St; small pizzas
from $16.50; ⊙11am-11pm Sun-Thu, to
midnight Fri & Sat; ⓜRed Line to Chicago)
Giordano's makes 'stuffed' pizza, a bigger, doughier version of deep dish. It's
awesome. For a slice of heaven, order
the 'special,' a stuffed pie with sausage,
mushroom, green pepper and onions.
Each pizza takes 45 minutes to bake.

Lou Malnati's (☎312-786-1000; www.
loumalnatis.com; 805 S State St; small pizzas
from $13; ⊙11am-11pm Sun-Thu, to midnight
Fri & Sat; ⓜRed Line to Harrison) Lou Malnati's is one of the city's premier deep-dish
pizza makers. In fact, it claims to have
invented the gooey behemoth (though
that's a matter of never-ending dispute).
Not in dispute: the deliciousness of Malnati's famed butter crust. Gluten-free
diners can opt for the sausage crust
(it's literally just meat, no dough). The
restaurant has outlets citywide.

Pequod's Pizza (☎773-327-1512; www.
pequodspizza.com; 2207 N Clybourn Ave;
small pizzas from $12; ⊙11am-2am Mon-Sat,
to midnight Sun; ☐9 to Webster) Like the
ship in *Moby Dick,* from which this
neighborhood restaurant takes its name,
Pequod's pan-style (akin to deep dish)
pizza is a thing of legend – head and
shoulders above chain competitors
because of its caramelized cheese,
generous toppings and sweetly flavored
sauce. Neon beer signs glow from the
walls, and Blackhawks jerseys hang from
the ceiling in the affably rugged interior.

✪ Near North

Xoco   Mexican $
(www.rickbayless.com; 449 N Clark St; mains
$9-14; ⊙8am-9pm Tue-Thu, to 10pm Fri & Sat;
ⓜRed Line to Grand) ✐ At celeb-chef Rick
Bayless' Mexican street-food restaurant
(pronounced '*show*-co') everything is

sourced from local small farms. Crunch into
warm churros (spiraled dough fritters) with
chili-spiked hot chocolate for breakfast,
crusty *tortas* (sandwiches, such as the
succulent mushroom and goat cheese) for
lunch and *caldos* (meal-in-a-bowl soups) for
dinner. Queues can be long; breakfast is the
least crowded time.

Billy Goat Tavern   Burgers $
(☎312-222-1525; www.billygoattavern.com; 430 N
Michigan Ave, lower level; burgers $4-8; ⊙6am-1am
Mon-Thu, to 2am Fri, to 3am Sat, 9am-2am Sun;
ⓜRed Line to Grand) *Tribune* and *Sun Times*
reporters have guzzled in the subterranean
Billy Goat for decades. Order a 'cheezborger'
and Schlitz beer and then look around at the
newspapered walls to get the scoop on infamous local stories, such as the Cubs' Curse.
The place is a tourist magnet, but a deserving
one. Follow the tavern signs that lead below
Michigan Ave to get here. Cash only.

Purple Pig   Mediterranean $$
(☎312-464-1744; www.thepurplepigchicago.
com; 500 N Michigan Ave; small plates $10-20;
⊙11:30am-midnight Sun-Thu, to 1am Fri & Sat;
✐; ⓜRed Line to Grand) The Pig's Magnificent
Mile location, wide-ranging meat and veggie
menu, and late-night serving hours make it
a crowd-pleaser. Milk-braised pork shoulder
is the hamtastic specialty. Dishes are meant
to be shared, and the long list of affordable
vinos gets the good times rolling at communal tables both indoors and out. Alas, there
are no reservations to help beat the crowds.

✪ Lincoln Park & Old Town

Alinea   Gastronomy $$$
(☎312-867-0110; www.alinearestaurant.com; 1723
N Halsted St; 10-/16-course menu from $165/285;
⊙5-10pm Wed-Sun; ⓜRed Line to North/Cly-
bourn) One of the world's best restaurants,
with three Michelin stars, Alinea brings on
multiple courses of molecular gastronomy.
Dishes may emanate from a centrifuge or be
pressed into a capsule, à la duck served with
a 'pillow of lavender air.' There are no reserva-
tions; instead Alinea sells tickets two to three
months in advance via its website. Check
Twitter (@Alinea) for last-minute seats.

Wicker Park & Bucktown

Irazu   Latin American **$**

(☏773-252-5687; www.irazuchicago.com; 1865 N
Milwaukee Ave; mains $11-15; ⏱11:30am-9:30pm
Mon-Sat; ⓜBlue Line to Western) Chicago's unassuming lone Costa Rican eatery turns out
burritos bursting with chicken, black beans
and fresh avocado, and sandwiches dressed
in a heavenly, spicy-sweet vegetable sauce.
Wash them down with an *avena* (a slurpable
oatmeal milkshake). For breakfast, the *arroz
con huevos* (peppery eggs scrambled into
rice) relieves hangovers. Irazu is BYOB with
no corkage fee. Cash only.

Dove's Luncheonette   Tex-Mex **$$**

(☏773-645-4060; www.doveschicago.com; 1545
N Damen Ave; mains $13-19; ⏱9am-9pm Mon-Thu,
8am-10pm Fri & Sat, 8am-9pm Sun; ⓜBlue Line
to Damen) Grab a seat at the retro counter
for Tex-Mex plates of pork-shoulder posole
and shrimp-stuffed sweet-corn tamales.
Dessert? It's pie, of course – maybe lemon
cream or peach jalapeño, depending on
what staff have baked that day. Soul music
spins on a record player, tequila flows from
the 70 bottles rattling behind the bar, and
presto: all is right in the world.

West Loop

Lou Mitchell's   Breakfast **$**

(☏312-939-3111; www.loumitchellsrestaurant.
com; 565 W Jackson Blvd; mains $9-14; ⏱5:30am-
3pm Mon, to 4pm Tue-Fri, 7am-4pm Sat, to 3pm
Sun; ♿; ⓜBlue Line to Clinton) A relic of Route
66, Lou's brings in elbow-to-elbow locals
and tourists for breakfast. The old-school
waitresses deliver fluffy omelets that hang
off the plate and thick-cut French toast with
a jug of syrup. They call you 'honey' and fill
your coffee cup endlessly. There's often a
queue to get in, but free doughnut holes
and Milk Duds help ease the wait.

Little Goat   Diner **$$**

(☏312-888-3455; www.littlegoatchicago.com;
820 W Randolph St; mains $10-19; ⏱7am-10pm
Sun-Thu, to midnight Fri & Sat; 🛜📶; ⓜGreen,
Pink Line to Morgan) *Top Chef* winner Steph-
anie Izard opened this diner for the foodie

masses across the street from her ever-
booked main restaurant, **Girl & the Goat**
(☏312-492-6262; www.girlandthegoat.com; 809
W Randolph St; small plates $9-16; ⏱4:30-11pm
Sun-Thu, to midnight Fri & Sat) ◢. Scooch into
a vintage booth and order off the all-day
breakfast menu. Better yet, try lunch and
dinner favorites such as the goat sloppy joe
with rosemary slaw or pork belly on scallion
pancakes. Izard's flavor combinations rule.

Roister   American **$$$**

(www.roisterrestaurant.com; 951 W Fulton Market;
mains $28-32; ⏱11:45am-2pm & 5-10:30pm
Mon-Thu, to 11pm Fri, 11:30am-3pm & 5-11pm Sat,
to 10:30pm Sun; ⓜGreen, Pink Line to Morgan)
Roister lets you eat the food of molecular
gastronomist Grant Achatz (the chef of
three-Michelin-star Alinea) on the cheap.
Here he cooks wild riffs on comfort foods
while a rip-roaring rock soundtrack blasts.
Dishes change and defy easy description –
like the 'whole chicken' served with thighs
fried, breast roasted and the rest melded
into a chicken salad – but they're all rich
and playful. Reserve ahead.

🍸 DRINKING & NIGHTLIFE

🍸 The Loop & Near North

Berghoff   Bar

(☏312-427-3170; www.theberghoff.com; 17 W
Adams St; ⏱11am-9pm Mon-Fri, 11:30am-9pm
Sat; ⓜBlue, Red Line to Jackson) The Berghoff
dates from 1898 and was the first spot in
town to serve a legal drink after Prohibition
(ask to see the liquor license stamped '#1').
Little has changed around the antique wood
bar since then. Belly up for frosty mugs of
the house-brand beer and order sauerbra-
ten, schnitzel and other old-world classics
from the adjoining German restaurant.

Arbella   Cocktail Bar

(☏312-846-6654; www.arbellachicago.com; 112 W
Grand Ave; ⏱5pm-midnight Sun & Mon, to 2am Thu
& Fri, to 3am Sat; ⓜRed Line to Grand) Named
for a 17th-century ship full of wine-guzzling
passengers, Arbella is an adventuresome
cocktail bar. Booze from around the globe
makes its way into the drinks, from rye to

Top Five for Architecture

Chicago Architecture Foundation (p136)

Willis Tower (p130)

Rookery (p130)

Chicago Cultural Center (p130)

360° Chicago (p131)

From left: Rookery (p130); Willis Tower (p130); Preston Bradley Hall, Chicago Cultural Center (p130)

rum, pisco to mezcal. Park yourself at a dark leather banquette, under sparkly globe lights, and taste-trip the night away in one of the city's warmest, coziest rooms.

Clark Street Ale House   Bar

(312-642-9253; www.clarkstreetalehouse. com; 742 N Clark St; ☺4pm-4am Mon-Fri, from 11am Sat & Sun; ☎; MRed Line to Chicago) Do as the retro sign advises and 'Stop & Drink.' Midwestern microbrews are the main draw. Work up a thirst on the free pretzels, order a three-beer sampler for $7 and cool off in the beer garden out back.

🍸 Lincoln Park & Old Town

Old Town Ale House   Bar

(312-944-7020; www.theoldtownalehouse.com; 219 W North Ave; ☺3pm-4am Mon-Fri, from noon Sat & Sun; MBrown, Purple Line to Sedgwick) Located near the Second City comedy club and the scene of late-night musings since the 1960s, this unpretentious neighborhood favorite lets you mingle with beautiful people and grizzled regulars, seated pint by pint under the nude-politician paintings. Classic jazz on the jukebox provides the soundtrack for the jovial goings-on. Cash only.

🍸 Wicker Park & Bucktown

Matchbox   Bar

(312-666-9292; 770 N Milwaukee Ave; ☺4pm-2am Mon-Thu, from 3pm Fri-Sun; MBlue Line to Chicago) Lawyers, artists and bums all squeeze in for retro cocktails. It's as small as – you got it – a matchbox, with about 10 bar stools; everyone else stands against the back wall. Barkeeps make the drinks from scratch. Favorites include the pisco sour and the ginger gimlet, ladled from an amber vat of homemade ginger-infused vodka.

🍸 West Loop

RM Champagne Salon   Bar

(312-243-1199; www.rmchampagnesalon.com; 116 N Green St; ☺5pm-midnight Mon-Thu, to 2am Fri & Sat, to 11pm Sun; MGreen, Pink Line to Morgan) This West Loop spot is a twinkling-light charmer for bubbles. Score a table in the cobblestoned courtyard and you'll feel transported to Paris.

Goose Island Brewery   Brewery

(www.gooseisland.com; 1800 W Fulton St; ☺2-8pm Thu & Fri, noon-6pm Sat & Sun; MGreen, Pink Line to Ashland) Goose Island

– Chicago's first craft brewer, launched in 1988 – is now owned by Anheuser-Busch InBev, so technically it's no longer a craft brewer. But it still acts like one, making excellent small-batch beers at this facility. The swanky mod-industrial taproom pours nine or so varieties; bring your own food to accompany them. Hour-long tours ($12) are available if you reserve in advance.

⭐ ENTERTAINMENT

Hot Tix (www.hottix.org) sells same-week drama, comedy and performing-arts tickets for half price (plus a $5 to $10 service charge). Book online or at the two Hot Tix outlets in the Loop. Check the *Chicago Reader* (www.chicagoreader.com) for listings.

Hideout   Live Music

(🎵773-227-4433; www.hideoutchicago.com; 1354 W Wabansia Ave; tickets $5-15; ☺5pm-2am Mon & Tue, from 4pm Wed-Fri, 7pm-3am Sat, hours vary Sun; 🚌72) Hidden behind a factory at the edge of Bucktown, this two-room lodge of indie rock and alt-country is well worth seeking out. The owners have nursed an outsider, underground vibe, and the place

feels like your grandma's rumpus room. Music and other events (talk shows, literary readings etc) take place nightly.

Buddy Guy's Legends   Blues

(🎵312-427-1190; www.buddyguy.com; 700 S Wabash Ave; tickets Sun-Thu $10, Fri & Sat $20; ☺5pm-2am Mon & Tue, from 11am Wed-Fri, noon-3am Sat, to 2am Sun; Ⓜ Red Line to Harrison) Top local and national acts wail on the stage of local icon Buddy Guy. The man himself usually plugs in his axe for a series of shows in January (tickets go on sale in November). The location is a bit rough around the edges, but the acts are consistently excellent.

Second City   Comedy

(🎵312-337-3992; www.secondcity.com; 1616 N Wells St; tickets $29-36; Ⓜ Brown, Purple Line to Sedgwick) Bill Murray, Stephen Colbert, Tina Fey and more honed their wit at this venue where shows take place nightly. The Mainstage and ETC stage host sketch revues (with improv thrown in); they're similar in price and quality. If you turn up around 10pm (on any night except Friday and Saturday) you can have yourself a bargain and watch the comics improv a set for free.

Detour: Hyde Park

Hyde Park is on Chicago's south side and makes for a leafy jaunt. As well as the University of Chicago's grand, Gothic campus, there are a couple of top sights. Take the Metra Electric Line trains from Millennium Station downtown, or bus 6 from State St in the Loop.

Museum of Science & Industry (MSI; ☑773-684-1414; www.msichicago.org; 5700 S Lake Shore Dr; adult/child $18/11; ☺9:30am-5:30pm Jun-Aug, shorter hours Sep-May; ▥) Geek out at the largest science museum in the Western Hemisphere. Highlights include a WWII German U-boat nestled in an underground display (tours $12 extra) and the Science Storms exhibit with a mock tornado and tsunami. Other popular exhibits include the baby chick hatchery, the minuscule furnishings in Colleen Moore's fairy castle, and the life-size shaft of a coal mine ($12 extra).

Robie House (☑312-994-4000; www.flwright.org; 5757 S Woodlawn Ave; adult/child $18/15; ☺10:30am-3pm Thu-Mon) Of the numerous Chicago buildings that Frank Lloyd Wright designed, none is more famous or influential than Robie House. Because its horizontal lines resembled the flat landscape of the Midwestern prairie, the style became known as 'Prairie style.' Inside are 174 stained-glass windows and doors, which you'll see on the hour-long tours (frequency varies, but there's usually at least one per hour).

iO Theater — Comedy
(☑312-929-2401; www.ioimprov.com/chicago; 1501 N Kingsbury St; tickets $5-16; ▥Red Line to North/Clybourn) One of Chicago's top-tier improv houses, iO is a bit edgier (and cheaper) than its competition, with four stages hosting bawdy shows nightly. Two bars and a beer garden add to the fun. The Improvised Shakespeare Company is awesome; catch them if you can.

Green Mill — Jazz
(☑773-878-5552; www.greenmilljazz.com; 4802 N Broadway; ☺noon-4am Mon-Fri, to 5am Sat, 11am-4am Sun; ▥Red Line to Lawrence) The timeless Green Mill earned its notoriety as Al Capone's favorite speakeasy (the tunnels where he hid the booze are still underneath the bar). Sit in one of the curved velvet booths and feel his ghost urging you on to another martini. Local and national jazz artists perform nightly; Sunday also hosts the nationally acclaimed poetry slam. Cash only.

BLUES — Blues
(☑773-528-1012; www.chicagobluesbar.com; 2519 N Halsted St; cover charge $7-10; ☺8pm-2am Wed-Sun; ▥Brown, Purple, Red Line to Fullerton) Long, narrow and high volume, this veteran blues club draws a slightly older crowd that soaks up every crackling, electrified moment. As one local musician put it, 'The audience here comes out to *understand* the blues.' Big local names grace the small stage.

Steppenwolf Theatre — Theater
(☑312-335-1650; www.steppenwolf.org; 1650 N Halsted St; ▥Red Line to North/Clybourn) Steppenwolf is Chicago's top stage for quality, provocative theater productions. The Hollywood-heavy ensemble includes Gary Sinise, John Malkovich, Martha Plimpton, Gary Cole, Joan Allen and Tracy Letts. A money-saving tip: the box office releases 20 tickets for $20 for each day's shows; they go on sale at 11am Monday to Saturday and at 1pm Sunday, and are available by phone.

ⓘ INFORMATION

Choose Chicago (www.choosechicago.com) Official tourism site with sightseeing and event info.

ⓘ GETTING THERE & AROUND

TO/FROM THE AIRPORT

O'Hare International Airport (ORD; www.fly chicago.com) Located 17 miles northwest of the Loop.

○ **Train** The Blue Line El train ($5) runs 24/7 and departs every 10 minutes or so. The journey to the city center takes 40 minutes.

○ **Shuttle** The **GO Airport Express** (www.airport express.com) shared-van service goes downtown for $35 per person. Vans run between 4am and 11:30pm, departing every 15 minutes. It takes an hour or more, depending on traffic.

○ **Taxi** Rides to the center take 30 minutes and cost around $50. Taxi queues can be lengthy, and the ride can take longer than the train, depending on traffic.

Chicago Midway Airport (MDW; www.flychicago. com) Located 11 miles southwest of the Loop.

○ **Train** The Orange Line El train ($3) runs between 4am and 1am. It departs every 10 minutes or so and reaches downtown in 30 minutes.

○ **Shuttle** The **GO Airport Express** (www. airportexpress.com) door-to-door shuttle goes downtown for $30. Vans run between 4am and 10:30pm. The journey takes approximately 50 minutes.

○ **Taxi** Rides to the center take 20 minutes or longer (depending on traffic) and cost $35 to $40.

BICYCLE

Divvy (www.divvybikes.com) has 5800 sky-blue bikes at 580 stations around Chicago. Kiosks issue 24-hour passes ($10) on the spot.

Bike rentals for longer rides (with accoutrements such as helmets and locks) start at around $18 for two hours. Try Bike Chicago (p135) or Bobby's Bike Hike (p135).

CAR & MOTORCYCLE

Downtown garages cost about $40 per day. On-street, metered parking costs from $2 per hour (in outlying areas) to $6.50 per hour (in the Loop).

PUBLIC TRANSPORTATION

Chicago Transit Authority (www.transit chicago.com) Runs the transport system.

○ The El (a system of elevated and subway trains) is the main way to get around. Red and Blue Lines operate 24/7, others between 4am and 1am.

○ The standard fare is $3 (except from O'Hare airport, where it costs $5) and includes two transfers. Enter the turnstile using a Ventra Ticket, which is sold from vending machines at train stations.

○ You can also buy a Ventra Card, aka a rechargeable fare card, at stations. It has a one-time $5 fee that gets refunded once you register the card. It knocks around 75¢ off the cost of each ride.

○ Unlimited ride passes (one-/three-day $10/20) are another handy option.

○ Buses cover areas that the El misses. Most run at least from early morning until 10pm; some go later. Some don't run on weekends.

TAXI & RIDE SHARE

Taxis are plentiful in the Loop, north to Lake View and northwest to Wicker Park/Bucktown. Fares start at $3.25 when you get into the cab, then it's $2.25 per mile. The first extra passenger costs $1; extra passengers after that are 50¢ apiece. Try **Checker Taxi** (☎ 312-243-2537; www. checkertaxichicago.com) if you need a pick-up. The ride-sharing companies Uber, Lyft and Via are also popular in Chicago.

TRAIN

Union Station (www.chicagounionstation.com; 225 S Canal St; Ⓜ Blue Line to Clinton) is the city's rail hub, located at the Loop's western edge. For public transportation onward, the Blue Line Clinton stop is a few blocks south (though not a good option at night). The Brown, Orange, Purple and Pink Line station at Quincy is about a half-mile east.

Ocean Drive (p155)

MIAMI

In this Chapter

Art Deco Historic District 148
Key Biscayne 152
Sights 154
Activities 160
Tours 160
Shopping 161
Eating 162
Drinking & Nightlife 167
Entertainment 168

Miami at a Glance...

Miami has so many different facets to its diverse neighborhoods that it's hard to believe it all fits in one place. By day you can admire incredible photorealistic murals in Wynwood, then spend the evening immersed in Afro Cuban jazz in Little Havana, perhaps followed by rooftop drinks atop the city's latest skyscraper. Crossing town you can't help feeling like you've passed into another city. Over in Miami Beach, you can endlessly wander around deco masterpieces, each one bursting with personality – best followed by late-afternoon strolls along the sands, when the golden light is mesmerizing.

Two Days in Miami

Start your trip with a tour around the Miami Beach deco district with the **Design Preservation League** (p160), and consider a visit to the **Wolfsonian-FIU** (p151) and **New World Center** (p154). On your second day, head to downtown Miami and take in the **art museum** (p155) and **HistoryMiami** (p155), as well as the **Brickell City Centre** (p157).

Four Days in Miami

On your third day, go to Little Havana and watch the locals slap dominoes at **Máximo Gómez Park** (p158). Then go to Wynwood to peruse galleries and dine like royalty at **Alter** (p165) or **Kyu** (p165). On day four, witness the full opulent fantasy of Miami at sites such as the **Vizcaya Museum** (p159) and the **Biltmore Hotel** (p158), or head out to **Key Biscayne** (p152) for a nature fix.

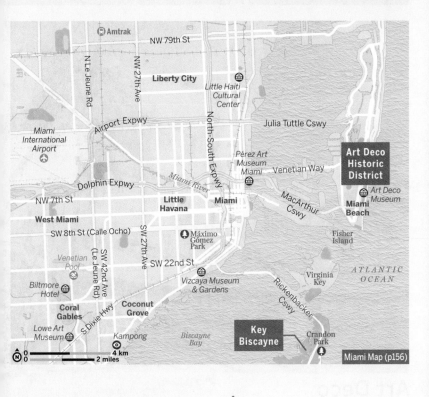

Amtrak
NW 79th St
N Le Jeune Rd
NW 27th Ave
Liberty City
Little Haiti Cultural Center
North–South Expwy
Julia Tuttle Cswy
Airport Expwy
Miami International Airport
Pérez Art Museum Miami
Venetian Way
Art Deco Historic District
Dolphin Expwy
Miami River
Art Deco Museum
NW 7th St
Little Havana
Miami
MacArthur Cswy
Miami Beach
West Miami
SW 8th St (Calle Ocho)
Máximo Gómez Park
Fisher Island
Venetian Pool
Le Jeune Rd
SW 42nd Ave
SW 27th Ave
SW 22nd St
ATLANTIC OCEAN
Biltmore Hotel
Vizcaya Museum & Gardens
Virginia Key
Coral Gables
S Dixie Hwy
Coconut Grove
Rickenbacker Cswy
Lowe Art Museum
Kampong
Biscayne Bay
Key Biscayne
Crandon Park
N
0   4 km
0   2 miles
Miami Map (p156)

Arriving in Miami

Miami International Airport Taxis ($35) and shared SuperShuttle vans (about $22) run to South Beach (40 minutes). The Miami Beach Airport Express (bus 150) costs $2.65 and makes stops all along Miami Beach.

Fort Lauderdale-Hollywood International Airport GO Airport Shuttle runs shared vans to Miami (around $25). A taxi costs around $75.

Sleeping

When the art-deco movement swept Miami Beach, hotels were some of the most important buildings impacted by the aesthetic. As such, it's fair to say hotels are the backbone of the area's rise to tourism prominence. The Magic City (and Miami Beach) offers the greatest range of accommodations in the state.

LITTLENYSTOCK / SHUTTERSTOCK ©

Art Deco Historic District

The world-famous Art Deco Historic District of Miami Beach is pure exuberance: architecture of bold lines, whimsical tropical motifs and a color palette that evokes all the beauty of the Miami landscape.

Great For...

☑ Don't Miss

Strolling the 700 block of Ocean Dr at night to soak up the best of the deco neon.

Among the 800 deco buildings listed on the National Register of Historic Places, each design is different, and it's hard not to be captivated when strolling among these restored beauties from a bygone era.

Background

For much of its history, Miami Beach was little more than an empty landscape of swaying palm trees, scrubland and sandy shoreline. It wasn't until the early 20th century that a few entrepreneurs began to envision transforming the island into a resort. Beginning in the 1920s, a few hotels rose up, catering to an elite crowd of wealthy industrialists vacationing from the north. And then disaster struck. In 1926 a hurricane left a devastating swath across the island and much of South Florida.

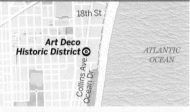

TIM GRAHAM / CONTRIBUTOR / GETTY IMAGES ©

**Art Deco
Historic District** ⊙

18th St

*ATLANTIC
OCEAN*

Collins Ave

Ocean Dr

❶ Need to Know

Many of the best deco buildings can be found between 11th and 14th Sts.

✕ Take a Break

Have your deco-district meal in the 11th Street Diner (p162), set in a 1940s train car.

★ Top Tip

Miami Design Preservation League (p160) runs excellent walking tours of the deco district.

When it was time to rebuild, Miami Beach would undergo a dramatic rebirth. This is where art deco enters from stage left. As luck would have it, at exactly that moment, a bold new style of architecture was all the talk in America, having burst onto the scene at a renowned fair known as the Exposition Internationale des Arts Décoratifs et Industriels Modernes held in Paris in 1925.

Over the next few years developers arrived in droves, and the building boom was on. Miami Beach would become the epicenter of this groundbreaking new design (which incidentally was not called 'art deco' in those days, but simply 'art moderne' or 'modernistic'). Hundreds of new hotels were built during the 1930s to accommodate the influx of middle-class tourists flooding into Miami Beach for a

slice of sand and sun. And the golden era of deco architecture continued until it all came to an end during WWII.

Deco Style

The art-deco building style was very much rooted in the times. The late 1920s and 1930s was an era of invention – of new automobiles, streamlined machines, radio antennae and cruise ships. Architects manifested these elements in the strong vertical and horizontal lines, at times coupled with zigzigs or sleek curves, all of which created the illusion of movement, of the bold forward march into the future.

In Miami Beach architects also incorporated more local motifs such as palm trees, flamingos and tropical plants. Nautical themes also appeared, with playful representations of ocean waves, sea horses, starfish and lighthouses. The style later became known as tropical deco.

Architects also came up with unique solutions to the challenges of building design in a hot, sun-drenched climate. Eyebrow-like ledges jutted over the windows, providing shade (and cooler inside temperatures), without obstructing the views. And thick glass blocks were incorporated into some building facades. These let in light while keeping out the heat – essential design elements in those days before air-conditioning.

The Best of Ocean Drive

One stretch of Ocean Dr has a collection of some of the most striking art-deco build-ings in Miami Beach. Between 11th and 14th Sts, you'll see many of the classic deco ele-ments at play in beautifully designed works – each bursting with individual personality. Close to 11th St, the **Congress Hotel** (1052 Ocean Dr) shows perfect symmetry in its three-story facade, with window-shading 'eyebrows' and a long marquee down the middle that's reminiscent of the grand movie palaces of the 1930s.

About a block north, the **Tides** (☏305-250-0784; www.tidessouthbeach.com; 1220 Ocean Dr; P ☀ 🛜 ⛵) is one of the finest of the nautical-themed hotels, with porthole windows over the entryway, a reception desk of Key limestone (itself imprinted with fossilized sea creatures), and curious arrows on the floor, meant to denote the ebb and flow of the tide.

Near 13th St, the **Cavalier** (☏305-673-1199; www.cavaliersouthbeach.com; 1320 Ocean Dr; P ☀ 🛜) plays with the seahorse theme, in stylized depictions of the sea creature, and also has palm-tree-like iconography. The **Carlyle** (1250 Ocean Dr) is another wor-

Villa Casa Casuarina

thy stop-off on Ocean Dr, with its futuristic styling, triple parapets and a *Jetsons* vibe.

Art Deco Museum

This small **museum** (www.mdpl.org/welcome-center/art-deco-museum; 1001 Ocean Dr; $5; ⊙10am-5pm Tue-Sun, to 7pm Thu) is one of the best places in town for an enlightening overview of the art-deco district. Through videos, photography, models and other displays you'll learn of the pioneering work of Barbara Capitman, who helped save these buildings from certain destruction back in the 1970s, and her collaboration with Leonard Horowitz, the talented artist who designed the pastel color palette that is an integral part of the design visible today.

The museum also touches on other key architectural styles in Miami, including Mediterranean Revival – typified by the **Villa Casa Casuarina** (☎786-485-2200; www.vmmiamibeach.com; 1116 Ocean Dr; P ❄ 🛜 ⛵) – and the post-deco boom of MiMo (Miami Modern), which emerged after WWII, and is particularly prevalent in North Miami Beach.

Wolfsonian-FIU

The imposing **Wolfsonian-FIU** (☎305-531-1001; www.wolfsonian.org; 1001 Washington Ave; adult/child $10/5, 6-9pm Fri free; ⊙10am-6pm Mon, Tue, Thu & Sat, to 9pm Fri, noon-6pm Sun, closed Wed), formerly the Washington Storage Company, is now an excellent design museum. Wealthy snowbirds of the 1930s stashed their pricey belongings here before heading back up north. Visit early in your stay to put the aesthetics of Miami Beach into context. It's one thing to see how wealth, leisure and the pursuit of beauty manifests in Miami Beach, but it's another to understand the roots and shadings of local artistic movements. By chronicling the interior evolution of everyday life, the Wolfsonian reveals how these trends were architecturally manifested in SoBe's exterior deco.

Which reminds us of the Wolfsonian's own noteworthy facade. Remember the Gothic-futurist apartment-complex-cum-temple-of-evil in *Ghostbusters*? Well, this imposing structure, with its grandiose 'frozen fountain' and lion-head-studded grand elevator, could serve as a stand-in for that set.

★ **Did You Know?**

The *Birdcage,* a 1996 comedy, was filmed at the Carlyle.

TRAVELVIEW / SHUTTERSTOCK ©

☑ **Don't Miss**

The **Art Deco Weekend** (www.artdecoweekend.com; Ocean Dr, btwn 1st St & 23rd St; ⊙mid-Jan) features guided tours, concerts, classic-auto shows, sidewalk cafes, arts and antiques.

Cape Florida Lighthouse

Key Biscayne

Key Biscayne is an easy getaway from Downtown Miami. But once you're here, you'll feel like you've been transported to a far-off tropical realm, with magnificent beaches, lush nature trails in state parks, and aquatic adventures aplenty.

Great For...

☑ Don't Miss

Join one of the monthly full-moon evening kayaking adventures offered by Virginia Key Outdoor Center (p160).

Start early in the day for the drive or bike ride out to this picturesque landscape, roughly 5 miles southeast of Downtown Miami (a 10-minute drive). Heading out along the Rickenbacker Causeway leads first to small Virginia Key, which has a few worthwhile sights – tiny beaches, a small mountain-bike park and pretty spots for kayaking.

The road continues to Key Biscayne, an island that's just 7 miles long with unrivaled views of the Miami skyline. As you pass over the causeway, note the small public beaches, picnic areas and fishing spots arranged on its margins.

Crandon Park

This 1200-acre **park** (☏305-361-5421; www.miamidade.gov/parks/parks/crandon_beach.asp; 6747 Crandon Blvd; per car weekday/

Raccoon, Bill Baggs Cape Florida State Park

ALEXANDER SPATARI / GETTY IMAGES ©

Miami ○

ATLANTIC OCEAN

Key Biscayne
◎

❶ Need to Know

Crandon Blvd is Key Biscayne's only real main road.

✕ Take a Break

There are several good places to dine in Bill Baggs state park, including **Boater's Grill** (📞305-361-0080; 1200 S Crandon Blvd; mains $14-32, burgers $7-10; ⊙9am-8pm Sun-Thu, to 10pm Fri & Sat).

★ Top Tip

The area gets busy on the weekends. To escape the crowds, come on a weekday.

weekend $5/7; ⊙sunrise-sunset; 🅿♿🐾) boasts Crandon Park Beach, a glorious stretch of sand that spreads for 2 miles. Much of the park consists of a dense coastal hammock (hardwood forest) and mangrove swamps. The beach here is clean and uncluttered by tourists, faces a lovely sweep of teal goodness and is regularly named one of the best beaches in the USA. Pretty cabanas at the south end of the park can be rented by the day ($40).

Bill Baggs Cape Florida State Park

If you don't make it to the Florida Keys, come to this **park** (📞305-361-5811; www.floridastateparks.org/capeflorida; 1200 S Crandon Blvd; per car/person $8/2; ⊙8am-sunset, lighthouse 9am-5pm; 🅿♿🐾) 🏊 for a taste of their unique island ecosystems. The 494-acre space is a tangled clot of tropical fauna and dark mangroves, all interconnected by sandy trails and wooden boardwalks, and surrounded by miles of pale ocean. A concession shack rents out kayaks, bikes, in-line skates, beach chairs and umbrellas.

At the state recreation area's southernmost tip, the 1845 brick Cape Florida Lighthouse is the oldest structure in Florida (it replaced another lighthouse that was severely damaged in 1836 during the Second Seminole War). Free tours run at 10am and 1pm Thursday to Monday.

Water Sports

One of the best reasons to visit this tropical hot spot is to get out on the water, whether on a kayak, stand up paddle board or sailboat. With special guided excursions out here, it pays to plan ahead. Be sure to check out if Virginia Key Outdoor Center (p160) has any trips planned while you're in the area.

⊙ SIGHTS

Miami's major sights aren't concentrated in one neighborhood. The most frequently visited area is South Beach, home to hot nightlife, beautiful beaches and art-deco hotels, but you'll find historic sites and museums in the Downtown area, art galleries in Wynwood and the Design District, old-fashioned hotels and eateries in Mid-Beach (in Miami Beach), more beaches on Key Biscayne, and peaceful neighborhood attractions in Coral Gables and Coconut Grove.

◎ South Beach

New World Center   Notable Building

(✆305-673-3330, tours 305-673-3331; www.newworldcenter.com; 500 17th St; tours $5; ◷tours 4pm Tue & Thu, 1pm Fri & Sat) Designed by Frank Gehry, this performance hall rises majestically out of a manicured lawn just above Lincoln Rd. Not unlike the ethereal power of the music within, the glass-and-steel facade encases characteristically Gehry-esque sail-like shapes within that help shape the magnificent acoustics and add to the futuristic quality of the concert hall. The grounds form a 2.5-acre public park aptly known as **SoundScape Park** (www.nws.edu; 500 17th St).

Jewish Museum of Florida-FIU   Museum

(✆305-672-5044; www.jmof.fiu.edu; 301 Washington Ave; adult/student & senior $6/5, Sat free; ◷10am-5pm Tue-Sun, closed Jewish holidays) Housed in a 1936 Orthodox synagogue that served Miami's first congregation, this small museum chronicles the rather large contribution Jews have made to the state of Florida. After all, it could be said that while Cubans made Miami, Jews made Miami Beach, both physically and culturally. Yet there were times when Jews were barred from the American Riviera they carved out of the sand, and this museum tells that story, along with some amusing anecdotes (like seashell Purim dresses).

Española Way Promenade   Area

(btwn 14th & 15th Sts) Española Way is an 'authentic' Spanish promenade...in the Florida theme-park spirit of authenticity. Oh, whatever; it's a lovely terracotta and cobbled arcade of rose-pink and Spanish-cream architecture, perfect for an alfresco meal with a side of people-watching at one of the many restaurants lining the strip.

World Erotic Art Museum   Museum

(✆305-532-9336; www.weam.com; 1205 Washington Ave; over 18yr $15; ◷11am-10pm Mon-Thu, to midnight Fri-Sun) In a neighborhood where no behavior is too shocking, the World Erotic Art Museum celebrates its staggering but artful pornography, including pieces by Rembrandt and Picasso. Back in 2005, 70-year-old Naomi Wilzig turned her 5000-piece erotica collection into a South Beach attraction.

WEAM takes itself seriously, which is part of the charm of this fascinating collection spanning the ages, from ancient sex manuals to Victorian peep-show photos to an elaborate four-poster (four-phallus rather) Kama Sutra bed, with carvings in wood depicting various ways (138 in fact) to get intimate. Other curiosities include the phallus bone of a whale with hand-carved wolf faces and the oversized sculpted genitals used as a murder weapon in *A Clockwork Orange*.

Miami Beach Botanical Garden   Gardens

(www.mbgarden.org; 2000 Convention Center Dr; suggested donation $2; ◷9am-5pm Tue-Sat) This lush but little-known 2.6 acres of plantings is operated by the Miami Beach Garden Conservancy, and is a veritable secret garden in the midst of the urban jungle – an oasis of palm trees, flowering hibiscus trees and glassy ponds. It's a great spot for a picnic.

◎ North Beach

Oleta River State Park   State Park

(✆305-919-1844; www.floridastateparks.org/oletariver; 3400 NE 163rd St; vehicle/pedestrian & bicycle $6/2; ◷8am-sunset; P🚶) Tequesta people were boating the Oleta River estuary as early as 500 BC, so you're just following in a long tradition if you canoe or kayak in this park. At almost 1000 acres, this is the largest urban park in the state and one of the best places in Miami to escape the madding crowd. Boat out to the local mangrove island, watch the eagles fly by, or just chill on the pretension-free beach.

Haulover Beach Park — Park

(☏305-947-3525; www.miamidade.gov/parks/haulover.asp; 10800 Collins Ave; per car Mon-Fri $5, Sat-Sun $7; ☺sunrise-sunset; P) Where are all those tanned men in gold chains and Speedos going? That would be the clothing-optional beach in this 40-acre park hidden from condos, highways and prying eyes by vegetation. There's more to do here than get in the buff, though; most of the beach is 'normal' (there's even a dog park) and is one of the nicer spots for sand in the area. The park is on Collins Ave about 4.5 miles north of 71st St.

◉ Downtown Miami

Pérez Art Museum Miami — Museum

(PAMM; ☏305-375-3000; www.pamm.org; 1103 Biscayne Blvd; adult/senior & student $16/12, 1st Thu & 2nd Sat of month free; ☺10am-6pm Fri-Tue, to 9pm Thu, closed Wed; P) The Pérez can claim fine rotating exhibits that concentrate on post-WWII international art, but just as impressive are its location and exterior. This art institution inaugurated Museum Park, a patch of land that overseas the broad blue swath of Biscayne Bay. Swiss architects Herzog & de Meuron designed the structure, which integrates tropical foliage, glass and metal – a melding of tropical vitality and fresh modernism that is a nice architectural analogy for Miami itself.

HistoryMiami — Museum

(☏305-375-1492; www.historymiami.org; 101 W Flagler St; adult/child $10/5; ☺10am-5pm Mon-Sat, from noon Sun; ♿) South Florida – a land of escaped slaves, guerrilla Native Americans, gangsters, land grabbers, pirates, tourists, drug dealers and alligators – has a special history, and it takes a special kind

📷 Cruising down Ocean Drive

Ocean Dr is the great cruising strip of Miami: an endless parade of classic cars, testosterone-sweating young men, peacock-like young women, street performers, vendors, those guys who yell unintelligible nonsense at everyone, celebrities pretending to be tourists, tourists who want to play celebrity, beautiful people, not-so-beautiful people, people people people and the best ribbon of art-deco preservation on the beach. Say 'Miami.' That image in your head? Probably Ocean Dr.

PHILIP LANGE / SHUTTERSTOCK ©

of museum to capture that narrative. This highly recommended place, located in the Miami-Dade Cultural Center, does just that, weaving together the stories of the region's successive waves of population, from Native Americans to Nicaraguans.

Patricia & Phillip Frost Museum of Science — Museum

(☏305-434-9600; www.frostscience.org; 1101 Biscayne Blvd; adult/child $28/20; ☺9am-6pm; P♿) This sprawling new Downtown museum spreads across 250,000 sq ft that includes a three-level aquarium, a 250-seat state-of-the-art planetarium and two distinct wings that delve into the wonders of science and nature. Exhibitions range from weather phenomena to creepy crawlies, feathered dinosaurs and vital-microbe displays, while Florida's fascinating Everglades and biologically rich coral reefs play starring roles.

Miami

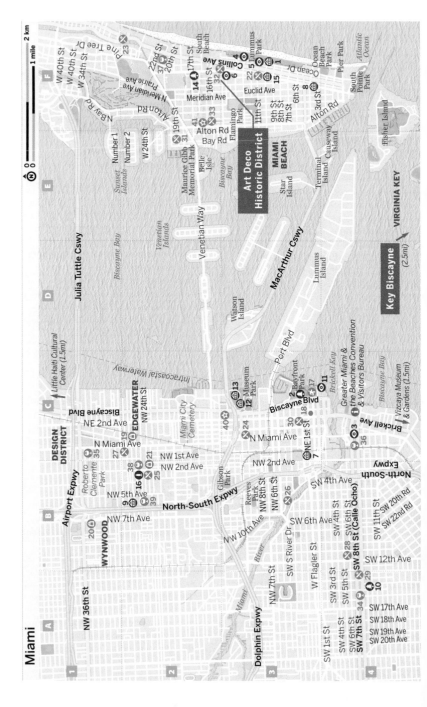

Miami

◎ Sights
1 Art Deco Museum F3
2 Bayfront Park..C3
3 Brickell City Centre....................................C4
4 Carlyle...F3
5 Congress Hotel...F3
6 Española Way Promenade.......................F3
7 HistoryMiami..C3
8 Jewish Museum of Florida-FIU.................F3
9 Margulies Collection at the
    Warehouse.. B2
10 Máximo Gómez Park A4
11 Miami Riverwalk C4
New World Center...........................(see 14)
12 Patricia & Phillip Frost Museum of
    Science..C3
13 Pérez Art Museum Miami C3
14 SoundScape Park F2
15 Wolfsonian-FIU..F3
16 Wynwood Walls B2

❶ Activities, Courses & Tours
Bike & Roll .... (see 1)
Miami Design Preservation
    League .... (see 1)
17 Tina Hills Pavilion C3
18 Urban Tour Host...C3

⬢ Shopping
19 Art by God C2
20 Brooklyn Vintage & Vinyl...........................B1
Guantanamera.................................... (see 34)
Havana Collection .... (see 34)
Malaquita.. (see 38)
Nomad Tribe.. (see 32)
21 Nomad Tribe... B2
Taschen...(see 41)

⊗ Eating
22 11th Street Diner... F3
23 27 Restaurant F2
24 All Day C3
25 Alter..B2
26 Casablanca...B3
27 Della Test Kitchen C2
28 Doce Provisions...B4
29 El Nuevo Siglo A4
Kyu...(see 16)
30 NIU Kitchen C3
Panther Coffee.................................... (see 25)
Panther Coffee.................................... (see 31)
31 Pubbelly E2
32 Taquiza F2
Verde..(see 13)
Wynwood Yard .... (see 27)
33 Yardbird F2

❺ Drinking & Nightlife
34 Ball & Chain.. A4
35 Bardot C1
36 Blackbird Ordinary C4
Bodega..(see 33)
Broken Shaker .... (see 23)
37 Sweet Liberty F2
38 Wood Tavern.. B2
39 Wynwood Brewing Company B2

◉ Entertainment
40 Adrienne Arsht Center for the
    Performing Arts.......................................C3
41 Colony Theater F2
Cubaocho ....(see 34)
Klipsch Amphitheater .... (see 2)
New World Symphony ....(see 14)
Tower Theater.................................... (see 10)

Bayfront Park   Park

(☏305-358-7550; www.bayfrontparkmiami.com;
301 N Biscayne Blvd) Few American parks can
claim to front such a lovely stretch of tur-
quoise (Biscayne Bay), but Miamians are
lucky like that. Notable park features are
two performance venues: the **Klipsch
Amphitheater** (www.klipsch.com/klipsch-
amphitheater-at-bayfront-park), which boasts
excellent views over Biscayne Bay and is
a good spot for live-music shows, and the
smaller 200-seat (lawn seating can accommodate 800 more) Tina Hills Pavilion,
which hosts free springtime performances.

Miami Riverwalk   Waterfront

This pedestrian walkway follows along
the northern edge of the river as it bisects
Downtown, and offers some peaceful
vantage points of bridges and skyscrapers
dotting the urban landscape. You can start
the walk at the south end of Bayfront Park
and follow it under bridges and along the
waterline till it ends just west of the SW 2nd
Ave Bridge.

Brickell City Centre   Area

(www.brickellcitycentre.com; 701 S Miami Ave;
⊙10am-9:30pm Mon-Sat, noon-7pm Sun) One

of the hottest new developments in Miami finally opened its doors in late 2016, after four long years of construction. The massive billion-dollar complex spreads across three city blocks, and it encompasses glittering residential towers, modernist office blocks and a soaring five-star hotel – the **EAST, Miami** (✆305-712-7000; www.east-miami.com; 788 Brickell Plaza; ❄🛜🏊). There's much to entice both Miami residents and visitors to the center, with restaurants, bars, a cinema and loads of high-end retailers (Ted Baker, All Saints, Kendra Scott).

◎ Wynwood & the Design District

Wynwood Walls Public Art

(www.thewynwoodwalls.com; NW 2nd Ave, btwn 25th & 26th Sts) FREE In the midst of rusted warehouses and concrete blah, there's a pastel-and-graffiti explosion of urban art. Wynwood Walls is a collection of murals and paintings laid out over an open courtyard that invariably bowls people over with its sheer color profile and unexpected location. What's on offer tends to change with the coming and going of major arts events such as **Art Basel** (www.artbasel.com/miami-beach; ⊙early Dec), but it's always interesting stuff.

**Margulies Collection
at the Warehouse** Gallery

(✆305-576-1051; www.margulieswarehouse.com; 591 NW 27th St; adult/student $10/5; ⊙11am-4pm Tue-Sat mid-Oct–Apr) Encompassing 45,000 sq ft, this vast not-for-profit exhibition space houses one of the best collections in Wynwood. Thought-provoking large-format installations are the focus at the Warehouse, and you'll see works by some of the leading 21st-century artists here.

◎ Little Havana

Máximo Gómez Park Park

(cnr SW 8th St & SW 15th Ave; ⊙9am-6pm) Little Havana's most evocative reminder of Old Cuba is Máximo Gómez Park, or

'Domino Park,' where the sound of elderly men trash-talking over games of chess is harmonized by the quick clack-clack of slapping dominoes. The jarring back-track, plus the heavy smell of cigars and a sunrise-bright mural of the 1994 Summit of the Americas, combine to make Máximo Gómez one of the most sensory sites in Miami (although it is admittedly one of the most tourist-heavy ones as well).

◎ Coral Gables

Fairchild Tropical Garden Gardens

(✆305-667-1651; www.fairchildgarden.org; 10901 Old Cutler Rd; adult/child/senior $25/12/18; ⊙9:30am-4:30pm; 🅿♿) If you need to escape Miami's madness, consider a green day in the country's largest tropical botanical garden. A butterfly grove, tropical plant conservatory and gentle vistas of marsh and keys habitats, plus frequent art installations from artists like Roy Lichtenstein, are all stunning. In addition to easy-to-follow, self-guided walking tours, a free 45-minute tram tours the entire park on the hour from 10am to 3pm (till 4pm weekends).

Biltmore Hotel Historic Building

(✆855-311-6903; www.biltmorehotel.com; 1200 Anastasia Ave; ⊙tours 1:30pm & 2:30pm Sun; 🅿) In the most opulent neighborhood of one of the showiest cities in the world, the Biltmore peers down her nose and says, 'hrmph.' It's one of the greatest of the grand hotels of the American Jazz Age, and if this joint were a fictional character from a novel, it'd be, without question, Jay Gatsby. Al Capone had a speakeasy on-site, and the Capone Suite is said to be haunted by the spirit of Fats Walsh, who was murdered here.

Lowe Art Museum Museum

(✆305-284-3535; www.miami.edu/lowe; 1301 Stanford Dr; adult/student/child $13/8/free; ⊙10am-4pm Tue-Sat, noon-4pm Sun) Your love of the Lowe, on the campus of the University of Miami, depends on your taste in art. If you're into modern and contemporary

Restaurant, Little Havana

works, it's good. If you're into the art and archaeology of cultures from Asia, Africa and the South Pacific, it's great. And if you're into pre-Columbian and Meso-american art, it's fantastic.

◎ Coconut Grove

Vizcaya Museum & Gardens — Historic Building

(☏305-250-9133; www.vizcayamuseum.org; 3251 S Miami Ave; adult/6-12yr/student & senior $18/6/12; ◷9:30am-4:30pm Wed-Mon; ℗) They call Miami the Magic City, and if it is, this Italian villa, the housing equivalent of a Fabergé egg, is its most fairy-tale resi- dence. In 1916 industrialist James Deering started a Miami tradition by making a ton of money and building ridiculously grandiose digs. He employed 1000 people (then 10% of the local population) and stuffed his home with 15th- to 19th-century furniture, tapestries, paintings and decorative arts; today the grounds are used for rotating contemporary-art exhibitions.

Kampong — Gardens

(☏305-442-7169; www.ntbg.org/tours/ kampong; 4013 Douglas Rd; adult/child $15/5; ◷tours by appointment only 10am-3pm Mon- Sat) David Fairchild, the Indiana Jones of the botanical world and founder of Fairchild Tropical Garden, would rest at the Kampong (Malay/Indonesian for 'village') in between journeys in search of beautiful and economically viable plant life. Today this lush garden is listed on the National Register of Historic Places and the lovely grounds serve as a classroom for the National Tropical Botanical Garden. Self-guided tours (allow at least an hour) are available by appointment, as are $20 one-hour guided tours.

◎ Little Haiti & the Upper East Side

Little Haiti Cultural Center — Gallery

(☏305-960-2969; www.littlehaiticulturalcenter. com; 212 NE 59th Tce; ◷10am-9pm Tue-Fri, 9am- 4pm Sat, 11am-7pm Sun) **FREE** This cultural center hosts an art gallery with often thought-provoking exhibitions from Haitian painters, sculptors and multimedia artists. You can also find dance classes, drama productions and a Caribbean-themed market during special events. The building itself is quite a confection of bold tropical colors, steep A-framed roofs and lacy decorative elements. Don't miss the mural in the palm-filled courtyard.

🟢 ACTIVITIES

Virginia Key Outdoor Center
Outdoors

(VKOC; www.vkoc.net; 3801 Rickenbacker Causeway, Virginia Key; kayak or bike hire 1st hour $25, each additional hour $10; ⊙9am-4:30pm Mon-Fri, from 8am Sat & Sun) This highly recommended outfitter will get you out on the water in a hurry with kayaks and stand up paddl boards, which you can put in the water just across from their office. The small mangrove-lined bay (known as Lamar Lake) has manatees, and makes for a great start to the paddle before you venture further out.

Venetian Pool
Swimming

(☑305-460-5306; www.coralgablesvenetianpool. com; 2701 De Soto Blvd; adult/child Sep-May $15/10, Jun-Aug $20/15; ⊙11am-5:30pm Tue-Fri, 10am-4:30pm Sat & Sun, closed Dec-Feb; 🎇) Just imagine: it's 1923, tons of rock have been quarried for one of the most beautiful neighborhoods in Miami, but now an ugly gash sits in the middle of the village. What to do? How about pump the irregular hole full of water, mosaic and tile up the whole affair, and make it look like a Roman emperor's aquatic playground?

Yoga by the Sea
Yoga

(www.thebarnacle.org; class $15; ⊙6:30-7:45pm Mon & Wed) A lovely open-air setting for yoga is on the grass overlooking the waterfront at the Barnacle Historic State Park. Hatha yoga classes happen twice weekly in the evenings. Bring your own mat.

BG Oleta River Outdoor Center
Water Sports

(☑786-274-7945; www.bgoletariveroutdoor. com; 3400 NE 163rd St; kayak/canoe hire per 90min $25/30; ⊙8am-1 hour before sunset; 🎇) Located in the Oleta River State Park, this outfitter hires out loads of water-sports gear; for a two-hour rental, options include single/tandem kayaks ($30/60), canoes ($35), stand up paddle boards ($40) and bikes (from $25).

Virginia Key North Point Trails
Mountain Biking

(3801 Rickenbacker Causeway, Virginia Key Beach North Point Park) **FREE** In a wooded section at the north end of the Virginia Key Beach North Point Park, you'll find a series of short mountain-bike trails, color coded for beginner, intermediate and advanced. It's free to use the trails, though you'll have to pay for parking at the Virginia Key Beach North Point Park to get here.

🟢 TOURS

History Miami Tours
Tours

(www.historymiami.org/city-tour; tours $30-60) Historian extraordinaire Dr Paul George leads fascinating walking tours, including culturally rich strolls through Little Haiti, Little Havana, Downtown and Coral Gables at twilight, plus the occasional boat trip to Stiltsville and Key Biscayne. Tours happen once a week or so. Get the full menu and sign up online.

Miami Design Preservation League
Walking

(MDPL; ☑305-672-2014; www.mdpl.org; 1001 Ocean Dr; guided tours adult/student $25/20; ⊙10:30am daily & 6:30pm Thu) Tells the stories and history behind the art-deco buildings in South Beach, with a lively guide from the Miami Design Preservation League. Tours last 90 minutes. Also offers tours of Jewish Miami Beach, Gay & Lesbian Miami Beach and a once-monthly tour (first Saturday at 9:30am) of the MiMo district in the North Beach area. Check website for details.

Urban Tour Host
Walking

(☎305-416-6868; www.miamiculturaltours.com; 25 SE 2nd Ave, Suite 1048; tours from $20) Urban Tour Host runs a program of custom tours that provide face-to-face interaction in all of Miami's neighborhoods. For something different, sign up for a Miami cultural community tour that includes Little Haiti and Little Havana, with opportunities to visit Overtown, Liberty City and Allpattah.

🔒 SHOPPING

Nomad Tribe
Clothing

(☎305-364-5193; www.nomadtribeshop. com; 2301 NW 2nd Ave; ◷noon-8pm) 🌱 This boutique earns high marks for carrying only ethically and sustainably produced merchandise. You'll find cleverly designed jewelry from Miami-based Kathe Cuervo, Osom brand socks (made of upcycled thread), ecologically produced graphic T-shirts from Thinking MU, and THX coffee and candles (which donates 100% of profits to nonprofit organizations) among much else.

Polished Coconut
Fashion & Accessories

(3444 Main Hwy; ◷11am-6pm Mon-Sat, noon-5pm Sun) 🌱 Colorful textiles from Central and South America are transformed into lovely accessories and home decor at this eye-catching store in the heart of Coconut Grove. You'll find handbags, satchels, belts, sun hats, pillows, bedspreads and table runners made by artisans inspired by traditional indigenous designs.

Taschen
Books

(☎305-538-6185; www.taschen.com; 1111 Lincoln Rd; ◷11am-9pm Mon-Thu, to 10pm Fri & Sat, noon-9pm Sun) An inviting well-stocked collection of art, photography, design and coffee-table books to make your home look that much smarter. A few volumes worth browsing include David Hockney's color-rich art books, the New Erotic Photography (always a great conversation starter) and Sebastião Salgado's lushly photographed human-filled landscapes.

💬 Little Haiti's Botanicas

If you pay a visit to Little Haiti, you might notice a few storefronts emblazoned with 'botanica' signs. Not to be confused with a plant store, a *botanica* is a *vodou* (voodoo) shop. *Botanicas* are perhaps the most 'foreign' sight in Little Haiti. Storefronts promise to help in matters of love, work and sometimes 'immigration services,' but trust us, there are no marriage counselors or INS guys in here. As you enter you'll probably get a funny look, but be courteous, curious and respectful and you should be welcomed.

Before you browse, forget stereotypes about pins and dolls. Like many traditional religions, *vodou* recognizes supernatural forces in everyday objects, and powers that are both distinct from and part of one overarching deity. Ergo, you'll see shrines to Jesus next to altars to traditional *vodou* deities. Notice the large statues of what look like people; these actually represent *loa* (pronounced lwa), intermediary spirits that form a pantheon below God in the *vodou* religious hierarchy. Drop a coin into a *loa* offering bowl before you leave, especially to Papa Legba, spirit of crossroads and, by our reckoning, travelers.

Botanica, Little Haiti
PETE M. WILSON / ALAMY STOCK PHOTO ©

Books & Books
Books

(☎305-442-4408; 265 Aragon Ave; ◷9am-11pm Sun-Thu, to midnight Fri & Sat) The best indie bookstore in South Florida is a massive emporium of all things literary. B&B hosts frequent readings and is generally just a fantastic place to hang out; there's also a good restaurant, with dining on a Mediterranean-like terrace fronting the shop.

Malaquita   Arts & Crafts

(www.malaquitadesign.com; 2613 NW 2nd Ave; ⊗11am-7pm) This artfully designed store has merchandise you won't find elsewhere, including lovely handblown vases, embroidered clothing, Meso-American tapestries, vibrantly painted bowls, handwoven palm baskets and other fair-trade objects – some of which are made by indigenous artisans in Mexico.

Brooklyn Vintage & Vinyl   Music

(www.facebook.com/brooklynvintageandvinyl; 3454 NW 7th Ave; ⊗noon-9pm Tue-Sat) Although it opened in late 2016, this record store on the edge of Wynwood has already attracted a following. It's mostly vinyl (plus some cassettes and a few T-shirts), with around 5000 records in the inventory. Staff can give good tips for exploring new music.

Guantanamera   Cigars

(www.guantanameracigars.com; 1465 SW 8th St; ⊗10:30am-8pm Sun-Thu, to midnight Fri & Sat) In a central location in Little Havana, Guantanamera sells high-quality handrolled cigars, plus strong Cuban coffee. It's an atmospheric shop, where you can stop for a smoke, a drink (there's a bar here) and some friendly banter. There's also live music here most nights. The rocking chairs in front are a fine perch for people-watching.

Sweat Records   Music

(⊉786-693-9309; www.sweatrecordsmiami.com; 5505 NE 2nd Ave; ⊗noon-10pm Mon-Sat, to 5pm Sun) Sweat's almost a stereotypical indie record store – there's funky art and graffiti on the walls, it sells weird Japanese toys, there are tattooed staff with thick glasses arguing over LPs and EPs you've never heard of and, of course, there's coffee and vegan snacks.

Havana Collection   Clothing

(⊉786-717-7474; 1421 SW 8th St; ⊗10am-6pm) One of the best and most striking collections of *guayaberas* (Cuban dress shirts)

in Miami can be found in this shop. Prices are high (plan on spending about $85 for a shirt), but so is the quality, so you can be assured of a long-lasting product.

Art by God   Gifts & Souvenirs

(⊉305-573-3011; www.artbygod.com; 60 NE 27th St; ⊗10am-5pm Mon-Fri, 11am-4pm Sat) Take a walk on the wild side at this sprawling warehouse full of relics of days past. Fossils, minerals and semiprecious stones play a supporting role to the more eye-catching draws: full-size giraffes, lions, bears and zebras in all their taxidermied glory.

⊗ EATING

Miami is a major immigrant entrepôt and a sucker for food trends. Thus you get a good mix of cheap ethnic eateries and high-quality top-end cuisine here, alongside some poor-value dross in touristy zones like Miami Beach. The best new areas for dining are in Downtown, Wynwood and Upper East Side; Coral Gables has great classic options.

⊗ South Beach

11th Street Diner   Diner $

(⊉305-534-6373; www.eleventhstreetdiner. com; 1065 Washington Ave; mains $10-20; ⊗7am-midnight Sun-Wed, 24hr Thu-Sat) You've seen the art-deco landmarks. Now eat in one: a Pullman-car diner trucked down from Wilkes-Barre, Pennsylvania – as sure a slice of Americana as a *Leave It to Beaver* marathon. The food is as classic as the architecture, with oven-roasted turkey, baby back ribs and mac 'n' cheese among the hits – plus breakfast at all hours.

Taquiza   Mexican $

(⊉305-748-6099; www.taquizamiami.com; 1506 Collins Ave; tacos $3.50-5; ⊗8am-midnight Sun-Thu, to 2am Fri & Sat) Taquiza has acquired a stellar reputation among Miami's street-food lovers. The takeout stand with a few outdoor tables serves up delicious perfection in its steak, pork, shrimp or veggie tacos (but no fish options) served on handmade blue-corn tortillas. They're small, so order a few.

Pubbelly   Fusion $$

(☎305-532-7555; www.pubbellyboys.com/
miami/pubbelly; 1418 20th St; sharing plates
$11-24, mains $19-30; ☺6pm-midnight Tue-Thu
& Sun, to 1am Fri & Sat; ☑) Pubbelly's dining
genre is hard to pinpoint, besides delicious.
It skews between Asian, North American and
Latin American, gleaning the best from all
cuisines. Examples? Try black-truffle risotto,
pork-belly dumplings or the mouthwatering
kimchi fried rice with seafood. Hand-crafted
cocktails wash down the dishes a treat.

Yardbird   Southern US $$

(☎305-538-5220; www.runchickenrun.com/mi-
ami; 1600 Lenox Ave; mains $18-38; ☺11am-mid-
night Mon-Fri, from 8:30am Sat & Sun; ☑)
Yardbird has earned a diehard following for
its delicious haute Southern comfort food.
The kitchen churns out some nice shrimp
and grits, St Louis–style pork ribs, charred
okra, and biscuits with smoked brisket, but
it's most famous for its supremely good
plate of fried chicken, spiced watermelon
and waffles with bourbon maple syrup.

⊗ North Beach

27 Restaurant   Fusion $$

(☎786-476-7020; www.freehandhotels.com/
miami/27-restaurant; 2727 Indian Creek Dr; mains
$17-28; ☺6:30pm-2am Mon-Sat, 11am-4pm &
6:30pm-2am Sun; ☑) This new spot sits on
the grounds of the very popular Broken
Shaker (p167), one of Miami Beach's
best-loved cocktail bars. Like the bar, the
setting is amazing – akin to dining in an old
tropical cottage, with worn wood floor-
boards, candlelit tables, and various rooms
slung with artwork and curious knickknacks, plus a lovely terrace. The cooking is
exceptional, and incorporates flavors from
around the globe.

Cafe Prima Pasta   Italian $$

(☎305-867-0106; www.cafeprimapasta.com;
414 71st St; mains $17-26; ☺5-11:30pm Mon-Sat,
4-11pm Sun) We're not sure what's better at
this Argentine-Italian place: the much-
touted pasta, which deserves every one
of the accolades heaped on it, or the
atmosphere, which captures the dignified

🛍 The Lincoln Road Experience

Lincoln Road Mall, an outdoor pedestrian thoroughfare between Alton Rd and
Washington Ave, is all about seeing and
being seen; there are times when Lincoln feels less like a road and more like a
runway. Carl Fisher, the father of Miami
Beach, envisioned the road as a Fifth
Ave of the South. Morris Lapidus, one of
the founders of the loopy, neo-baroque
Miami Beach style, designed much of
the mall, including shady overhangs,
waterfall structures and traffic barriers
that look like the marbles a giant might
play with.

---

sultriness of Buenos Aires. You can't go
wrong with the small, well-curated menu,
with standouts like gnocchi formaggi,
baked branzino, and squid-ink linguine with
seafood in a lobster sauce.

⊗ Downtown Miami

All Day   Cafe $

(www.alldaymia.com; 1035 N Miami Ave; coffee
$3.50, breakfast $10-14; ☺7am-7pm Mon-Fri,
from 9am Sat & Sun; �) All Day is one of the
best places in the Downtown area to linger
over coffee or breakfast – no matter the
hour. Slender Scandinavian-style chairs,
wood-and-marble tables and the Françoise
Hardy soundtrack lend an easygoing vibe to
the place.

Casablanca   Seafood $$

(www.casablancaseafood.com; 400 N River Dr;
mains $15-34; ☺11am-10pm Sun-Thu, to 11pm Fri
& Sat) Perched over the Miami River, Casablanca serves up some of the best seafood
in town. The setting is a big draw – tables
on a long wooden deck just above the water,
with the odd seagull winging past. But the
fresh fish is the real star here.

Verde   American $$

(☎786-345-5697; www.pamm.org/dining;
1103 Biscayne Blvd, mains $13-19; ☺11am-5pm

Fri-Tue, to 9pm Thu, closed Wed; 🐾) Inside the Pérez Art Museum Miami (p155), Verde is a local favorite for its tasty market-fresh dishes and great setting – with outdoor seating on a terrace overlooking the bay. Crispy mahimahi tacos, pizza with squash blossoms and goat cheese, and grilled endive salads are among the temptations.

NIU Kitchen   Spanish $$

(📞786-542-5070; www.niukitchen.com; 134 NE 2nd Ave; sharing plates $14-25; ⏰noon-3:30pm & 6-10pm Mon-Fri, 1-4pm & 6-11pm Sat, 6-10pm Sun; 🐾) NIU is a stylish living-room-sized restaurant serving up delectable contemporary Spanish cuisine. It's a showcase of culinary pyrotechnics, featuring complex sharing plates with clipped Catalan names like Ous (poached eggs, truffled potato foam, *jamón ibérico* and black truffle) or Toninya (smoked tuna, green guindillas and pine nuts). Wash it all down with good wine.

🟠 Wynwood & the Design District

Panther Coffee   Cafe $

(📞305-677-3952; www.panthercoffee.com; 2390 NW 2nd Ave; coffees $3-6; ⏰7am-9pm Mon-Sat, from 8am Sun; 🛜) Miami's best independent coffee shop specializes in single-origin, small-batch roasts, fired up to perfection. Aside from sipping on a zesty brewed-to-order Chemex-made coffee (or a creamy latte), you can enjoy microbrews, wines and sweet treats. The front patio is a great spot for people-watching.

Wynwood Yard   Food Trucks $

(www.thewynwoodyard.com; 56 NW 29th St; mains $7-14; ⏰noon-11pm Tue-Thu, to 1am Fri-Sun; 🛜🐾) 🍴 On a once vacant lot, the Wynwood Yard is something of an urban oasis for those who want to enjoy a bit of casual open-air eating and drinking. Around a dozen different food trucks park here, offering gourmet mac 'n' cheese, cruelty-free salads, meaty schnitzel plates, zesty tacos, desserts and more. There's also a bar, and often live music.

Cuban sandwich (p166)

Kyu
Fusion $$

(☎786-577-0150; www.kyumiami.com; 251 NW 25th St; sharing plates $17-38; ⊗noon-11:30pm Mon-Sat, 11am-10:30pm Sun, bar till 1am Fri & Sat; 🅿) ✿ One of the best new restaurants in Wynwood, Kyu has been dazzling locals and food critics alike with its creative, Asian-inspired dishes, most of which are cooked up over the open flames of a wood-fired grill. The buzzing, industrial space is warmed up via artful lighting and wood accents (tables and chairs, plus shelves of firewood for the grill).

Alter
Modern American $$$

(☎305-573-5996; www.altermiami.com; 223 NW 23rd St; set menu 5/7 courses $69/89; ⊗7-11pm Tue-Sun) This new spot, which has garnered much praise from food critics, brings creative high-end cooking to Wynwood courtesy of its award-winning young chef Brad Kilgore. The changing menu showcases Florida's high-quality ingredients from sea and land in seasonally inspired dishes with Asian and European accents. Reserve ahead.

⊗ Little Havana

El Nuevo Siglo
Latin American $

(1305 SW 8th St; mains $8-12; ⊗7am-8pm) Hidden inside a supermarket of the same name, El Nuevo Siglo draws foodie-minded locals who come for delicious cooking at excellent prices – never mind the unfussy ambience. Grab a seat at the shiny black countertop and nibble on roast meats, fried yucca, tangy Cuban sandwiches, grilled snapper with rice, beans and plantains, and other daily specials.

El Carajo
Spanish $$

(☎305-856-2424; www.el-carajo.com; 2465 SW 17th Ave; tapas $5-15; ⊗noon-10pm Mon-Wed, to 11pm Thu-Sat, 11am-10pm Sun; 🅿) Pass the Pennzoil please. We know it is cool to tuck restaurants into unassuming spots, but the Citgo station on SW 17th Ave? Really? Really. Walk past the motor oil into a Granadan wine cellar and try not to act too fazed. And now the food, which is absolutely incredible.

Doce Provisions
Modern American $$

(☎786-452-0161; www.doceprovisions.com; 541 SW 12th Ave; mains $11-25; ⊗noon-3:30pm & 5-10pm Mon-Thu, noon-3:30pm & 5-11pm Fri, noon-11pm Sat, 11am-9pm Sun) For a break from old-school Latin eateries, stop in at Doce Provisions, which has more of a Wynwood vibe than a Little Havana one. The stylish industrial interior sets the stage for dining on creative American fare – rock shrimp mac 'n' cheese, fried chicken with sweet plantain waffle, short rib burgers and truffle fries – plus local microbrews.

⊗ Coral Gables

Threefold
Cafe $$

(☎305-704-8007; 141 Giralda Ave; mains $13-19; ⊗8am-4:30pm; 🎅🅿) Coral Gables' most talked-about cafe is a buzzing, Aussie-run charmer that serves up perfectly pulled espressos (and a good flat white), along with creative breakfast and lunch fare. Start the morning with waffles and berry compote, smashed avocado toast topped with feta, or a slow-roasted leg of lamb with fried eggs.

Frenchie's Diner
French $$

(☎305-442-4554; www.frenchiesdiner.com; 2618 Galiano St; mains lunch $14-24, dinner $24-34; ⊗11am-3pm & 6-10pm Tue-Sat) Tucked down a side street, it's easy to miss this place. Inside, Frenchie's channels an old-time American diner vibe, with black-and-white checkered floors, a big chalkboard menu, and a smattering of old prints and mirrors on the wall. The cooking, on the other hand, is a showcase for French bistro classics.

⊗ Coconut Grove

Last Carrot
Vegetarian $

(☎305-445-0805; 3133 Grand Ave; mains $6-8; ⊗10:30am-6pm Mon-Sat, 11am-4:30pm Sun; 🅿🕎) Going strong since the 1970s, the Last Carrot serves up fresh juices, delicious pita sandwiches, avocado melts, veggie burgers and famous spinach pies, all amid old-Grove neighborliness. The Carrot's endurance next to massive CocoWalk is testament to

🍽 Miami Specialties

Cuban Sandwich

The traditional Cuban sandwich, also known as a *sandwich mixto,* is not some slapdash creation. It's a craft best left to the experts – but here's some insight into how they do it. Correct bread is crucial – it should be Cuban white bread: fresh, soft and easy to press. The insides (both sides) should be buttered and layered (in the following order) with sliced pickles, slices of roast Cuban pork, ham (preferably sweet-cured ham) and baby Swiss cheese. Then it all gets pressed in a hot *plancha* (sandwich press) until the cheese melts.

Arepas

The greatness of a city can be measured by many yardsticks. The arts. Civic involvement. Infrastructure. What you eat when you're plowed at 3am. In Miami, the answer is often enough *arepas,* delicious South American corn cakes that can be stuffed (Venezuelan-style) or topped (Colombian-style) with any manner of deliciousness; generally, you can't go wrong with cheese.

Stone Crabs

The first reusable crustacean: only one claw is taken from a stone crab – the rest is tossed back in the sea (the claw regrows in 12 to 18 months, and crabs plucked again are called 'retreads'). The claws are so perishable that they're always cooked before selling. For straight-out-of-the-ocean freshness, try them in Everglades City.

the quality of its good-for-your-body food served in a good-for-your-soul setting.

Coral Bagels   Deli $

(☎305-854-0336; 2750 SW 26th Ave; mains $7-11; ☺6:30am-3pm Mon-Fri, 7am-4pm Sat & Sun; P 🍴) Although it's out of the way (1 mile north of Coconut Grove's epicenter), this is

a great place to start the day. The buzzing little deli serves proper bagels, rich omelets and decadent potato pancakes with apple sauce and sour cream. You'll be hard pressed to spend double digits, and you'll leave satisfied.

Boho   Mediterranean $$

(☎305-549-8614; 3433 Main Hwy; mains $19-26, pizzas $12-17; ☺noon-11pm Mon-Fri, from 10am Sat & Sun) This Greek-run charmer is helping to lead the culinary renaissance in Coconut Grove, serving up fantastic Mediterranean dishes, including tender marinated octopus, creamy risotto, thin-crust pizzas drizzled with truffle oil and zesty quinoa and beet salads. The setting invites long, leisurely meals with its jungle-like wallpaper, big picture windows and easygoing vibe.

Spillover   Modern American $$

(☎305-456-5723; www.spillovermiami.com; 2911 Grand Ave; mains $13-25; ☺11:30am-10pm Sun-Tue, to 11pm Wed-Sat; 🐾🍴) Tucked down a pedestrian strip near the CocoWalk, the Spillover serves up locally sourced seafood and creative bistro fare in an enticing vintage setting (cast-iron stools and recycled doors around the bar, suspenders-wearing staff, brassy jazz playing overhead). Come for crab cakes, buffalo shrimp tacos, spear-caught fish and chips, or a melt-in-your-mouth lobster Reuben.

✦ Little Haiti & the Upper East Side

Chef Creole   Haitian $

(☎305-754-2223; www.chefcreole.com; 200 NW 54th St; mains $7-20; ☺11am-10pm Mon-Sat) When you need Caribbean food on the cheap, head to the edge of Little Haiti and this excellent takeout shack. Order up fried conch, oxtail or fish, ladle rice and beans on the side, and you'll be full for a week. Enjoy the food on nearby picnic benches while Haitian music blasts out of tinny speakers – as island an experience as they come.

Phuc Yea   Vietnamese $

(☎305-602-3710; www.phucyea.com; 7100 Biscayne Blvd; ☺6pm-midnight Tue-Sat, 11:30am-

3:30pm & 6-9pm Sun) Not unlike its cheeky name, Phuc Yea pushes boundaries with its bold and deliciously executed Vietnamese cooking – served up in a graffiti-smeared and hip-hop loving setting. You too can heed the call to get 'Phuc'd up!' (undoubtedly a good thing since 'phuc' means 'blessings and prosperity') by indulging in lobster summer rolls, fish curry, spicy chicken wings and other great sharing plates.

Mina's   Mediterranean $$

(☏786-391-0300; www.minasmiami.com; 749 NE 79th St; mains $16-30, sharing plates $6-16; ⊙5-10pm Tue-Thu, to 11pm Fri, noon-11pm Sat, 11am-9pm Sun; ☞) Soaring ceilings, vintage travel posters and a friendly vibe set the stage for a memorable meal at Mina's. The Mediterranean menu is great for sharing, with creamy hummus, refreshing dolmas, spanakopita (spinach-filled pastries) and toothsome fried calamari among the great starters.

🍷 DRINKING & NIGHTLIFE

Too many people assume Miami's nightlife is all about being wealthy and attractive and/or phony. Disavow yourself of this notion, which only describes a small slice of the scene in South Beach. Miami has an intense variety of bars to pick from that range from grotty dives to beautiful – but still laid-back – lounges and nightclubs.

Blackbird Ordinary   Bar

(☏305-671-3307; www.blackbirdordinary.com; 729 SW 1st Ave; ⊙3pm-5am Mon-Fri, 5pm-5am Sat & Sun) Far from ordinary, the Blackbird is an excellent bar, with great cocktails (the London Sparrow, with gin, cayenne, lemon juice and passion fruit, goes down well) and an enormous courtyard. The only thing 'ordinary' about the place is the sense that all are welcome for a fun and pretension-free night out.

Sweet Liberty   Bar

(www.mysweetliberty.com; 237 20th St; ⊙4pm-5am Mon-Sat, from noon Sun) A much-loved local haunt near Collins Park, Sweet Liberty

has all the right ingredients for a fun night out: friendly, easygoing bartenders who whip up excellent cocktails (try a mint julep), great happy-hour specials (including 75¢ oysters) and a relaxed, pretension-free crowd. The space is huge, with flickering candles, a long wooden bar and the odd band adding to the cheer.

Broken Shaker   Bar

(☏305-531-2727; ⊙6pm-3am Mon-Fri, 2pm-3am Sat & Sun) Craft cocktails are having their moment in Miami, and if mixology is in the spotlight, you can bet Broken Shaker is sharing the glare. Expert bartenders run this spot, located in the back of the **Freehand Miami hotel** (www.thefreehand.com; 2727 Indian Creek Dr; ❋☞⊠), which takes up one closet-sized indoor niche and a sprawling plant-filled courtyard of excellent drinks and beautiful people.

Bodega   Cocktail Bar

(☏305-704-2145; www.bodegasouthbeach.com; 1220 16th St; ⊙noon-5am) Bodega looks like your average hipster Mexican joint – serving up delicious tacos ($3 to $5) from a con- verted Airstream trailer to a party-minded crowd. But there's actually a bar hidden behind that blue porta potty door on the right. Head inside (or join the long line on weekends) to take in a bit of old-school glam in a sprawling drinking den.

Wynwood Brewing
Company   Microbrewery

(☏305-982-8732; www.wynwoodbrewing.com; 565 NW 24th St; ⊙noon-10pm Sun & Mon, to midnight Tue-Sat) The beer scene has grown in leaps and bounds in Miami, but this warmly lit spot, which was the first craft brewery in Wynwood, is still the best. The family-owned 15-barrel brewhouse has friendly and knowledgeable staff, excellent year-round brews (including a blonde ale, a robust porter and a top-notch IPA) and seasonal beers, and there's always a food truck parked outside.

Bardot   Club

(☏305-576-5570; www.bardotmiami.com; 3456 N Miami Ave; ⊙8pm-3am Tue & Wed, to 5am

Art Walks: Nightlife Meets Art

Ever-flowing (not always free) wine and beer, great art, a fun crowd and no cover charge (or velvet rope): welcome to the wondrous world where art and nightlife collide. The Wynwood and Design District Art Walks are among the best ways to experience an alternative slice of Miami culture. Just be careful, as a lot of galleries in Wynwood are separated by short drives (the Design District is more walkable). Art Walks take place on the second Saturday of each month, from 7pm to 10pm (some galleries stretch to 11pm); when it's all over, lots of folks repair to Wood Tavern (p168) or Bardot (p167). Visit www.artofmiami. com/maps/art-walks for information on participating galleries.

Wynwood mural
IMAGE COURTESY OF WYNWOOD WALLS, MARTHA COOPER ©

Thu-Sat) You really should see the interior of Bardot before you leave the city. It's all sexy French vintage posters and furniture (plus a pool table) seemingly plucked from a private club that serves millionaires by day, and becomes a scene of decadent excess by night. The entrance looks to be on N Miami Ave, but it's actually in a parking lot behind the building.

Ball & Chain   Bar

(www.ballandchainmiami.com; 1513 SW 8th St; ☺noon-midnight Mon-Wed, to 3am Thu-Sat, 2-10pm Sun) The Ball & Chain has survived several incarnations over the years. Back in 1935, when 8th St was more Jewish than Latino, it was the sort of jazz joint Billie Hol-

iday would croon in. That iteration closed in 1957, but the new Ball & Chain is still dedicated to music and good times – specifically, Latin music and tropical cocktails.

Wood Tavern   Bar

(☎305-748-2828; www.woodtavernmiami.com; 2531 NW 2nd Ave; ☺5pm-3am Tue-Sat, 3pm-midnight Sun) So many new bars in Miami want to be casual but cool; Wood is one of the few locales achieving this Golden Mean of atmosphere and aesthetic. Food specials are cheap, the beer selection is excellent and the crowd is friendly – this Wood's got the right grain.

Churchill's   Bar

(☎305-757-1807; www.churchillspub.com; 5501 NE 2nd Ave; ☺3pm-3am Sun-Thu, to 5am Fri & Sat) A Miami icon that's been around since 1979, Churchill's is a Brit-owned pub in the midst of what could be Port-au-Prince. There's a lot of live music here, mainly punk, indie and more punk. Not insipid modern punk either: think the Ramones meets the Sex Pistols.

⊕ ENTERTAINMENT

Adrienne Arsht Center for the Performing Arts   Performing Arts

(☎305-949-6722; www.arshtcenter.org; 1300 Biscayne Blvd; ☺box office 10am-6pm Mon-Fri, and 2 hours before performances) This magnificent venue manages to both humble and enthrall visitors. Today the Arsht is where the biggest cultural acts in Miami come to perform; a show here is a must-see on any Miami trip. There's an Adrienne Arsht Center stop on the Metromover.

Cubaocho   Live Performance

(☎305-285-5880; www.cubaocho.com; 1465 SW 8th St; ☺11am-10pm Tue-Thu, to 3am Fri & Sat) Jewel of the Little Havana Art District, Cubaocho is renowned for its concerts, with excellent bands from across the Spanish-speaking world. It's also a community center, art gallery and research outpost for all things Cuban. The interior resembles an old Havana cigar bar, yet the walls are decked out in artwork that references both the classical past of Cuban art and its avant-garde future.

New World Symphony
Classical Music

(NWS; ☑305-673-3330; www.nws.edu; 500 17th St) Housed in the New World Center (p154) – a funky explosion of cubist lines and geometric curves, fresh white against the blue Miami sky – the acclaimed New World Symphony holds performances from October to May. The deservedly herald-ed NWS serves as a three- to four-year preparatory program for talented musicians from prestigious music schools.

Tower Theater
Cinema

(☑305-237-2463; www.towertheatermiami.com; 1508 SW 8th St) This renovated 1926 land-mark theater has a proud deco facade and a handsomely renovated interior, thanks to support from the Miami-Dade Community College. In its heyday, it was the center of Little Havana social life and, via the films it showed, served as a bridge between im-migrant society and American pop culture. Today it frequently shows independent and Spanish-language films (sometimes both).

Colony Theater
Performing Arts

(☑305-674-1040, box office 800-211-1414; www. colonymb.org; 1040 Lincoln Rd) The Colony is an absolute art-deco gem, with a classic marquee and Inca-style crenellations, which looks like the sort of place gangsters would go to watch *Hamlet*. This treasure now serves as a major venue for performing arts – from comedy and occasional musicals to theatrical dramas, off-Broadway produc-tions and ballet – as well as hosting movie screenings and small film festivals.

❶ INFORMATION

The **Greater Miami & the Beaches Convention & Visitors Bureau** (☑305-539-3000; www.mi-amiandbeaches.com; 701 Brickell Ave, 27th fl; ☺8:30am-6pm Mon-Fri) offers loads of info on

---

✷ The Full Moon Drum Circle

If there's a full moon, check out the beach between 79th and 85th Sts – a big, boisterous drum circle that is held here doubles as a full-moon party. The beat tends to start between 8:30pm and 9:30pm, and can run well into the wee hours. That said, drinking (and the consumption of other substances) is technically illegal on the beach, and police have broken up the event before. Still, it tends to be a pretty fun party that shouldn't be missed if you're in the area and want to see an incredible moonset.

Miami and keeps up to date with the latest events and cultural offerings.

MEDICAL SERVICES
Coral Gables Hospital (☑305-445-8461; 3100 Douglas Rd, Coral Gables) A community-based facility with many bilingual doctors.

CVS Pharmacy This chain has many 24-hour pharmacies, including one in **South Beach** (☑305-538-1571; 1421 Alton Rd; ☺24hr).

Miami Beach Community Health Center (Stanley C Meyers Center; ☑305-538-8835; www. miamibeachhealth.org; 710 Alton Rd, South Beach; ☺7am-5pm Mon-Fri) Walk-in clinic with long lines.

Mount Sinai Medical Center (☑305-674-2121, emergency room 305-674-2200; www.msmc.com; 4300 Alton Rd; ☺24hr) The area's best emergen-cy room. Be aware that you must eventually pay, and fees are high.

❶ GETTING THERE & AWAY

The majority of travelers come to Miami by air, although it's feasible to arrive by car, bus or even train. Miami is a major international airline hub, with flights to many cities across the USA, Latin America and Europe. Most flights come into Miami International Airport (MIA), although many are also directed to Fort Lauderdale-Hollywood International Airport (FLL).

Colony Theater (p169)

AIR

Located 6 miles west of Downtown, the busy **Miami International Airport** (MIA; ☑305-876-7000; www.miami-airport.com; 2100 NW 42nd Ave) has three terminals and serves over 40 million passengers each year. Around 60 airlines fly into Miami. The airport is open 24 hours and is laid out in a horseshoe design. There are left-luggage facilities on two concourses at MIA, between B and C, and on G; prices vary according to bag size.

Around 26 miles north of Downtown Miami, **Fort Lauderdale-Hollywood International Airport** (FLL; ☑866-435-9355; www.broward.org/airport; 320 Terminal Dr) is also a viable gateway airport to the Florida region.

CAR & MOTORCYCLE

Driving to Florida is easy; there are no international borders or entry issues. Incorporating Florida into a larger USA road trip is very common, and having a car while in Miami can be very handy.

ⓘ GETTING AROUND

TO/FROM THE AIRPORT

From Miami International Airport, taxis charge a flat rate, which varies depending on where you're heading. It's $22 to Downtown, Coconut Grove or Coral Gables; $35 to South Beach; and $44 to Key Biscayne. Count on 40 minutes to South Beach in average traffic, and about 25 minutes to Downtown.

Metro buses leave from Miami Airport Station (connected by electric rail to the airport) and run throughout the city; fares are $2.25. The Miami Beach Airport Express (bus 150) costs $2.65 and makes stops along Miami Beach, from 41st to the southern tip. You can also take the **SuperShuttle** (☑305-871-8210; www.supershuttle.com) shared-van service, which will cost about $22 to South Beach. Be sure to reserve a seat the day before.

From Fort Lauderdale-Hollywood International Airport, count on at least 45 minutes from the airport to Downtown by taxi, and at least an hour for the ride to South Beach. Prices are metered. Expect to pay about $75 to South Beach and $65 to Downtown. Alternatively, shared van service is available from the airport with **GO Airport Shuttle** (☏800-244-8252; www.go-airportshuttle.com). Prices are around $25 to South Beach.

BICYCLE

Citi Bike (☏305-532-9494; www.citibikemiami.com; 30min/1hr/2hr/4hr/1-day rental $4.50/6.50/10/18/24) is a bike-share program where you can borrow a bike from scores of kiosks spread around Miami and Miami Beach. Miami is flat, but traffic can be horrendous (abundant and fast-moving), and there isn't much biking culture (or respect for bikers) just yet. Free paper maps of the bike network are available at some kiosks, or you can find one online. There's also a handy iPhone app that shows you where the nearest stations are.

For longer rides, clunky Citi Bikes are not ideal (no helmet, no lock and only three gears).

Other rental outfits:

Bike & Roll (☏305-604-0001; www.bikemiami.com; 210 10th St; hire per 2hr/4hr/day from $10/18/24, tours $40; ☉9am-7pm) Also does bike tours.

Brickell Bikes (☏305-373-3633; www.brickellbikes.com; 70 SW 12th St; bike hire per 4/8 hr $20/25; ☉10am-7pm Mon-Fri, to 6pm Sat)

BUS

Miami's local bus system is called **Metrobus** (☏305-891-3131; www.miamidade.gov/transit/routes.asp; tickets $2.25) and though it has an extensive route system, service can be pretty spotty. Each bus route has a different schedule and routes generally run from about 5:30am to 11pm, though some are 24 hours. Rides cost $2.25 and must be paid in exact change (coins or a combination of bills and coins) or with an Easy Card (available for purchase from Metrorail stations and some shops and pharmacies). An easy-to-read route map is available online. Note that if you have to transfer buses, you'll have to pay the fare each time if paying in cash. With an Easy Card, transfers are free.

CAR & MOTORCYCLE

If you drive around Miami, there are a few things to know. Miami Beach is linked to the mainland by four causeways built over Biscayne Bay. They are, from south to north: the MacArthur (the extension of US Hwy 41 and Hwy A1A); Venetian ($1.75 toll); Julia Tuttle and John F Kennedy. There's also a $1.75 toll over the Rickenbacker Causeway to Key Biscayne. The tolls are automated, so ask about hiring a Sunpass if you're renting a vehicle.

The most important north–south highway is I-95, which ends at US Hwy 1 south of Downtown Miami. US Hwy 1, which runs from Key West all the way north to Maine, hugs the coastline. It's called Dixie Hwy south of Downtown Miami and Biscayne Blvd north of Downtown Miami. The Palmetto Expwy (Hwy 826) makes a rough loop around the city and spurs off below SW 40th St to the Don Shula Expwy (Hwy 874, a toll road). Florida's Turnpike Extension makes the most western outer loop around the city. Hwy A1A becomes Collins Ave in Miami Beach.

TROLLEY

A new free bus service has hit the streets of Miami, Miami Beach, Coconut Grove, Little Havana and Coral Gables, among other locations. The Trolley (www.miamigov.com/trolley) is actually a hybrid-electric bus disguised as an orange and green trolley. There are numerous routes, though they're made for getting around neighborhoods and not *between* them.

The most useful for travelers are the following:

Biscayne Travels along Biscayne Blvd; handy for transport from Brickell to Downtown and up to the edge of Wynwood.

Brickell Connects Brickell area (south of the Miami River in the Downtown area) with the Vizcaya Museum & Gardens.

Coral Way Goes from Downtown (near the Freedom Tower) to downtown Coral Gables.

Wynwood Zigzags through town, from the Adrienne Arsht Center for the Performing Arts up through Wynwood along NW 2nd Ave to 29th St.

Clockwise from top left: Ocean Drive (p150); Venetian Pool (p160); Biltmore Hotel (p158); Lincoln Road Mall (p163)

Clockwise from left: Haulover Beach Park (p155); cigars; Brickell City Centre (p158); Ocean Drive (p150)

ORLANDO & WALT DISNEY WORLD® RESORT

In this Chapter

Walt Disney World® Resort 180
Universal Orlando Resort 186
Orlando...192
Winter Park..196

Orlando & Walt Disney World® Resort at a Glance...

If Orlando were a Disney character, it's fair to say that it would be like Dory (of Nemo fame) and lack a bit of confidence. It's so easy to get caught up in Greater Orlando – in the isolated, constructed worlds of Disney or Universal Orlando (for which, let's face it, you're probably here) – that you forget all about the downtown city of Orlando itself. It has a lot to offer: lovely tree-lined streets, a rich performing-arts and museum scene, several fantastic gardens and nature preserves, fabulous cuisine and a delightfully slower pace devoid of manic crowds.

Two Days in Orlando

Assuming you're here for some theme-park fun, you can easily kill two days at either Walt Disney World® Resort or Universal Orlando. If you're at the former, pick two out of these three: **Magic Kingdom** (p180), **Epcot** (p182) or the **Animal Kingdom** (p183). At **Universal** (p186), everywhere is fun, but don't miss the Wizarding World of Harry Potter.

Four Days in Orlando

If you still want another world of imagination, we recommend **Legoland® Florida Resort** (p193). Otherwise, spend day three hitting up the **Mennello Museum of American Art** (p192), and make sure you catch a show at the **Enzian Theater** (p195) or **Mad Cow** (p195). On the fourth day, go to Winter Park and enjoy the **Charles Hosmer Morse Museum** (p196) and locavore dining.

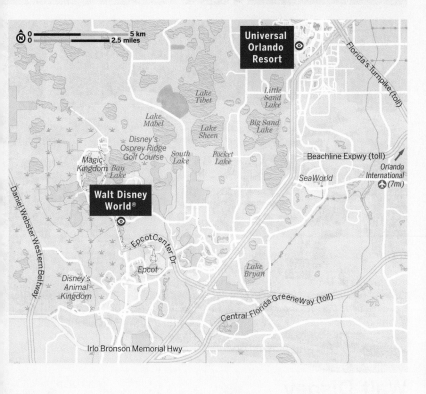

Arriving in Orlando

Orlando lies 285 miles from Miami; the fastest and most direct route is a 4½-hour road trip via Florida's Turnpike.

Orlando International Airport Handles more passengers than any other airport in Florida. Serves Walt Disney World Resort, the Space Coast and the Orlando area.

Orlando Sanford International Airport Small airport 30 minutes north of downtown Orlando and 45 minutes north of Walt Disney World® Resort.

Sleeping

Downtown Orlando has some lovely privately owned options, which can be a relief from the resorts. Walt Disney World Resort and Universal Orlando both offer on-site resort hotels with all kinds of enticing perks. While the town itself is a nice escape, Winter Park's accommodation is limited to two hotels. Kissimmee has chain hotels within easy driving of the theme parks, but note those in Historic Downtown Kissimmee are too far away to be useful.

Walt Disney World® Resort

Cinderella's Castle. Spaceship Earth. The Tree of Life. These are the symbols of magical lands that together make up Walt Disney World® Resort, which loudly proclaims itself the Happiest Place on Earth.

Great For...

☑ Don't Miss

Waving to all of your favorite characters during the Festival of Fantasy (p184) parade.

Magic Kingdom

When most people think of Walt Disney World Resort, they're thinking of one of the four theme parks – the **Magic Kingdom** (1180 Seven Seas Dr; $100-119, prices vary daily; ⊙9am-11pm, hours vary; 🚊Disney, ⛴Disney, 🚊Disney). This is the Disney of commercials, of princesses and pirates, of dreams come true; this is quintessential old-school Disney with classic rides such as It's a Small World and Space Mountain.

At its core is Cinderella's Castle, the iconic image (this overused phrase is used correctly here) of the TV show. Remember when Tinkerbell dashed across the screen as fireworks burst across the castle turrets?

You'll see it as soon as you enter the park and emerge onto Main Street, USA. A horse-drawn carriage and an old-fashioned

Mickey, Minnie, Goofy and Donald at the
circus-themed Pete's Silly Sideshow (no
FastPass+).

Haunted Mansion

A ramblin' 19th-century mansion houses
Haunted Mansion, the only real ride in Liberty Square. Cruise slowly past the haunted
dining room, where apparitions dance
across the stony floor, but beware of those
hitchhiking ghosts – don't be surprised if
they jump into your car uninvited. While
mostly it's lighthearted ghosty goofiness,
kids may be frightened by the spooky pre-
ride dramatics.

Pirates of the Caribbean

Hop on a slow-moving boat and ride
through the dark and shadowy world.
Drunken pirates sing pirate songs, sleep
among the pigs and sneer over their empty
whiskey bottles, but unless you're scared
of the dark or growling marauders, it's a
giggle, not a scream. And Jack Sparrow
looks so incredibly lifelike that you'll swear
it's Johnny Depp himself.

Sorcerers of the Magic Kingdom

Sorcerers of the Magic Kingdom is a wildly
popular, self-paced treasure-hunt-styled
experience in which participants join Merlin
in his efforts to find and defeat Disney
villains. Players receive a key card that
activates hidden game portals throughout

car run for the first hour from the park
entrance to the castle (though most people
walk), and from there, paths lead to the
four 'lands' – Fantasyland, Tomorrowland,
Adventureland and Frontierland, as well as
two other areas: Liberty Square and Main
Street, USA.

Fantasyland

Quintessential Disney and home to the
sweet Winnie-the-Pooh, Peter Pan, Dumbo,
Ariel and Snow White–themed rides,
Fantasyland is the highlight of any Disney
trip for both the eight-and-under crowd
and grown-ups looking for a nostalgic taste
of classic Disney. Keep an eye out for Cinderella, Mary Poppins, Alice in Wonderland
and other favorites hanging out throughout
Fantasyland, or hop in line to see princesses at Fairytale Hall (FastPass+) and

Magic Kingdom, as well as a map and spell cards used to cast spells at these portals. Stop by the firehouse by the front entrance on Main Street, USA, or behind the Christmas shop in Liberty Square to sign up. Free with theme-park admission.

Epcot

With no roller coasters screeching overhead, no parades, no water rides and plenty of water, things here run a bit slower in **Epcot** (200 Epcot Center Dr; $100-119, prices vary daily; ⊙11am-9pm, hours vary) than in the rest of Walt Disney World Resort. Slow down and enjoy. Smell the incense in Morocco, listen to the Beatles in the UK and sip miso in Japan.

The park is divided into two sections situated around a lake. Future World has Epcot's only two thrill rides plus several pavilions with attractions, restaurants and character greeting spots. World Showcase comprises 11 re-created nations featuring country-specific food, shopping and entertainment.

Spaceship Earth

Inside what people joke is a giant golf ball landmark at the front entrance, Spaceship Earth is a bizarre, kitschy slow-moving ride past animatronic scenes depicting the history of communication from cave painting to computers. Yes, it sounds boring, and yes, it sounds weird. But it's surprisingly funny and a cult favorite. In recent years they've tried to modernize it with an interactive questionnaire about your travel interests, but we like the retro aspects better.

Disney's Animal Kingdom

World Showcase

Who needs the hassle of a passport and jet lag when you can travel the world right here at Walt Disney World Resort? At World Showcase you can wander around the lake and visit 11 countries. You can throw back a tequila in Mexico, munch on a pizza in Italy and muscle up against a troll in Norway. And don't miss the retro rides into the 'future.'

Disney's Animal Kingdom

Set apart from the rest of Disney both in miles and in tone, **Animal Kingdom** (2101 Osceola Pkwy; $100-119, prices vary daily; ⏱9am-7pm, hours vary; 🚇Disney) attempts

> ★ **Top Tip**
>
> Call ☎407-939-3463 to make reservations at table-service restaurant throughout Walt Disney World® Resort.

to blend theme park and zoo, carnival and African safari, with a healthy dose of Disney characters, storytelling and transformative magic.

Short trails around Animal Kingdom's Discovery Island lead to quiet spots along the water, where a handful of benches make a great place to relax with a snack. Keep an eye out for animals such as tortoises and monkeys.

Finding Nemo: The Musical

Arguably the best show at Walt Disney World Resort, this sophisticated 40-minute musical theater performance features massive and elaborate puppets on stage and down the aisles, incredible set design and great acting. The music was composed by Robert Lopez and Kristen Anderson-Lopez, who also wrote *Frozen's* Academy Award–winning 'Let It Go,' and the spectacular puppets were created by Michael Curry, the creative and artistic force behind the puppets in Broadway's *The Lion King*.

Kilimanjaro Safaris

Board a jeep and ride through the African Savannah, pausing to look at zebras, lions, giraffes, alligators and more, all seemingly roaming free. Sometimes you'll have to wait to let an animal cross the road, and if you're lucky, you'll see babies or some raucous activity. These are not classic Disney auto-animatronic creatures, but real, live animals.

Disney Parades, Fireworks & Light Shows

It takes a little bit of planning to coordinate your schedule to hit Disney's parades and nighttime spectaculars. Note that times

> ☑ **Don't Miss**
>
> The Build a Better Mousetrip website (www.buildabettermousetrip.com) has planning advice and a schedule of free outdoor screenings of Disney movies.

vary according to day and season. In addition to the following cornerstones, check www.disneyworld.disney.go.com for holiday celebrations and specialty parties.

Festival of Fantasy (Magic Kingdom; theme-park admission required; ⊙morning & afternoon daily, hours vary; 🚌Disney, 🚤Disney, 🚌Lynx 50, 56) Elaborate floats and dancing characters, including Dumbo, Peter Pan and Sleeping Beauty.

IllumiNations: Reflections of Earth (Epcot; theme-park admission required; ⊙nightly, hours vary; 🚌Disney, 🚤Disney, 🚌Lynx 50, 56) This fiery narrative, with a light show and fireworks, features a massive globe illuminated with LED lights in the center of Epcot's World Showcase Lagoon.

Happily Ever After (Magic Kingdom) This fireworks-and-light-show extravaganza (often promoted as the 'Night-time Spectacular') was about to be launched with a bang at the time of research.

Fantasmic (Hollywood Studios; theme-park admission required; ⊙nightly; 👪; 🚌Disney, 🚤Disney) Dramatic and overhyped water, music and light show has a vague, rather disconnected and confusing plot in which Mickey Mouse proves victorious over a cast of Disney villains.

Star Wars: A Galactic Spectacular A firework and light show topped off with projected clips of the Star Wars on the Chinese Theatre.

Rivers of Light Animal Kingdom's recently introduced light show that features its beautiful baobab tree, the 'tree of life.'

Ticketing Options

One-day tickets are valid for entry to Magic Kingdom. Separate one-day tickets at slightly lower prices are valid for Epcot, Hollywood Studios or Animal Kingdom.

Multiday tickets are valid for one theme park per day for each day of the ticket (you can leave and re-enter the park, but you can't enter another park).

Park Hopper gives same-day entry to any or all of the four Walt Disney World Resort parks. Fair warning: hopping between four parks requires a lot of stamina. Two parks a day is more feasible.

Park Hopper Plus is the same as Park Hopper, but you can toss in Blizzard Beach, Typhoon Lagoon and Oak Trail Golf Course. The number of places you can visit increases the more days you buy (eg a four-day ticket allows four extra visits; a five-day ticket allows five).

FastPass+ & MagicBand

FastPass+ is designed to allow guests to plan their days in advance and reduce time spent waiting in line. Visitors can reserve a specific time for up to three attractions per

Main Street, Magic Kingdom (p180)

day through My Disney Experience (www.disneyworld.disney.go.com), accessible online or by downloading the free mobile app. There are also kiosks in each park where you can make reservations.

Resort guests receive a MagicBand – a plastic wristband that serves as a room key, park entrance ticket, FastPass+ access and room charge. As soon as you make your room reservation, you can set up your My Disney Experience account and begin planning your day-by-day Disney itinerary. Your itinerary, including any changes you make online or through the mobile app, will automatically be stored in your wristband.

★ **Top Tip**
Avoid the lunchtime queues: buy a sandwich on the way and picnic at your leisure.

Universal Orlando Resort

Pedestrian-friendly Universal Orlando Resort has got spunk, spirit and attitude. It's comparable to Walt Disney World® Resort, but Universal does everything just a bit more smoothly, as well as being smaller and easier to navigate.

Great For...

☑ Don't Miss

The Wizarding World of Harry Potter (p187) – likely to be the best theme-park experience you'll ever encounter.

The Universal Orlando Resort consists of three theme parks: Islands of Adventure, with the bulk of the thrill rides; Universal Studios, with movie-based attractions and shows; and Volcano Bay, a state-of-the-art water park.

Islands of Adventure

Islands of Adventure is just plain fun. Scream-it-from-the-rooftops, no-holds-barred, laugh-out-loud kind of fun. Superheroes zoom by on motorcycles, roller coasters whiz overhead and plenty of rides will get you soaked. The park is divided into distinct areas, including the dinosaur-themed Jurassic Park and the cartoon-heavy Toon Island.

Suess Landing

ℹ **Need to Know**

☏407-363-8000; www.universalorlando.
com; 1000 Universal Studios Plaza; single park
adult 1/2 days $105/185, child $100/175, both
parks adult/child $155/150; ◷daily, hours
vary; ⊡Lynx 21, 37 & 40, ⊛Universal

✕ **Take a Break**

Each Universal resort has high-quality
bars and restaurants that you can enjoy
even if you're not a guest.

★ **Top Tip**

If possible, visit during low season; avoid
Christmas through early January, March
and summer.

coasters twist and loop; inspired by the first task
of the Triwizard Tournament.

Flight of the Hippogriff (Express Pass)
Family-friendly coaster passes over Hagrid's Hut
– don't forget to bow to Buckbeak!

The Incredible Hulk Coaster

Follow the screams to this massive loop-
dee-loop coaster. There's no clickity-
clackity building of suspense on this beast
– you climb in, buckle up, and zoom, off
you launch, from zero to 67mph. Climb up
150ft and fly down through a zero-gravity
roll. It was reopened in 2016 with new 'en-
hancements,' including a new vehicle and a
high-tech scientific facility with a 'Gamma
Core' as the entrance.

Seuss Landing

Drink Moose Juice or Goose Juice and
peruse shelves of Dr Seuss books before
riding through The Cat in the Hat or around
and around on an elephant-bird from
Horton Hears a Who. In Seuss Landing, the
Lorax guards his truffula trees, Thing One
and Thing Two make trouble and creatures
from all kinds of Seuss favorites adorn the
shops and the rides. There are four rides, a

Wizarding World of Harry Potter – Hogsmeade

Poke along the cobbled streets and impossibly crooked buildings of Hogsmeade,
sip frothy Butterbeer, munch on Cauldron
Cakes and mail a card via Owl Post, all in
the shadow of Hogwarts Castle. The detail
and authenticity tickle the fancy at every
turn, from the screeches of the mandrakes
in the shop windows to the groans of
Moaning Myrtle in the bathroom – keep
your eyes peeled for magical happenings.

**Harry Potter and the Forbidden
Journey** Feel the cold chill of Dementors and
soar over the castle in a Quidditch match on this
simulated masterpiece.

Dragon Challenge (Express Pass) Gut-churning
orange-and-blue roller

storytelling performance and the wonderful If I Ran the Zoo interactive splash play area.

Universal Studios

Divided geographically by film-inspired and region-specific architecture and ambience, and themed as a Hollywood backlot, Universal Studios has shows and magnificently designed, simulation-heavy rides dedicated to silver-screen and TV icons. Drink Duff beer, a Homer favorite, in Springville; ride the Hogwarts Express into Diagon Alley; and challenge the host of *The Tonight Show* to a scavenger hunt.

Wizarding World of Harry Potter

Diagon Alley

Diagon Alley, lined with magical shops selling robes, Quidditch supplies, wands, scaly creatures and more, leads to the massive Gringotts Bank. Detour through the blackness of Knockturn Alley, where only dark wizards go to buy their supplies, hydrate with an elixir of Fire Protection Potion poured into Gilly Water, try a scoop of Butterbeer ice cream and, when you hear the grumblings of the bank's ferocious dragon, perched on the top, be prepared for his fiery roar.

The massive Harry Potter landmarks of Hogwarts and Gringotts house the lines for the respective rides, but are also in and of themselves marvelously themed in great detail. In Hogwarts, the queue winds through the corridors of the school, past talking portraits and Dumbledore's office, and at Gringotts the towering goblin bank tellers look you in the eye. Note: there is a route, too, for those who want to enter without doing the ride, so nobody misses out!

Simpsons Ride

Escape from Gringotts Wind through the bank, with its massive marble columns and goblin tellers, and hop on a combination coaster and simulation ride through Gringotts.

Ollivander's Wand Shop Floor-to-ceiling shelves crammed with dusty wand boxes set the scene for a 10-minute show in which the wand chooses the wizard (note that there is also an Ollivander's show in Hogsmeade).

London

To enter the Wizarding World of Harry Potter, you must, of course, start in London.

MIAMI2YOU / SHUTTERSTOCK ©

Like the rest of Universal Studios, it's themed with great detail to create a sense of place – and it isn't just any London, it's the London of JK Rowling's imagination, the London shared by wizards and muggles alike. There are no traditional rides, but you catch the Hogwarts Express from King's Cross Station here.

The Simpsons Ride

The *Simpsons* creators James Brooks and Matt Groening helped create a simulated extravaganza into Krusty the Clown's techno-colored theme park, Krustyland. Sideshow Bob, escaped from prison, is chasing you and the Simpsons through the park, and you must zip down coasters, spin on kiddie rides and cruise down water slides as you try to escape.

Revenge of the Mummy

A high-thrill indoor coaster combines roller-coaster speed and twists with in-your-face special effects. Head deep into ancient Egyptian catacombs in near pitch black, but don't anger Imhotep the mummy – in his wrath he flings you past fire, water and more. The deep growl of the mummy, screeching of bats and unexpected twists add to the creepy thrills to take this several notches beyond your classic coaster.

Themed Bars at Universal Orlando

Hog's Head Pub (Islands of Adventure; drinks $4-8, theme-park admission required; ⊙11am-park closing) Butterbeer, frozen or frothy, real beer on tap, pumpkin cider and more. Keep an eye on that hog over the bar – he's more real than you think!

Duff Brewery (Springfield; snacks $5-12, theme-park admission required; ⌚11am-park closing; 📶) Outdoor lagoonside bar serving Homer Simpson's beer of choice, on tap or by the bottle, and Springfield's signature Flaming Moe.

Moe's Tavern (Springfield; drinks $3-9, theme-park admission required; ⌚11am-park closing; 📶) Brilliantly themed Simpsons bar with Isotopes memorabilia, the Love Tester and Bart Simpson crank-calling the red rotary phone; it's as if you walked straight into your TV to find yourself at Homer's favorite neighborhood joint.

Volcano Bay

This is Universal Resort's third theme park – a water park – launched in 2017. Modeled on a Pacific island, the main feature of this tropical oasis is a colossal volcano through and down which, you guessed it, run watery thrills and spills. Among the 18 attractions are winding rivers with family raft rides, pools and two intertwining slides, but the main attraction is the Ko'okiri Body Plunge. At a hair-raising 125ft, it's the tallest trap-door body plunge ride in North America.

Express Pass

Avoid lines at designated Islands of Adventure and Universal Studios rides by flashing your Express Pass at the separate Express Pass line. The standard one-day pass (for one park $50 to $60; for two parks from $65) allows one-time Express Pass access to each attraction. Alternatively, purchase the bundled two-day Park-to-Park Ticket Plus Unlimited Express (from $220), which includes admission to both parks and unlimited access to Express Pass rides. With this, you can go to any ride, any time you like, as often as you like.

If you are staying at one of Universal Orlando's deluxe resort hotels – Universal Orlando's Loews Portofino Bay, Hard Rock or Loews Royal Pacific Resort – up to five guests in each room automatically receive an Unlimited Express Pass. A limited number of passes per day are available online or at the park gates. Check www.universalorlando. com for a calendar of prices and black-out dates. Note that Unlimited Express Passes are sold bundled to park admission online, but, if they're available, you can add them to an existing ticket at the park.

CityWalk

Across the canal from the three theme parks is **CityWalk** (www.citywalk.com; ⌚7am-2am, hours vary), Universal's entertainment district comprising a pedestrian mall with restaurants, clubs, bars, a multiplex movie theater, miniature golf and shops. Live music and *mucho* alcohol sums up the entertainment options here. Although nights can be packed with partying 20-somethings, there's a distinct family-friendly vibe and several bars have reasonable food. Oh, and although it

Moe's Tavern

feels like a partying theme park in its own right, you can come here even if you're not visiting the Universal theme parks.

Delancy Street Preview Center

Some Universal Orlando visitors could be pulled from the crowds and asked to go to the Delancy Street Preview Center (in the New York section of Universal Studios) to watch clips from a TV pilot or movie and to give their opinions. It's a way of testing potential new shows – and the best part is participants are compensated for their time. As in money. They're looking for a particular demographic based on the material, and it's not always open, but if you stop by and ask you just may be what they want.

☑ Don't Miss

For some downtime or a picnic, a fenced-in grassy area with shade trees and views across the lagoon sits just across from the entrance to Universal Studios' Woody Woodpecker's KidZone.

★ Top Tip

Pick up a free map (listing the attractions, with a schedule outlining events, shows and locations of free character interactions) at each park entrance.

PHOTOSOUNDS / SHUTTERSTOCK ®

Orlando

Many visitors never reach downtown Orlando, distracted by the hype and sparkle of Cinderella and Hogwarts, but those who do discover a pretty, leafy city, blessed with a great field-to-fork eating scene and world-class museums.

⊙ SIGHTS & ACTIVITIES

Mennello Museum of American Art   Museum

(📞407-246-4278; www.mennellomuseum.org; 900 E Princeton St, Loch Haven Park, Downtown; adult/child 6-18yr $5/1; ⊙10:30am-4:30pm Tue-Sat, from noon Sun; 🚌Lynx 125, 🚉Florida Hospital Health Village) Tiny but excellent lakeside art museum featuring the work of Earl Cunningham, whose brightly colored images, a fusion of pop and folk art, leap off the canvas. Visiting exhibits often feature American folk art. Every four months there's a new exhibition, everything from a Smithsonian collection to a local artist.

Harry P Leu Gardens   Gardens

(📞407-246-2620; www.leugardens.org; 1920 N Forest Ave, Audubon Park; adult/child 4-18yr $10/3; ⊙9am-5pm, last admission 4:30pm; 🚌Lynx 38, 8, 50) Camelias, roses, orange groves and desert plants cover 50 acres, as well as plenty of grassy spots for a lakeside picnic. Pick up supplies at the trendy East End Market, a half-mile east of the entrance gate on Corrine Dr. Tours of Leu House, an 18th-century mansion (later owned by the Leu family), run every half-hour from 10am to 3:30pm. See the website for details on outdoor movies, storytelling and live music.

Orlando Museum of Art   Museum

(📞407-896-4231; www.omart.org; 2416 N Mills Ave, Loch Haven Park; adult/child $15/5; ⊙10am-4pm Tue-Fri, from noon Sat & Sun; 🚻; 🚌Lynx 125, 🚉Florida Hospital Health Village) Founded in 1924, Orlando's grand and blindingly white center for the arts boasts a fantastic collection – both permanent and temporary – and hosts an array of adult and family-friendly art events and classes.

The popular First Thursday ($10), from 6pm to 9pm on the first Thursday of the month, celebrates local artists with regional work, live music and food from Orlando restaurants.

West Orange Trail Bikes & Blades   Cycling

(📞407-877-0600; www.orlandobikerental. com; 17914 State Rd 438, Winter Garden; bikes per hr $7-11, per day $30-50, per week $99-149, delivery/pick-up $40; ⊙9am-5pm Mon-Fri, from 7:30am Sat & Sun) This bike shop lies 20 miles west of Orlando and sits at the beginning of the West Orange Trail. It offers bike rental and comprehensive information, both online and on-site, on biking in and around Orlando.

⊕ TOURS

Central Florida Nature Adventures   Kayaking

(📞352-589-7899; www.kayakcentralflorida. com; 2-3hr per person $64; 🚻) Run by local residents and nature lovers, Jenny and Kenny, these small nature tours make for a relaxing paddle among the alligators, turtles, herons and egrets. They will meet you at different launch sites depending on the tour you choose.

⊗ EATING

East End Market   Market $

(📞231-236-3316; www.eastendmkt.com; 3201 Corrine Dr, Audubon Park; ⊙10am-7pm Tue-Sat, 11am-6pm Sun; 🚻🚻) 🌿 Look for the raised vegetable beds and picnic tables outside this little earthy, organic, hip collection of locally sourced eateries and markets.

Inside there's Lineage, a fabulous coffee stand (it's worth it for a good brew); Local Roots Farm Store, specializing in an 'all Florida all year' theme and offering flights of Florida beer and wine at the tiny bar; Gideon's Bakehouse, with fabulous cakes and cookies; the excellent raw-vegan bar Skybird Juicebar & Experimental Kitchen; and more.

Dandelion
Communitea Café   Vegetarian $

(📞407-362-1864; www.dandelioncommunitea.
com; 618 N Thornton Ave, Thornton Park; mains
$10-14; ⏱11am-10pm Mon-Sat, to 5pm Sun;
🍴🏍) 🌱 Unabashedly crunchy and defini-
tively organic, this pillar of the sprouts and
tempeh and green-tea dining scene serves
up creative and excellent plant-based fare
in a refurbished old house that invites folks
to sit down and hang out.

Urbain 40   American $$

(📞407-872-2640; http://urbain40.com; 8000
Via Dellagio Way, Restaurant Row) Tap into your
inner classy selves and transport yourself
back to the 1940s, where classic martinis
were downed like water by besuited clients
who sat on blue leather bar stools. This
stunning old-style American brasserie
manages to re-create this (without contriv-
ance) and serves up great cuisine as well
as ambience. Do not miss the char-roasted
mussels ($12).

Rusty Spoon   American $$

(📞407-401-8811; www.therustyspoon.com; 55 W
Church St, Downtown; mains $15-31; ⏱11am-
3pm Mon-Fri, 5-10pm Sun-Thu, to 11pm Fri &
Sat; 🍴) 🌱 Airy, handsome and inviting,
with a brick wall covered in giant photos
of farm animals, a trendy urban vibe and
an emphasis on simply prepared, locally
sourced produce. Kind of pub classics with
delightful (and much more sophisticated)
twists. If it's on the menu, don't bypass the
chocolate s'mores dessert. (We say
no more.)

Slate   American $$

(📞407-500-7528; www.slateorlando.com; 8323
W Sand Lake Rd, Restaurant Row; mains $14-38;
⏱11am-12:30pm & 5-10pm Mon-Fri, 10:30am-
3pm & 5-11pm Sat, 10:30am-3pm & 5-9pm Sun)
One of Orlando's newest and trendiest
places, it's buzzy, noisy and draws a chatty
crowd after crusty pizza (straight from
the large, copper oven) or contemporary
dishes from brisket to diver scallops. There
are several seating areas, from a communal
table to the wood room, a verandah-style
space with a fireplace.

👪 Getting to Legoland®
Florida Resort

In Winter Haven, about 50 miles southwest of Orlando, **Legoland® Florida
Resort** (📞863-318-5346; http://florida.
legoland.com; 1 Legoland Way; 1-/2-day
tickets adult $93/113, child 3-12yr $86/106;
⏱10am-5pm; 🏍; 🚌Legoland Shuttle) is a
joy. With manageable crowds, and no
bells and whistles, this lakeside theme
park maintains an old-school vibe – you
don't have to plan like a general to enjoy
a day here, and it's strikingly stress-free.
This is about fun (and yes, education) in
a colorful and interactive environment.
Rides and attractions, including the attached water park, are best for children
aged two to 12 years. Opening hours
vary seasonally.

Highlights include Flight School,
a coaster that zips you around with
your feet dangling free, and Miniland,
a Lego re-creation of iconic American
landmarks and cities. There are a few
remnants from the park's history as the
site of Cypress Gardens (circa 1936),
including lovely botanical gardens. The
water-ski show has a bizarre and rather
silly pirate theme, and the Cartoon
Network's *Legends of Chima* inspires an
entire section.

Don't miss the Imagination Zone, a
wonderful interactive learning center
heavily staffed with skilled Lego makers
happy to help children of all ages create
delights with their blocks.

Legoland Shuttle ($5; booking 24
hours ahead is essential) runs daily from
I-Drive 360 (near the Orlando Eye).

Miniland
© 2016 CHIP LITHERLAND PHOTOGRAPHY INC.

🍴 Buying Groceries

While most Orlando hotel rooms have small refrigerators, only deluxe Disney hotels provide them free of charge.

Whole Foods Market Philips Crossing (☑407-355-7100; www.wholefoodsmarket. com/stores/orlando; 8003 Turkey Lake Rd, Restaurant Row; ⊗8am-10pm) Organic fare, a salad bar, brick-oven pizza and more. There's another store at 1989 Aloma Ave, Winter Park.

Fresh Market (☑407-294-1516; www. thefreshmarket.com; 5000 Dr Phillips Blvd, Restaurant Row; ⊗8am-9pm) Excellent grocery store with organic and local produce.

DoveCote   French $$

(http://dovecoteorlando.com/; 390 N Orange Ave, Suite 110; lunch mains $12-24, dinner mains $16-30; ⊗11:30am-2:30pm & 5:30-10pm) One of the hottest tickets in Orlando sits tidily within the city's Bank of America building. It's an all-things-to-all-people kind of spot with a brasserie and a coffee stop, plus plenty of cocktails. 'Comfort French' is often used to describe the cuisine.

Stubborn Mule   Modern American $$

(www.thestubbornmuleorlando.com; 100 S Eola Dr, Suite 103, Downtown; mains $19-28; ⊗11am-11pm Tue-Sat, 11am-9pm Sun) A trendy and very popular gastropub that serves handcrafted cocktails with flair (yes, plenty of mules) and good ol' locally sourced, delicious food that's nothing but contemporary. It serves up the likes of polenta cakes and smoked Gouda grits and roasted winter vegetables. It's the new kid on the block and one definitely worth visiting.

K Restaurant   American $$$

(☑407-872-2332; www.krestaurant.net; 1710 Edgewater Dr, College Park; mains $18-40; ⊗5-9pm Mon-Thu, 5:30-10pm Fri & Sat, 5:30-8pm Sun; ☑) ☞ Chef and owner Kevin Fonzo,

one of Orlando's most celebrated and established field-to-fork foodie stars, earns local and national accolades year after year, but this neighborhood favorite remains wonderfully unassuming. There's a wrap-around porch, and a lovely little terrace, and herbs and vegetables come from the on-site garden.

🍸 DRINKING & NIGHTLIFE

Icebar   Bar

(☑407-426-7555; www.icebarorlando.com; 8967 International Dr; entry at door/advance online $20/15; ⊗5pm-midnight Mon-Wed, to 1am Thu, to 2am Fri-Sun; 🚋I-Trolley Red Line Stop 18 or Green Line Stop 10) More classic Orlando gimmicky fun. Step into the 22°F (-5°C) ice house, sit on the ice seat, admire the ice carvings, sip the icy drinks. Coat and gloves are provided at the door (or upgrade to the photogenic faux fur for $10), and the fire room, bathrooms and other areas of the bar are kept at normal temperature.

Adults over 21 welcome anytime; folks aged between eight and 20 are allowed between 7pm and 9pm only.

Hanson's Shoe Repair   Cocktail Bar

(☑407-476-9446; www.facebook.com/han-sonsshoerepair; 3rd fl, 27 E Pine St, Downtown; cocktails $12; ⊗8pm-2am Tue-Thu & Sat, from 7pm Fri) In a city saturated with over-the-top theming from Beauty and the Beast to Harry Potter, it shouldn't be surprising that you can walk from 21st-century Downtown Orlando into a Prohibition-era speakeasy, complete with historically accurate cocktails and a secret password for entry. To get in, call for the password.

Wally's Mills Ave Liquors   Bar

(☑407-896-6975; www.wallysonmills.com; 1001 N Mills Ave, Thornton Park; ⊗7:30am-2am) It's been around since the early '50s, before Orlando became Disney, and while its peeling, naked-women wallpaper could use some updating, it wouldn't be Wally's without it. Nothing flashy, nothing loud, just a tiny, windowless, smoky bar with a jukebox

Mennello Museum of American Art (p192)

and cheap, strong drinks – as much a dark dive as you'll find anywhere. And yes, it opens at 7:30*am*.

✪ ENTERTAINMENT

Enzian Theater — Cinema

(☏407-629-0054; www.enzian.org; 1300 S Orlando Ave, Maitland; adult/child $10/8; ☉5pm-midnight Tue-Fri, noon-midnight Sat & Sun) The envy of any college town, this clapboard-sided theater screens independent and classic films, and has the excellent **Eden Bar** (☏407-629-1088; mains $10-16; ☉11am-11pm Sun-Thu, to 1am Fri & Sat; ✍) ✔ restaurant, featuring primarily local and organic fare. Have a veggie burger and a beer on the patio underneath the cypress tree or opt for table service in the theater.

Mad Cow Theatre — Theater

(☏407-297-8788; www.madcowtheatre.com; 54 W Church, Downtown; tickets from $26) A model of inspiring regional theater, with classic and modern performances in a downtown Orlando space (located on the 2nd floor).

John & Rita Lowndes Shakespeare Center — Theater

(☏407-447-1700; www.orlandoshakes.org; 812 E Rollins St, Loch Haven Park; tickets $13-65) Set on the shores of Lake Estelle in grassy Loch Haven Park, this lovely theater includes three intimate stages hosting professional classics such as *Pride and Prejudice* and *Beowulf,* excellent children's theater and up-and-coming playwrights' work.

ℹ INFORMATION

Official Visitor Center – Visit Orlando
(☏407-363-5872; www.visitorlando.com; 8723 International Dr; ☉8:30am-6pm; 🚍I-Ride Trolley Red Line 15) Legitimate discount attraction tickets through its website (or turn up in person for daily deals) and the best source for information on theme parks, accommodations, outdoor activities, performing arts and more.

ⓘ GETTING THERE & AWAY

Amtrak (www.amtrak.com; 1400 Sligh Blvd) Offers daily trains south to Miami (from $46) and north to New York City (from $144).

Greyhound (📞407-292-3424; www.greyhound. com; 555 N John Young Pkwy) Serves numerous cities from Orlando.

Orlando International Airport (MCO; 📞407-825-8463; www.orlandoairports.net; 1 Jeff Fuqua Blvd) About 10 miles south of town.

Orlando Sanford International Airport (📞407-585-4000; www.orlandosanfordairport.com; 1200 Red Cleveland Blvd) Situated around 25 miles northeast of town.

ⓘ GETTING AROUND

Lymmo (www.golynx.com; free; ⊙6am-10pm Mon-Thu, to midnight Fri, 10am-midnight Sat, to 10pm Sun) circles downtown Orlando for free with stops near Lynx Central Station on Garland Ave, near SunRail's Church St Station, at Central and Magnolia, Jefferson and Magnolia, and outside the Westin Grand Bohemian on Orange Ave.

Winter Park

Founded in the mid-19th century and home to the small liberal-arts school Rollins College, bucolic Winter Park concentrates some of Orlando's best-kept secrets – including several of the city's most talked about restaurants and field-to-fork favorites – within a few shaded, pedestrian-friendly streets. Shops, wine bars and sidewalk cafes line Park Ave.

◎ SIGHTS

Charles Hosmer Morse Museum of American Art   Museum
(📞407-645-5311; www.morsemuseum.org; 445 N Park Ave; adult/child $6/free; ⊙9:30am-4pm Tue-Sat, from 1pm Sun, to 8pm Fri Nov-Apr; 🚼) Internationally famous, this stunning and delightful museum houses the world's most comprehensive collection of Louis Comfort Tiffany art. Highlights include the chapel interior designed by the artist for

the 1893 World's Columbian Exhibition in Chicago; 10 galleries filled with architectural and art objects from Tiffany's Long Island home, Laurelton Hall; and an installation of the Laurelton's Daffodil Terrace.

Albin Polasek Museum & Sculpture Gardens   Museum
(www.polasek.org; 633 Osceola Ave; adult/child $5/free; ⊙10am-4pm Tue-Sat, from 1pm Sun) Listed on the National Register of Historic Places and perched on the shore of Lake Osceola, this small yellow villa was home to Czech sculptor Albin Polasek. The house serves as a small museum of his life and work, and the gardens house some of his sculptures. Also hosts rotating exhibitions.

ⓖ TOURS

Scenic Boat Tour   Boating
(📞407-644-4056; www.scenicboattours.com; 312 E Morse Blvd; adult/child $14/7; ⊙hourly 10am-4pm; 🚼) One of the best ways to appreciate the under-the-radar beauty and classic Florida escape of Winter Park is to meander over to Lake Osceola for a one-hour boat tour. You learn much about the area's history and gossip about the houses on the lake. Hop on an 18-passenger pontoon and cruise through Winter Park's tropical canals and lakes, past mansions, Rollins College and other sights.

ⓐ SHOPPING

Rifle Paper Co   Stationery
(📞407-622-7679; www.riflepaperco.com; 558 W New England Ave; ⊙9am-6pm Mon-Fri, 10am-5pm Sat) This tiny retail space, started by a husband and wife team in 2009, sells lovely paper stationery products. It now also ships internationally.

Lighten Up Toy Store   Toys
(📞407-644-3528; 348 S Park Ave; ⊙10am-5pm Mon-Sat) Small but well-stocked toy store with classics such as marbles and kazoos, outdoor toys including Frisbees, boomerangs and kites, and restaurant-perfect activity and picture books. There's

an entire wall of games and puzzles and, for those rainy days stuck in the hotel, 'furniture-friendly bow and arrow rockets.'

🌑 EATING & DRINKING

Ethos Vegan Kitchen Vegan $

(📞407-228-3898; www.ethosvegankitchen.com; 601b S New York Ave; mains $7-14; ⏰11am-11pm Mon-Fri; 🌿) 🍴 The welcome sign at this meat-free stop says 'get off at Platform One' for a vegan arrival. Ethos Vegan Kitchen offers a range of delights such as pizza with broccoli, banana peppers, zucchini and seitan; meat-free shepherd's pie; pecan-encrusted eggplant; homemade soups and various sandwiches with names such as A Fungus Among Us and Hippie Wrap.

Croissant Gourmet Cafe $

(📞407-622-7753; www.facebook.com/the croissantgourmet; 120 E Morse Blvd; mains $8-12; ⏰7am-6pm Sun-Thu, to 8pm Fri & Sat, kitchen closes 6pm daily) Befitting Winter Park's European vibe, start the day with coffee and a pastry at the tiny Paris-perfect Croissant Gourmet. There are classic éclairs, delicious blueberry tarts and massive cinnamon twists, as well as sweet and savory crepes, traditional French breakfasts and lunches, and wine by the glass.

Ravenous Pig American $$$

(📞407-628-2333; www.theravenouspig.com; 565 W Fairbanks; mains $14-32; ⏰11:30am-3pm & 5-10pm Mon-Sat, 10:30am-3pm & 5-9pm Sun) 🍴 The cornerstone of Orlando's restaurant trend for locally sourced food, this chef-owned hipster spot moved to its new location in 2016. Here it's all about letting the food do the talking: locavore, omnivore, carnivore – take your pick. Really ravenous pigs can get their teeth into the pork porterhouse or the local seafood (the shrimp and grits is a must; $15). Don't miss.

Prato Italian $$$

(📞407-262-0050; www.prato-wp.com; 124 N Park Ave; mains $16-33; ⏰11:30am-4:30pm Mon & Tue, to 11pm Wed-Sat, to 10pm Sun) A hopping go-to spot with high ceilings, exposed beams and a bar expanding the length of the room. Offers inspired interpretations of classic Italian dishes, house-cured meats and excellent wood-oven pizza ($16).

Wine Room Wine Bar

(📞407-696-9463; www.thewineroomonline.com; 270 S Park Ave; tastings from $2.50; ⏰2pm-midnight Mon-Wed, from noon Thu, 11:30am-1:30am Fri & Sat, noon-11pm Sun) It's a bit of a gimmick, but you purchase a wine card and put as much money on it as you'd like. Then simply slide your card into the automated servers for whichever wine looks good, press the button for a taste or a full glass, and enjoy. More than 150 wines, arranged by region and type.

ℹ️ GETTING THERE & AWAY

From downtown Orlando, take I-4 to Fairbanks Ave and head east for about 2 miles to Park Ave.

Orlando's **SunRail** (www.sunrail.com) stops at downtown Winter Park.

Lynx 102 services Orange Ave from downtown Orlando to Winter Park.

NEW ORLEANS

In this Chapter

Mardi Gras	202
St Charles Avenue Streetcar	206
Sights	208
Tours	212
Shopping	212
Eating	213
Drinking & Nightlife	216
Entertainment	216

New Orleans at a Glance...

New Orleans is something, and somewhere, else. Founded by the French and administered by the Spanish (and then by the French again), she is, with her sidewalk cafes and iron balconies, one of America's most European cities. But she is also, with her vodou (voodoo), Mardi Gras Indians, brass bands and gumbo, the most African and Caribbean city in the country.

However you see it, one fact is certain: the things that make life worth living – eating, drinking and the making of merriment – are the air that New Orleans breathes.

Two Days in New Orleans

Spend day one in the French Quarter. Wander around **Jackson Square** (p208) and explore the **Cabildo** (p208). Grab dinner and drinks in the area, followed by live music at **Preservation Hall** (p216). On day two, head to Uptown and shop along Magazine St. Then check out the Garden District, popping into **Lafayette Cemetery No 1** (p212) and hopping onto the **St Charles Avenue Streetcar** (p206).

Four Days in New Orleans

On day three, soak up the Marigny's vibe. Gape at the Mississippi River from **Crescent Park** (p211) and peruse cool crafts at the **Frenchmen Art Market** (p211). On day four meander around the Tremé – don't miss the **Backstreet Cultural Museum** (p208) or **Willie Mae's** (p213) fried chicken. Head up Esplanade Ave to **City Park** (p209) and wander around the **New Orleans Museum of Art** (p209).

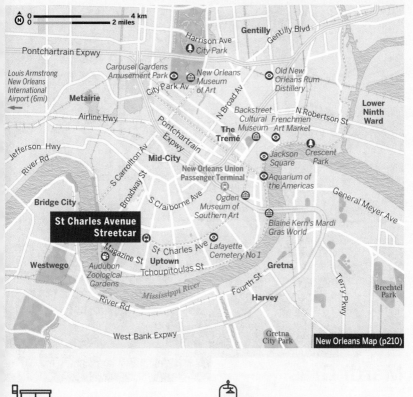

New Orleans Map (p210)

Arriving in New Orleans

Louis Armstrong New Orleans International Airport Taxis to the Central Business District (CBD) cost $36, or $15 per passenger for three or more passengers. Shuttle buses cost $24 per person. The E2 bus takes you to Carrollton and Tulane Ave in Mid-City for $2.

Where to Stay

Big hotels are found in the French Quarter and CBD; they tend to have a more boutique, historical feel in the French Quarter, while CBD properties are more modern. Intimate (and quirky) guesthouses and B&Bs are the norm in the Garden District, Uptown, Faubourg Marigny and the Bywater.

Mardi Gras

Weird pageantry, West African rituals, Catholic liturgy and massive parade floats, all culminating in the single-most exhausting and exhilarating day of your life – happy Mardi Gras!

Great For...

☑ Don't Miss

The all-female Muses krewe, who take over St Charles Ave in one of the best early parades.

Pagan Beginnings

Carnival's pagan origins are deep. Pre-spring festivals of unabashed sexuality and indulgence of appetite are not a rarity around the world, and neither is the concept of denying these appetites as a means of reasserting human forbearance in the face of animalistic cravings. After trying unsuccessfully to suppress these traditions, the early Catholic Church co-opted the spring rite and slotted it into the Christian calendar. Carnival kickoff is rife with costuming, cross-dressing, mistaken identities and satirical, often crude, pokes at people in power. This attitude persists into Fat Tuesday (Mardi Gras).

Modern Mardi Gras

During the mid-19th century, a growing number of krewes (a deliberately quirky

CHUCK WAGNER / SHUTTERSTOCK ©

Zulu appeared in 1909, with members initially calling themselves the Tramps and parading on foot. By 1916, when the Zulu Social Aid & Pleasure Club was incorporated, the krewe brought floats, and its antics deliberately spoofed the pomposity of elite white krewes.

Today's 'superkrewes' began forming in the 1960s. Endymion debuted as a modest neighborhood parade in 1967; now its parades and floats are the largest around, with nearly 2000 riders and with one of its immense floats measuring 240ft in length.

Throw Me Something!

During Mardi Gras, enormous floats crowded with riders representing the city's Carnival krewes proceed up and down thoroughfares such as St Charles Ave and Canal St. The float riders toss 'throws' to the waiting crowds; throws range from strings of beads to plastic cups, blinking baubles and stuffed animals. Here are some locally recognized rules for throw-catching:

○ First: Locals never bare their breasts for beads. Most find it crude, and there are kids around.

○ Second: If there's a young kid near you, move, or be prepared to give the kid whatever you catch.

○ Third: Many locals will say they'd never touch a throw that hit the street, but we've

spelling of 'crews,' or clubs) supplied Mardi Gras with both structure and spectacle; the former made the celebration easily accessible, while the latter gave it popularity and notoriety outside of New Orleans. Rex first appeared in 1872, Momus a year later, and Proteus in 1882. Mythological and sometimes satirical themes defined the parades, making these processions coherent theatrical works on wheels. These old-line krewes were (and for the most part remain) highly secretive societies comprising the city's wealthiest, most powerful men.

Many enduring black traditions emerged around the turn of the 20th century. The spectacular Mardi Gras Indians began to appear in 1885; today their elaborate feathered costumes, sewn as a tribute to Native American warriors, are recognized as pieces of folk art. The black krewe of seen more than a few sneakily bend over to scoop up a cup or a unique string of beads. Rest assured it's not the done thing – even if it is occasionally, well, done.

Twelve Days of Parades

The parade season is a 12-day period beginning two Fridays before Fat Tuesday. Early parades are charming, neighborly processions that whet your appetite for the later parades, which increase in size and grandeur.

Krewe du Vieux By parading before the official parade season and marching on foot, Krewe du Vieux is permitted to pass through the French Quarter. Notoriously bawdy and satirical. Usually held three Saturdays before Fat Tuesday.

Le Krewe d'Etat The name is a clever, satirical pun: d'Etat is ruled by a dictator rather than a king.

Muses An all-women's krewe that parades down St Charles Ave with thousands of members and some imaginative, innovative floats; their throws include coveted hand-decorated shoes.

Mardi Gras weekend is lit up by the entrance of the superkrewes, who arrive with their monstrous floats and endless processions of celebrities, as flashy as a Vegas revue.

Endymion On Saturday night this megakrewe stages its spectacular parade and 'Extravaganza,' as it calls its ball in the Superdome.

Bacchus On Sunday night the Bacchus super-krewe wows an enraptured crowd along

St Charles Ave with its celebrity monarch and a gorgeous fleet of crowd-pleasing floats.

Zulu On Mardi Gras morning Zulu rolls along Jackson Ave, where folks set up barbecues on the sidewalk and krewe members distribute their prized hand-painted coconuts.

The 'King of Carnival,' Rex, waits further Uptown; it's a much more restrained affair, with the monarch himself looking like he's been plucked from a deck of cards.

★ Top Tip

For Mardi Gras or Jazz Fest (www. nojazzfest.com; ⊘Apr), **reserve accommodations six months to a year in advance.**

Walking Krewe Review

Some of the best parades of Carnival Season are put on by DIY bohemian walking krewes, groups of friends who create a grassroots show. Casual observers are always welcome to participate. Just bring a costume!

Barkus Dress up your furry friends for this all-pet parade (www.barkus.org).

Box of Wine Crazily costumed revelers march up St Charles Ave ahead of the Bacchus (god of wine) parade, distributing free wine from boxes along the way.

Intergalactic Krewe of Chewbacchus Dress up as your favorite sci-fi character at this wonderful parade for geeks, nerds and other people we might hang out with on weekends (www.chewbacchus.org).

Red Beans & Rice On Lundi Gras, folks dress up in costumes made from dry beans or as Louisiana food items.

Society of St Anne Traditionally made up of artists and bohemians, St Anne marches on Mardi Gras morning from the Bywater to the Mississippi and features the best costumes of Carnival Season.

Costume Contests

Mardi Gras is a citywide costume party, and many locals take a dim view of visitors who crash the party without one. For truly fantastic outfits, march with the Society of St Ann on Mardi Gras morning. This collection of artists and misfits prides itself on its DIY outfits, which seem to have marched out of a collision between a David Bowie video and a '60s acid trip. The creativity and pageantry on display really needs to be seen to be believed.

★ Did You Know?

The Presbytère (p208) has a permanent exhibit on the Mardi Gras where you can learn everything you ever wanted to know about the festival.

St Charles Avenue Streetcar

Clanging through this bucolic corridor comes the St Charles Avenue Streetcar, a mobile bit of urban transportation history, bearing tourists and commuters along a street as important to American architecture as Frank Lloyd Wright.

Great For...

☑ Don't Miss

Tulane and Loyola Universities and several historic churches and synagogues on the streetcar route.

The Streetcar

The clang and swoosh of the **St Charles Avenue Streetcar** (📞504-248-3900, TTY 504-827-7832; www.norta.com; per ride $1.25; 👪) is as essential to Uptown and the Garden District as live oaks and mansions. New Orleanians are justifiably proud of their moving monument, which began life as the nation's second horse-drawn streetcar line, the New Orleans & Carrollton Railroad, in 1835.

In 1893 the line was among the first streetcar systems in the country to be electrified. Now it is one of the few streetcars in the USA to have survived the automobile era. Millions of passengers utilize the streetcar every day despite the fact the city's bus service tends to be faster. In many ways, the streetcar is the quintessential vehicle for New Orleans public trans-

St Charles
Avenue
Streetcar

❶ Need to Know

Streetcars arrive every 15 minutes or so, 24 hours a day. The cost per ride is $1.25.

✕ Take a Break

Surrey's Juice Bar (p215) sits a few blocks away from the streetcar's route, prime for a meaty pit stop.

★ Top Tip

The Jazzy Pass provides unlimited rides on streetcars for one ($3) or three ($9) days; see www.norta.com.

portation: slow, pretty and, if not entirely efficient, extremely atmospheric.

The fleet of antique cars survived the hurricanes of 2005 and today full service has been restored all the way to South Carrollton Ave. In recent times the line has carried more than 3 million passengers a year.

St Charles Avenue

It's only slightly hyperbolic to claim St Charles Ave is the most beautiful street in the USA. Once you enter the Garden District, the entire street is shaded under a tunnel of grand oak trees that look like they could have wiped the floor with an orc army in a Tolkien novel (ie they're old, and they're big).

Gorgeous houses, barely concealed behind the trees, belong to the most aristocratic elite of the city. Those same

elite often ride in the floats that proceed along St Charles during Carnival season; look up to the tree branches and you'll see many are laden with shiny beads tossed from Mardi Gras floats. Within the Neutral Ground, or median space that houses the streetcar tracks, you'll often see joggers and families passing through the verdant corridor. By far the best way of experiencing this cityscape is via the slow, antique rumble of the streetcar; freed from driving, you can gaze on all the beauty.

Some of the most elegant buildings to keep an eye out for:

Elms Mansion (3029 St Charles Ave)

Smith House (4534 St Charles Ave)

'Wedding Cake' House (5807 St Charles Ave)

Milton Latter Memorial Library (5120 St Charles Ave)

⊙ SIGHTS

◎ French Quarter

Jackson Square   Square

(Decatur & St Peter Sts) Sprinkled with lazing loungers, surrounded by sketch artists, fortune-tellers and traveling performers, and watched over by cathedrals, offices and shops plucked from a Parisian fantasy, Jackson Sq is one of America's great town greens and the heart of the Quarter. The identical, block-long Pontalba Buildings overlook the scene, and the nearly identical Cabildo and Presbytère structures flank the impressive St Louis Cathedral, which fronts the square.

Cabildo   Museum

(📞800-568-6968, 504-568-6968; http://louisianastatemuseum.org/museums/the-cabildo; 701 Chartres St; adult/student/child under 12yr $6/5/free; ⊙10am-4:30pm Tue-Sun, closed Mon; 👪) The former seat of government in colonial Louisiana now serves as the gateway to exploring the history of the state in general, and New Orleans in particular. It's also a magnificent building in its own right; the elegant Cabildo marries elements of Spanish colonial architecture and French urban design better than most buildings in the city. Exhibits range from Native American tools, to 'Wanted' posters for escaped slaves, to a gallery's worth of paintings of stone-faced old New Orleanians.

St Louis Cathedral   Cathedral

(📞504-525-9585; www.stlouiscathedral.org; Jackson Sq; donations accepted, self-guided tour $1; ⊙8am-4pm, mass noon Mon-Fri, 5pm Sat, 9am & 11am Sun) One of the best examples of French architecture in the country, this triple-spired cathedral is dedicated to Louis IX, the French king sainted in 1297; it's the most innocuous bit of Gallic heritage in the heart of an American city. In addition to hosting black, white and Creole Catholic congregants, St Louis has also attracted those who, in the best New Orleanian tradition, mix their influences, such as *vodou* (voodoo) queen Marie Laveau.

Historic New Orleans Collection   Museum

(THNOC; 📞504-523-4662; www.hnoc.org; 533 Royal St; admission free, tours $5; ⊙9:30am-4:30pm Tue-Sat, 10:30am-4:30pm Sun, tours 10am, 11am, 2pm & 3pm Tue-Sat) A combination of preserved buildings, museums and research centers all rolled into one, the Historic New Orleans Collection is a good introduction to the history of of the city. The complex is anchored by its Royal St campus, which presents a series of regularly rotating exhibits and occasional temporary exhibits. Some of the artifacts on offer include an original Jazz Fest poster, transfer documents of the Louisiana Purchase, and utterly disturbing slave advertisements.

Presbytère   Museum

(📞800-568-6968, 504-568-6968; http://louisianastatemuseum.org/museums/the-presbytere; 751 Chartres St; adult/student $6/5; ⊙10am-4:30pm Tue-Sun, closed Mon) ✈ The lovely Presbytère building, designed in 1791 as a rectory for the St Louis Cathedral, serves as New Orleans' Mardi Gras museum. You'll find there's more to the city's most famous celebration than wanton debauchery – or, at least, discover the many levels of meaning behind the debauchery. There's an encyclopedia's worth of material on the krewes, secret societies, costumes and racial histories of the Mardi Gras tapestry, all intensely illuminating and easy to follow.

◎ Mid-City & the Tremé

Backstreet Cultural Museum   Museum

(📞504-522-4806; www.backstreetmuseum.org; 1116 Henriette Delille St; per person $10; ⊙10am-4pm Tue-Sat) Mardi Gras Indian suits grab the spotlight with dazzling flair – and finely crafted detail – in this informative museum, which examines the distinctive elements of African American culture in New Orleans. The museum isn't terribly big – it's the former Blandin's Funeral Home – but if you have any interest in the suits and rituals of Mardi Gras Indians as well as Second Line parades and Social Aid & Pleasure Clubs (the local black community version of civic associations), you need to stop by.

City Park   Park

(☎504-482-4888; www.neworleanscitypark. com; Esplanade Ave & City Park Ave; P) Live oaks, Spanish moss and lazy bayous frame this masterpiece of urban planning. Three miles long and one wide, dotted with gardens, waterways, bridges and home to a captivating art museum, City Park is bigger than Central Park in NYC, and is New Orleans' prettiest green space. Although a planned golf course has tampered with the park's natural beauty, some areas still feel like a slightly tamed expression of the forest and Louisiana wetlands that are the natural backdrop of the city.

New Orleans
Museum of Art   Museum

(NOMA; ☎504-658-4100; www.noma.org; 1 Collins Diboll Circle; adult/child 7-17yr $12/6; ☺10am-6pm Tue-Thu, to 9pm Fri, 10am-5pm Sat, 11am-5pm Sun) Inside City Park, this elegant museum was opened in 1911 and is well worth a visit both for its special exhibitions, gorgeous marble atrium, and top-floor galleries of African, Asian, Native American and Oceanic art. Its **sculpture garden** (☺10am-6pm Mon-Fri, to 5pm Sat & Sun) FREE contains a cutting-edge collection in lush, meticulously planned grounds.

Louis Armstrong Park   Park

(835 N Rampart St; ☺sunrise-sunset) The entrance to this massive park has got to be one of the greatest gateways in the US, a picturesque arch that ought rightfully be the final set piece in a period drama about Jazz Age New Orleans. The original Congo Sq is here, as well as a Louis Armstrong statue and a bust of Sidney Bechet. The **Mahalia Jackson Theater** (☎504-525-1052, box office 504-287-0350; www.mahaliajacksontheater.com; 1419 Basin St) hosts opera and Broadway productions. The park often hosts live music festivals throughout the year.

St Louis Cemetery No 1   Cemetery

(☎504-525-3377; www.saveourcemeteries.org/st-louis-cemetery-no-1; 1300 St Louis St; guided

New Orleans for Children

In addition to the enormous green space of City Park and the carnival atmosphere of Jackson Square, these are good bets for entertaining kids:

Audubon Zoological Gardens (☎504-861-2537; www.auduboninstitute.org; 6500 Magazine St; adult/child 2-12yr/senior $23/18/20; ☺10am-5pm Mon-Fri, to 6pm Sat & Sun; P) This wonderful zoo contains African, Asian and South American landscapes and fauna, as well as the ultra-cool Louisiana Swamp exhibit, full of alligators, bobcats, foxes, bears and otters. During the summer months, part of the zoo becomes a dedicated water park for the kids.

Aquarium of the Americas (☎504-581-4629; www.auduboninstitute.org; 1 Canal St; adult/senior/child $30/25/22; ☺10am-5pm Tue-Sun;) Part of the Audubon Institute, the immense Aquarium of the Americas is loosely regional, with exhibits that delve beneath the surface of the Mississippi River, Gulf of Mexico, Caribbean Sea and far-off Amazon rainforest. The impressive Great Maya Reef lures visitors into a 30ft-long clear tunnel running through a 'submerged' Mayan city, home to exotic fish. Upstairs, the penguin colony, the sea-horse gallery and a tank for playful otters are perennially popular. In the Mississippi River Gallery, look for the rare white alligator.

tour adult/child $20/free; ☺tours 10am, 11:30am & 1pm Mon-Sat, 10am Sun) This cemetery received the remains of many early Creoles, who were buried above-ground in family tombs due to the shallow water table. The supposed grave of *vodou* queen Marie Laveau is here, scratched with 'XXX's from spellbound devotees. By request of the family that owns the tomb, do not add to this graffiti; to do so is also illegal. Cemetery visitation is limited to relatives of the interred and approved tours, which can be arranged

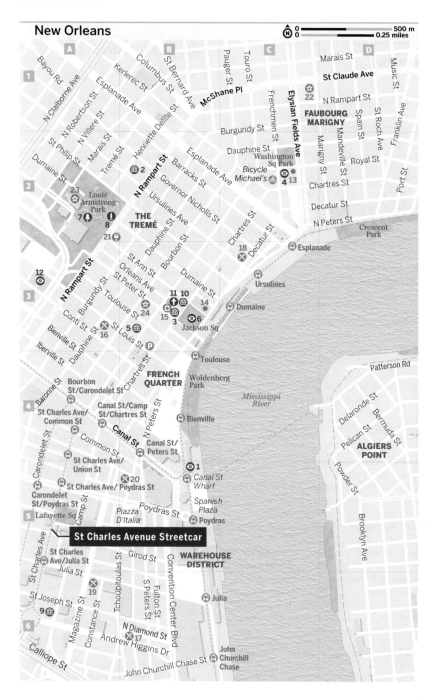

New Orleans

0 — 500 m
0 — 0.25 miles

New Orleans

◎ Sights
 1 Aquarium of the Americas..........................B5
 2 Backstreet Cultural Museum B2
 3 Cabildo...B3
 4 Frenchmen Art Market...............................C2
 5 Historic New Orleans Collection B3
 6 Jackson Square...B3
 7 Louis Armstrong Park A2
 8 Louis Armstrong Statue.............................A2
 9 Ogden Museum of Southern Art..............A6
10 Presbytère..B3
11 St Louis Cathedral B3
12 St Louis Cemetery No 1..............................A3

◎ Activities, Courses & Tours
13 Confederacy of Cruisers C2
14 Friends of the Cabildo B3

◎ Shopping
15 Faulkner House Books................................B3

◎ Eating
16 Bayona...A3
17 Cochon Butcher..B6
18 Coop's Place..C3
19 Peche Seafood Grill......................................A6
20 Restaurant August B5

◎ Drinking & Nightlife
21 Tonique..A2

◎ Entertainment
22 AllWays Lounge C1
23 Mahalia Jackson Theater A2
24 Preservation Hall B3
    Spotted Cat .... (see 4)

via Save Our Cemeteries and booked via that organization's website.

◎ Faubourg Marigny & Bywater

Frenchmen Art Market   Market

(☏504-941-1149; www.frenchmenartmarket.com; 619 Frenchmen St; ⊙7pm-1am Thu-Sat, 6pm-midnight Sun) ✿ Independent artists and artisans line this alleyway market, which has built a reputation as one of the finest spots in town to find a unique gift to take home as your New Orleans souvenir. 'Art,' in this case, includes clever T-shirts, hand-crafted jewelry, trinkets and, yes, a nice selection of prints and original artwork.

Crescent Park   Park

(☏504-636-6400; www.crescentparknola.org; Piety, Chartres & Mazant Sts; ⊙6am-6:30pm, to 7:30pm mid-Mar–early Nov; ℗) ✿ This waterfront park is our favorite spot in the city for taking in the Mississippi. Enter over the enormous arch at Piety and Chartres Sts, or at the steps at Marigny and N Peters, and watch the fog blanket the nearby skyline. A promenade meanders past an angular metal and concrete conceptual 'wharf' (placed next to the burned remains of the former commercial wharf). A dog park is located near the Mazant St entrance.

◎ CBD & Warehouse District

Ogden Museum of Southern Art   Museum

(☏504-539-9650; www.ogdenmuseum.org; 925 Camp St; adult/child 5-17yr $13.50/6.75; ⊙10am-5pm Wed-Mon, to 8pm Thu) One of our favorite museums in the city manages to be beautiful, educational and unpretentious all at once. New Orleans entrepreneur Roger Houston Ogden has assembled one of the finest collections of Southern art anywhere, which includes impressionist landscapes, outsider folk-art quirkiness and contemporary installation work. On Thursday nights, pop in for Ogden after Hours, when you can listen to great Southern musicians and sip wine with a fun-loving, arts-obsessed crowd in the midst of the masterpieces.

Blaine Kern's Mardi Gras World   Museum

(☏504-475-2057; www.mardigrasworld.com; 1380 Port of New Orleans Pl; adult/senior/child 2-11yr $20/16/13; ⊙tours 9:30am-4:30pm; ⋒) We dare say Mardi Gras World is one of the happiest places in New Orleans by day – but at night it must turn into one of the most terrifying funhouses this side of Hell. It's all those *faces,* the dragons, clowns, kings and fairies, leering and dead-eyed... That said, we love touring Mardi Gras World – the studio warehouse of Blaine Kern (Mr Mardi

What is Vodou?

Vodou (voodoo), as a faith, comes from West Africa. It is a belief system that stresses ancestor worship and the presence of the divine via a pantheon of spirits and deities. Slaves from Africa and the Caribbean brought *vodou* to Louisiana, where it melded with Roman Catholicism. One faith stressed saints and angels, the other ancestor spirits and supernatural forces; all came under the rubric of *vodou*.

The most well-known *vodou* practitioner was Marie Laveau, a 19th-century mixed race woman who married a Haitian free person of color. The legends surrounding Laveau are legion, but she is popularly associated with leading *vodou* rituals near Bayou St John and providing magic spells for high-class New Orleans women. It's a fair bet much of this folklore was sensationalized by the popular press of the time; stories of magic brown-skinned women performing devilish rituals sold newspapers and magazines, at least more so than a sober recording of a religion that mixed Western Christianity and African ancestor worship.

Gras) and family, who have been making jaw-dropping parade floats since 1947. Tours last 30 to 45 minutes.

Garden District & Central City

Lafayette Cemetery No 1   Cemetery

(Washington Ave, at Prytania St; ⊙7am-3pm) Shaded by groves of lush greenery, this cemetery exudes a strong sense of Southern subtropical Gothic. Built in 1833, it is divided by two intersecting footpaths that form a cross. Look out for the crypts built by fraternal organizations such as the Jefferson Fire Company No 22, which took care of their members and their families in large shared tombs. Some of the wealthier family tombs were built of marble, with elaborate

details, but most were constructed simply of inexpensive plastered brick.

TOURS

Confederacy of Cruisers   Cycling

(☎504-400-5468; www.confederacyofcruisers. com; 634 Elysian Fields Ave; tours $49-89) Our favorite bicycle tours in New Orleans set you up on cruiser bikes that come with fat tires and padded seats for Nola's flat, pot-holed roads. The main 'Creole New Orleans' tour takes in the best architecture of the Marigny, Bywater, Esplanade Ave and the Tremé. Confederacy also does a 'History of Drinking' tour (for those 21 and over) and a tasty culinary tour.

Friends of the Cabildo   Walking

(☎504-523-3939; www.friendsofthecabildo.org; 523 St Ann St; adult/student $20/15; ⊙10am & 1:30pm Tue-Sun) ❢ These walking tours are led by knowledgeable (and often funny) docents who will give you a great primer on the history of the French Quarter, the stories behind some of the most famous streets and details of the area's many architectural styles. Tours depart from the 1850 House Museum Store.

SHOPPING

Faulkner House Books   Books

(☎504-524-2940; www.faulknerhousebooks.com; 624 Pirate's Alley; ⊙10am-6pm) The erudite owner of this former residence of author William Faulkner sells rare first editions and new titles in an airy, elegant, charming independent bookshop.

Magazine Antique Mall   Antiques

(☎504-896-9994; www.magazineantiquemall. com; 3017 Magazine St; ⊙10:30am-5:30pm, noon-5:30pm Sun) Scary baby dolls. Hats. Chandeliers. Coca-Cola memorabilia. Inside this overstuffed emporium, rummagers are likely to score items of interest in the dozen or so stalls, where independent dealers peddle an intriguing and varied range of antique bric-a-brac. Bargain hunters aren't likely to have much luck, though.

⊗ EATING

This city finds itself in its food; meals are both expressions of identity and bridges between the city's many divisions.

⊗ French Quarter

Coop's Place   Cajun $$

(🖉504-525-9053; www.coopsplace.net; 1109 Decatur St; mains $8-20; ⊙11am-3am) Coop's is an authentic Cajun dive but more rocked out. Make no mistake: it's a grotty chaotic place, the servers have attitude and the layout is annoying. But it's worth it for the food: rabbit jambalaya, chicken with shrimp and *tasso* (smoked ham) in a cream sauce – there's no such thing as 'too heavy' here. No patrons under 21.

Bayona   Louisianan $$$

(🖉504-525-4455; www.bayona.com; 430 Dauphine St; mains $28-34; ⊙11:30am-1:30pm Wed-Sun, plus 6-9:30pm Mon-Thu, 5:30-10pm Fri & Sat; 🖉) Bayona is one of our favorite splurges in the Quarter. It's rich but not overwhelming, classy but unpretentious, innovative without being precocious, and all round just a very fine spot for a meal. The menu changes regularly, but expect fresh fish, fowl and game prepared in a way that comes off as elegant and deeply cozy at the same time.

⊗ Mid-City & the Tremé

Parkway Tavern   Sandwiches $

(🖉504-482-3047; www.parkwaypoorboys.com; 538 Hagan Ave; po'boys mains $8-13; ⊙11am-10pm Wed-Mon; P🖉) Who makes the best po'boy in New Orleans? Honestly, who can say? But tell a local you think the top sandwich comes from Parkway and you will get, at the least, a nod of respect. The roast beef in particular – a craft some would say is dying among the great po'boy makers – is messy as hell and twice as good.

Willie Mae's Scotch House   Southern US $

(🖉504-822-9503; www.williemaesnola.com; 2401 St Ann St; fried chicken $11; ⊙10am-5pm Mon-Sat) Willie Mae's has been dubbed the best fried chicken in the world by the James Beard Foundation, the Food Network and other media, and in this case, the hype isn't far off – this is superlative fried bird. The white beans are also amazing. The drawback is everyone knows about it, so expect long lines, sometimes around the block.

Dooky Chase   Creole $$

(🖉504-821-0600; www.dookychaserestaurant. com; 2301 Orleans Ave; buffet $20, mains $20-25; ⊙11am-3pm Tue-Thu, 11am-3pm & 5-9pm Fri) Ray Charles wrote 'Early in the Morning' about Dooky's; civil rights leaders used it as informal headquarters in the 1960s; and Barack Obama ate here after his inauguration. Leah Chase's labor of love is the backbone of the Tremé, and her buffets are the stuff of legend, a carnival of top-notch gumbo and excellent fried chicken served in a white-linen dining room.

⊗ Faubourg Marigny & Bywater

Pizza Delicious   Italian $

(🖉504-676-8482; www.pizzadelicious.com; 617 Piety St; pizza by slice from $2.25, whole pie from $15; ⊙11am-11pm Tue-Sun; 🖉🖉🖉) 'Pizza D's' pies are thin-crust, New York–style and *good*. The preparation is pretty simple, but the ingredients are fresh as the morning and consistently top-notch. An easy, family-friendly ambience makes for a lovely spot for casual dinner, and it serves some good beer too if you're in the mood. Vegan pizza available. The outdoor area is pet-friendly.

Bacchanal   Modern American $

(🖉504-948-9111; www.bacchanalwine.com; 600 Poland Ave; mains $8-18, cheese from $6; ⊙11am-11pm Sun-Thu, to midnight Fri & Sat) From the outside, Bacchanal looks like a leaning Bywater shack; inside are racks of wine and stinky but sexy cheese. Musicians play in the garden, while cooks dispense delicious meals on paper plates from the kitchen in the back; on any given day you may try chorizo-stuffed dates or seared diver scallops that will blow your gastronomic mind.

Red's Chinese   Chinese $$

(🖉504-304-6030; www.redschinese.com; 3048 St Claude Ave; mains $5-17; ⊙noon-11pm) Red's has upped the Chinese cuisine game in New Orleans in a big way. The chefs aren't afraid to add lashings of Louisiana flavor, yet this isn't what we'd call 'fusion' cuisine. The food is grounded deeply in spicy Sichuan flavors, which pairs well with the occasional flash of cayenne. The General Lee's chicken is stupendously good.

CBD & Warehouse District

Cochon Butcher   Sandwiches $

(☏504-588-7675; www.cochonbutcher.com; 930 Tchoupitoulas St; mains $10-14; ⊙10am-10pm Mon-Thu, to 11pm Fri & Sat, to 4pm Sun) Tucked behind the slightly more formal Cochon, this sandwich and meat shop calls itself a 'swine bar and deli.' We call it one of our favorite sandwich shops in the city. From the savory sandwiches to the fun-loving cocktails, this welcoming place encapsulates the best of New Orleans.

Peche Seafood Grill   Seafood $$

(☏504-522-1744; www.pecherestaurant.com; 800 Magazine St; small plates $9-14, mains $14-27; ⊙11am-10pm Sun-Thu, to 11pm Fri & Sat) Coastal seafood dishes are prepared simply here, but unexpected flourishes – whether from salt, spices or magic – sear the deliciousness onto your taste buds. The vibe is convivial, with a happy, stylish crowd sipping and savoring among the exposed-brick walls and wooden beams. A large whole fish, made for sharing, is a signature preparation, but we recommend starting with the smoked tuna dip and the fried bread with sea salt.

Restaurant August   Creole $$$

(☏504-299-9777; www.restaurantaugust.com; 301 Tchoupitoulas St; lunch $23-42, dinner $37-47, 5-course tasting menu per person $97, with wine pairings $147; ⊙5-10pm daily, 11am-2pm Fri; ☏) For a little romance, reserve a table at Restaurant August, an outpost of chef John Besh's restaurant empire. This converted 19th-century tobacco warehouse, with its flickering candles and warm, soft shades, earns a nod for most aristocratic dining room in New Orleans, but somehow manages to be both intimate and lively. Delicious meals take you to another level of gastronomic perception. The signature speckled trout Pontchartrain is layered with lump crabmeat, wild mushrooms and hollandaise.

⊗ Garden District & Central City

Surrey's Juice Bar American $

(☎504-524-3828; www.surreysnola.com; 1418 Magazine St; breakfast & lunch $6.50-13; ☺8am-3pm; ☝) Surrey's makes a simple bacon-and-egg sandwich taste – and look – like the most delicious breakfast you've ever been served. And you know what? It probably *is* the best. Boudin biscuits; eggs scrambled with salmon; biscuits swimming in salty sausage gravy; and a shrimp, grits and bacon dish that should be illegal. And the juice, as you might guess, is blessedly fresh.

⊗ Uptown & Riverbend

Ba Chi Canteen Vietnamese $

(☎504-373-5628; www.facebook.com/bachi canteenla; 7900 Maple St; mains $4-15; ☺11am-2:30pm & 5:30-9pm Mon-Wed, 11am-2:30pm & 5:30-10pm Thu & Fri, 11am-3:30pm & 5:30-10pm Sat, closed Sun; ☝) Do not be skeptical of the bacos. These pillowy bundles of deliciousness – a *banh bao* crossed with a taco – successfully merge the subtle seasonings of Vietnamese fillings with the foldable convenience of a taco-shaped steamed flour

bun. Pho and banh mi – dubbed po'boys here – round out the menu.

Boucherie Southern US $$

(☎504-862-5514; www.boucherie-nola.com; 1506 S Carrollton Ave; lunch $12-23, dinner $15-26; ☺11am-3pm Tue-Sat, 5:30-9:30pm Mon-Sat, 10:30am-2:30pm Sun) The thick, glistening cuts of bacon on the BLT can only be the work of the devil – or chef Nathanial Zimet, whose house-cured meats and succulent Southern dishes are lauded citywide. Savor boudin balls with garlic aioli, blackened shrimp in bacon vinaigrette, and smoked Wagyu brisket with gloriously stinky garlic-Parmesan fries. The Krispy Kreme bread pudding with rum syrup is a wonder.

Clancy's Creole $$$

(☎504-895-1111; www.clancysneworleans.com; 6100 Annunciation St; lunch $17-20, dinner $28-40; ☺11:30am-2pm Thu & Fri, 5-10:30pm Mon-Sat) This white-tablecloth neighborhood restaurant embraces style, the good life and Creole cuisine with a chattering *joie de vivre* and top-notch service. The city's professional set comes here to gossip and savor the specialties: fried oysters and brie, veal

★ Top Five for Eating

Coop's Place (p213)

Dooky Chase (p213)

Bayona (p213)

Clancy's (p215)

Boucherie (p215)

From left: Seafood gumbo (p352); Market food stall; po'boys (Southern-style sandwiches)

Detour: Old New Orleans Rum Distillery

A short drive north of the Marigny is the **Old New Orleans Rum Distillery** (☏504-945-9400; www.oldneworleansrum. com; 2815 Frenchmen St; admission $15; ☺tours noon, 2pm & 4pm Mon-Sat, 2pm & 4pm Sun). Founded by local artist James Michalopoulos and friends, the distillery makes great spirits that you'll find in most local bars. You can sample all of them, including a rare vintage unavailable outside the factory, on an entertaining 45-minute distillery tour. Warning: there's a lot of free rum available, so you may want to visit on a full stomach.

The distillery offers a complimentary shuttle from the French Market (behind the Organic Banana stall) at 10:30am, 1:30pm and 3:30pm Monday to Saturday, and at 1:30pm and 3:30pm on Sunday.

BRENT HOFACKER / SHUTTERSTOCK ©

with crabmeat and béarnaise, and lobster and mushroom risotto. Want to go where the locals go? Come here, and dress up a little. Reservations recommended.

🍸 DRINKING & NIGHTLIFE

Tonique   Bar
(☏504-324-6045; www.bartonique.com; 820 N Rampart St; ☺noon-2am) Tonique is a bartender's bar. Seriously, on a Sunday night, when the weekend rush is over, we've seen no less than three of the city's top bartenders arrive here to unwind. Why? Because this gem mixes some of the best drinks in the

city, and it has a spirits menu as long as a Tolstoy novel to draw upon.

NOLA Brewing   Brewery
(☏504-301-1117; www.nolabrewing.com; 3001 Tchoupitoulas St; ☺taproom 11am-11pm, tours 2-3pm Fri, to 4pm Sat & Sun) This cavernous brewery welcomes guests throughout the weekend for a free brewery tour that kicks off with sloshy cups of craft brew and a food truck or two out front. The rest of the week? Stop by the taproom, which has plenty of beers on tap and a roof deck.

Twelve Mile Limit   Bar
(☏504-488-8114; www.facebook.com/twelve. mile.limit; 500 S Telemachus St; ☺5pm-2am Mon-Wed, 11am-2am Thu & Fri, 10am-2am Sat, 10am-midnight Sun) Twelve Mile is simply a great bar. It's staffed by people who have the skill, both behind the bar and in the kitchen, to work in four-star spots, but who chose to set up shop in a neighborhood, for a neighborhood. The mixed drinks are excellent, the match of any mixologist's cocktail in Manhattan, and the vibe is super accepting.

✪ ENTERTAINMENT

Tipitina's   Live Music
(☏504-895-8477; www.tipitinas.com; 501 Napoleon Ave; cover $5-20) 'Tips,' as locals call it, is one of New Orleans' great musical meccas. The legendary Uptown nightclub, which takes its name from Professor Longhair's 1953 hit single, is the site of some of the city's most memorable shows, particularly when big names such as Dr John come home to roost. Outstanding music from local talent packs 'em in year-round.

Preservation Hall   Jazz
(☏504-522-2841; www.preservationhall.com; 726 St Peter St; cover Sun-Thu $15, Fri & Sat $20, reserved seats $34-45; ☺showtimes 8pm, 9pm & 10pm Mon-Wed, 6pm, 8pm, 9pm & 10pm Thu-Sun) Preservation Hall, housed in a former art gallery that dates to 1803, is one of the most storied live-music venues in New Orleans. The resident performers, the Preservation Hall Jazz Band, are ludicrously tal-

ented, and regularly tour around the world. 'The Hall' dates to 1961, when Barbara Reid and Grayson 'Ken' Mills formed the Society for the Preservation of New Orleans Jazz.

Maple Leaf Bar   Live Music

(☎504-866-9359; www.mapleleafbar.com; 8316 Oak St; cover around $10; ⊙3pm-late) The premier nighttime destination in the Riverbend area, the legendary Maple Leaf's dimly lit, pressed-tin caverns are the kind of environs you'd expect from a New Orleans juke joint. Work up a sweat on the small dancefloor or relax at the bar in the next room. The Rebirth Brass Band plays Tuesdays, starting between 10pm and 11pm.

Spotted Cat   Live Music

(www.spottedcatmusicclub.com; 623 Frenchmen St; ⊙2pm-2am Mon-Fri, noon-2am Sat & Sun) The Cat might just be your smoky dream of a New Orleans jazz club, a thumping sweatbox where drinks are served in plastic cups, impromptu dances break out at the drop of a feathered hat, and the music is always exceptional. Fair warning, though, it can get crowded.

AllWays Lounge   Theater

(☎504-218-5778; www.theallwayslounge.net; 2240 St Claude Ave; ⊙6pm-2am Sun-Thu, to 4am Fri & Sat) In a city full of funky music venues, the AllWays stands out as one of the funkiest. On any night of the week you may see experimental guitar, local theater, thrash-y rock, live comedy or a '60s-inspired shagadelic dance party. Also, drinks are super cheap.

ⓘ INFORMATION

New Orleans Convention & Visitors Bureau

(☎504-566-5003; www.neworleanscvb.com; 2020 St Charles Ave; ⊙8:30am-5pm) Both the CVB's website and the office are good resources on New Orleans tourism.

ⓘ GETTING THERE & AROUND

TO/FROM THE AIRPORT

Louis Armstrong New Orleans International Airport (MSY; ☎504-303-7500; www.flymsy.com; 900 Airline Hwy; ☎) is located in the suburb of Kenner, 13 miles west of the city.

Most visitors take the Airport Shuttle to and from the airport. It offers frequent service between the airport and downtown hotels, although it can be time-consuming, especially if your hotel is the last stop.

A taxi ride downtown costs a flat rate of $36 for one or two passengers or $15 per person for three or more passengers.

If your baggage is not too unwieldy and you're in no hurry, Jefferson Transit (www.jefferson transit.org) offers the cheapest ride downtown aboard its **E2 Airport Downtown Express** (fare $2). The ride to New Orleans follows city streets and stops approximately every two blocks. On weekdays, until 6:52pm, the bus goes all the way to Tulane and Loyola Ave, at the edge of downtown and the French Quarter; on weekends it will only get you as far as the corner of Tulane St and Carrollton Ave. From there it's a cheap cab ride to the French Quarter.

BICYCLE

Flat New Orleans is easy to cycle – you can cross the entirety of town in 45 minutes. **Bicycle Michael's** (☎504-945-9505; www.bicycle michaels.com; 622 Frenchmen St; per day from $35; ⊙10am-5pm Sun-Tue & Thu, to 7pm Fri & Sat) rents wheels from its shop in the Marigny.

PUBLIC TRANSPORTATION

Streetcars (aka trolleys or trams) have made a comeback in New Orleans, with four lines serving key routes in the city. They are run by the Regional Transit Authority (www.norta.com). Fares cost $1.25 – have exact change – or purchase a Jazzy Pass (one-/three-day unlimited rides $3/9), which is also good on buses. Streetcars run about every 15 to 20 minutes, leaning toward every 30 minutes later at night.

Bus service is decent, but limited. Most visitors only use buses when venturing uptown or out to City Park. Fare is $1.25 plus 25¢ per transfer.

TAXI

For a taxi, call **United Cabs** (☎504-522-9771; www.unitedcabs.com).

In this Chapter

Congress Avenue
Bridge Bat Colony 222
Bob Bullock Texas
State History Museum 224
Sights... 228
Activities... 229
Tours 229
Shopping 231
Eating.. 232
Drinking & Nightlife........................ 235
Entertainment................................. 236

Austin at a Glance...

A big city with a small-town heart, Austin earns the love with great music, culinary prowess, whip-smart locals and a sociable streak that's impossible to resist.

Quality live performances go down every night in its countless bars and clubs. The laid-back food scene is awesome, with busted-up food trucks, down-home barbecue joints and whimsical farm-to-table restaurants cooking up glory. There's heaps of outdoor action on the lakes and trails. And it's all wrapped in a funky, artsy, eccentric package. Austin keeps on keeping it weird.

Two Days in Austin

Start at the **Bob Bullock Texas State History Museum** (p224). Wander Guadalupe St for lunch and groovy murals, then cool off at **Barton Springs Pool** (p229). After dark, plug into Austin's live-music scene downtown. On day two, explore the **Texas State Capitol** (p228). Head to South Congress for lunch and shopping. Stroll the **Ann & Roy Butler Trail** (p228). If it's summer, don't miss the **bat colony** (p222). End at **Broken Spoke** (p236).

Four Days in Austin

On day three, visit the **Lyndon Baines Johnson (LBJ) Library & Museum** (p228), go hiking at **Mt Bonnell** (p229) and chow in one of the city's many barbecue joints. Check out the **Lady Bird Johnson Wildflower Center** (p229) on day four, followed by more South Congress action at **Güero's Taco Bar** (p234) and the **Continental Club** (p236).

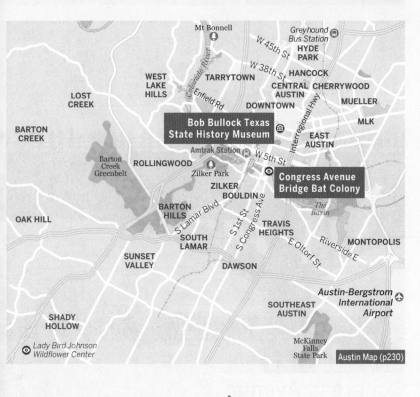

Mt Bonnell

Greyhound
Bus Station

W 45th St

HYDE
PARK

Colorado River

W 38th St

WEST
LAKE
HILLS

TARRYTOWN

HANCOCK

LOST
CREEK

Enfield Rd

CENTRAL
AUSTIN

CHERRYWOOD

DOWNTOWN

MUELLER

BARTON
CREEK

MLK

**Bob Bullock Texas
State History Museum**

EAST
AUSTIN

Interregional Hwy

Amtrak Station

W 5th St

Barton
Creek
Greenbelt

ROLLINGWOOD

Zilker Park

**Congress Avenue
Bridge Bat Colony**

ZILKER

BOULDIN

The
Basin

S Lamar Blvd

BARTON
HILLS

OAK HILL

S 1st St

S Congress Ave

TRAVIS
HEIGHTS

SOUTH
LAMAR

MONTOPOLIS

Riverside E

SUNSET
VALLEY

E Oltorf St

DAWSON

Austin-Bergstrom
International
Airport

SOUTHEAST
AUSTIN

SHADY
HOLLOW

Lady Bird Johnson
Wildflower Center

McKinney
Falls
State Park

Austin Map (p230)

Arriving in Austin

**Austin-Bergstrom International
Airport** The limited-stop Airport Flyer
(bus 100) goes to downtown and the
University of Texas (UT; $1.25, departing
every 30 minutes, 20 minutes to downtown, 35 minutes to UT). SuperShuttle
offers a shared-van service to downtown hotels for about $14 one way. Taxis
cost from $25 to $30.

Where to Stay

Most lodgings are in South Austin,
Downtown and the UT & Central Austin
area. South Austin holds the funky
mother lode, with excellent boutique
hotels. Artsy B&Bs cluster around UT
& Central Austin. For budgeteers, a
handful of hostels dot the city. Prices
skyrocket during SXSW (mid-March),
the Formula 1 Grand Prix (late October
or November) and Austin City Limits
Festival (October).

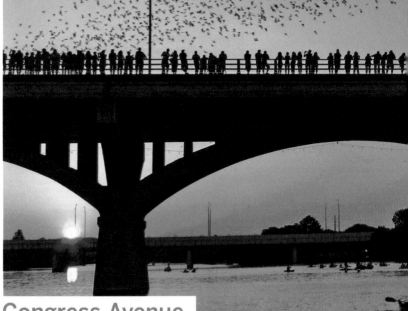

Congress Avenue Bridge Bat Colony

Bat Story

Looking like a special effect from a B movie, a funnel cloud of up to 1.5 million Mexican free-tailed bats swarms from under the Congress Avenue Bridge nightly from late March to early November.

The Congress Avenue Bridge was built in 1910. After improvements to the bridge in 1980, a colony of Mexican free-tailed bats moved in. Apparently the bats like the bridge's nooks and crannies for roosting. These tiny winged mammals live in Mexico in the winter then migrate north when Austin warms up. They typically swarm out at twilight to feed. The colony is made up entirely of female and young animals. Such is the bat density that bat radars have detected bat columns up to 10,000 bat feet (3050m) high. In June, each female gives birth to one pup, and every night at dusk, the families take to the skies in search of food.

Great For...

☑ Don't Miss

Bat Conservation International (www. batcon.org) runs programs throughout the bat season.

Bat Colony

❶ Need to Know

Congress Ave; ☉sunset Apr-Nov

✕ Take a Break

Many good restaurants line S Congress Ave south of the bridge. Try Hopdoddy Burger Bar (p233).

★ Top Tip

To find out what time the bats will emerge, call the Bat Hotline on ☏512-327-9721 ext 3.

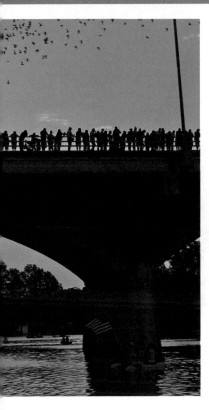

Bat Viewing from Land

It's become an Austin tradition to head to Lady Bird Lake to watch the bats swarm out to feed on an estimated 10,000lb to 20,000lb of insects per night. The swarm looks a lot like a fast-moving, black, chittering river. Best places on land for viewing? One easy spot is the sidewalk on the eastern side of the bridge. You can also try the grassy lawn behind the Austin-American Statesman building at 305 S Congress Ave, on the southeast end of the bridge. Parking in the Statesman lot is $6 for four hours. Don't miss this nightly show. The best viewing is in August.a

Bat Cruises & Kayak Tours

To add a little adventure to your bat watching, view the bats from a boat or kayak on Lady Bird Lake. During bat season, **Lone Star Riverboat** (☏512-327-1388; www.lonestarriverboat.com; adult/child $10/7; ☉Mar–mid-Dec) offers nightly sunset bat-watching trips on its 32ft electric cruiser. The company's dock is on the south shore of Lady Bird Lake near the Hyatt; **Capital Cruises** (☏512-480-9264; www.capitalcruises.com; adult/child $10/5) also runs tours. **Live Love Paddle** (www.livelovepaddle) and **Congress Avenue Kayaks** (www.congresskayaks.com) offer guided evening bat tours.

Bob Bullock Texas State History Museum

This is no dusty historical museum. Big and glitzy, it shows off the Lone Star State's history, from when it used to be part of Mexico up to the present.

Great For...

☑ Don't Miss

The not-so-pretty Goddess of Liberty in her display.

La Belle: The Ship That Changed History

A new permanent exhibit on the 1st floor showcases the history – and the recovered hull – of *La Belle*, a French ship that sank off the Gulf Coast in the 1680s, changing the course of Texas history. Exhibits explore the ship's remarkable story: sent by King Louis XIV of France under the command of René-Robert Cavelier, Sieur de la Salle, *La Belle* was one of four vessels carrying 400 passengers to the new world, where they were to establish a colony and trade routes. All four ships were eventually lost, with *La Belle* sinking off the Texas coast in 1686. Archaeologists have recovered 1.4 million artifacts; muskets, glass beads and farming tools are currently on display.

W Martin Luther King Jr Blvd

University of Texas at Austin

Bob Bullock Texas State History Museum ◎

Colorado St

W 18th St

N Congress Ave

❶ Need to Know

☎512-936-8746; www.thestoryoftexas. com; 1800 Congress Ave; adult/child $13/9; ⊙9am-5pm Mon-Sat, noon-5pm Sun

✖ Take a Break

Grab at beer at **Scholz Garten** (☎512-474-1958; 1607 San Jacinto Blvd; ⊙11am-11pm).

★ Top Tip

The always compelling Blanton Museum of Art (p228) is across the street, so save an hour to check it out.

Story of Texas

The Texas History galleries are the core of the museum, and more than 700 artifacts are displayed across three floors. The 1st floor focuses on *La Belle*, while exhibits on the 2nd floor trace Texas history from 1821 to 1936. A statue of Texas statesman and hero Sam Houston marks the entrance.

As you explore, you'll discover more about Texas booster Stephen F Austin (check out his pine desk) and learn more about the Alamo, Texas Comanches and the lives of African Americans. Oil and cattle exhibits are highlights on the 3rd floor while the Austin City Limits display livens up the scene with music.

IMAX & The Star of Destiny

The museum also houses Austin's first IMAX theater (check website for listings; adult/child four to 17 years $9/7) and the Texas Spirit Theater (adult/child four to 17 years $5/4). The Texas Spirit Theater is where you can see *The Star of Destiny*, a 15-minute special-effects film that's simultaneously high-tech and hokey fun.

South Congress Stroll

You won't find any chain stores along S Congress Ave, and the indie shops here are truly unique. People-watching is superb.

Start Lucy in Disguise
Finish Tesoros Trading Co
Distance 0.1 mile
Duration 1 hour

6 Colorful and unique arts-and-crafts, many with a Latin influence, stock **Tesoros Trading Co** (☎512-447-7500; 1500 S Congress Ave; ☺11am-6pm Sun-Fri, 10am-6pm Sat)

W Monroe St

Classic Photo Allens Boots' (p231) neon sign

3 Towering aisles of men's and women's cowboy boots beckon at **Allens Boots** (p231).

W Milton St

4

4 Willy Wonka would be impressed by **Big Top Candy Shop** (p232), crammed with sweet delights.

0 100 m
0 0.05 miles

Take a Break... Güero's Taco Bar (p234) Good-time margaritas and Tex-Mex food.

W Elizabeth St

FINISH 6

E Elizabeth St

START 1

2

The Church on Congress Avenue

3

E Monroe St

S Congress Ave

5

E Milton St

1 At **Lucy in Disguise** (512-444-2002; www.lucyindisguise.com; 1506 S Congress Ave; 11am-7pm Mon-Sat, noon-6pm Sun) costumes and vintage duds highlight the joyful weirdness of Austin.

2 Quirky wares fill **Uncommon Objects** (p231), an enticing antique mall with 20-plus vendors.

5 South Congress Hotel (www.southcongresshotel.com; 1603 S Congress Ave) is prime for minimalist-cool decor and people-watching patios.

◉ SIGHTS

◎ Downtown

Texas State
Capitol   Historic Building
(📞512-463-5495, tours 512-463-0063; cnr 11th
St & Congress Ave; ⏰7am-10pm Mon-Fri, 9am-
8pm Sat & Sun; 🚻) **FREE** Built in 1888 from
sunset-red granite, this state capitol is the
largest in the US, backing up the ubiquitous
claim that everything is bigger in Texas.
If nothing else, take a peek at the lovely
rotunda – be sure to look up at the dome –
and try out the whispering gallery created
by its curved ceiling.

Mexic-Arte Museum   Museum
(📞512-480-9373; www.mexic-artemuseum.org;
419 Congress Ave; adult/child under 12yr/student
$5/1/4; ⏰10am-6pm Mon-Thu, to 5pm Fri &
Sat, noon-5pm Sun) This wonderful, eclectic
downtown museum features works from
Mexican and Mexican American artists in
exhibitions that rotate every two months.
The museum's holdings include carved
wooden masks, modern Latin American
paintings, historic photographs and contemporary art. Don't miss the back gallery,
where new and experimental talent is
shown. Admission is free on Sundays.

◎ South Austin
Zilker Park   Park
(📞512-974-6700; www.austintexas.gov/
department/zilker-metropolitan-park; 2100
Barton Springs Rd; ⏰5am-10pm; 🚻) This
350-acre park is a slice of green heaven,
lined with hiking and biking trails. The park
also provides access to the famed Barton
Springs natural swimming pool and **Barton
Creek Greenbelt** (www.austintexas.gov; 3753
S Capital of Texas Hwy). Find boat rentals, a
miniature train, a playground and a botanical garden, too.

On weekends from April to early September, admission is $5 per car. The park
celebrated its centennial in 2017.

Ann & Roy Butler
Hike-and-Bike Trail
& Boardwalk   Viewpoint, Architecture
(www.austintexas.gov; 1820 Lakeshore Blvd;
⏰5am-midnight; 🚻🐾) You can gaze at the
downtown skyline from a series of photo-
genic boardwalks on this scenic 10-mile
trail, which loops around Lady Bird Lake.
Shorten the loop by crossing the lake on
one of several bridges. You'll find restrooms,
water fountains and waste bags for your
pet along the way. Check the city's Parks
& Recreation webpage (www.austintexas.
gov/department/parks-and-recreation) for
parking lots, trail access points and ADA
accessible entrances. Austin old-timers
may refer to the trail as the Lady Bird Trail
or the Town Lake Trail.

◎ University of Texas
& Central Austin
Blanton Museum of Art   Museum
(📞512-471-5482; www.blantonmuseum.org; 200
E Martin Luther King Jr Blvd; adult/child $9/free;
⏰10am-5pm Tue-Fri, 11am-5pm Sat, 1-5pm Sun)
A big university with a big endowment is
bound to have a big art collection, and now,
finally, it has a suitable building to show it
off properly. With one of the best university
art collections in the USA, the Blanton
showcases a variety of styles. It doesn't go
very in-depth into any of them, but then
again you're bound to find something of
interest.

Lyndon Baines Johnson (LBJ)
Library & Museum   Museum
(📞512-721-0200; www.lbjlibrary.org; 2313 Red
River St; adult/child 13-17yr/senior $8/3/5;
⏰9am-5pm) A major renovation has brought
the museum into the new millennium
with interactive exhibits and audiovisual
displays. Fortunately, they didn't lose the
hokey, animatronic LBJ that regales visitors
with the president's recorded stories –
although they did stir some controversy
when they changed him out of his ranch
duds into a suit much more befitting an
animatronic of his stature.

⦿ Market District, Clarksville & North Austin

HOPE Outdoor Gallery   Gallery

(Graffiti Park at Castle Hill; http://hopecampaign. org; 11th St & Baylor St; ⊙9am-7pm) For a wild collision of colors and art, make your way to this sprawling collection of graffiti that's been spray-painted across multilevel concrete ruins. The on-site open-air gallery here is run by the HOPE Foundation, a collection of creatives who support education. To add your own art, email murals@ hopecampaign.org for a permit. Note that the property could be closed or repurposed at any time, so get there now.

⦿ West Austin

Mt Bonnell   Park

(Covert Park; ☑512-974-6700; www.austintexas. gov; 3800 Mt Bonnell Rd) On the weekend, you might find yourself tiptoeing around a wedding ceremony at Mt Bonnell, the highest point in the city at 775ft. This pretty overlook has impressed day-trippers since the 1830s. At sunset, climb the short but steep stairway for broad views of Lake Austin (a section of the Colorado River) and the homes along the nearby hillsides. From the summit, follow the trail both left and right for a variety of views.

✪ ACTIVITIES

Barton Springs Pool   Swimming

(☑512-867-3080; 2201 Barton Springs Rd; adult/ child $8/3; ⊙5am-10pm) Hot? Not for long. Even when the temperature hits 100, you'll be shivering in a jiff after you jump into this icy-cold natural-spring pool. Draped with century-old pecan trees, the area around the pool is a social scene in itself, and the place gets packed on hot summer days.

Lady Bird Lake   Canoeing

(☑512-459-0999; www.rowingdock.com; 2418 Stratford Dr; ⊙9am-6pm) Named after former first lady 'Lady Bird' Johnson, Lady Bird Lake looks like a river. And no wonder: it's actually a dammed-off section of the Colorado River that divides Austin into north

Lady Bird Johnson Wildflower Center

Anyone with an interest in Texas' flora and fauna should make the 20-minute drive to the wonderful gardens of the **Lady Bird Johnson Wildflower Center** (☑512-232-0100; www.wildflower.org; 4801 La Crosse Ave; adult/child 5-17yr/student & senior $10/4/8; ⊙9am-5pm Tue-Sun), southwest of downtown Austin. The center, founded in 1982 with the assistance of Texas' beloved former first lady, has a display garden featuring every type of wildflower and plant that grows in Texas, separated by geographical region, with an emphasis on Hill Country flora. Spring is the best time to visit, but there's something in bloom all year.

The Wildflower Center hosts a variety of events during National Wildflower Week in May.

Purple coneflower
JIM AND LYNNE WEBER / SHUTTERSTOCK ©

and south. Get on the water at the rowing dock, which rents kayaks, canoes and stand up paddle boards from $10 to $20 per hour Monday to Thursday, with higher prices on weekends and during major events.

⊙ TOURS

Texpert Tours   Tours

(☑512-383-8989; www.texperttours.com; per hr from $100) For an interesting alternative to your stereotypical, run-of-the-mill bus and van tour, try Texpert Tours, led by affable public-radio host Howie Richey (aka the 'Texas Back Roads Scholar'). Historical anecdotes, natural history and environmental

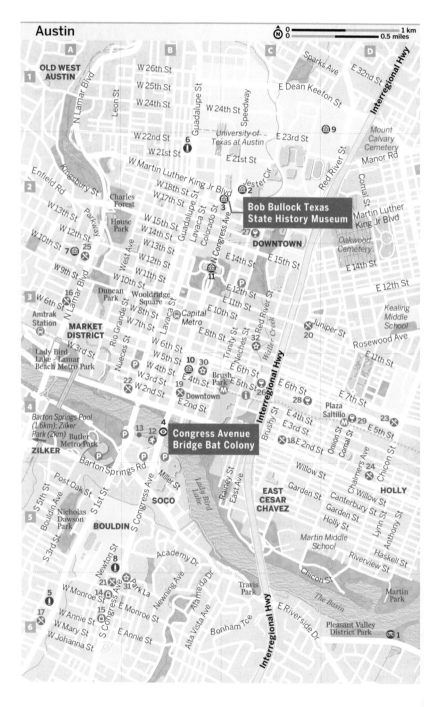

Austin

N 0 ——————— 1 km
   0 ——————— 0.5 miles

OLD WEST AUSTIN 1

W 26th St
W 25th St
W 24th St
W 22nd St
W 21st St

Leon St
Guadalupe St
Speedway

W 24th St

University of Texas at Austin

6

E 32nd St
E Dean Keeton St
E 23rd St

9

Interregional Hwy

Mount Calvary Cemetery
Manor Rd
Red River St
Comal St

Enfield Rd
Kingsbury St
Charles Forest
House Park

W Martin Luther King Jr Blvd
W 18th St
W 17th St
W 15th St
W 14th St
W 13th St
W 12th St
W 11th St
W 10th St

Jester Cir

2

3

Bob Bullock Texas State History Museum

Martin Luther King Jr Blvd
Oakwood Cemetery
E 14th St

Guadalupe St
Lavaca St
Colorado St
N Congress Ave

27

DOWNTOWN

E 15th St
E 14th St

W 13th St
W 12th St
Enfield Rd
W 10th St
West Ave

7   25

W 9th St

16

Duncan Park

Woolridge Square

Capital Metro

E 12th St
E 11th St
E 10th St

11

E 12th St
Red River St
Juniper St

20

Kealing Middle School
Rosewood Ave
E 11th St

Amtrak Station

MARKET DISTRICT

Lady Bird Lake - Lamar Beach Metro Park

W 6th St
N Lamar Blvd
Rio Grande St
Nueces St
Lavaca St

W 8th St
W 7th St
W 6th St
W 5th St
W 4th St
W 3rd St
W 2nd St

10 30

22

19

Downtown

Trinity St
Neches St

E 8th St

Brush Park
E 5th St

32

E 6th St

26

28

E 7th St

Plaza Saltillo

29 23

Congress Avenue Bridge Bat Colony

Barton Springs Pool (1.6km); Zilker Park (2km)
Butler Metro Park

ZILKER

13 12

4

Barton Springs Rd

Miller St

Lady Bird Lake

Rainey St
East Ave

18 E 2nd St

E 4th St
E 3rd St

Onion St
Comal St
Chalmers Ave
Chicon St

24

HOLLY

Post Oak St
S 5th St
S 1st St
Bouldin Ave

Nicholas Dawson Park

BOULDIN

S Congress Ave
Academy Dr
Newton St

8

21   14
31 Park La

5

17

15

W Monroe St
W Annie St
W Mary St
W Johanna St

S Congress Ave
E Monroe St
E Annie St

Alta Vista Ave
Newning Ave
Alameda Dr

SOCO

Willow St

EAST CESAR CHAVEZ

Garden St
Canterbury St
Willow St
Garden St
Holly St

Martin Middle School

Riverview St

Chicon St

Travis Park

Bonham Tce

Chicon St

Interregional Hwy
E Riverside Dr
The Basin

Pleasant Valley District Park

1

Martin Park
Lynn St
Anthony St
Haskell St

A   B   C   D

Austin

◎ Sights
1 Ann & Roy Butler Hike-and-Bike
    Trail & Boardwalk.................................D6
2 Blanton Museum of Art...........................C2
3 Bob Bullock Texas State History
    Museum...C2
4 Congress Avenue Bridge Bat
    Colony...B4
5 Greetings from Austin Mural....................A6
6 Hi, How Are You Mural.............................B2
7 Hope Outdoor Gallery..............................A3
8 I Love You So Much Mural........................A5
9 Lyndon Baines Johnson (LBJ)
    Library & Museum D1
10 Mexic-Arte Museum B4
11 Texas State Capitol.................................B3

◎ Activities, Courses & Tours
12 Capital Cruises..B4
    Historic Walking Tours......................(see 11)
13 Lone Star Riverboat................................B4

◎ Shopping
14 Allens Boots..A6
15 Big Top Candy Shop A6
    Lucy in Disguise................................(see 14)
    Tesoros Trading Co ....(see 14)
    Uncommon Objects............................(see 14)
    Waterloo Records ....(see 16)

◎ Eating
16 Amy's Ice Creams A3
17 Bouldin Creek Coffee House.....................A6
18 Cenote...C4
19 Coopers Old Time Pit Bar-B-Cue B4
20 Franklin Barbecue C3
21 Güero's Taco Bar......................................A6
    Hopdoddy Burger Bar........................(see 21)
22 Lamberts...B4
23 Thai-Kun at Whisler's..............................D4
24 Veracruz All Natural.................................D5
25 Wink..A3

◎ Drinking & Nightlife
26 Easy Tiger..C4
    Hotel San José ....(see 8)
27 Scholz Garten C2
28 Violet Crown Social Club..........................C4
    Whisler's..(see 23)
29 White Horse...D4

◎ Entertainment
30 Antone's..B4
31 Continental Club......................................B6
32 Stubb's Bar-B-Q C3

tips are all part of the educational experience. A three-hour tour of central Austin takes visitors to the state capitol, the Governor's Mansion and the top of Mt Bonnell.

Historic Walking Tours   Walking
(☏512-474-5171; www.tspb.state.tx.us/plan/tours/tours.html; ◷9am Tue & Thu-Sat, 11am & 1pm Sun) FREE One of the best deals around are the free Historic Walking Tours of downtown Austin, which leave from the capitol's south steps. Tours last between 60 and 90 minutes. Make reservations at least 48 hours in advance either online or by phone through the visitor center.

🅐 SHOPPING

Uncommon Objects   Vintage
(☏512-442-4000; 1512 S Congress Ave; ◷11am-7pm Sun-Thu, to 8pm Fri & Sat) 'Curious oddities' is what they advertise at this

quirky antique store that sells all manner of fabulous knickknacks, all displayed with an artful eye. More than 20 different vendors scour the state to stock their stalls, so there's plenty to look at.

Waterloo Records   Music
(☏512-474-2500; www.waterloorecords.com; 600 N Lamar Blvd; ◷10am-11pm Mon-Sat, from 11am Sun) If you want to stock up on music, this is the record store. There are sections reserved just for local bands, and listening stations featuring Texas, indie and alt-country acts.

Allens Boots   Fashion & Accessories
(☏512-447-1413; 1522 S Congress Ave; ◷9am-8pm Mon-Sat, noon-6pm Sun) In hip South Austin, family-owned Allens sells row upon row of traditional cowboy boots for ladies, gents and kids. A basic pair costs from $100 or so, while somethin' fancy runs a few hundred dollars.

From left: Canoeing, Barton Creek Greenbelt (p228); Kite flying, Zilker Park (p228); Texas State Capitol (p228)

Big Top Candy Shop — Food

(www.bigtopcandyshop.tumblr.com; 1706 S Congress Ave; ⊙11am-7pm Sun-Thu, 11am-8pm Fri. 10am-9pm Sat; 👶) If you're trying to tame your sweet tooth, don't step into this colorful candy emporium where old-school treats like Squirrel Nut Zippers and Charleston Chews jostle for your attention with gummy bears and caramel coffee truffles. And yes, you can get a malt at the soda fountain.

🅧 EATING

🅧 Downtown

Coopers Old Time
Pit Bar-B-Cue — Barbecue $$

(📞512-474-2145; www.coopersbbqaustin.com; 217 Congress Ave; beef ribs & brisket per lb $18, other meats vary; ⊙11am-10pm) The downtown lunch crowd has discovered this new outpost of beloved Cooper's Bar-B-Cue in Llano. Pick your meat at the counter (paid by the pound) then add sides. We're partial to the jalapeño mac-and-cheese, which you won't want to share. The baked beans and the white bread are always free.

Lamberts — Barbecue $$$

(📞512-494-1500; www.lambertsaustin.com; 401 W 2nd St; lunch $12-19, dinner $19-42; ⊙11am-2:30pm Mon-Sat, to 2pm Sun, 5:30-10pm Sun-Wed, to 10:30pm Thu-Sat) Torn between barbecue and fine dining? Lambert's serves intelligent updates of American comfort-food classics – some might call it 'uppity barbecue' – in a historic stone building run by Austin chef Lou Lambert.

🅧 East Austin

Franklin Barbecue — Barbecue $

(📞512-653-1187; www.franklinbarbecue.com; 900 E 11th St; sandwiches $6-10, ribs/brisket per lb $17/20; ⊙11am-2pm Tue-Sun) This famous BBQ joint only serves lunch, and only till it runs out – usually well before 2pm. In fact, to avoid missing out, you should join the line – and there will be a line – by 10am (9am on weekends). Just treat it as a tailgating party: bring beer or mimosas to share and make friends.

Veracruz All Natural — Mexican $

(📞512-981-1760; www.veracruztacos.com; 1704 E Cesar Chavez St; tacos $3-4, mains $8; ⊙7am-

3pm) Two sisters from Mexico run this East Austin taco truck (an old bus), which may serve the best tacos in town. Step up to the window, order a *migas* breakfast taco (you must!) then add a quesadilla or torta for variety. Take your buzzer – yep, this food truck has a buzzer – and grab a picnic table.

Thai-Kun at Whisler's   Thai $

(512-719-3332; www.thaikun.com; 1816 E 6th St; mains $7-10; 4pm-1:45am) The beef panang curry is, simply put, amazing. Served from a colorful food truck behind Whisler's cocktail bar, this spicy curry is one of a half-dozen noodle and curry dishes on the menu, all under the oversight of chef Thai Changdong. The food truck was named one of the best new restaurants in America by *Bon Appetit!*

Cenote   Cafe $

(1010 E Cesar Chavez St; mains $8-15; 7am-10pm Mon-Fri, from 8am Sat, 8am-4pm Sun;) One of our favorite cafes in Austin, Cenote uses seasonal, largely organic ingredients in its simple but delicious anytime fare. Come for housemade granola and yogurt with fruit, banh mi sandwiches and couscous curry. The cleverly shaded patio is a fine

retreat for a rich coffee or a craft beer (or perhaps a handmade popsicle from Juju).

Dai Due   American $$$

(512-719-3332; www.daidue.com; 2406 Manor Rd; breakfast & lunch $13-22, dinner $22-84; 10am-3pm & 5-10pm Tue-Sun) Even your basic eggs-and-sausage breakfast is a meal to remember at this lauded restaurant, where all the ingredients are from farms, rivers and hunting grounds in Texas, as well as the Gulf of Mexico. Supper Club dinners spotlight limited items like wild game and foraged treats. Like your cut of meat? See if they have a few pounds to go, at the attached butcher shop.

South Austin

Hopdoddy Burger Bar   Burgers $

(512-243-7505; www.hopdoddy.com; 1400 S Congress Ave; burgers $7-13; 11am-10pm Sun-Thu, to 11pm Fri & Sat) People line up around the block for the burgers, fries and shakes – and it's not because burgers, fries and shakes are hard to come by in Austin. It's because this place slathers tons of love into everything it makes, from the humanely

🍴 Food Trailers

From epicurean Airstreams to regular old taco trucks, food trailers are kind of a big deal in Austin, and wandering from one to another is a fun way to experience the local food scene. They travel in packs, and here is where they tend to congregate:

South Austin Trailer Park and Eatery This seems to be a rather settled trailer community, with a fence, an official name, a sign and picnic tables.

East Austin This area has its own little enclave, conveniently located right among all the bars on the corner of E 6th and Waller Sts.

Rainey Street A cluster of food trucks is ready to serve the downtown hordes downing beers at nearby bars.

Food trucks, South Congress
KYLIE MCLAUGHLIN / GETTY IMAGES ©

raised beef to the locally sourced ingredients to the fresh-baked buns. The sleek, modern building is pretty sweet, too.

Ramen Tatsu-ya   Ramen $
(☎512-893-5561; www.ramen-tatsuya.com; 1234 S Lamar Blvd; ramen $10; ⏰11am-10pm) With its communal tables, loud indie music and hustling efficiency, we wouldn't say this busy ramen joint is a relaxing experience, but darn, is it good. Step up to the counter – there will be a line – and take your pick of seven noodle-and-veggie-loaded broths. Like it spicy? Order the Mi-So-Hot. You can also add spicy or sweet 'bombs' to vary the flavor.

Bouldin Creek
Coffee House   Vegetarian $
(☎512-416-1601; www.bouldincreekcafe.com; 1900 S 1st St; mains $6-10; ⏰7am-midnight Mon-Fri, 8am-midnight Sat & Sun; 🛜🅿) You can get your veggie chorizo tacos or a potato leek omelet all day long at this buzzing vegan-vegetarian eatery. It's got an eclectic South Austin vibe and is a great place for people-watching, finishing your novel or joining a band.

Güero's Taco Bar   Tex-Mex $$
(☎512-447-7688; www.gueros.com; 1412 S Congress Ave; breakfast $5-7, lunch & dinner $10-34; ⏰11am-10pm Mon-Wed, to 11pm Thu & Fri, 8am-11pm Sat, to 10pm Sun) Set in a former feed-and-seed store from the late 1800s, Güero's is an Austin classic and always draws a crowd. It may not serve the best Tex-Mex in town but with its free chips and salsa, refreshing margaritas and convivial vibe, we can almost guarantee a fantastic time. And the food? Try the homemade corn tortillas and chicken tortilla soup.

✖ University of Texas & Central Austin

Via 313   Pizza $$
(☎512-358-6193; www.via313.com; 3016 Guadalupe St; pizzas $10-29; ⏰11am-11pm Sun-Thu, to 11pm Fri & Sat) What? Why is my pizza a square? Because it's Detroit-style, baby, meaning it's cooked in a square pan, plus there's caramelized cheese on the crust and sauce layered over the toppings. And after just one bite of one of these rich favorites, we guarantee you'll forget all geometric concerns. Good craft beer selection too.

✖ Market District, Clarksville & North Austin

Amy's Ice Creams   Ice Cream $
(☎512-480-0673; www.amysicecreams.com; 1012 W 6th St; ice cream $3.25-6; ⏰11:30am-midnight Sun-Thu, to 1am Fri & Sat) It's not just the ice cream we love; it's the toppings that get pounded and blended in, violently but lovingly, by the staff wielding a metal scoop in each hand. Look for other locations on

Guadalupe St north of the UT campus, on South Congress near all the shops, or at the airport for a last-ditch fix.

Kerbey Lane Café American $

(☏512-451-1436; www.kerbeylanecafe.com; 3704 Kerbey Lane; breakfast $6-13, lunch & dinner $9-13; ◷6:30am-11pm Mon-Thu, 24hr from 6:30am Fri-11pm Sun; ☏⛹) Kerbey Lane is a longtime Austin favorite, fulfilling round-the-clock cravings for anything from gingerbread pancakes to black-bean tacos to mahimahi. Try the addictive Kerbey Queso while you wait. (They have vegan queso, too!) There are several other locations around town, but this location in a homey bungalow is the original and has the most character.

Uchiko Japanese $$$

(☏512-916-4808; www.uchikoaustin.com; 4200 N Lamar Blvd; small plates $4-28, sushi rolls $10-16; ◷5-10pm Sun-Thu, to 11pm Fri & Sat) Not content to rest on his Uchi laurels, chef Tyson Cole opened this North Lamar restaurant that describes itself as 'Japanese farmhouse dining.' But we're here to tell you, it's hard to imagine being treated to fantastic and unique delicacies such as these and enjoying this sort of bustling ambience in any Japanese farmhouse. Reservations are highly recommended.

Wink Fusion $$$

(☏512-482-8868; 1014 N Lamar Blvd; mains $17-33; ◷6-9:30pm Mon-Wed, 5:30-9:30pm Thu-Sat) Date night? At this intimate gem hidden behind Whole Earth Provision Co, diners are ushered to tables underneath windows screened with Japanese rice paper, then presented with an exceptional wine list. The chef-inspired fare takes on a nouveau fusion attitude that is equal parts modern French and Asian. For a special splurge, try the five-course ($68) tasting menu.

DRINKING & NIGHTLIFE

Downtown

Easy Tiger Beer Garden

(www.easytigeraustin.com; 709 E 6th St; ◷11am-2am) The one bar on Dirty 6th that all locals love? Easy Tiger, an inside-outside beer garden overlooking Waller Creek. The place welcomes all comers with an upbeat communal vibe. Craft beers are listed on the chalkboard. And the artisanal sandwiches? Baked on tasty bread from the bakery upstairs (7am to 2am). The meat is cooked in-house.

East Austin

Whisler's Cocktail Bar

(☏512-480-0781; www.whislersatx.com; 1816 E 6th St; ◷4pm-2am) If vampires walk the streets of East Austin, then this dark and moody cocktail bar is surely where they congregate before a night of feeding. And we don't quite trust that taxidermied boar overlooking the bar from his lofty perch. Head to the patio for a less intimate scene, as well as live music. There's a fantastic Thai food truck out back.

White Horse Honky-Tonk

(☏512-553-6756; www.thewhitehorseaustin.com; 500 Comal St; ◷3pm-2am) Ladies, you will be asked to dance at this East Austin honky-tonk, where two-steppers and hipsters mingle like siblings in a diverse but happy family. Play pool, take a dance lesson or step outside to sip a microbrew on the patio. Live music nightly, and whiskey on tap. We like this place.

South Austin

ABGB Beer Garden

(Austin Beer Garden Brewery; ☏512-298-2242; www.theabgb.com; 1305 W Oltorf St; ◷11:30am-11pm Tue-Thu, 11:30am-midnight Fri, noon-midnight Sat, noon-10pm Sun; ☏⛹) Want a place to meet your friends for beer and conversation? Then settle in at a picnic table inside or out at this convivial brewery and beer garden that's also known for its great food. The boar, tasso and spinach pizza? Oh yes, you do want a slice of this thin-crusted specialty pie ($4). Live music Tuesday and Wednesday, and Friday through Sunday.

Hotel San José Bar

(☏512-852-2350; 1316 S Congress Ave; ◷noon-midnight) Transcending the hotel-bar

Detour: Barbecue Trail

They call it the **Texas Barbecue Trail** (www.texasbbqtrails.com): 80 artery-clogging miles worth of the best brisket, ribs and sausage Texas has to offer, stretching from Taylor (36 miles north-east of Austin) down to Luling, passing through Elgin and Lockhart along the way. Marketing gimmick? Perhaps. Do our stomachs care? They do not. If your schedule or limited appetite make driving two hours and eating at 12 different barbecue restaurants unfeasible, make a beeline for brisket in Lockhart, or, if it's hot sausage you crave, Elgin is your best bet.

Coopers Old Time Pit Bar-B-Cue (p232)
JORDAN ADKINS / SHUTTERSTOCK ©

genre, this is actually a cool, Zen-like outdoor patio that attracts a chill crowd, and it's a nice place to hang if you want to actually have a conversation. Service can be leisurely, but maybe that's OK for an oasis?

🍸 Market District, Clarksville & North Austin

Ginny's Little Longhorn Saloon — Bar

(📞512-524-1291; www.thelittlelonghornsaloon.com; 5434 Burnet Rd; ⏰5pm-midnight Tue & Wed, to 1am Thu-Sat, 2-10pm Sun) This funky little cinder-block building is one of those dive bars that Austinites love so very much – and did even before it became nationally famous for chicken-shit bingo on Sunday night. The place gets so crowded during bingo that you can barely see the darn

chicken – but, hey, it's still fun. The overflow crowd is out back.

Mean Eyed Cat — Bar

(📞512-920-6645; www.themeaneyedcat.com; 1621 W 5th St; ⏰11am-2am) We're not sure if this watering hole is a legit dive bar or a calculated dive bar (it opened in 2004). Either way, a bar dedicated to Johnny Cash has our utmost respect. Inside, Man in Black album covers, show posters and other knickknackery adorn the walls of this former chainsaw repair shop. A 300-year-old live oak anchors the lively patio.

✪ ENTERTAINMENT

Music is the town's leading nighttime attraction, and a major industry. You can get heaps of information from Thursday's *Austin Chronicle* or the *Austin American-Statesman's* Austin 360 website (www.austin360.com).

Broken Spoke — Live Music

(www.brokenspokeaustintx.net; 3201 S Lamar Blvd; ⏰11am-11:30pm Tue, to midnight Wed & Thu, to 1:30am Fri & Sat) George Strait once hung from the wagon-wheel chandeliers at the wooden-floored Broken Spoke, a true Texas honky-tonk. Not sure of your dance moves? Take a lesson. They're offered from 8pm to 9pm Wednesday through Saturday. As the sign inside says: 'Please do Not!!!! Stand on the Dance Floor.'

Continental Club — Live Music

(📞512-441-2444; www.continentalclub.com; 1315 S Congress Ave; ⏰4pm-2am Mon-Fri, from 3pm Sat & Sun) No passive toe-tapping here; this 1950s-era lounge has a dancefloor that's always swinging with some of the city's best local acts. On most Monday nights you can catch local legend Dale Watson and his Lone Stars (10:15pm).

Stubb's Bar-B-Q — Live Music

(📞512-480-8341; www.stubbsaustin.com; 801 Red River St; ⏰11am-10pm Mon-Thu, to 11pm Fri & Sat, 10:30am-9pm Sun) Stubb's has live music almost every night, with a great mix of premier local and touring acts from across the musical spectrum. Many warm-weather shows are held out back along Waller Creek. There are two stages, a smaller stage indoors and a larger backyard venue.

Antone's
Live Music

(www.facebook.com/antonesnightclub; 305 E 5th St; ☺showtimes vary) A key player in Austin's musical history, Antone's has attracted the best of the blues and other popular local acts since 1975. All ages, all the time.

Saxon Pub
Live Music

(☑512-448-2552; www.thesaxonpub.com; 1320 S Lamar Blvd) The super-chill Saxon Pub, presided over by 'Rusty,' a huge knight who sits out the front, has music every night, mostly Texas performers in the blues-rock vein. A great place to kick back, drink a beer and discover a new favorite artist.

ℹ INFORMATION

Austin Visitor Information Center (☑512-478-0098; www.austintexas.org; 602 E 4th St; ☺9am-5pm Mon-Sat, from 10am Sun) Helpful staff, free maps, extensive racks of information brochures and restrooms. There's also a fun collection of Austin souvenirs, from bat magnets to T-shirts to art.

ℹ GETTING THERE & AROUND

TO/FROM THE AIRPORT

Austin-Bergstrom International Airport (AUS; www.austintexas.gov/airport) is about 10 miles southeast of downtown. Capital Metro runs a limited-stop Airport Flyer (bus 100) service between the airport and downtown and UT for $1.25 each way, with departures every 30 minutes. It takes at least 20 minutes to get downtown from the airport, and 35 minutes to reach the UT campus. **SuperShuttle** (☑800-258-3826; www.supershuttle.com) offers a shared-van service from the airport to downtown hotels for about $14 one way. A taxi between the airport and downtown costs $25 to $30.

BICYCLE

Cycling around downtown, South Congress and the UT campus is doable. The city offers bike sharing, with more than 40 **Austin B-cycle** (www.austin.bcycle.com) stations scattered around town. Rates are $12 for 24-hour access or $15 for three consecutive days.

CAR & MOTORCYCLE

Downtown, the best parking deal is at the **Capitol Visitors Parking Garage** (1201 San Jacinto Blvd). It's free for the first two hours, and only $1 per half-hour after that, maxing out at $12.

PUBLIC TRANSPORTATION

Austin's handy public-transit system is run by **Capital Metro** (CapMetro; ☑512-474-1200, transit store 512-389-7454; www.capmetro.org; transit store 209 W 9th St; ☺transit store 7:30am-5:30pm Mon-Fri). Regular city buses (not the more expensive express routes) cost $1.25.

RIDE SHARE

Uber and Lyft are not available in Austin. For ride sharing, try **Fare** (www.ridefare.com), **Fasten** (www.fasten.com) or the nonprofit **Ride Austin** (www.rideaustin.com).

TAXI

You usually need to call for a cab (rather than flag one down). The flag drops at $2.50, then it's $2.40 for each additional mile. Larger companies include **Yellow Cab** (☑512-452-9999) and **Austin Cab** (☑512-478-2222) .

Human-powered bicycle taxis (aka pedicabs) are available downtown on 6th St and around the Warehouse District. The drivers, who are typically young students or musicians, work entirely for tips, so be generous.

LAS VEGAS

In this Chapter

Cruising The Strip.............................242
Vegas Shows.....................................246
Sights & Activities.............................248
Eating..249
Drinking & Nightlife...........................250
Entertainment..................................251

Las Vegas at a Glance...

Vegas, baby! An oasis of indulgence dazzling in the desert. This is the only place you can spend the night partying in ancient Rome, wake up for brunch beneath the Eiffel Tower, watch an erupting volcano at sunset and get married in a pink Cadillac. Double down with the high rollers, browse couture or sip a frozen vodka martini from a bar made of ice – it's all here for the taking.

So, is Vegas America's dirty little secret or its dream factory? It is, of course, both – and remains a bastion of hangover-inducing weekends for people from all walks of life.

Two Days in Las Vegas

It's all about the Strip. On day one, check out the casino and beach at **Mandalay Bay** (p244), the mind-blowing lobby at the **Cosmopolitan** (p244), the unmissable fountains at the **Bellagio** (p245), and **Caesars Palace** (p245) for a show. On day two, visit the **LINQ Promenade** (p248), the marbled **Venetian** (p245) and the Wynn to see **Le Rêve the Dream** (p251).

Four Days in Las Vegas

Explore Downtown Vegas on day three, taking in the **Mob Museum** (p248), **Neon Museum** (p248) and **Fremont Street Experience** (p248). Sip at the hipster-haven **Beauty Bar** (p250). On day four, seek out the **Pinball Hall of Fame** (p248). Afterward, head back to the Strip for more action at the casinos, shows and cocktail bars.

Arriving in Las Vegas

McCarran International Airport Shuttle buses run to Strip hotels from $7 one-way, $9 to Downtown and off-Strip hotels. You'll pay at least $20 plus tip for a taxi to the Strip.

Driving Most travelers approach the Strip (Las Vegas Blvd) off the I-15 Fwy. Try to avoid exiting onto busy Flamingo Rd; opt for quieter Tropicana Ave or Spring Mountain Rd.

Where to Stay

Downtown is cheaper, but the Strip is where the action is. Properties east and west of the Strip have their merits, though you'll need wheels to get around. Always ask whether the hotel will be undergoing renovations during your visit and whether or not the swimming pool will be open.

Cruising the Strip

The Strip, a 4.2-mile stretch of S Las Vegas Blvd lined with hulking casino hotels and megaresorts, is so hypnotizing that few visitors venture beyond it – this is where Vegas is at.

Great For...

ℹ **Need to Know**

See www.lasvegas.com for the lowdown on restaurants, bars and events.

The Strip is what happens when you take the ideals of freedom and abundance to their extremes. It's the epicenter in a vortex of limitless potential, where almost anything goes and time becomes elastic. Heads spin at the endless sales pitches: some get lucky, many have such a good time that they don't seem to mind incinerating their hard-earned cash. Magic dwells in this garden of extraordinary delight, but finding *yours* can be tricky: the Strip excels at distraction.

Casinos

Mandalay Bay (702-632-7700; www.mandalaybay.com; 3950 S Las Vegas Blvd; 24hr) Since opening in 1999, in place of the former 50s-era Hacienda, Mandalay Bay has anchored the southern Strip. Its theme may be tropical, but it sure ain't tacky, nor is its 135,000-sq-ft casino.

Well-dressed sports fans find their way to the upscale race and sports book near the high-stakes poker room. Refusing to be pigeonholed, the Bay's standout attractions are many and include the multilevel **Shark Reef Aquarium** (www.sharkreef. com; adult/child $25/19; 10am-8pm Sun-Thu, to 10pm Fri & Sat), day spas and the unrivaled **Mandalay Bay Beach** (pool 8am-5pm, Moorea Beach Club 11am-6pm).

Cosmopolitan (702-698-7000; www.cosmopolitanlasvegas.com; 3708 S Las Vegas Blvd; 24hr) Hipsters who thought they were too cool for Vegas finally have a place to go where they don't need irony to endure – or enjoy – the aesthetics of the Strip. Like the new Hollywood 'It' girl, the Cosmopolitan casino looks absolutely fabulous at all times. A steady stream of ingenues and entourages parade through the lobby (with some

Bellagio's Conservatory & Botanical Gardens

of the coolest design elements we've seen) along with anyone else who adores contemporary art and design.

Bellagio (☎888-987-6667; www.bellagio.com; 3600 S Las Vegas Blvd; ◷24hr) The Bellagio experience transcends its decadent casino floor of high-limit gaming tables and in excess of 2300 slot machines; locals say odds here are less than favorable. A stop on the World Poker Tour, Bellagio's tournament-worthy poker room offers kitchen-to-gaming-table delivery around-the-clock. Most, however, come for the property's stunning architecture, interiors and amenities, including the **Conservatory & Botanical Gardens** (◷24hr) FREE, **Gallery of Fine Art** (adult/

✕ Take a Break

Hit the roof for views and cocktails at Skyfall Lounge (p250).

child under 12yr $18/free; ◷10am-8pm, last entry 7:30pm), unmissable **Fountains of Bellagio** (◷shows every 30min 3-8pm Mon-Fri, noon-8pm Sat, 11am-7pm Sun, every 15min 8pm-midnight Mon-Sat, from 7pm Sun) FREE and the 2000-plus hand-blown glass flowers embellishing the hotel lobby.

Caesars Palace (☎866-227-5938; www.caesarspalace.com; 3570 S Las Vegas Blvd; ◷24hr) Caesars Palace claims that its smartly renovated casino floor has more million-dollar slots than anywhere in the world, but its claims to fame are more numerous than that. Entertainment heavyweights Celine Dion and Elton John 'own' its custom-built **Colosseum theater** (www.thecolosseum.com; tickets $55-500), fashionistas saunter around the **Shops at Forum** (www.simon.com/mall/the-forum-shops-at-caesars-palace/stores; ◷10am-11pm Sun-Thu, to midnight Fri & Sat), while Caesars group hotel guests quaff cocktails in the Garden of the Gods Pool Oasis. By night, megaclub **Omnia** (www.omnianightclub.com; cover female/male $20/40; ◷10pm-4am Tue & Thu-Sun) is the *only* place to get off your face this side of Ibiza.

Venetian (☎702-414-1000; www.venetian.com; 3355 S Las Vegas Blvd; ◷24hr) The Venetian's regal 120,000-sq-ft casino has marble floors, hand-painted ceiling frescoes and 120 table games, including a high-limit lounge and an elegant no-smoking poker room, where women are especially welcome (unlike at many other poker rooms in town). When combined with its younger, neighboring sibling **Palazzo** (☎702-607-7777; www.palazzo.com; 3325 S Las Vegas Blvd; ◷24hr), the properties claim the largest casino space in Las Vegas. Unmissable on the Strip, a highlight of this miniature replica of Venice is to take a **gondola ride** (shared ride per person $29, child under 3yr free, private 2-passenger ride $116; ◷indoor 10am-11pm Sun-Thu, to midnight Fri & Sat, outdoor rides 11am-10pm) down its Grand Canal.

★ Top Tip

Ride-share services offered by a glut of eager drivers are the cheapest and most efficient way to get around.

O by Cirque du Soleil

VERONIQUE VIAL ©

Vegas Shows

Whether you hanker for Britney Spears, Celine Dion, feats of underwater acrobatics or erotic burlesque, you can bet it's on stage in Vegas. Larger-than-life production shows are the main stock-in-trade.

Great For...

☑ Don't Miss

Le Rêve the Dream (p251) takes place in an enormous, custom-built swimming pool at the Wynn.

All Kinds of Shows

The whirling **Cirque du Soleil** (☑877-924-7783; www.cirquedusoleil.com/las-vegas; discount tickets from $49, full-price from $69) empire keeps expanding, most recently with the addition of two musical-themed spectaculars – *Beatles LOVE* and *Michael Jackson ONE* – and the fantastical variety show *Zarkana*. The much-ballyhooed invasion of the Strip by Broadway showstoppers has slowed, although big productions like *Jersey Boys* and *Mamma Mia!* still sweep through town for limited runs.

This is Vegas, so there's first-rate comedy, too, as well as heavyweight rock stars in constant rotation. Resident shows of late have included Celine Dion, Carlos Santana,

VERONIQUE VIAL ©

❶ Need to Know

The city's tourism website (www.las vegas.com) let's you search what's on by date and price.

✕ Take a Break

Parasol Up & Parasol Down (p251) makes a fine pit stop for cool cocktail.

★ Top Tip

Downtown's Fremont Street Experience (p248) puts on a heck of a show — and it's free.

Tue-Sun) lights up a big-top circus tent outside Caesars Palace.

Ticket Outlets

Be aware that most Vegas ticket outlets apply a surcharge for each ticket sold.

Tix 4 Tonight (www.tix4tonight.com) All but the biggest-ticket shows are up for grabs at these same-day, discount ticket outlets, but you must show up in person (no online or phone sales). Get in line before 10am for the best selection of shows and seats. Check the website for a list of handy outlet locations around town.

Vegas.com (www.vegas.com) Sells tickets to a variety of high-profile and low-budget shows, special events and touring exhibitions, as well as nightclub VIP and front-of-the-line passes.

Ticketmaster (www.ticketmaster.com) A broker for megaconcerts and sporting events.

Guns N' Roses and Britney Spears. Mega-resort venues host a veritable who's-who of famous faces and voices throughout the year.

Old-school production shows at smaller casinos feature a variety of hokey song, dance and magic numbers that often don't follow a story line. Capitalizing on Sin City's reputation, there's also a grab-bag of erotically themed shows, from rock musicals to late-night pin-up revues, all featuring topless showgirls.

Sin City's new breed of bawdy, hilarious variety shows are staged cabaret-style in unusual venues, mostly on the Strip:
Absinthe (☏800-745-3000; www.absinthe vegas.com; tickets $99-125; ⏾8pm & 10pm

⊙ SIGHTS & ACTIVITIES

⊙ The Strip

Stratosphere Thrill Rides   Amusement Park

(🕿702-383-5210; www.stratospherehotel.com/Attractions/Thrill-Rides; Stratosphere; elevator adult $20, incl 3 thrill rides $35, all-day pass $40; ⊙10am-1am Sun-Thu, to 2am Fri & Sat; 🚇Sahara) The world's highest thrill rides await, a whopping 110 stories above the Strip. Big Shot straps riders into completely exposed seats that zip up the tower's pinnacle, while Insanity spins riders out over the tower's edge. X-Scream leaves you hanging 27ft over the edge, 866ft above ground. For a real adrenaline rush, save your dough for **SkyJump** (🕿702-380-7777; www.skyjump lasvegas.com; per jump $120; ⊙10am-1am Sun-Thu, to 2am Fri & Sat).

LINQ Promenade   Street

(www.caesars.com/linq; ⊙24hr; P♿; 🚇Flamingo or Harrah's/Linq) You'll be delighted by the fun vibe of the Strip's newest outdoor pedestrian promenade, where you can browse the latest LA fashions, gorge yourself on cupcakes, jaburritos (where sushi rolls meet burritos!) and fish and chips, go bowling, ride the **High Roller** (🕿702-322-0591; www.caesars.com/linq; adult/child from $22/9, after 5pm $32/19; ⊙11:30am-2am, rock out to live music, or sip pints on lazy patios beneath the desert sun.

⊙ Downtown

Mob Museum   Museum

(🕿702-229-2734; www.themobmuseum.org; 300 Stewart Ave; adult/child $24/14; ⊙9am-9pm; P; 🚇Deuce) It's hard to say what's more impressive: the museum's physical location in a historic federal courthouse where mobsters sat for federal hearings in 1950–51, the fact that the board of directors is headed up by a former FBI Special Agent, or the thoughtfully curated exhibits telling the story of organized crime in America. In addition to hands-on FBI equipment and mob-related artifacts, the museum boasts a series of multimedia exhibits featuring interviews with real-life Tony Sopranos.

Neon Museum – Neon Boneyard   Museum

(🕿702-387-6366; www.neonmuseum.org; 770 N Las Vegas Blvd; 1hr tour adult/child $19/15, after dark $26/22; ⊙tours daily, schedules vary; 🚇113) This nonprofit project is doing what almost no one else does: saving Las Vegas' history. Book ahead for a fascinating guided walking tour of the 'Neon Boneyard,' where irreplaceable vintage neon signs – Las Vegas' original art form – spend their retirement. Start exploring at the visitor center inside the salvaged La Concha Motel lobby, a mid-century modern icon designed by African American architect Paul Revere Williams. Tours are usually given throughout the day, but are most spectacular at night.

Fremont Street Experience   Street

(🕿702-678-5600; www.vegasexperience.com; Fremont St Mall; ⊙shows hourly dusk-midnight or 1am; 🚇Deuce, SDX) FREE A five-block pedestrian mall, between Main St and N Las Vegas Blvd, topped by an arched steel canopy and filled with computer-controlled lights, the Fremont Street Experience has brought life back Downtown. Every evening, the canopy is transformed by light-and-sound shows enhanced by 550,000 watts of wraparound sound and a larger-than-life screen lit up by 12.5-million synchronized LEDs. Soar through the air on ziplines strung underneath the canopy from **Slotzilla** (www.vegasexperience.com/slotzilla-zip-line; lower line $25, upper line $45; ⊙1pm-1am Sun-Thu, to 2am Fri & Sat; ♿), a 12-story, slot-machine-themed platform. Gaudy, yes. Weird, yes. Busy: always.

⊙ East of the Strip

Pinball Hall of Fame   Museum

(🕿702-597-2627; www.pinballmuseum.org; 1610 E Tropicana Ave; per game 25¢-$1; ⊙11am-11pm Sun-Thu, to midnight Fri & Sat; ♿; 🚇201) You may have more fun at this no-frills arcade than playing slot machines back on the Strip. Tim Arnold shares his collection of 200-plus vintage pinball and video games with the public. Take time to read the handwritten curatorial cards explaining the unusual history behind these restored machines.

✖ EATING
⊗ The Strip
Ramen-ya Katana · Ramen $

(📞702-586-6889; www.ramen-katanaya.com; 3615 S Las Vegas Blvd, Grand Bazaar Shops; meals $9-14; ⊙9:30am-1am; ❋) Granted, purists who follow the Japanese religion of ramen might get picky, but we won't. In a sea of complicated, overpriced and prohibitive dining, Katana offers humble bowls of hot broth swimming with hearty noodles at *almost* normal prices, on the center Strip. In true San Franciscan fashion, they've even thrown sushi burritos on the menu. Winning!

Peppermill · Diner $$

(📞702-735-4177; www.peppermilllasvegas.com; 2985 S Las Vegas Blvd; mains $8-32; ⊙24hr; 🚍Deuce) Slide into a crescent-shaped booth at this retro casino coffee shop and revel in the old-school Vegas atmosphere. You can eavesdrop on Nevada cowboys and downtown politicos digging into a gigantic late-night bite or early breakfast. For tropical tiki drinks, step into the Peppermill's **Fireside Lounge** (📞702-735-7635; ⊙24hr).

Searsucker Las Vegas · Gastropub $$

(📞702-866-1800; www.searsucker.com/las-vegas; Caesars Palace; mains $12-32; ⊙5pm-midnight) Searsucker is a heavy hitter serving punchy small plates and killer cocktails in casual, cowboy-tinged digs on Caesars (p245) gaming floor. Daily happy hour and a modern American menu that has something for everyone.

Morimoto · Fusion $$$

(📞702-891-1111; www.mgmgrand.com; MGM Grand; mains $24-75; ⊙5-10pm) Iron Chef Masaharu Morimoto's latest Vegas incarnation is in his eponymous showcase restaurant, which pays homage to his Japanese roots and the cuisine of this city that has

propelled him to legend status around the world. Dining here is an experience in every possible way and, we think, worth every penny.

⊗ Downtown
Carson Kitchen · American $$

(📞702-473-9523; www.carsonkitchen.com; 124 S 6th St; tapas & mains $8-22; ⊙11:30am-11pm Thu-Sat, to 10pm Sun-Wed; 🚍Deuce) This tiny eatery with an industrial theme of exposed beams, bare bulbs and chunky share tables hops with downtowners looking to escape

💬 Gambling Terms

All in To bet everything you've got.

Ante A starting wager required to play table games.

Comps Freebies (eg buffet passes, show tickets, hotel rooms) given to players.

Cooler An unlucky gambler who makes everyone else lose.

Double down In blackjack, to double your bet after getting your first two cards.

Eye in the sky High-tech casino surveillance systems.

Fold To throw in your cards and stop betting.

High roller A gambler who bets big (aka 'whale').

Let it ride To roll over a winning wager into the next bet.

Low roller A small-time gambler (eg who likes penny slot machines).

Marker Credit-line debt owed to a casino.

One-armed bandit Old-fashioned nickname for a slot machine.

Pit boss A card dealer's supervisor on the casino floor.

Sucker bet A gamble on nearly impossible odds.

Toke A tip or gratuity.

Going to the Chapel

If you're thinking of officially tying the knot in Las Vegas and want to know what's required, contact Clark County's **Marriage License Bureau** (☏702-671-0600; www.clarkcountynv.gov/Depts/clerk/Services/Pages/MarriageLicenses.aspx; 201 E Clark Ave; marriage license from $60; ☺8am-midnight), which gets jammed during crunch times such as weekends, holidays and 'lucky number' days. For an inexpensive, no-fuss civil ceremony, make an appointment with the county's **Office of Civil Marriages** (☏702-671-0577; www.clarkcountynv.gov/depts/clerk/services/pages/civilmarriages.aspx; 330 S 3rd St, 6th fl; wedding ceremonies from $75; ☺2-6pm Sun-Thu, 10am-9pm Fri, 12:30-9pm Sat).

Expect to pay at least $200 for a basic ceremony at an old-school Vegas wedding chapel. Operating for more than 50 years, **Graceland Wedding Chapel** (☏702-382-0091; www.gracelandchapel.com; 619 S Las Vegas Blvd; ☺9am-11pm) created the original Elvis wedding. **Little Church of the West** (☏702-739-7971; www.littlechurchlv.com; 4617 S Las Vegas Blvd; ☺8am-11pm) features a quaint, quiet little wooden chapel built in 1942 and pictured in *Viva Las Vegas*. At zany **Viva Las Vegas Wedding Chapel** (☏702-384-0771; www.vivalasvegasweddings.com; 1205 S Las Vegas Blvd; P), you can invite your family and friends to watch your wacky themed ceremony broadcast live online.

the mayhem of Fremont St or the Strip's high prices. Excellent shared plates include rainbow cauliflower, watermelon and feta salad and decadent mac 'n' cheese, and there's a creative 'libations' menu.

Grotto   Italian $$
(☏702-386-8341; www.goldennugget.com; 129 Fremont St E, Golden Nugget; pizza $12-15, mains $19-35; ☺11:30am-midnight Sun-Thu, to 1am Fri & Sat; ⊒Deuce, SDX) At this Italian trattoria covered in painted murals, you'll be drawn to the sunlight-filled patio next to the Nugget's shark-tank water slide and swimming pool. Wood-oven-fired, thin-crust pizzas, heavy pastas, and chicken, fish, veal and steak dishes are accompanied by a 200-bottle list of Italian wines. Happy hour runs 2pm to 6pm daily.

🍷 DRINKING & NIGHTLIFE

Skyfall Lounge   Bar
(☏702-632-7575; www.delanolasvegas.com; Delano; ☺5pm-midnight Sun-Thu, to 1:30am Fri & Sat) Enjoy unparalleled views of the southern Strip from this rooftop bar atop Mandalay Bay's **Delano** (☏877-632-7800; P ❄ @ 🛜 ⛲ 🐾) hotel. Sit and sip cocktails as the sun sets over the Spring Mountains to the west, then dance the night away to mellow DJ beats, spun from 9pm.

Beauty Bar   Bar
(☏702-598-3757; www.thebeautybar.com; 517 Fremont St E; cover free-$10; ☺9pm-4am; ⊒Deuce) Swill a cocktail or just chill with the cool kids inside the salvaged innards of a 1950s New Jersey beauty salon. DJs and live bands rotate nightly, spinning everything from tiki lounge tunes, disco and '80s hits to punk, metal, glam and indie rock. Check the website for special events like 'Karate Karaoke.' There's often no cover charge.

Commonwealth   Bar
(☏702-445-6400; www.commonwealthlv.com; 525 Fremont St E; ☺7pm-late Tue-Sat; ⊒Deuce) It might be a little too cool for school but,

whoa, that Prohibition-era interior is worth a look: plush booths, softly glowing chandeliers, Victorian-era bric-a-brac and a saloon bar. Imbibe your old-fashioned cocktails on the rooftop patio overlooking the Fremont East scene. They say there's a secret cocktail bar within the bar, but you didn't hear that from us.

Parasol Up & Parasol Down
Cocktail Bar

(☏702-770-3392; www.wynnlasvegas.com; Wynn; ⏱11am-3am Sun-Thu, to 4am Fri & Sat, Parasol Down 11am-2am; 🚌Deuce) Stepping into the whimsical jewel-hued Parasol Up feels something like walking into a glamorous version of *Alice in Wonderland*, complete with bright, almost psychedelic flowers. Cozy up on a plush ruby-red loveseat and gaze out at the glassy Lake of Dreams. Down the fairy-tale-like curved escalator, Parasol Down's seasonal outdoor patio is the perfect spot for cucumber and ginger-infused martinis.

⭐ ENTERTAINMENT

Blue Man Group   Live Performance

(☏702-262-4400; www.blueman.com; tickets $80-190; ⏱shows at 7pm & 9:30pm; 👪) Art, music and technology combine with a dash of comedy in one of Vegas' most popular, family-friendly shows at the **Luxor** (☏702-262-4000; www.luxor.com; 3900 S Las Vegas Blvd; ⏱24hr; 🅿).

Le Rêve the Dream
Theater

(☏702-770-9966; http://boxoffice.wynnlasvegas.com; Wynn; tickets $105-205; ⏱shows at 7pm & 9:30pm Fri-Tue) Underwater acrobatic feats by scuba-certified performers are the centerpiece of this intimate 'aqua-in-the-round' theater, which holds a one-million-gallon swimming pool. Critics call it a less-inspiring version of Cirque's *O*, while devoted fans find the romantic underwater tango, thrilling high dives and visually spectacular adventures to be

superior. Beware: the cheapest seats are in the 'splash zone.'

ℹ INFORMATION

Las Vegas Convention & Visitors Authority

(LVCVA; ☏702-892-7575; www.lasvegas.com; 3150 Paradise Rd; ⏱8am-5:30pm Mon-Fri; 🚌Las Vegas Convention Center) The hotline provides up-to-date information about shows, attractions, activities and more; staff may help with finding last-minute accommodations.

ℹ GETTING THERE & AROUND

TO/FROM THE AIRPORT

McCarran International Airport (LAS; ☏702-261-5211; www.mccarran.com; 5757 Wayne Newton Blvd; 🚗) sits near the south end of the Strip.

The easiest and cheapest way to get to your hotel is by airport shuttle (one-way to Strip/Downtown hotels from $7/9) or a shared ride-share service (from $10). As you exit baggage claim, look for shuttle bus kiosks lining the curb; prices and destinations are clearly marked. Taxis hover at $15 to $25 for the Strip and upwards of $20 for Downtown, plus tip.

PUBLIC TRANSPORTATION

○ Bus Deuce buses to/from downtown stop every block or two along the Strip. A 24-hour pass costs $8.

○ Tram Free air-conditioned trams operate on three routes: one connects the Bellagio, CityCenter and the Monte Carlo; another links Treasure Island and the Mirage, while a third travels between Excalibur, Luxor and Mandalay Bay.

TAXI & RIDE SHARE

It's illegal to hail a cab but there are taxi stands at almost every casino hotel and shopping mall. Rides cost at least $20, plus tip.

Uber and Lyft are by far the best way to get around Vegas, and even cheaper when traveling with others.

GRAND CANYON NATIONAL PARK

In this Chapter

South Rim Overlooks...........................256
South Rim...258
North Rim...260
Flagstaff..262

Grand Canyon National Park at a Glance...

No matter how much you read about the Grand Canyon or how many photographs you've seen, nothing really prepares you for the sight of it. One of the world's seven natural wonders, it's so startlingly familiar and iconic you can't take your eyes off it. The canyon's immensity, the sheer intensity of light and shadow at sunrise or sunset, even its very age, scream for superlatives.

Snaking along its floor are 277 miles of the Colorado River, which has carved the canyon over the past six million years and exposed rocks up to two billion years old.

Two Days at Grand Canyon South Rim

On day one, see the sun rise at **Yaki Point** (p257). Stroll the **Rim Trail** (p258) from Mather Point to **Yavapai Geology Museum** (p258), and have lunch at **El Tovar Dining Room & Lounge** (p259). Later, catch the sunset at **Hopi Point** (p256). The next day, hike on the **South Kaibab Trail** (p258). Wrap up with a drive east along Desert View Dr, stopping at viewpoints and **Desert View Watchtower** (p256).

Two Days at Grand Canyon North Rim

On day one, arrive early and get your first canyon eyeful at **Bright Angel Point** (p260). Bring a picnic, or grab a sandwich at **Deli in the Pines** (p261), then hike along the **Widforss Trail** (p261). Have a meal at **Grand Canyon Lodge** (p261). On day two hike along the **North Kaibab Trail** (p260) or have a picnic at **Marble Viewpoint** (p260). Then saddle up with **Canyon Trail Rides** (p261).

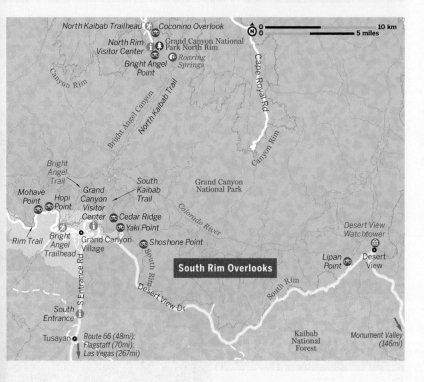

North Kaibab Trailhead Coconino Overlook

North Rim Visitor Center Grand Canyon National Park North Rim

Bright Angel Point Roaring Springs

Canyon Rim

Bright Angel Canyon

North Kaibab Trail

Cape Royal Rd

Canyon Rim

Bright Angel Trail

Mohave Point

Hopi Point

Grand Canyon Visitor Center

South Kaibab Trail

Grand Canyon National Park

Colorado River

Cedar Ridge

Yaki Point

Rim Trail

Bright Angel Trailhead

Grand Canyon Village

Shoshone Point

S Entrance Rd

South Rim Overlooks

South Rim Dr

Desert View Dr

South Rim

Desert View Watchtower

Lipan Point

Desert View

South Entrance

Tusayan

Route 66 (48mi);
Flagstaff (70mi);
Las Vegas (267mi)

Kaibab National Forest

Monument Valley (146mi)

0 — 10 km
0 — 5 miles

Arriving in Grand Canyon National Park

South Rim The more accessible entry point. Grand Canyon Village is at its heart, accessed via Hwy 64, south to Flagstaff (79 miles, partly on Hwy 180) and east to Hwy 89. A scheduled bus service or bookable shuttle also ply this route.

North Rim Access is via Hwy 67. It's a 215-mile, four- to five-hour drive to the South Rim; or take the Trans-Canyon Shuttle.

Where to Stay

South Rim Has three campgrounds and six hotels. **Xanterra** (☎928-638-3283, 303-297-2757, 888-297-2757; www.grandcanyonlodges.com) operates all park lodges. Reserve well ahead. If everything is booked up, consider Tusayan (7 miles south), Valle (30 miles south) or Williams (60 miles south).

North Rim There's one lodge and one campground. More options are another 60 miles north in Kanab, UT.

View from Lipan Point

OLGS / SHUTTERSTOCK ©

South Rim Overlooks

The views from the South Rim are stunners. Each overlook has its individual beauty – a dizzyingly sheer drop, a view of river rapids or a felicitous arrangement of jagged temples and buttes.

Great For...

☑ Don't Miss

Mohave and Hopi Points: these are the two to view if you're short on time.

Top Five Overlooks

Mohave Point (www.nps.gov/grca; Hermit Rd; 🚐Hermits Rest) Overlooks the river and three rapids; great for sunrise or sunset.

Hopi Point (www.nps.gov/grca; Hermit Rd; 🚐Hermits Rest) Gorgeous sunset spectacle; juts further into the canyon than any other South Rim overlook, offering magnificent east–west views. During the summer peak, there can be more than a thousand people waiting for shuttle pick-up after sunset.

Lipan Point (www.nps.gov/grca; Desert View Dr) Offers expansive views and an excellent perch for sunset.

Desert View Watchtower (www.nps.gov/grca; Desert View, East Entrance; ⊘8am-sunset mid-May–Aug, 9am-6pm Sep–mid-Oct, 9am-5pm mid-Oct–Feb, 8am-6pm Mar–mid-May) The marvelously worn winding staircase of Mary

South Kaibab Trail (p258)

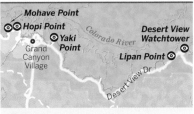

❶ Need to Know

Park entry (vehicle $30, shuttle-bus passenger $15) is valid for seven days at both rims.

✕ Take a Break

Fuel up on pancakes, fresh trout and more at El Tovar Dining Room & Lounge (p259).

★ Top Tip

Check the park website (www.nps. gov/grca) for updates on sights and events.

Colter's 70ft stone tower, built in 1932, leads to the highest spot on the rim (7522ft). Unparalleled views take in not only the canyon and the Colorado River, but also the San Francisco Peaks, Navajo Reservation and Painted Desert.

Yaki Point (www.nps.gov/grca; Yaki Point Rd, off Desert View Dr; ☐ Kaibab/Rim) A favorite spot for watching the sunrise; it's accessible year-round by shuttle or bicycle only, so it tends to be quieter.

Reading the Formations

Many visitors are eager to identify the formations that layer the canyon. The distinctive sequence of color and texture is worth learning, as you'll see it from each viewpoint.

Kaibab limestone Starting at the top, a layer of creamy white Kaibab limestone caps the rim on both sides of the canyon.

Toroweap formation The vegetated slope between Kaibab limestone above and the massive Coconino cliffs below.

Coconino sandstone Note how sandstone erodes differently from limestone when you see these sheer 350ft cliffs.

Hermit shale Next lies a slope of crumbly red Hermit shale; today it supports a distinctive band of shrubs and trees.

Supai Group Just below the Hermit shale are the red cliffs and ledges of the Supai Group, similar in composition and color, but differing in hardness.

Redwall limestone This next layer is one of the canyon's most prominent features; the huge red cliff forms a dividing line between forest habitats above and desert habitats below.

Finally comes the small slope of Muav limestone, followed by the greenish Bright Angel shale and Tapeats sandstone, the last and oldest layer.

South Rim

If you don't mind bumping elbows with other travelers, you'll be fine on the accessible and (comparatively) developed Grand Canyon South Rim. Infrastrucure is abundant: you'll find an entire village worth of lodging, restaurants, bookstores, libraries, a supermarket and a deli.

◎ SIGHTS

Shoshone Point   Viewpoint
(www.nps.gov/grca; Desert View Dr) Walk 1 mile along the mostly level dirt road to marvelously uncrowded Shoshone Point, a rocky promontory with some of the canyon's best views. This viewpoint is unmarked; look for the small parking lot about 1.2 miles east of Yaki Point.

Yavapai Geology
Museum   Museum
(☏928-638-7890; www.nps.gov/grca; Grand Canyon Village; ☺8am-7pm Mar-May & Sep-Nov, to 6pm Dec-Feb, to 8pm Jun-Aug; 🚻; 🚆Kaibab/Rim) **FREE** Views don't get much better than those unfolding behind the plate-glass windows of this little stone building at Yavapai Point. Handy panels identify and explain the various formations before you, and displays (including a scale model) highlight the canyon's multilayered geologic history.

✪ ACTIVITIES

Bright Angel Trail   Hiking
The most popular of the corridor trails is the beautiful Bright Angel Trail. The steep and scenic 7.8-mile descent to the Colorado River is punctuated with four logical turnaround spots. The trailhead is just west of **Bright Angel Lodge** (www.nps.gov/grca; Village Loop Dr; 🚆Village) **FREE**.

Rim Trail   Hiking
(www.nps.gov/grca; 🚻; 🚆Hermits Rest, 🚆Village, 🚆Kaibab/Rim) Beginning in Grand Canyon Village, the popular Rim Trail follows the rim west 13 miles to Hermits Rest, dipping in and out of scrubby pines and connecting a series of scenic points and his-

torical sights. Portions are paved, and every viewpoint is accessed by one of the three shuttle routes.

South Kaibab Trail   Hiking
(Yaki Point Rd, off Desert View Dr; 🚆Kaibab/Rim) The South Kaibab is one of the park's prettiest trails, combining stunning scenery and unobstructed 360-degree views with every step. Steep, rough and wholly exposed, ascents during summer can be dangerous, and during this season rangers discourage all but the shortest day hikes – otherwise it's a grueling 7-mile round-trip to the Colorado River.

⊕ TOURS

Canyon Vistas Mule Rides   Tours
(☏888-297-2757, same day/next day reservations 928-638-3283; www.grandcanyonlodges.com; Bright Angel Lodge; 3hr mule ride $135, 1-/2-night mule ride incl meals & accommodations $552/788; ☺rides available year-round, hours vary) This outfit takes groups of up to 20 mules 4 miles along the East Rim Trail. If you want to descend into the canyon, the only option is an overnight trip to Phantom Ranch. These trips follow the Bright Angel Trail 10.5 miles (5½ hours) down, spend one or two nights at Phantom Ranch, and return 7.8 miles (five hours) along the South Kaibab Trail.

Rim View Walk   Hiking
(www.nps.gov/grca; Grand Canyon Village; ☺8:30am Mon, Wed & Fri Jun-Aug) This two-hour ranger-led walk along a paved two-mile section of the Rim Trail examines natural history and contemporary Grand Canyon issues.

✖ EATING

Yavapai Lodge
Restaurant   American $
(☏928-638-6421; www.visitgrandcanyon.com; 11 Yavapai Lodge Rd, Yavapai Lodge; breakfast $7-9, lunch & dinner $13-16; ☺6am-10pm May-Sep, shorter hours rest of year; 🚻; 🚆Village) The restaurant at the Yavapai Lodge serves barbecue and sandwiches as well as beer and

wine. Place your order, pick up your drinks, and your number will get called when the food is ready.

El Tovar Dining Room & Lounge   American $$$

(📞928-638-2631; www.grandcanyonlodges. com; National Historic Landmark District; mains $20-30; ⊗restaurant 6-10:30am, 11am-2pm & 4:30-10pm, lounge 11am-11pm; 🚹; 🚊Village) Dark-wood tables are set with china and white linen, eye-catching murals spotlight American Indian tribes and huge windows frame views of the Rim Trail and canyon beyond. Breakfast options include El Tovar's pancake trio (buttermilk, blue cornmeal and buckwheat pancakes with pine-nut butter and prickly pear syrup), and blackened trout with two eggs.

Arizona Room   American $$$

(📞928-638-2631; www.grandcanyonlodges.com; 9 Village Loop Dr, Bright Angel Lodge; lunch $13-16, dinner $22-28; ⊗11:30am-3pm & 4:30-10pm Jan-Oct; 🚹; 🚊Village) Antler chandeliers hang from the ceiling and picture windows over-look the Rim Trail and canyon beyond. Try to get on the waitlist when the doors open at 4:30pm, because by 4:40pm you may have an hour's wait – reservations are not accepted. Agave/citrus-marinated chicken, oven-roasted squash and ribs with chipotle barbecue give a Western vibe.

ℹ️ INFORMATION

Grand Canyon Visitor Center (📞928-638-7888; www.nps.gov/grca; Visitor Center Plaza, Grand Canyon Village; ⊗9am-5pm; 🚊Village, 🚊Kaibab/ Rim) The South Rim's main visitor center: on the plaza here, bulletin boards and kiosks display information about ranger programs, the weather, tours and hikes. Inside is a ranger-staffed information desk, a lecture hall and a theater screening a 20-minute movie *Grand Canyon: A Journey of Wonder*.

ℹ️ GETTING THERE & AWAY

Grand Canyon National Park Airport, in Tusayan just south of the park's south entrance, handles

Rafting the Colorado River

Rafting the Colorado is an epic, adrenaline-pumping adventure.

OARS (📞800-346-6277, 209-736-4677; www.oars.com; 6- to 7-day Upper Canyon oar trip from $2658, 14- to 18-day Full Canyon dory trips from $5661) One of the best in the canyon, OARS boasts the best guide-to-guest ratio (1:4). With oar, paddle and dory trips, and carbon-offset options, OARS offers more elegance than most – they claim you'll eat better with them than you do at home – and partners with local artisans.

Arizona Raft Adventures (📞800-786-7238, 928-526-8200; www.azraft.com; 6-day Upper Canyon hybrid/paddle trips $2097/2197, 10-day Full Canyon motor trips $3160) This multigenerational family-run outfit offers motor, paddle, oar and hybrid (both paddling and floating) trips. Music fans can join one of the folk and bluegrass trips, with professional pickers and banjo players providing background music.

Wilderness River Adventures (📞800-992-8022, 928-645-3296; www.riveradven-tures.com; 6-day full-Canyon motor trips $2525, 12-day full-Canyon oar trips $3900) Wilderness River Adventures' hybrid trips give rafters the chance to be active and relaxed, combining hands-on paddling with floating. It partners with Green Thread, an environmental organi-zation operating in national parks. Save hundreds of dollars on quoted rates by using the 'Pay Now' option online.

ELEN ARRIGO / SHUTTERSTOCK ©

charter flights, scenic flights and helicopters, and can get you to Boulder City or Las Vegas.

🚹 GETTING AROUND

CAR

Grand Canyon Village is very congested in summer. Day-trippers should park in one of the four lots at the Grand Canyon Visitor Center, or ride the shuttle from Tusayan to the visitor center, then catch a shuttle into the Village.

SHUTTLE

Free shuttle buses ply three routes along the South Rim. In the pre-dawn hours, shuttles run every half-hour or so and typically begin running about an hour before sunrise; check the *Guide* for current sunrise and sunset information. From early morning until after sunset, buses run every 15 minutes.

Hermits Rest Route Shuttle (Red) www.nps. gov/grca; ⊗Mar-Nov

Hikers' Express Bus www.nps.gov/grca; Grand Canyon Village; ⊗5am, 6am & 7am May & Sep, 4am, 5am & 6am Jun-Aug, 6am, 7am & 8am Apr & Oct, 8am, 9am & 10am Nov-Mar

Kaibab/Rim Route Shuttle (Orange) www. nps.gov/grca; Visitor Center Plaza, Grand Canyon Village

Tusayan Route Shuttle (Purple) www.nps.gov/ grca; ⊗8am-9:30pm mid-May–early Sep

Village Route Shuttle (Blue) www.nps.gov/grca; Grand Canyon Village

North Rim

Solitude reigns supreme on the North Rim. All you'll find here are a classic rimside lodge, campground, motel and general store, plus miles of trails carving through meadows thick with wildflowers, willowy aspen and towering ponderosa pines. You'll also find peace, room to breathe and a less fettered Grand Canyon experience.

👁 SIGHTS

Bright Angel Point   Viewpoint
(www.nps.gov; North Rim) Short, easy and spectacular (it's just a 0.5-mile round-trip),

the paved trail to Bright Angel Point is a Grand Canyon must. Beginning from the back porch of the Grand Canyon Lodge, it goes to a narrow finger of an overlook with fabulous views.

**Grand Canyon National
Park North Rim**   National Park
(www.nps.gov/grca; per vehicle $30, per motorcycle $25, per bicycle, pedestrian or shuttle-bus passenger $15; ⊗mid-May–mid-Oct) The park's remote, wild and ravishing North Rim is far less developed, and sees far fewer visitors that its southern counterpart. In part this is due to seasonal closure: at these altitudes (8000ft) the winter snows force a winter closure of all services between October 15 and May 15. The road from Jacob Lake stays open longer, for day use and car camping – usually until the end of November.

Marble Viewpoint   Viewpoint
A favorite of the many Kaibab National Forest overlooks, this viewpoint makes a spectacular picnic or camping spot. From the 1-acre meadow, covered with Indian paintbrush and hiding Coconino sandstone fossils, views extend over the eastern edge of the canyon to the paper-flat expanse beyond. This is not a quintessential Grand Canyon overlook that you'll see in postcards or Grand Canyon books. Instead, you're looking down to where the Colorado first cuts into the rocks from Lees Ferry.

The road seems to end at an overlook; be sure to take the narrow road through the woods to the right about 0.25 miles to Marble Viewpoint.

🚴 ACTIVITIES

North Kaibab Trail   Hiking
(North Rim) The North Kaibab Trail is the North Rim's only maintained rim-to-river trail and connects with trails to the South Rim. The first 4.7 miles are the steepest, dropping 3050ft to Roaring Springs – a popular all-day hike.

If you prefer a shorter day hike below the rim, walk just 0.75 miles down to Coconino Overlook or 2 miles to the Supai Tunnel to get a taste of steep inner-canyon hiking. The 28-mile round-trip to the Colorado River is a multiday affair.

Cape Final Trail   Hiking
To join this easy 4-mile round-trip, which offers incredible views of the canyon, find the trailhead in an unpaved car park on the east side of the Cape Royal Rd, about 2.5 miles north of the Cape Royal car park.

Widforss Trail   Hiking
The moderate Widforss Trail (10 miles round-trip) meanders through stands of spruce, white fir, ponderosa pine and aspen to Widforss Point. Tall trees offer shade, fallen limbs provide pleasant spots to relax, and you likely won't see more than a few people along the trail. Though the total elevation change is only 440ft, rolling terrain makes this six-hour hike a moderate challenge.

🍂 TOURS

Canyon Trail Rides   Tours
(☎435-679-8665; www.canyonrides.com; North Rim; 1hr/half-day mule ride $45/90; ☺schedules vary mid-May–mid-Oct) You can make reservations anytime for the upcoming year but, unlike mule trips on the South Rim, you can usually book a trip upon your arrival at the park; just duck inside the Grand Canyon Lodge to the Mule Desk. Rides don't reach the Colorado River, but the half-day trip gives a taste of life below the rim.

✖ EATING & DRINKING

Deli in the Pines   Cafeteria $
(☎928-638-2611; lunch & dinner $7-15; ☺10:30am-9pm mid-May–mid-Oct) The name is a bit misleading: this isn't a deli, but a small cafeteria adjacent to the Grand Canyon Lodge serving takeaway salads and sandwiches to pack for a hike or picnic. There's also pizza, soft-serve ice cream, and a handful of daily specials like chili and pulled pork.

Grand Canyon Lodge
Dining Room   American $$
(☎May-Oct 928-638-2611, Nov-Apr 928-645-6865; www.grandcanyonforever.com; breakfast $8-11, lunch $10-13, dinner $18-28; ☺6:30-10:30am, 11:30am-2:30pm & 4:30-9:30pm May 15-Oct 15; ⚡🐾) Although seats beside the window are wonderful, views from the dining room are so huge it really doesn't matter where you sit. While the solid dinner menu includes buffalo steak, western trout and several vegetarian options, don't expect great culinary memories – the view is the thing. Make reservations in advance of your arrival to guarantee a spot for dinner.

Grand Canyon
Cookout Experience American $$$
(☎928-638-2611; Grand Canyon Lodge; adult/child 6-15yr $30/15; ☺5:45-9pm Jun 1-Sep 30; 🐾) Feast on smoked beef brisket, roasted chicken, skillet cornbread and all the fixings – served with a side of Western songs and jokes. It's cheesy, but it's a lot of fun, old-school National Park–style, and it's great for kids. Take the Bridle Trail from the Grand Canyon Lodge to the cookout site, or catch the complimentary train or shuttle van.

Coffee Shop & Rough
Rider Saloon   Coffee, Bar
(www.grandcanyonforever.com; Grand Canyon Lodge; ☺5:30-10:30am & 11:30am-10:30pm) If you're up for an early morning hike, stop for coffee or a quick breakfast at the cozy Coffee Shop – a space that morphs back into a saloon by noon, serving beer, wine and mixed drinks, plus sandwiches, wraps and pizza. Teddy Roosevelt memorabilia lines the walls (and inspires the cocktails), honoring his role in the history of the park.

ℹ INFORMATION

North Rim Visitor Center (☎928-638-7888; www.nps.gov/grca; ☺8am-6pm May 15-Oct 15) Beside Grand Canyon Lodge, this is the place to get information on the park, and the starting point for ranger-led nature walks.

North Rim Scenic Drive

Driving on the North Rim involves miles of slow, twisty roads through dense stands of evergreens and aspen to get to the most spectacular overlooks. From Grand Canyon Lodge, drive north for about 3 miles, then take the signed turn east to Cape Royal and Point Imperial and continue for 5 miles to a fork in the road called the Y.

From the Y it's another 15 miles south to Cape Royal (7876ft) past overlooks, picnic tables and an Ancestral Puebloan site. A 0.6-mile paved path, lined with piñon, cliffrose and interpretive signs, leads from the parking lot to a natural arch and Cape Royal Point, arguably the best view from this side of the canyon.

Point Imperial, the park's highest overlook at 8803ft, is reached by following Point Imperial Rd from the Y for an easy 3 miles. Expansive views include Nankoweap Creek, the Vermilion Cliffs, the Painted Desert and the Little Colorado River.

Mt Hayden, Point Imperial
JOE WEST / SHUTTERSTOCK ©

❶ GETTING THERE & AWAY

The only access road to the Grand Canyon North Rim is Hwy 67, which closes with the first snowfall and reopens in spring after the snowmelt (exact dates vary).

Although only 11 miles from the South Rim as the crow flies, it's a grueling 215-mile, four- to five-hour drive on winding desert roads between here and Grand Canyon Village. You can drive yourself or take the **Trans-Canyon Shuttle**

(☏928-638-2820, 877-638-2820; www.trans-canyonshuttle.com; one-way rim to rim $90, one-way South Rim to Marble Canyon $80). Reserve at least two weeks in advance.

Flagstaff

Flagstaff's laid-back charms are many, from a pedestrian-friendly historic downtown crammed with eclectic vernacular architecture and vintage neon, to hiking and skiing. Throw in a healthy appreciation for craft beer, freshly roasted coffee beans and an all-around good time and you have the makings of the perfect northern Arizonan escape.

◉ SIGHTS & ACTIVITIES

Sunset Crater Volcano National Monument Volcano
(☏928-526-0502; www.nps.gov/sucr; Park Loop Rd 545; car/motorcycle/bicycle or pedestrian $20/15/10; ⏰9am-5pm Nov-May, from 8am Jun-Oct) Around AD 1064 a volcano erupted on this spot, spewing ash across 800 sq miles, spawning the Kana-A lava flow and forcing farmers to vacate lands tilled for 400 years. Now the 8029ft Sunset Crater is quiet, and mile-long trails wind through the Bonito lava flow (formed c 1180), and up Lenox Crater (7024ft). More ambitious hikers and bikers can ascend O'Leary Peak (8965ft; 8 miles round-trip), or there's a gentle, 0.3-mile, wheelchair-accessible loop overlooking the petrified flow.

Lowell Observatory Observatory
(☏main phone 928-774-3358, recorded information 928-233-3211; www.lowell.edu; 1400 W Mars Hill Rd; adult/senior/child 5-17yr $15/14/8; ⏰10am-10pm Mon-Sat, to 5pm Sun; ♿) Sitting atop a hill just west of downtown, this national historic landmark – famous for the first sighting of Pluto, in 1930 – was built by Percival Lowell in 1894. Weather permitting, visitors can stargaze through on-site telescopes, including the famed 1896 Clark Telescope, the impetus behind the now-accepted theory of an expanding universe. Kids will love the paved Pluto Walk,

which meanders through a scale model of our solar system.

Absolute Bikes
Cycling

(🖉928-779-5969; www.absolutebikes.net; 202 E Rte 66; bike rentals per day from $39; ⏰9am-7pm Mon-Fri, 9am-6pm Sat, 10am-4pm Sun Apr-Thanksgiving, shorter hours Dec-Mar) Visit these super-friendly gearheads for the inside track on the local mountain-biking scene, and to hire wheels for the surrounding trails.

🍴 EATING

Tourist Home Urban Market
Cafe $

(🖉928-779-2811; www.touristhomeurbanmarket. com; 52 S San Francisco St; mains $10-12; ⏰6am-8pm; 🍴) Housed in a beautifully renovated 1926 house that was originally home to Basque sheepherder immigrants, this upscale market cafe serves up the best breakfast in a town full of excellent morning vittles. Try the Hash Bowl: eggs any style served on breakfast potatoes and accompanied by chorizo, spiced beets and a cilantro pesto.

Pizzicletta
Pizza $

(🖉928-774-3242; www.pizzicletta.com; 203 W Phoenix Ave; pizzas $11-15; ⏰5-9pm Sun-Thu, to 10pm Fri & Sat) Tiny Pizzicletta, where the excellent thin-crusted wood-fired pizzas are loaded with gourmet toppings like arugula and aged prosciutto, is housed in a sliver of a white-brick building. Inside there's an open kitchen, one long table with iron chairs, Edison bulbs and industrial surrounds. You can order in while you enjoy some suds at **Mother Road Brewing Company** (🖉928-774-9139; www.motherroadbeer.com; 7 S Mikes Pike; ⏰2-9pm Mon-Thu, 2-10pm Fri, noon-10pm Sat, noon-9pm Sun) next door.

Macy's
Cafe $

(🖉928-774-2243; www.macyscoffee.net; 14 S Beaver St; breakfast/lunch $6/7; ⏰6am-6pm;

🛜🍴) The delicious coffee at this Flagstaff institution – house roasted in the original, handsome, fire-engine-red roaster in the corner – has kept local students and caffeine devotees buzzing since the 1980s. The vegetarian menu includes many vegan choices, along with traditional cafe grub like pastries, steamed eggs, waffles, yogurt and granola, salads and veggie sandwiches.

🍷 DRINKING & NIGHTLIFE

Museum Club
Bar

(🖉928-526-9434; www.themuseumclub.com; 3404 E Rte 66; ⏰11am-2am) This honky-tonk roadhouse on Route 66 has been kicking up its heels since 1936. Inside what looks like a huge log cabin you'll find a large wooden dancefloor, animal mounts and an elixir-filled mahogany bar. The origins of the name? In 1931 it housed a taxidermy museum.

Hops on Birch
Pub

(🖉928-774-4011; www.hopsonbirch.com; 22 E Birch Ave; ⏰1:30pm-12:30am Mon-Thu, to 2am Fri, noon-2am Sat, noon-12:30am Sun) Simple and handsome, Hops on Birch has 34 rotating beers on tap, live music five nights a week and a friendly local-crowd vibe. In classic Flagstaff style, dogs are as welcome as humans.

ℹ️ GETTING THERE & AWAY

Hwy 180 is the most direct route northwest to Tusayan and the South Rim (80 miles), while Hwy 89 beelines north to Cameron (59 miles), where it meets Hwy 64 heading west to the canyon's East Entrance.

Arizona Shuttle (🖉928-226-8060, 800-888-2749; www.arizonashuttle.com) and **Flagstaff Shuttle & Charter** (🖉888-215-3105; www.flag shuttle.com) have shuttles that run between Flagstaff, Grand Canyon National Park, Williams, Sedona and Phoenix's Sky Harbor International Airport.

LOS ANGELES

In this Chapter

Santa Monica Pier.............................268
Hollywood..270
Griffith Park.......................................274
Sights...278
Eating...281
Drinking & Nightlife..........................285
Entertainment...................................286

Los Angeles at a Glance...

Ruggedly good looking, deeply creative, with a sunny disposition to boot...if LA were on Tinder, the app would crash. This is a city of incredible energy, architectural riches and some of the best places to eat and drink in the nation. Despite the plastic cliches, LA is one of the world's great cultural cities, home to exceptional art collections, world-shaking architecture and an extraordinary melting pot of cultures. But it's the incomparable beauty of its setting that sets it apart. Here, the rat race comes with sweeping beaches, mountain vistas and bewitching sunsets.

Two Days in Los Angeles

Start in **Hollywood** (p270) by walking all over your favorite stars on the **Hollywood Walk of Fame** (p273), snapping pics of the iconic **Capitol Records Tower** (p272) and pressing up against famous hands outside **Grauman's Chinese Theatre** (p273). On day two, hit the streets of rapidly evolving Downtown LA. Check out the stunning new **Broad** (p278) art museum and the **Grammy Museum** (p278).

Four Days in Los Angeles

With two more days in town, you'll want to get a taste of beach life, by walking around Santa Monica, a hip and eccentric enclave of surfers and tourists surrounding its world-famous **pier** (p268). Get a dose of nature at **Griffith Park** (p274). Finally, explore the incredible **Getty Center** (p278), a spectacular synergy of art, architecture, landscaping and views.

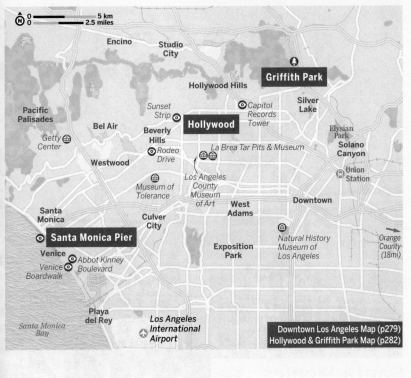

N 0 ⸺ 5 km
0 ⸺ 2.5 miles

Encino

Studio City

Hollywood Hills

🌳 **Griffith Park**

Pacific Palisades

Sunset Strip ◉

◉ Capitol Records Tower

Silver Lake

Bel Air

Beverly Hills

Hollywood

Elysian Park

Getty 🏛 Center

◉ Rodeo Drive

La Brea Tar Pits & Museum 🏛🏛

Solano Canyon

Westwood

🏛 Museum of Tolerance

Los Angeles County Museum of Art

🚉 Union Station

Santa Monica

Culver City

West Adams

Downtown

◉ **Santa Monica Pier**

🏛 Natural History Museum of Los Angeles

Orange County (18mi) →

Venice ◉ Venice ◉ Boardwalk

Abbot Kinney Boulevard

Exposition Park

Playa del Rey

Santa Monica Bay

✈ **Los Angeles International Airport**

Downtown Los Angeles Map (p279)
Hollywood & Griffith Park Map (p282)

Arriving in Los Angeles

Los Angeles International Airport
Shuttle buses, taxis and ride-sharing services are conveniently located at the terminals. Door-to-door shuttles charge $23, $28 and $17 for trips to Santa Monica, Hollywood and Downtown, respectively. Curbside dispatchers summon taxis that have flat rates to most popular neighborhoods (ie $47 to Downtown LA, $35 to Santa Monica).

Where to Stay

LA is huge, and your interests will determine where you want to stay. Do your research before booking a room or house. Do you want to be within stumbling distance of hot spot bars and clubs, near major cultural sites, or by the ocean?

EDUARDO FREDERIKSEN / 500PX ©

Santa Monica Pier

Santa Monica is LA's cute, alluring, hippie-chic little sister, its karmic counterbalance and, to many, its salvation. This is where you'll encounter the picturesque oceanside California you've seen in the movies.

Great For...

☑ Don't Miss

The beautiful, hand-painted horses of the 1922 carousel at the entrance to Santa Monica Pier.

Surrounded by LA on three sides and the Pacific on the fourth, SaMo is a place where real-life Lebowskis sip white Russians next to martini-swilling Hollywood producers, celebrity chefs dine at family-owned taquerias, and soccer moms and career bachelors shop at abundant farmers markets. All the while, kids, out-of-towners and those who love them flock to wide beaches and the pier, where the landmark Ferris wheel and roller coaster welcome one and all.

Once the very end of the mythical Route 66, and still the object of a tourist love affair, the Santa Monica Pier dates back to 1908 and is the city's most compelling landmark. There are arcades and carnival games, and the pier comes alive with free concerts (Twilight Dance Series) and outdoor movies in the summertime.

❶ Need to Know

☎310-458-8901; www.santamonicapier.org

✖ Take a Break

Try The Godmother, the Queen of All Sandwiches, at **Bay Cities** (www.baycitiesitaliandeli.com; 1517 Lincoln Blvd; sandwiches $5-9; ⊘9am-6pm Tue-Sun; ℗), the best Italian deli in LA.

★ Top Tip

The best way to get around is by bicycle; you'll find rentals by the day or hour.

Pacific Park

Kids get their kicks at **Pacific Park** (☎310-260-8744; www.pacpark.com; 380 Santa Monica Pier; per ride $5-10, all-day pass adult/child under 8yr $32/18; ⊘daily, seasonal hours vary; 🐾; Ⓜ Expo Line to Downtown Santa Monica), a small amusement park with a solar-powered Ferris wheel, kiddy rides, midway games and food stands. Check the website for discount coupons.

Aquarium

If you peer under the pier – just below the carousel – you'll find Heal the Bay's **Santa Monica Pier Aquarium** (☎310-393-6149; www.healthebay.org; 1600 Ocean Front Walk; adult/child $5/free; ⊘2-6pm Tue-Fri, 12:30-6pm Sat & Sun; 🐾; Ⓜ Expo Line to Downtown Santa Monica) 🐾. Sea stars, crabs, sea urchins and other critters and crustaceans scooped from the bay are on display in their adopted touch-tank homes. For a fin-filled frenzy, stop by the shark tanks for feedings of those multifanged beasts.

South of the Pier

South of the pier is the **Original Muscle Beach** (www.musclebeach.net; 1800 Ocean Front Walk; ⊘sunrise-sunset), where the Southern California exercise craze began in the mid-20th century. New equipment now draws a fresh generation of fitness fanatics. Close by, the search for the next Bobby Fischer is on at the **International Chess Park** (☎310-458-8450; www.smgov.net; Ocean Front Walk at Seaside Tce; ⊘sunrise-sunset). Anyone can join in.

Following the South Bay Bicycle Trail, a paved bike and walking path, south for about 1.5 miles takes you straight to Venice Beach. Bikes or in-line skates are available to rent on the pier and at beachside kiosks.

Grauman's Chinese Theatre (p273)

Hollywood

No other corner of LA is steeped in as much mythology as Hollywood. You'll find the Walk of Fame, Capitol Records and Grauman's Chinese Theatre, where the entertainment deities have been immortalized in concrete.

Great For...

ⓘ Need to Know

Many of Hollywood's tourist attractions gravitate around the intersection of Hollywood Blvd and Highland Ave.

☑ **Don't Miss**

Stepping into the shoe prints of your favorite movie star at Grauman's Chinese Theatre.

Most of Hollywood's main tourist attractions are steps away from the intersection of Hollywood Blvd and Highland Ave (serviced by metro Red Line).

Capitol Records Tower

Vine St is where you'll find the **Capitol Records Tower** (Map p282; 1750 Vine St) **FREE**. You'll have no trouble recognizing this iconic 1956 structure, one of LA's great mid-century buildings. Designed by Welton Becket, it resembles a stack of records topped by a stylus blinking out 'Hollywood' in Morse code. Some of music's biggest stars have recorded hits in the building's basement studios, among them Nat King Cole, Frank Sinatra and Capitol's current heavyweight, Katy Perry. Outside on the sidewalk, Garth Brooks and John Lennon have their stars.

Hollywood Museum

For a taste of Old Hollywood, do not miss this musty temple to the stars, its four floors crammed with movie and TV costumes and props. The **museum** (Map p282; ☎323-464-7776; www.thehollywood museum.com; 1660 N Highland Ave; adult/child $15/5; ⊙10am-5pm Wed-Sun; Ⓜ Red Line to Hollywood/Highland) is housed inside the Max Factor Building, built in 1914 and relaunched as a glamorous beauty salon in 1935. At the helm was Polish-Jewish businessman Max Factor, Hollywood's leading authority on cosmetics. And it was right here that he worked his magic on Hollywood's most famous screen queens.

Hollywood Walk of Fame

Grauman's Chinese Theatre

Ever wondered what it's like to be in George Clooney's shoes? Just find his footprints in the forecourt of this world-famous **movie palace** (TCL Chinese Theatres; Map p282; ☎323-461-3331; www.tclchinesetheatres.com; 6925 Hollywood Blvd; guided tour adult/senior/child $16/13.50/8; 🚻; Ⓜ Red Line to Hollywood/Highland). The exotic pagoda theater – complete with temple bells and stone heaven dogs from China – has shown movies since 1927 when Cecil B DeMille's the *King of Kings* first flickered across the screen.

> **✗ Take a Break**
>
> One of the oldest dive bars in Hollywood, the **Frolic Room** (Map p282; ☎323-462-5890; 6245 Hollywood Blvd; ⊙11am-2am; Ⓜ Red Line to Hollywood/Vine) remains a hit.

Hollywood Walk of Fame

The **Hollywood Walk of Fame** (Map p282; www.walkoffame.com; Hollywood Blvd; Ⓜ Red Line to Hollywood/Highland) runs along Hollywood Blvd, as well as along Vine St a mile to the east. Big Bird, Bob Hope, Marilyn Monroe and Aretha Franklin are among the stars being sought out, worshipped, photographed and stepped on along the Hollywood Walk of Fame. Since 1960 more than 2600 performers – from legends to bit-part players – have been honored with a pink-marble sidewalk star.

Paramount Studios

Star Trek, Indiana Jones and *Shrek* are among the blockbusters that originated at Paramount, the country's second-oldest movie studio and the only one still in Hollywood proper. Two-hour **tours** (Map p282; ☎323-956-1777; www.paramount studiotour.com; 5555 Melrose Ave; tours from $55; ⊙tours 9:30am-5pm, last tour 3pm) of the studio complex are offered year-round, taking in the back lots and sound stages. Guides are usually passionate and knowledgeable, offering fascinating insight into the studio's history and the movie-making process in general.

OSCITY / SHUTTERSTOCK ©, HOLLYWOOD™ & DESIGN © HOLLYWOOD CHAMBER OF COMMERCE

> **★ Top Tip**
>
> Take the metro (Red Line); if driving, park at the Hollywood & Highland mall.

Griffith Observatory

TRAVELVIEW / SHUTTERSTOCK ©

Griffith Park

A gift to the city in 1896 by mining mogul Griffith J Griffith, and five times the size of New York's Central Park, Griffith Park is one of the country's largest urban green spaces.

It's easy to spend a whole day in this sprawling park, which contains an outdoor theater, zoo, observatory, two museums, golf courses, playgrounds, 53 miles of hiking trails, Batman's caves and the Hollywood sign.

Griffith Observatory

LA's landmark 1935 observatory opens a window onto the universe from its perch on the southern slopes of Mt Hollywood. Its planetarium claims the world's most advanced star projector, while its astronomical touch displays explore some mind-bending topics, from the evolution of the telescope and the ultraviolet X-rays used to map our solar system to the cosmos itself. Then, of course, there are the views (on clear days) of the entire LA basin, surrounding mountains and Pacific Ocean.

Great For...

☑ Don't Miss

The observatory's rooftop viewing platform has prime-time views of LA and the Hollywood Hills.

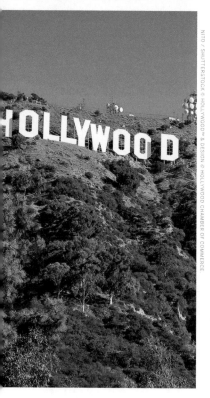

NITO / SHUTTERSTOCK ® © HOLLYWOOD™ & DESIGN © HOLLYWOOD CHAMBER OF COMMERCE

❶ Need to Know

☏323-644-2050; www.laparks.org; 4730 Crystal Springs Dr; ◷5am-10pm, trails sunrise-sunset

✕ Take a Break

Follow the signposted 0.6-mile hike to Fern Dell Dr for lunch at **Trails** (Map p282; ☏323-871-2102; 2333 Fern Dell Dr, Los Feliz; pastries $3-4, meals $5-9; ◷8am-5pm; 🛜👶), an outdoor cafe with made-from-scratch treats.

★ Top Tip

Parking is plentiful and free here – unlike most sights in LA.

You can peer into the Zeiss Telescope on the east side of the roof where sweeping views of the Hollywood Hills and the gleaming city below are especially spectacular at sunset. After dark, staff wheel additional telescopes out to the front lawn for stargazing.

Inside the building, grab a seat in the Planetarium – the aluminum-domed ceiling becomes a massive screen where lasers are projected to offer a tour of the cosmos, while another laser-projection show allows you to search for water, and life, beyond earth. Downstairs, the Leonard Nimoy Event Horizon Theater screens a fascinating 24-minute documentary about the observatory's history, including an extraordinary engineering feat that saw the entire building lifted from its foundations during its expansion in the early 2000s.

If relying on public transit, hop on the DASH Observatory shuttle bus, which runs between Vermont/Sunset metro station on the Red Line and the observatory. Buses run every 20 minutes from noon to 10pm on weekdays and 10am to 10pm on weekends.

Hollywood Sign

LA's most famous landmark first appeared in the hills in 1923 as an advertising gimmick for a real-estate development called 'Hollywoodland.' Each letter is 50ft tall and made of sheet metal. Once aglow with 4000 light bulbs, the sign even had its own caretaker who lived behind the 'L' until 1939.

In 1932 a struggling young actress named Peggy Entwistle leapt her way into local lore from the letter 'H.' The last four letters were lopped off in the '40s as the sign started to crumble. In the late '70s, Alice Cooper and Hugh Hefner joined forces with fans to save the symbol, and Hef was back at it again in 2010 when the hills behind the sign became slated for a housing development.

Architectural Masterpieces

Filled with amazing buildings, eateries and museums, Downtown LA is one of the most exciting neighborhoods for a stroll.

Start Verve
Finish Grand Central Market
Distance 2.5 miles
Duration Three Hours

5 Gape in wonder at **Broad** (p278), Downtown's most extraordinary building.

4 Step inside for a look at the opulent interiors of **Millennium Biltmore Hotel** (213-624-1011; www.thebiltmore.com; 506 S Grand Ave), which has appeared in *Ghostbusters*, *Fight Club* and *Mad Men*.

3 Pershing Square (www.laparks. org; 532 S Olive St), LA's first public park, was recently redone by French landscape architecture firm Agence Ter.

2 Architect Claud Beelman's extraordinary 1929 **Eastern Columbia Building** (www.eastern columbiahoa.com; 849 S Broadway) is a masterpiece of art moderne architecture.

Take a Break... Grand Park (www.grandparkla.org; 227 N Spring St) **is a great place to catch your breath and post some pics using the free wi-fi.**

Classic Photo A selfie outside the glittering facade of the Walt Disney Concert Hall (p278).

6 Frank Gehry's showstopping masterpiece, **Walt Disney Concert Hall** (p278), is home to the LA Philharmonic.

7 Grand Central Market (p278) is in a lovely beaux-arts building and has been satisfying appetites since 1917.

1 Start the tour with a steaming cup from Santa Cruz micro-roastery **Verve** (☎213-455-5991; www.vervecoffee.com; 833 S Spring St; ⊗7am-7pm Mon-Fri, to 8pm Sat & Sun).

Ⓝ 0 — 500 m
0 — 0.25 miles

⊙ SIGHTS

◎ Downtown Los Angeles

Downtown is divided into numerous areas. Bunker Hill is home to major modern-art museums and the Walt Disney Concert Hall. To the east is City Hall and, further east still, Little Tokyo. Southeast of Little Tokyo lies the trendy Arts District. Broadway is flanked by glorious heritage buildings, while the city's oldest colonial buildings flank Olvera St, north of City Hall and the 101 freeway. Further north still is Chinatown.

Broad   Museum

(Map p279; ☑213-232-6200; www.thebroad. org; 221 S Grand Ave; ⊙11am-5pm Tue & Wed, to 8pm Thu & Fri, 10am-8pm Sat, to 6pm Sun; P ✢; M Red/Purple Lines to Civic Center/Grand Park) **FREE** From the instant it opened in September 2015, the Broad (rhymes with 'road') became a must-visit for contemporary-art fans. It houses the world-class collection of local philanthropist and billionaire real-estate honcho Eli Broad and his wife Edythe, with more than 2000 postwar pieces by dozens of heavy hitters, including Cindy Sherman, Jeff Koons, Andy Warhol, Roy Lichtenstein, Robert Rauschenberg, Keith Haring and Kara Walker.

Grammy Museum   Museum

(Map p279; ☑213-765-6800; www.grammy museum.org; 800 W Olympic Blvd; adult/child $13/11; ⊙10:30am-6:30pm Mon-Fri, from 10am Sat & Sun; P ✢) It's the highlight of LA Live. Music lovers will get lost in interactive exhibits, which define, differentiate and link musical genres. Spanning three levels, the museum's rotating exhibitions might include threads worn by the likes of Michael Jackson, Whitney Houston and Beyonce, scribbled words from the hands of Count Basie and Taylor Swift and instruments once used by world-renowned rock deities. Inspired? Interactive sound chambers allow you to try your own hand at singing, mixing and remixing.

Grand Central Market   Market

(Map p279; www.grandcentralmarket.com; 317 S Broadway; ⊙8am-10pm; M Red/Purple Lines to Pershing Sq) LA's Grand Central Market has been satisfying appetites since 1917. Originally leased to the Ville de Paris department store, this was the city's first fireproof, steel-reinforced commercial building, designed by prolific architect John Parkinson and once home to an office occupied by Frank Lloyd Wright. Lose yourself in its bustle of neon signs, stalls and counters, peddling everything from fresh produce and nuts, to sizzling Thai street food, hipster egg rolls, artisanal pasta and specialty coffee.

Walt Disney
Concert Hall   Notable Building

(Map p279; ☑323-850-2000; www.laphil.org; 111 S Grand Ave; ⊙guided tours usually noon & 1:15pm Thu-Sat, 10am & 11am Sun; M Red/ Purple Lines to Civic Center/Grand Park) **FREE** A molten blend of steel, music and psychedelic architecture, this iconic concert venue is the home base of the Los Angeles Philharmonic, but has also hosted contemporary bands such as Phoenix and classic jazz musicians such as Sonny Rollins. Frank Gehry pulled out all the stops: the building is a gravity-defying sculpture of heaving and billowing stainless steel.

◎ Beverly Hills & Around

Getty Center   Museum

(☑310-440-7300; www.getty.edu; 1200 Getty Center Dr, off I-405 Fwy; ⊙10am-5:30pm Tue-Fri & Sun, to 9pm Sat; P ✢; ☐734, 234) **FREE** In its billion-dollar, in-the-clouds perch, high above the city grit and grime, the Getty Center presents triple delights: a stellar art collection (everything from medieval triptychs to baroque sculpture and impressionist brushstrokes), Richard Meier's cutting-edge architecture, and the visual splendor of seasonally changing gardens. Admission is free, but parking is $15 ($10 after 3pm).

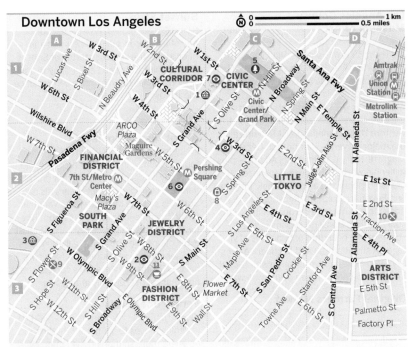

Downtown Los Angeles

◎ **Sights**
1 Broad B1
2 Eastern Columbia Building B3
3 Grammy Museum A3
4 Grand Central Market C2
5 Grand Park C1
6 Pershing Square B2
7 Walt Disney Concert Hall C1

🛍 **Shopping**
8 Last Bookstore in Los Angeles C2

🍴 **Eating**
9 Broken Spanish A3
10 Manuela D2

🍷 **Drinking & Nightlife**
11 Verve B3

Museum of Tolerance Museum
(📞reservations 310-772-2505; www.museum
oftolerance.com; 9786 W Pico Blvd; adult/senior/
student $15.50/12.50/11.50, Anne Frank Exhibit
adult/senior/student $15.50/13.50/12.50;
◎10am-5pm Sun-Wed & Fri, to 9:30pm Thu, to
3:30pm Fri Nov-Mar; 🅿) Run by the Simon
Wiesenthal Center, this powerful, deeply
moving museum uses interactive technology to engage visitors in discussion and
contemplation around racism and bigotry.
Particular focus is given to the Holocaust,

with a major basement exhibition that
examines the social, political and economic
conditions that led to the Holocaust as well
as the experience of the millions persecuted. On the museum's 2nd floor, another
major exhibition offers an intimate look into
the life and impact of Anne Frank.

◎ West Hollywood & Mid-City

Top of the list for any visit to LA is Museum
Row, as Wilshire Blvd is known between
about Fairfax and La Brea Aves.

Los Angeles County Museum of Art
Museum

(LACMA; Map p282; ☏323-857-6000; www.
lacma.org; 5905 Wilshire Blvd, Mid-City; adult/
child $15/free, 2nd Tue each month free; ⊗11am-
5pm Mon, Tue & Thu, to 8pm Fri, 10am-7pm Sat
& Sun; P; ☐Metro lines 20, 217, 720, 780 to
Wilshire & Fairfax) The depth and wealth of
the collection at the largest museum in the
western US is stunning. LACMA holds all
the major players – Rembrandt, Cézanne,
Magritte, Mary Cassat, Ansel Adams – plus
millennia worth of Chinese, Japanese,
pre-Columbian and ancient Greek, Roman
and Egyptian sculpture. Recent acquisi-
tions include massive outdoor installations
such as Chris Burden's *Urban Light* (a
surreal selfie backdrop of hundreds of vintage LA streetlamps) and Michael Heizer's
Levitated Mass, a surprisingly inspirational
340-ton boulder perched over a walkway.

Original Farmers Market
Market

(Map p282; ☏323-933-9211; www.farmers
marketla.com; 6333 W 3rd St, Fairfax District;
⊗9am-9pm Mon-Fri, to 8pm Sat, 10am-7pm Sun;
P 🖼) Long before the city was flooded with
farmers markets, there was *the* farmers
market. Fresh produce, roasted nuts,
doughnuts, cheeses, blinis – you'll find
them all at this 1934 landmark. Casual and
kid-friendly, it's a fun place for a browse,
snack or people-watching.

La Brea Tar Pits & Museum
Museum

(Map p282; www.tarpits.org; 5801 Wilshire Blvd,
Mid-City; adult/student & senior/child $12/9/5,
1st Tue of month Sep-Jun free; ⊗9:30am-5pm;
P 🖼) Mammoths, saber-toothed cats and
dire wolves used to roam LA's savannah in
prehistoric times. We know this because of
an archaeological trove of skulls and bones
unearthed here at the La Brea Tar Pits, one
of the world's most fecund and famous
fossil sites. A museum has been built here,
where generations of young dino-hunters
have come to seek out fossils and learn
about paleontology from docents and
demonstrations in on-site labs.

Sunset Strip
Street

(Map p282; Sunset Blvd) A visual cacophony of billboards, giant ad banners and
neon signs, the sinuous stretch of Sunset
Blvd running between Laurel Canyon and
Doheny Dr has been nightlife central since
the 1920s.

◎ Venice

Abbot Kinney Boulevard
Area

(☐Big Blue Bus line 18) Abbot Kinney, who
founded Venice in the early 1900s, would
probably be delighted to find that one of
Venice's best-loved streets bears his name.
Sort of a seaside Melrose with a Venetian
flavor, the mile-long stretch of Abbot Kinney Blvd between Venice Blvd and Main St
is full of upscale boutiques, galleries, lofts
and sensational restaurants. A few years
back, *GQ* named it America's coolest street,
and that cachet has only grown since.

Venice Boardwalk
Waterfront

(Ocean Front Walk; Venice Pier to Rose Ave) Life
in Venice moves to a different rhythm and
nowhere more so than on the famous Venice Boardwalk, officially known as Ocean
Front Walk. It's a freak show, a human zoo
and a wacky carnival alive with Hula-hoop
magicians, old-timey jazz combos, solo
distorted garage rockers and artists (good
and bad) – as far as LA experiences go, it's
a must.

◎ Malibu & Pacific Palisades

El Matador State Beach
Beach

(☏818-880-0363; 32215 Pacific Coast Hwy,
Malibu; P) Arguably Malibu's most stunning
beach, where you park on the bluffs and
stroll down a trail to sandstone rock towers
that rise from emerald coves. Topless
sunbathers stroll through the tides, and
dolphins breech the surface beyond the
waves. It's been impacted by coastal
erosion, but you can still find a sliver of dry
sand tucked against the bluffs.

Getty Villa
Museum

(☏310-430-7300; www.getty.edu; 17985
Pacific Coast Hwy, Pacific Palisades; ⊗10am-

5pm Wed-Mon; P ; line 534 to Coastline Dr) FREE Stunningly perched on an ocean-view hillside, this museum in a replica 1st-century Roman villa is an exquisite, 64-acre showcase for Greek, Roman and Etruscan antiquities. Dating back 7000 years, they were amassed by oil tycoon J Paul Getty. Galleries, peristiles, courtyards and lushly landscaped gardens ensconce all manner of friezes, busts and mosaics, millennia-old cut, blown and colored glass and brain-bending geometric configurations in the Hall of Colored Marbles. Other highlights include the Pompeii fountain and Temple of Herakles.

Exposition Park & South Los Angeles

Watts Towers Landmark

(213-847-4646; www.wattstowers.us; 1761-1765 E 107th St, Watts; adult/child 13-17yr & senior/child under 13yr $7/3/free; tours 11am-3pm Thu & Fri, 10:30am-3pm Sat, noon-3pm Sun; P; M Blue Line to 103rd St) The three Gothic spires of the fabulous Watts Towers rank among the world's greatest monuments of folk art. In 1921 Italian immigrant Simon Rodia set out 'to make something big' and then spent 33 years cobbling together this whimsical free-form sculpture from concrete, steel and a motley assortment of found objects: green 7-Up bottles to sea shells, tiles, rocks and pottery.

EATING

Downtown Los Angeles

Guisados Tacos $

(323-264-7201; www.guisados.co; 2100 E Cesar Chavez Ave, Boyle Heights; tacos from $2.75; 10:30am-8pm Mon-Thu, to 9pm Fri, 9am-9pm Sat, 9am-5pm Sun; M Gold Line to Mariachi Plaza) Guisados' citywide fame is founded on its *tacos de guisados:* warm, thick, nixtamal tortillas made to order and topped with sultry, smoky, slow-cooked stews. Do yourself a favor and order the sampler plate ($7.25), a democratic mix of six mini tacos. The *chiles torreados* (blistered, charred chili) taco is a must for serious spice lovers.

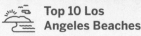

Top 10 Los Angeles Beaches

Leo Carrillo Families love this summer-camp-style beach with stimulating tide pools, cliff caves, nature trails and great swimming.

El Matador An intimate, remote hideaway with sandstone spires that rise from the swirling azure sea.

Westward Beach Malibu locals favor this wide, blond beach for crystal water, resident dolphin pods and sea lion colonies.

Zuma Two miles of pearly sand. Mellow swells make for perfect bodysurfing.

Paradise Cove The site of a kitschy beach restaurant, Paradise Cove is close enough to Point Dume to get set-piece rock formations and mellow waves.

Santa Monica Wide slab of sand where beach-umbrella-toting families descend like butterfly swarms on weekends to escape the inland heat.

Venice Beach The wide beaches south of the Venice Pier are an oft-ignored gem with excellent bodysurfing.

Manhattan Beach A brassy SoCal beach with a high flirt factor and hardcore surfers hanging by the pier.

Hermosa Beach LA's libidinous, seemingly never-ending beach party with hormone-crazed hard bodies getting their game on.

Malaga Cove This crescent-shaped, cliff-backed shoreline is the only sandy Palos Verdes beach easily accessible by the hoi polloi.

Malibu beach
THOMAS BARRAT / SHUTTERSTOCK ©

Hollywood & Griffith Park

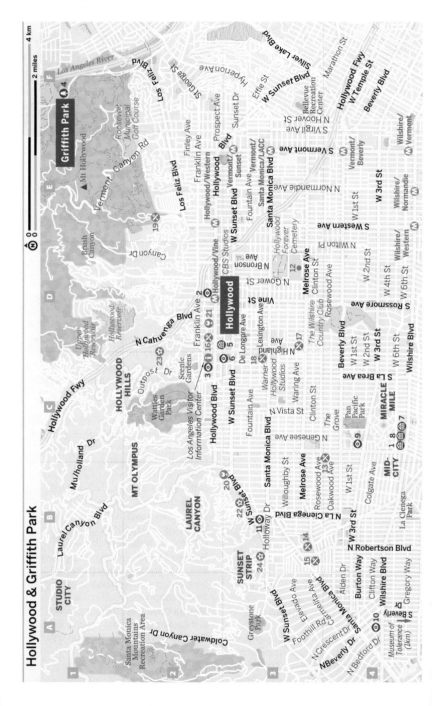

Hollywood & Griffith Park

◎ **Sights**
1 Academy Museum C4
   Anderton Court .... (see 10)
2 Capitol Records Tower D2
3 Grauman's Chinese Theatre C2
4 Griffith Park F1
5 Hollywood Museum D2
6 Hollywood Walk of Fame C3
7 La Brea Tar Pits & Museum C4
8 Los Angeles County Museum of Art C4
9 Original Farmers Market C4
10 Rodeo Drive A4
11 Sunset Strip B3
   Via Rodeo .... (see 10)

◎ **Activities, Courses & Tours**
12 Paramount Pictures D3
   Red Line Tours .... (see 5)
   TMZ Celebrity Tour .... (see 3)

◎ **Shopping**
   Hollywood & Highland .... (see 3)

◎ **Eating**
13 Canter's C4
14 Catch LA B3
15 Gracias Madre B3
16 Musso & Frank Grill D2
17 Petit Trois D3
18 Salt's Cure C3
19 Trails E2

◎ **Drinking & Nightlife**
   Abbey .... (see 14)
20 Bar Marmont B3
21 Dirty Laundry D2
   Frolic Room .... (see 2)

◎ **Entertainment**
22 Comedy Store B3
23 Hollywood Bowl D2
24 Whisky-a-Go-Go B3

Manuela   Modern American $$

(Map p279; ☑323-849-0480; www.manuela-la.com; 907 E 3rd St; ☺5:30-10pm Sun-Thu, to 11pm Fri & Sat, also 11:30am-3:30pm Wed-Fri & 10am-4pm Sat & Sun; 🛜) Young Texan chef Wes Whitsell heads this deserving it-kid inside the Hauser & Wirth arts complex. The woody warmth of the loft-like space is echoed in the oft-tweaked menu, a beautiful fusion of local ingredients and smoky southern accents. Pique the appetite with a house-pickled appetizer then lose yourself in deceptively simple soul-stirrers like sultry pork ragù over flawless polenta.

Broken Spanish   Mexican $$$

(Map p279; ☑213-749-1460; http://brokenspanish.com; 1050 S Flower St; mains $22-49; ☺5:30-10pm Sun-Thu, to 11pm Fri & Sat; 🛜) Despite retro design nods such as concrete blocks, macrame plant hangers and terra-cotta lampshades, Ray Garcia's sleek Downtown eatery is all about confident, contemporary Mexican cooking. From the *chochoyoes* (masa dumplings with green garlic and pasilla pepper) to a rich, intense dish of mushrooms with black garlic, flavors are clean and intriguing, and the presentation polished.

◎ Hollywood

Musso & Frank Grill   Steak $$

(Map p282; ☑323-467-7788; www.mussoandfrank.com; 6667 Hollywood Blvd; mains $15-52; ☺11am-11pm Tue-Sat, 4-9pm Sun; Ⓟ; Ⓜ Red Line to Hollywood/Highland) Hollywood history hangs in the thick air at Musso & Frank Grill, Tinseltown's oldest eatery (since 1919). Charlie Chaplin used to knock back vodka gimlets, Raymond Chandler penned scripts in the high-backed booths, and movie deals were made on the old phone at the back (the booth closest to the phone is favored by Jack Nicholson and Johnny Depp).

Petit Trois   French $$

(Map p282; ☑323-468-8916; http://petittrois.com; mains $14-36; ☺noon-10pm Sun-Thu, to 11pm Fri & Sat; Ⓟ) Good things come in small packages...like tiny, no-reservations Petit Trois! Owned by acclaimed TV chef Ludovic Lefebvre, its two long counters (the place is too small for tables) are where food lovers squeeze in for smashing, honest, Gallic-inspired grub, from a ridiculously light Boursin-stuffed omelet to a showstopping double cheeseburger served with a stand-out foie gras–infused red-wine Bordelaise.

Salt's Cure
Modern American $$

(Map p282; [phone]323-465-7258; http://saltscure.com; 1155 N Highland Ave; mains $17-34; [time]11am-11pm Mon-Thu, to midnight Fri, 10am-midnight Sat, 10am-11pm Sun) Wood-paneled, concrete-floored Salt's Cure is an out, proud locavore. From the in-season vegetables to the house-butchered and cured meats, the menu celebrates all things Californian. Expect sophisticated takes on rustic comfort grub, whether it's capicollo with chili paste or tender duck breast paired with impressively light oatmeal griddle cakes and blackberry compote.

 Santa Monica

Erven
Vegan $$

([phone]310-260-2255; www.ervenrestaurant.com; 514 Santa Monica Blvd; sandwiches $7-15, snacks $5, dinner mains $15-21; [wifi]; [M]Expo Line to Downtown Santa Monica) [icon] In this city that teems with vegetarian and vegan dining, chef Nick Erven's restaurant ticks it up a few notches in this airy, modern space. Lunch and dinner are different experiences – counter service versus refined sit-down, with different menus – and there's a marketplace counter that's open even when the kitchen is closed.

Milo & Olive
Italian $$

([phone]310-453-6776; www.miloandolive.com; 2723 Wilshire Blvd; dishes $7-20; [time]7am-11pm) We love this place for its small-batch wines, incredible pizzas, terrific breakfasts (creamy polenta and poached eggs anyone?), breads and pastries, all of which you may enjoy at the marble bar or shoulder to shoulder with new friends at one of two common tables. It's a cozy, neighborhood joint so it doesn't take reservations.

Cassia
Southeast Asian $$$

([phone]310-393-6699; 1314 7th St; appetizers $12-24, mains $18-77; [time]5-10pm Sun-Thu, to 11pm Fri & Sat; [P]) Ever since it opened in 2015, open, airy Cassia has made about every local and national 'best' list of LA restaurants. Chef Bryant Ng draws on his Chinese-Singaporean heritage in dishes such as kaya toast (with coconut jam, butter and a slow-cooked egg), 'sunbathing' prawns, and the encompassing Vietnamese *pot au feu:*

Fish tacos

short-rib stew, veggies, bone marrow and delectable accompaniments.

West Hollywood & Mid-City

Gracias Madre　Vegan, Mexican **$$**
(Map p282; ☏323-978-2170; www.gracias madreweho.com; 8905 Melrose Ave, West Hollywood; mains lunch $10-13, dinner $12-18; ⏱11am-11pm Mon-Fri, from 10am Sat & Sun; ☑) Gracias Madre shows just how tasty – and chichi – organic, plant-based Mexican cooking can be. Sit on the gracious patio or in the cozy interior and feel good as you eat healthy: sweet potato flautas, coconut 'bacon,' plantain 'quesadillas,' plus salads and bowls. We're consistently surprised at innovations like cashew 'cheese,' mushroom 'chorizo' and heart-of-palm 'crab cakes.'

Canter's　Deli **$$**
(Map p282; ☏323-651-2030; www.cantersdeli.com; 419 N Fairfax Ave, Mid-City; ⏱24hr; ℗) As old-school delis go, Canter's is hard to beat. A fixture in the traditionally Jewish Fairfax district since 1931, it serves up the requisite pastrami, corned beef and matzo ball soup with a side of sass by seen-it-all waitresses, in a rangy room with deli and bakery counters up front.

Catch LA　Fusion **$$$**
(Map p282; ☏323-347-6060; http://catch restaurants.com/catchla; 8715 Melrose Ave, West Hollywood; shared dishes $11-31, dinner mains $28-41; ⏱11am-3pm Sat & Sun, 5pm-2am daily; ℗) An LA-scene extraordinaire. You may well find sidewalk paparazzi stalking celebrity guests and a doorman to check your reservation, but all that's forgotten once you're up in this 3rd-floor rooftop restaurant-bar above WeHo. The Pacific Rim–inspired menu features super-creative cocktails and shared dishes such as truffle sashimi, black-cod lettuce wraps, and scallop and cauliflower with tamarind brown butter.

 Movie-Star Tours

TMZ Celebrity Tour (Map p282; ☏844-869-8687; www.tmz.com/tour; 6925 Hollywood Blvd; adult/child $54/44; ⏱tours departing Hard Rock Cafe Hollywood 12:15pm, 3pm & 5:30pm Thu-Tue, 12:15pm & 3pm Wed; Ⓜ Red Line to Hollywood/Highland) Cut the shame; we know you want to spot celebrities, glimpse their homes and laugh at their dirt. Join this super-fun tour imagined by the paparazzi made famous. Tours run for two hours, and you'll likely meet some of the TMZ stars...and perhaps even celebrity guests on the bus.

Red Line Tours (Map p282; ☏323-402-1074; www.redlinetours.com; 6708 Hollywood Blvd; adult/child from $25/15; ⏱75min Hollywood Behind-the-Scenes Tour 10am, noon, 2pm & 4pm; Ⓜ Red Line to Hollywood/Highland) Learn the secrets of Hollywood on Red Line's 'edutaining' Hollywood Behind-the-Scenes Tour, a 75-minute walking tour that comes with nifty headsets to cut out traffic noise. Guides use a mix of anecdotes, fun facts, trivia and historical and architectural data to keep their charges entertained.

Upgrades include the Total Hollywood Experience (adult/child $72/52), which consists of both the walking tour and a two-hour bus tour of celebrity homes.

🍸 DRINKING & NIGHTLIFE

Abbey　Gay & Lesbian
(Map p282; ☏310-289-8410; www.theabbey weho.com; 692 N Robertson Blvd, West Hollywood; ⏱11am-2am Mon-Thu, from 10am Fri, from 9am Sat & Sun) It's been called the best gay bar in the world, and who are we to argue? Once a humble coffeehouse, the Abbey has expanded into WeHo's bar/club/restaurant of record. Always a party, it has so many

Shopaholic Essentials

It might be pricey and unapologetically pretentious, but no trip to LA would be complete without a saunter along **Rodeo Drive** (Map p282), the famous three-block ribbon of style where sample-size fembots browse for Gucci and Dior. Fashion retailer Fred Hayman opened the strip's first luxury boutique, Giorgio Beverly Hills, at No 273 back in 1961. Famed for its striped white-and-yellow awning, the store allowed its well-heeled clients to sip cocktails while shopping and have their purchases home delivered in a Rolls-Royce.

Downtown, what started as a one-man operation out of a Main St storefront is now **Last Bookstore in Los Angeles** (Map p279; 213-488-0599; www.lastbookstorela.com; 453 S Spring St; ⊙10am-10pm Mon-Thu, to 11pm Fri & Sat, to 9pm Sun), California's largest new-and-used bookstore, spanning two levels of an old bank building. Eye up the cabinets of rare books before heading upstairs, home to a horror-and-crime book den, a book tunnel and a few art galleries to boot. The store also houses a terrific vinyl collection.

Rodeo Drive
CHIARA SALVADORI / GETTY IMAGES ©

different flavored martinis and mojitos that you'd think they were invented here, plus a full menu of upscale pub food (mains $14 to $21).

Dirty Laundry Bar

(Map p282; 323-462-6531; http://dirty laundrybarla.com; 1725 N Hudson Ave; ⊙10pm-2am Tue-Sat; Ⓜ Red Line to Hollywood/Vine) Under a cotton-candy-pink apartment block of no particular import is this funky den of musty odor, low ceilings, exposed pipes and good times. There's fine whiskey, funkalicious tunes on the turntables and plenty of eye-candy peeps with low inhibitions. Alas, there are also velvet rope politics at work here, so reserve a table to make sure you slip through.

Bar Marmont Bar

(Map p282; 323-650-0575; www.chateau marmont.com; 8171 Sunset Blvd, Hollywood; ⊙6pm-2am) Elegant, but not stuck up; been around, yet still cherished. With high ceilings, molded walls and terrific martinis, the famous and the wish-they-weres still flock here. If you time it right you might see celebs – the Marmont doesn't share who (or else they'd stop coming – get it?). Come midweek. Weekends are for amateurs.

✪ ENTERTAINMENT

Geffen Playhouse Theater

(310-208-5454; www.geffenplayhouse.com; 10886 Le Conte Ave, Westwood) American magnate and producer David Geffen forked over $17 million to get his Mediterranean-style playhouse back into shape. The center's season includes both American classics and freshly minted works, and it's not unusual to see well-known film and TV actors treading the boards.

Hollywood Bowl Concert Venue

(Map p282; 323-850-2000; www.hollywood bowl.com; 2301 N Highland Ave; rehearsals free, performance costs vary; ⊙Jun-Sep) Summers in LA just wouldn't be the same without alfresco melodies under the stars at the Bowl, a huge natural amphitheater in the Hollywood Hills. Its annual season – which usually runs from June to September –

includes symphonies, jazz bands and iconic acts such as Blondie, Bryan Ferry and Angélique Kidjo. Bring a sweater or blanket as it gets cool at night.

Echo   Live Music
(www.attheecho.com; 1822 W Sunset Blvd, Echo Park; cover varies) Eastsiders hungry for an eclectic alchemy of sounds pack this crowded dive, basically a sweaty bar with a stage and a back patio. On the music front, expect anything from indie and electronica, to dub reggae and dream and power pop. Monday nights are dedicated to up-and-coming local bands, with regular club nights including Saturday's always-a-blast Funky Sole party.

Saturdays Off the 405   Live Music
(www.getty.edu; Getty Center; ⊙6-9pm Sat May-Sep) From May to September, the Getty Center courtyard fills with evening crowds for a delicious collision of art, brilliant live acts and beat-pumping DJ sets.

ⓘ INFORMATION

Los Angeles Visitor Information Center
(Map p282; ☏323-467-6412; www.discover losangeles.com; Hollywood & Highland, 6801 Hollywood Blvd; ⊙8am-10pm Mon-Sat, 9am-7pm Sun; Ⓜ Red Line to Hollywood/Highland) The main tourist office for LA. Maps, brochures and lodging information, plus tickets to theme parks and attractions.

ⓘ GETTING THERE & AWAY

AIR

The main LA gateway is **Los Angeles International Airport** (LAX; www.lawa.org/welcomeLAX. aspx). Its nine terminals are linked by the free LAX Shuttle A, leaving from the lower (arrival) level of each terminal. Cabs and hotel and car-rental shuttles also stop here.

CAR & MOTORCYCLE

If you're driving, there are several ways to enter the metropolitan area.

From San Francisco and Northern California, the fastest route is the I-5 through San Joaquin Valley. Hwy 101 is slower but more picturesque, while the most scenic, and slowest, route is via Hwy 1 (Pacific Coast Hwy, or PCH).

From San Diego and other points south, I-5 is the obvious route. Near Irvine, I-405 branches off I-5 and takes a westerly route to Long Beach and Santa Monica, bypassing Downtown LA entirely.

ⓘ GETTING AROUND

TO/FROM THE AIRPORT

Door-to-door shuttles, such as those operated by **Prime Time** (☏800-733-8267; www.primetime shuttle.com) and **Super Shuttle** (☏800-258-3826; www.supershuttle.com), charge $23, $28 and $17 for trips to Santa Monica, Hollywood and Downtown, respectively.

Curbside dispatchers can summon a taxi for you. The flat rate to Downtown LA is $47, while going to Santa Monica costs $30 to $35, to West Hollywood around $40 and to Hollywood $50, plus the $4 LAX surcharge.

LAX FlyAway (☏866-435-9529; www.lawa. org/FlyAway) buses travel nonstop for $9.75 to Downtown's Patsaouras Transit Plaza at Union Station (45 minutes), Hollywood (one to 1½ hours) and beyond.

CAR & MOTORCYCLE

Unless time is short, or money is extremely tight, you'll want to spend some time behind the wheel, although this means contending with some of the worst traffic in the country. Avoid rush hour (7am to 9am and 3:30pm to 6pm). Valet parking at nicer restaurants and hotels is commonplace ($3.50 to $10).

SAN FRANCISCO

In this Chapter

Golden Gate Bridge 292
Historic Cable Cars........................... 294
Alcatraz 296
Ferry Building 300
Chinatown 302
Sights 306
Eating.. 312
Drinking & Nightlife.......................... 315
Entertainment.................................. 318

San Francisco at a Glance...

Grab your coat and a handful of glitter, and enter the land of fog and fabulousness. So long, inhibitions; hello, San Francisco.

California is one grand, sweeping gesture – a long arm hugging the Pacific – and the 7-by-7-mile peninsula of San Francisco is a thumb pointed optimistically upwards. Look up and you'll notice San Francisco's crooked Victorian rooflines, wind-sculpted treetops and fog tumbling over the Golden Gate Bridge. Heads are perpetually in the clouds atop San Francisco's 43 hills, with exhilarating views from Telegraph Hill's garden-lined stairways and windswept hikes around Land's End.

Two Days in San Francisco

On day one, hop aboard the Powell-Mason **cable car** (p295) and hold on for hills and thrills. Have lunch in the **Ferry Building** (p301), then catch your prebooked ferry to **Alcatraz** (p297). On day two, get the camera ready for vistas of the **Golden Gate Bridge** (p292). Walk across, or visit Golden Gate Park and the **California Academy of Sciences** (p307).

Four Days in San Francisco

Start day three in **Chinatown**. Hit **Fisherman's Wharf** (p311) in the afternoon; take the Powell-Hyde cable car past zigzagging **Lombard Street** (p307) to **Maritime National Historical Park** (p312). On day four have a taco in the Mission, explore hippie-historic **Haight Street** (p311), and end the evening at **Specs** (p316) or another North Beach bar.

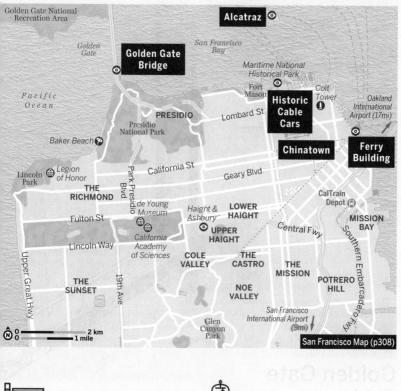

Arriving in San Francisco

San Francisco International Airport
Fast rides to downtown SF on BART cost $8.95; door-to-door shuttle vans cost $17 to $20, plus tip; taxis cost $40 to $55.

Oakland International Airport (OAK)
BART from the airport to downtown SF costs $10.20; taxis cost $60 to $80 to SF destinations.

Sleeping

San Francisco hotel rates are among the world's highest. Plan ahead – well ahead – and grab bargains when you see them. Given the choice, San Francisco's boutique properties beat chains for a sense of place – but take what you can get at a price you can afford.

Golden Gate Bridge

The city's most spectacular icon towers 80 stories above the roiling waters of the Golden Gate, the narrow entrance to San Francisco Bay. When the fog clears it reveals magnificent views.

Great For...

☑ Don't Miss

There's a cross-section of suspension cable behind the Bridge Pavilion Visitor Center.

San Franciscans have passionate perspectives on every subject, especially their signature landmark, though everyone agrees it's a good thing the Navy didn't get its way over the bridge's design – naval officials preferred a hulking concrete span, painted with caution-yellow stripes, over the soaring art-deco design of architects Gertrude and Irving Murrow and engineer Joseph B Strauss, which, luckily, won the day.

Construction

Nobody thought it could happen. Not until the early 1920s did the City of San Francisco seriously investigate building a bridge over the treacherous, windblown strait. The War Department owned the land on both sides and didn't want to take chances with ships: safety and solidity were its goals. But the green light was given to the counter-

Golden Gate Bridge

PACIFIC OCEAN

101

ℹ Need to Know

✏toll information 877-229-8655; www.golden
gatebridge.org/visitors; Hwy 101; northbound
free, southbound $6.50-7.50; 🚌28, all Golden
Gate Transit buses

✕ Take a Break

You'll find refreshments only at the SF
end of the bridge by the Bridge Pavilion.

★ Top Tip

For on-site information, drop into
the Bridge Pavilion Visitor Center
(✆415-426-5220; www.ggnpc.org; Gate
Bridge toll plaza; ⏰9am-7pm Jun-Aug, to
6pm Sep-May).

proposal by Strauss and the Murrows for
a subtler suspension span, economic in
form, that harmonized with the natural
environment.

Before the War Department could insist
on an eyesore, laborers dove into the
treacherous riptides of the bay and got the
bridge under way in 1933. Just four years
later workers balancing atop swaying cables completed what was then the world's
longest suspension bridge – nearly 2 miles
long, with 746ft suspension towers, higher
than any construction west of New York.

Which View?

As far as best views go, cinema buffs
believe Hitchcock got it right: seen from
below at Fort Point, the 1937 bridge induces
a thrilling case of vertigo. Fog aficionados
prefer the north-end lookout at Marin's

Vista Point, to watch gusts billow through
bridge cables like dry ice at a Kiss concert.

To see both sides of the Golden Gate
debate, hike or bike the 1.7-mile span. Muni
bus 28 runs to the parking lot, and pedestrians and cyclists can cross the bridge
on sidewalks. For drivers, bridge tolls are
billed electronically to your vehicle's license
plate; see www.goldengate.org/tolls.

Walking & Cycling Over the Bridge

Pedestrians take the eastern sidewalk.
Dress warmly! From the parking area and
bus stop (off Lincoln Blvd), a pathway leads
past the toll plaza, then it's 1.7 miles across.
If the 3.4-mile round-trip seems too much,
take a bus to the north side via Golden Gate
Transit, then walk back.

By bicycle, ride from the toll-plaza
parking area toward the Roundhouse,
then follow signs to the western sidewalk,
reserved for bikes only.

Historic Cable Cars

Offering million-dollar vistas and the promise of adventure, cable cars are the way to explore San Francisco. These ratcheting wonders bring you lurching into the heart of the city's best neighborhoods.

Great For...

☑ Don't Miss

The California St cable car rumbles through Chinatown and past Old St Mary's Cathedral.

Carnival rides can't compare to cable cars, San Francisco's vintage public transit. Novices slide into strangers' laps – cable cars were invented in 1873, long before seat belts – but regular commuters just grip leather hand-straps, lean back and ride downhill slides like pro surfers. On this trip, you'll master the San Francisco stance and conquer SF hills without breaking a sweat.

Powell-Hyde Cable Car

At the Powell St Cable Car Turnaround, you'll see operators turn the car atop a revolving wooden platform and a vintage kiosk where you can buy an all-day Muni Passport for $21, instead of paying $7 per ride. Board the red-signed Powell-Hyde cable car and begin your 338ft ascent of Nob Hill.

ELIZA SNOW / GETTY IMAGES / ISTOCKPHOTO ©

❶ Need to Know

Powell-Mason cars are quickest to reach Fisherman's Wharf, but Powell-Hyde cars are more scenic.

✖ Take a Break

After the ride, visit the Ferry Building (p301), where champagne-and-oyster happy hour awaits.

★ Top Tip

If you're planning to stop en route, get a Muni Passport for $21 per day.

Nob Hill

As your cable car lurches uphill, you can imagine horses struggling up this slippery crag. Nineteenth-century city planners were skeptical of inventor Andrew Hallidie's 'wire-rope railway' – but after more than a century of near-continuous operation, his wire-and-hemp cables have seldom broken. Hallidie's cable cars even survived the 1906 earthquake and fire that destroyed 'Snob Hill' mansions, returning the faithful to the rebuilt Grace Cathedral (p307) – hop off to say hello to SF's gentle patron, St Francis, carved by sculptor Beniamino Bufano.

Lombard Street

Back on the Powell-Hyde car, enjoy Bay views as you careen past crooked, flower-lined Lombard St (p307) toward Fisherman's Wharf. The waterfront terminus is named for Friedel Klussmann, who saved cable cars from mayoral modernization plans in 1947. She did the math: cable cars brought in more tourism dollars than they cost in upkeep. The mayor demanded a vote – and lost to 'the Cable Car Lady' by a landslide. For her funeral in 1986, cable cars citywide were draped in black.

Fisherman's Wharf

At the wharf, emerge from the submarine USS *Pampanito* (p312) to glimpse SF as sailors used to. Witness Western saloon brawls in vintage arcade games at the Musée Mécanique (p311).

Alcatraz

From its 19th-century founding to detain Civil War deserters and Native American dissidents until its closure by Bobby Kennedy in 1963, Alcatraz was America's most notorious jail.

Great For...

☑ **Don't Miss**

For maximum chill factor, book the spooky twilight jailhouse tour.

Alcatraz: for over 150 years, the name has given the innocent chills and the guilty cold sweats. Over the decades, it's been the nation's first military prison, a forbidding maximum-security penitentiary and disputed territory between Native American activists and the FBI.

It all started innocently enough back in 1775, when Spanish lieutenant Juan Manuel de Ayala sailed the San Carlos past the 22-acre island he called Isla de Alcatraces (Isle of the Pelicans). In 1859 a new post on Alcatraz became the first US West Coast fort, and soon proved handy as a holding pen for Civil War deserters, insubordinates and those who had been court-martialed. By 1902 the four cell blocks of wooden cages were rotting, unsanitary and otherwise ill-equipped for the influx of US soldiers convicted of war crimes in the Philippines.

⊙ Need to Know

☑Alcatraz Cruises 415-981-7625; www.nps.
gov/alcatraz; tours adult/child 5-11yr day
$37.25/23, night $44.25/26.50; ⊘ferries
depart Pier 33 half-hourly 8:45am-3:50pm,
night tours 5:55pm & 6:30pm

✕ Take a Break

Codmother Fish & Chips (☑415-
606-9349; 2824 Jones St; mains $5-10;
⊘11:30am-5pm Mon & Wed-Sat, to 2:30pm
Sun; ⊟47, ⊟Powell-Mason, ⓂF) is a little
food truck right by the Alcatraz departure docks.

★ Top Tip

For Alcatraz Cruises, book a month
ahead for day visits, two to three
months for night tours.

The army began building a new concrete
military prison in 1909, but upkeep was
expensive and the US soon had other
things to worry about: WWI, financial ruin
and flappers.

In 1922, when the 18th Amendment to
the Constitution declared selling liquor
a crime, rebellious Jazz Agers weren't
prepared to give up their tipple – and gangsters kept the booze coming. Authorities
were determined to make a public example
of criminal ringleaders, and in 1934 the Federal Bureau of Prisons took over Alcatraz as
a prominent showcase for its crime-fighting
efforts. 'The Rock' averaged only 264
inmates, but its roster read like a list of
America's Most Wanted. A-list criminals
doing time on Alcatraz included Chicago
crime boss Al 'Scarface' Capone, dapper
kidnapper George 'Machine Gun' Kelly,

hot-headed Harlem mafioso and sometime
poet 'Bumpy' Johnson, and Morton Sobell,
the military contractor found guilty of Soviet espionage along with Julius and Ethel
Rosenberg.

Today, first-person accounts of daily life
in the Alcatraz lockup are included on the
excellent self-guided audio tour provided
by Alcatraz Cruises. But take your head-
phones off for just a moment and notice
the sound of carefree city life traveling
across the water: this is the torment that
made perilous escapes into riptides worth
the risk. Though Alcatraz was considered
escape-proof, in 1962 the Anglin brothers and Frank Morris floated away on a
makeshift raft and were never seen again.
Security and upkeep proved prohibitively
expensive, and finally the island prison was
abandoned to the birds in 1963.

Alcatraz

A HALF-DAY TOUR

Book a ferry from Pier 33 and ride 1.5 miles across the bay to explore America's most notorious former prison. The trip itself is worth the money, providing stunning views of the city skyline. Once you've landed at the ❶ **Ferry Dock & Pier**, you begin the 580yd walk to the top of the island and prison; if you need assistance to reach the top, there's a twice-hourly tram.

As you climb toward the ❷ **Guardhouse**, notice the island's steep slope; before it was a prison, Alcatraz was a fort. In the 1850s, the military quarried the rocky shores into near-vertical cliffs. Ships could then only dock at a single port, separated from the main buildings by a sally port (a drawbridge and moat in what became the guardhouse). Inside, peer through floor grates to see Alcatraz's original prison.

Volunteers tend the brilliant ❸ **Officers' Row Gardens**, an orderly counterpart to the overgrown rose bushes surrounding the burned-out shell of the ❹ **Warden's House**. At the top of the hill, by the front door of the ❺ **Main Cellhouse**, beautiful shots unfurl all around, including a view of the ❻ **Golden Gate Bridge**. Above the main door of the administration building, notice the ❼ **historic signs & graffiti**, before you step inside the dank, cold prison to find the ❽ **Frank Morris cell**, former home to Alcatraz's most notorious jail-breaker.

TOP TIPS

➡ Book at least one month prior for self-guided daytime visits, longer for ranger-led night tours. For info on garden tours, see www.alcatraz gardens.org.

➡ Be prepared to hike; a steep path ascends from the ferry landing to the cell block. Most people spend two to three hours on the island. You need only reserve for the outbound ferry; take any ferry back.

➡ There's no food (just water) but you can bring your own; picnicking is allowed at the ferry dock only. Dress in layers as weather changes fast and it's usually windy.

ADRIEN_G / SHUTTERSTOCK ©

Historic Signs & Graffiti

During their 1969–71 occupation, Native Americans graffitied the water tower: 'Home of the Free Indian Land.' Above the cellhouse door, examine the eagle-and-flag crest to see how the red-and-white stripes were changed to spell 'Free.'

DOPTIS / SHUTTERSTOCK ©

Warden's House

Fires destroyed the warden's house and other structures during the Indian Occupation. The government blamed the Native Americans; the Native Americans blamed agents provocateurs acting on behalf of the Nixon administration to undermine public sympathy.

Parade Grounds

Officers' Row Gardens

In the 19th century soldiers imported topsoil to beautify the island with gardens. Well-trusted prisoners later gardened – Elliott Michener said it kept him sane. Historians ornithologists and archaeologists choose today's plants.

Main Cellhouse

During the mid-20th century, the maximum-security prison housed the day's most notorious troublemakers, including Al Capone and Robert Stroud, the 'Birdman of Alcatraz' (who actually conducted his ornithology studies at Leavenworth).

View of the Golden Gate Bridge

The Golden Gate Bridge stretches wide on the horizon. Best views are from atop the island at Eagle Plaza, near the cellhouse entrance, and at water level along the Agave Trail (September to January only).

Power House

Recreation Yard

Water Tower

⑥

Officers' Club

⑤

⑧

Guardhouse

Alcatraz's oldest building dates to 1857 and retains remnants of the original drawbridge and moat. During the Civil War the basement was transformed into a military dungeon – the genesis of Alcatraz as a prison.

⑦

Lighthouse ③

④

Guard Tower

②

Frank Morris Cell

Peer into cell 138 on B-Block to see a recreation of the dummy's head that Frank Morris left in his bed as a decoy to aid his notorious – and successful – 1962 escape from Alcatraz.

①

Ferry Dock & Pier

A giant wall map helps you get your bearings. Inside nearby Building 64, short films and exhibits provide historical perspective on the prison and details about the Native American Occupation.

Ferry Building

Global food trends start in San Francisco. To sample tomorrow's menu today, wander through the city's monument to trailblazing, sustainable food. The Ferry Building has the best bites from Northern California.

Other towns have gourmet ghettos, but San Francisco puts its love of food front and center at the Ferry Building. The once-grand port was overshadowed by a 1950s elevated freeway – until the overpass collapsed in 1989's Loma Prieta earthquake. The Ferry Building survived and became a symbol of San Francisco's reinvention, marking your arrival at America's forward-thinking food frontier.

History

The trademark 240ft tower greeted dozens of ferries daily after its 1898 inauguration. But with the opening of the Bay and Golden Gate Bridges, ferry traffic subsided in the 1930s. An overhead freeway was built, obscuring the building's stately facade and turning it black with exhaust fumes. Only after the 1989 earthquake did city planners

Great For...

☑ Don't Miss

During the Saturday farmers markets top chefs jostle for first pick of rare heirloom varietals.

MICHAEL URMANN / SHUTTERSTOCK ©

ⓘ Need to Know

📞415-983-8030; www.ferrybuildingmarket
place.com; cnr Market St & the Embarcadero;
🕙10am-7pm Mon-Fri, 8am-6pm Sat, 11am-
5pm Sun; 🚼; 🚌2, 6, 9, 14, 21, 31, Ⓜ Embarcadero, Ⓑ Embarcadero

✕ Take a Break

Slurp the sea's bounty at **Hog Island
Oyster Company** (📞415-391-7117; www.
hogislandoysters.com; 4 oysters $14; 🕙11am-
9pm) 🍴.

★ Top Tip

You can still catch a ferry here and
crossing the sparkling bay is a great
escape.

realize what they'd been missing: with its
grand halls and bay views, this was the
perfect place for a new public commons.

Foodie Hot Spot

Today the grand arrivals hall tempts
commuters to miss the boat and get on
board with SF's latest culinary trends
instead. Indoor kiosks sell locally roasted
espresso, artisan cheese and cured meats,
plus organic ice-cream flavors to match
– that's right, Vietnamese coffee, cheese
and prosciutto. People-watching wine bars
and award-winning restaurants are further
enticements to stick around, and raise a
toast to San Francisco.

Ferry Building Farmers Market

Even before Ferry Building renovations
were completed in 2003, the **Ferry
Plaza**

Farmers Market (📞415-291-3276; www.
cuesa.org; street food $3-12; 🕙10am-2pm Tue &
Thu, from 8am Sat; 🚼🍴) 🍴 began operating
out front on the sidewalk. Soon the foodie
action spread to the bayfront plaza, with
50 to 100 local food purveyors catering
to hometown crowds three times a week.
While locals sometimes grumble that
the prices are higher here than at other
markets, there's no denying that the Ferry
Plaza market offers seasonal, sustainable,
handmade gourmet treats and specialty
produce not found elsewhere.

Join SF's legions of professional chefs
and semiprofessional eaters, and taste-test
the artisan goat cheese, fresh-pressed California olive oil, wild boar and organic pluots
for yourself. The Saturday morning farmers
market offers the best people-watching –
it's not uncommon to spot celebrities – but
arrive early if you're shopping, before those
pesky *Top Chef* contestants snap up the
best finds.

PHOTO UA / SHUTTERSTOCK ©

Chinatown

Dumplings and rare teas are served under pagoda roofs on Chinatown's main streets – but its historic back alleys are filled with temple incense, mah-jongg tile clatter and distant echoes of revolution.

Great For...

☑ Don't Miss

Hearing mah-jongg tiles, temple gongs and Chinese orchestras as you wander the Chinatown Alleyways.

Grant Avenue

Enter through the Dragon's Gate, donated by Taiwan in 1970, and you'll find yourself on the street formerly known as Dupont in its notorious red-light heyday. The pagoda-topped 'Chinatown deco' architecture beyond this gate was innovated by Chinatown merchants, led by Look Tin Ely, in the 1920s – a pioneering initiative to lure tourists with a distinctive modern look.

Now it's hard to believe that this souvenir-shopping strip was once lined with brothels – at least until you see the fascinating displays at the **Chinese Historical Society of America** (CHSA; 📞415-391-1188; www.chsa.org; 965 Clay St; adult/student/child $15/10/free; ⊙11am-4pm Wed-Sun; 👫; 🚌1, 8, 30, 45, 🚋California, Powell-Mason, Powell-Hyde).

Tin How Temple, Waverly Place

Ross Alley
Washington St
Grant Ave
Spofford
Alley
Portsmouth
Sq
Waverly
Place
Clay St
Commercial St

❶ Need to Know

Key bus routes to Chinatown include 1, 8, 30 and 45. The California St cable car passes through the neighborhood's southern end.

✕ Take a Break

Picking up where Jack Kerouac left off at Li Po (p316), a historic Beat hangout.

★ Top Tip

Parking is tough. There's public parking underneath Portsmouth Sq and at the Good Luck Parking Garage.

Waverly Place

Grant Ave may be the economic heart of Chinatown, but its soul is Waverly Place, lined with historic clinker-brick buildings and flag-festooned temple balconies. Due to 19th-century race-based restrictions, family associations and temples were built right on top of the barber shops, laundries and restaurants lining these two city blocks. Through good times and bad, Waverly Pl stood its ground, and services have been held here since 1852.

Chinatown Alleyways

The 41 historic alleyways packed into Chinatown's 22 blocks have seen it all since 1849: gold rushes and revolution, incense and opium, fire and icy receptions. In clinker-brick buildings lining these narrow backstreets, temple balconies jut out over

bakeries, laundries and barbers – there was nowhere to go but up in Chinatown after 1870, when laws limited Chinese immigration, employment and housing. **Chinatown Alleyway Tours** (☏415-984-1478; www.china townalleywaytours.org; Portsmouth Sq; adult/student $26/16; ⏱tours 11am Sat; ♿; ☐1, 8, 10, 12, 30, 41, 45, ☒California, Powell-Mason, Powell-Hyde) and **Chinatown Heritage Walking Tours** (☏415-986-1822; www.cccsf. us; Chinese Culture Center, Hilton Hotel, 3rd fl, 750 Kearny St; group tour adult $25-30, student $15-20, private tour 1-4 people $60; ⏱tours 10am, noon & 2pm Tue-Sat; ♿; ☐1, 8, 10, 12, 30, 41, 45, ☒California, Powell-Mason, Powell-Hyde) offer community-supporting, time-traveling strolls through defining moments in American history.

Sun Yat-sen once plotted the overthrow of China's Manchu dynasty at Spofford Alley, and, during Prohibition, this was the site of turf battles over local bootlegging and protection rackets. Around sundown a Chinese orchestra strikes up a tune and the clicking of a mah-jongg game begins.

JUDY BELLAH / GETTY IMAGES ©

North Beach Beat Walk

This tour of the North Beach hits all the literary hot spots from San Francisco's Beat scene.
Start City Lights Books
Finish Specs
Distance 1.5 miles
Duration Two hours

3 Look for parrots in the tree-tops and octogenarians in tai chi stances on the lawn at **Washington Square** (http://sfrecpark.org/destination/washington-square).

Columbus Ave

Union St

Stockton St

Jasper Pl

Green St

Vallejo St

Powell St

Broadway

2 With opera on the jukebox and potent espresso, **Caffe Trieste** (p316) is where Francis Ford Coppola allegedly drafted the *Godfather*.

Classic Photo Browsing the shelves at City Lights

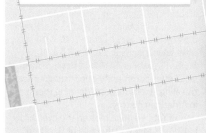

1 Pick up a copy of Allen Ginsberg's *Howl* at **City Lights Books** (p310), home of Beat poetry and free speech.

4 Bob Kaufman Alley is a peaceful place that's named after the legendary street-corner poet.

Filbert St

Union St

Green St

Kearny St

Vallejo St   Vallejo Steps

Grant Ave

Romolo Pl

Broadway

START

Jack Kerouac Al

Columbus Ave

Montgomery St

Grant Ave

Washington St

FINISH

5 Beat Museum (p311) is where visitors are all (to quote Ginsberg) 'angelheaded hipsters burning for the ancient heavenly connection.'

6 Specs (p316) is the jumping-off point for a literary bar crawl through the neighborhood.

Take a Break... Follow the lead of Kerouac and Ginsberg and toss one back at Li Po (p316).

400 m
0.2 miles

◎ SIGHTS

Most major museums are downtown, though Golden Gate Park is home to the de Young Museum and the California Academy of Sciences. The city's most historic districts are the Mission, Chinatown, North Beach and the Haight. Galleries are clustered downtown and in North Beach, the Mission, Potrero Flats and Dogpatch. You'll find hilltop parks citywide, but Russian, Nob and Telegraph Hills are the highest and most panoramic.

◎ Downtown & Civic Center

Asian Art Museum   Museum

(☏415-581-3500; www.asianart.org; 200 Larkin St; adult/student/child $15/10/free, 1st Sun of month free; ◷10am-5pm Tue, Wed & Fri-Sun, to 9pm Thu; ♿; ⓂCivic Center, ⒷCivic Center) Imaginations race from ancient Persian miniatures to cutting-edge Japanese minimalism through three floors spanning 6000 years of Asian art. Besides the largest collection outside Asia – 18,000 works – the museum offers excellent programs for all ages, from shadow-puppet shows and tea tastings with star chefs to mixers with cross-cultural DJ mash-ups.

SF Camerawork   Gallery

(☏415-487-1011; www.sfcamerawork.org; 1011 Market St, 2nd fl; ◷noon-6pm Tue-Sat; ☒6, 7, 9, 21, ⒷCivic Center, ⓂCivic Center) **FREE** Since 1974, this nonprofit art organization has championed experimental photo-based imagery beyond classic B&W prints and casual digital snapshots. Since moving into this spacious new Market St gallery, Camerawork's far-reaching exhibitions have examined memories of love and war in Southeast Asia, taken imaginary holidays with slide shows of vacation snapshots scavenged from the San Francisco Dump and showcased SF-based Iranian American artist Sanaz Mazinani's mesmerizing Islamic-inspired photo montages made of tiny Donald Trumps.

San Francisco Museum of Modern Art   Museum

(SFMOMA; ☏415-357-4000; www.sfmoma.org; 151 3rd St; adult/under 18yr/student $25/free/19; ◷10am-5pm Fri-Tue, to 9pm Thu; public

Grace Cathedral

spaces from 9am; 🚹; 🚌5, 6, 7, 14, 19, 21, 31, 38, Ⓜ Montgomery, Ⓑ Montgomery) The expanded SFMOMA is a mind-boggling feat, tripled in size to accommodate a sprawling collection of modern masterworks and 19 concurrent exhibitions over 10 floors – but, then again, SFMOMA has defied limits ever since its 1935 founding. SFMOMA was a visionary early investor in then-emerging art forms, including photography, installations, video, performance art, and (as befits a global technology hub) digital art and industrial design. Even during the Depression, SFMOMA envisioned a world of vivid possibilities, starting in San Francisco.

Luggage Store Gallery   Gallery

(📞415-255-5971; www.luggagestoregallery.org; 1007 Market St; ⊙noon-5pm Wed-Sat; 🚌5, 6, 7, 21, 31, Ⓜ Civic Center, Ⓑ Civic Center) Like a dandelion pushing through sidewalk cracks, this plucky nonprofit gallery has brought signs of life to one of the Tenderloin's toughest blocks for two decades. By giving SF street artists a gallery platform, the Luggage Store helped launch graffiti-art star Barry McGee, muralist Rigo and street photographer Cheryl Dunn. Find the graffitied door and climb to the 2nd-floor gallery, which rises above the street without losing sight of it.

◉ Golden Gate Park

California Academy of Sciences   Museum

(📞415-379-8000; www.calacademy.org; 55 Music Concourse Dr; adult/student/child $35/30/25; ⊙9:30am-5pm Mon-Sat, from 11am Sun; 🅿🚹; 🚌5, 6, 7, 21, 31, 33, 44, Ⓜ N) 🍃 Architect Renzo Piano's 2008 landmark LEED-certified green building houses 40,000 weird and wonderful animals in a four-story rainforest, split-level aquarium and planetarium all under a 'Living Roof' of California wildflowers.

de Young Museum   Museum

(📞415-750-3600; http://deyoung.famsf.org; 50 Hagiwara Tea Garden Dr; adult/child $15/free, 1st Tue of month free; ⊙9:30am-5:15pm Tue-Sun, to 8:45pm Fri Apr-Nov; 🚹; 🚌5, 7, 44, Ⓜ N) Follow sculptor Andy Goldsworthy's artificial fault line in the sidewalk into Herzog & de

Meuron's sleek, copper-clad building that's oxidizing green to blend into the park. Don't be fooled by the de Young's camouflaged exterior: shows here boldly broaden artistic horizons, from Oceanic ceremonial masks and trippy hippie handmade fashion to James Turrell's domed 'Skyspace' installation, built into a hill in the sculpture garden. Ticket includes free same-day entry to the **Legion of Honor** (📞415-750-3600; http://legionofhonor.famsf.org; 100 34th Ave; adult/child $15/free, discount with Muni ticket $2, 1st Tue of month free; ⊙9:30am-5:15pm Tue-Sun; 🚹; 🚌1, 2, 18, 38).

◉ Nob Hill, Russian Hill & Fillmore

Cable Car Museum   Historic Site

(📞415-474-1887; www.cablecarmuseum.org; 1201 Mason St; donations appreciated; ⊙10am-6pm Apr-Sep, to 5pm Oct-Mar; 🚹; 🚋 Powell-Mason, Powell-Hyde) **FREE** Hear that whirring beneath the cable-car tracks? That's the sound of the cables that pull the cars, and they all connect inside the city's long-functioning cable-car barn. Grips, engines, braking mechanisms...if these warm your gearhead heart, you'll be besotted with the Cable Car Museum.

Lombard Street   Street

(🚋 Powell-Hyde) You've seen the eight switchbacks of Lombard St's 900 block in a thousand photographs. The tourist board has dubbed it 'the world's crookedest street,' which is factually incorrect: Vermont St in Potrero Hill deserves that award, but Lombard is much more scenic, with its red-brick pavement and lovingly tended flowerbeds. It wasn't always so bent; before the arrival of the car it lunged straight down the hill.

Grace Cathedral   Church

(📞415-749-6300; www.gracecathedral.org; 1100 California St; suggested donation adult/child $3/2, services free; ⊙8am-6pm Mon-Sat, to 7pm Sun, services 8:30am, 11am & 6pm Sun; 🚌1, 🚋 California) The city's Episcopal cathedral has been rebuilt three times since the gold rush; the current French-inspired, reinforced-concrete cathedral took 40 years to complete. The

San Francisco

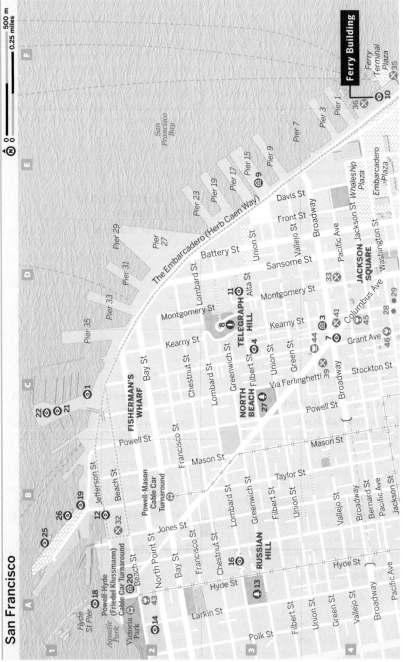

San Francisco

◎ **Sights**
1 Aquarium of the Bay C1
2 Asian Art Museum B8
3 Beat Museum D4
4 Bob Kaufman Alley C3
5 Cable Car Museum C5
6 Chinese Historical Society of
America C5
7 City Lights Books C4
8 Coit Tower...D3
9 Exploratorium E3
10 Ferry Building F4
11 Filbert Street Steps..................................D3
12 Fisherman's Wharf B2
13 George Sterling Park A3
14 Ghirardelli Square A2
15 Grace Cathedral B5
16 Lombard Street A3
17 Luggage Store Gallery C7
18 Maritime National Historical Park..............A1
19 Musée Mécanique B1
20 National Park Visitors Center A2
21 Pier 39..C1
22 San Francisco Carousel C1
23 San Francisco Museum of Modern
Art D7
24 SF Camerawork C7
25 SS Jeremiah O'Brien.................................B1
26 USS Pampanito B1
27 Washington Square C3

◎ **Activities, Courses & Tours**
28 Chinatown Alleyway Tours D4
29 Chinatown Heritage Walking
Tours..D4

30 Emperor Norton's Fantastic Time
Machine C6

✖ **Eating**
31 Acquerello A5
32 Codmother Fish & Chips B2
33 Cotogna D4
34 farm:table B6
35 Ferry Plaza Farmers Market F4
36 Hog Island Oyster Company F4
37 In Situ E6
38 Mister Jiu's C5
39 Molinari C4
40 Swan Oyster Depot A5
41 Tosca Cafe..D4

◎ **Drinking & Nightlife**
42 Aunt Charlie's Lounge...............................C7
43 Buena Vista Cafe A2
44 Caffe Trieste C4
45 Comstock Saloon D4
46 Li Po...C4
47 Pagan Idol D5
48 Smuggler's Cove A8
Specs..(see 41)
49 Tonga Room..C5
50 Top of the Mark..C5

◎ **Entertainment**
51 Giants Stadium F8

spectacular stained-glass windows include a series dedicated to human endeavor, including Albert Einstein uplifted in swirling nuclear particles. Check the website for events on the indoor and outdoor labyrinths, including candlelit meditation services and yoga, plus inclusive weekly spiritual events, such as Thursday Evensong.

◎ North Beach & Chinatown
Coit Tower   Public Art
(📞415-249-0995; www.sfrecpark.org; Telegraph Hill Blvd; nonresident elevator fee adult/child $8/5; ⊙10am-6pm Apr-Oct, to 5pm Nov-Mar; 🚌39) The exclamation mark on San Francisco's skyline is Coit Tower, with 360-degree views of downtown and wraparound 1930s Works Progress Administration (WPA) murals

glorifying SF workers. Initially denounced as Communist, the murals are now a national landmark. For a wild-parrot's panoramic view of San Francisco 210ft above the city, take the elevator to the tower's open-air platform. To glimpse seven recently restored murals up a hidden stairwell on the 2nd floor, join the 11am tour Wednesday or Saturday (free; donations welcome).

City Lights Books   Cultural Center
(📞415-362-8193; www.citylights.com; 261 Columbus Ave; ⊙10am-midnight; 🚶; 🚌8, 10, 12, 30, 41, 45, 🚋Powell-Mason, Powell-Hyde) Free speech and free spirits have flourished here since 1957, when City Lights founder and poet Lawrence Ferlinghetti and manager Shigeyoshi Murao won a landmark ruling defending their right to publish Allen

Ginsberg's magnificent epic poem *Howl*. Celebrate your freedom to read freely in the designated Poet's Chair upstairs overlooking Jack Kerouac Alley, load up on zines on the mezzanine and entertain radical ideas downstairs in the new Pedagogies of Resistance section.

Filbert Street Steps   Architecture

(🏛39) Halfway through the steep climb up the Filbert Street Steps to Coit Tower, you might wonder if it's all worth the trouble. Take a breather and notice what you're passing: hidden cottages along Napier Lane's wooden boardwalk, sculpture-dotted gardens in bloom year-round and sweeping Bay Bridge vistas. If you need further encouragement, the wild parrots in the trees have been known to interject a few choice words your gym trainer would probably get sued for using.

Beat Museum   Museum

(📞800-537-6822; www.kerouac.com; 540 Broadway; adult/student $8/5, walking tours $25; ⏰museum 10am-7pm, walking tours 2-4pm Sat; 🚌8, 10, 12, 30, 41, 45, 🚋Powell-Mason) The closest you can get to the complete Beat experience without breaking a law. The 1000-plus artifacts in this museum's literary-ephemera collection include the sublime (the banned edition of Ginsberg's *Howl*, with the author's own annotations) and the ridiculous (those Kerouac bobblehead dolls are definite head-shakers). Downstairs, watch Beat-era films in ramshackle theater seats redolent with the odors of literary giants, pets and pot. Upstairs, pay your respects at shrines to individual Beat writers.

◉ The Haight

Haight Street   Street

(Haight St, btwn Fillmore & Stanyan Sts; 🚌7, 22, 33, 43, Ⓜ N) Was it the fall of 1966 or the winter of '67? As the Haight saying goes, if you can remember the Summer of Love, dude, you probably weren't there. The fog was laced with pot, sandalwood incense and burning draft cards, entire days were spent contemplating Day-Glo Grateful

Dead posters, and the corner of Haight and Ashbury Sts became the turning point for an entire generation.

◉ The Marina, Fisherman's Wharf & the Piers

Exploratorium   Museum

(📞415-528-4444; www.exploratorium.edu; Pier 15; adult/child $30/20, 6-10pm Thu $15; ⏰10am-5pm Tue-Sun, over 18yr only 6-10pm Thu; 🅿♿; Ⓜ E, F) � Is there a science to skateboarding? Do toilets really flush counterclockwise in Australia? Find out things you'll wish you learned in school at San Francisco's thrilling hands-on science museum. Combining science with art and investigating human perception, the Exploratorium nudges you to question how you perceive the world around you. The setting is thrilling: a 9-acre, glass-walled pier jutting straight into San Francisco Bay, with large outdoor portions you can explore free of charge, 24 hours a day.

Baker Beach   Beach

(📞10am-5pm 415-561-4323; www.nps.gov/prsf; ⏰sunrise-sunset; 🅿; 🚌29, PresidiGo Shuttle) Picnic amid wind-sculpted pines, fish from craggy rocks or frolic nude at mile-long Baker Beach, with spectacular views of the Golden Gate. Crowds come weekends, especially on fog-free days; arrive early. For nude sunbathing (mostly straight girls and gay boys), head to the north. Families in clothing stick to the south, nearer parking. Mind the currents and the c-c-cold water.

Fisherman's Wharf   Pier

(www.fishermanswharf.org; ♿; 🚌19, 30, 47, 49, 🚋Powell-Mason, Powell-Hyde, Ⓜ E, F) **FREE** Fisherman's Wharf – the Embarcadero and Jefferson St waterfront running from Pier 29 to Van Ness Ave – includes the following sights: **Pier 39** (📞415-705-5500; www.pier39.com; cnr Beach St & the Embarcadero), the **Musée Mécanique** (📞415-346-2000; www.museemechanique.org; Pier 45, Shed A; ⏰10am-8pm), the San Francisco Maritime National Historical Park, the **National Park Visitors Center** (📞415-447-5000; www.nps.gov/safr; 499 Jefferson St; ⏰9:30am-5:30pm)

EOROY / SHUTTERSTOCK ©

From left: San Francisco Museum of Modern Art (p306); bowl of seafood stew; Pier 39 (p311), Fisherman's Wharf

FREE, **USS *Pampanito*** (☎415-775-1943, tickets 855-384-6410; www.maritime.org/pamphome.htm; Pier 45; adult/child/family $20/10/45; ⊙9am-8pm Thu-Tue, to 6pm Wed), **SS *Jeremiah O'Brien*** (☎415-554-0100; www.ssjeremiahobrien.org; Pier 45; adult/child/family $20/10/40; ⊙9am-4pm), the **Aquarium of the Bay** (☎415-623-5300; www.aquariumofthebay.org; Pier 39; adult/child/family $24.95/14.95/70; ⊙9am-8pm late May-early Sep, shorter hours low season), the **San Francisco Carousel** (www.pier39.com; Pier 39; rides $3; ⊙11am-7pm) and **Ghirardelli Square** (☎415-775-5500; www.ghirardellisq.com; 900 North Point St; 10am-9pm).

Maritime National Historical Park   Historic Site

(☎415-447-5000; www.nps.gov/safr; 499 Jefferson St, Hyde St Pier; 7-day ticket adult/child $10/free; ⊙9:30am-5pm Oct-May, to 5:30pm Jun-Sep; ⊞; ☐19, 30, 47, ☐Powell-Hyde, ⓂF) Four historic ships are floating museums at this maritime national park, Fisherman's Wharf's most authentic attraction. Moored along Hyde Street Pier, standouts include the 1891 schooner *Alma*, which hosts guided sailing trips in summer; 1890 steamboat

Eureka; paddlewheel tugboat *Eppleton Hall*; and iron-hulled *Balclutha*, which brought coal to San Francisco. It's free to walk the pier; pay only to board ships.

✖ EATING

✖ Downtown & Civic Center

farm:table   American $

(☎415-292-7089; www.farmtablesf.com; 754 Post St; dishes $6-9; ⊙7:30am-2pm Tue-Fri, 8am-3pm Sat & Sun; ☞; ☐2, 3, 27, 38) ● A ray of sunshine in the concrete heart of the city, this plucky little storefront showcases seasonal California organics in just-baked breakfasts and farmstead-fresh lunches. Check the menu on Twitter (@farmtable) for today's homemade cereals, savory tarts and game-changing toast – mmmm, ginger peach and mascarpone on whole-wheat sourdough. Tiny space, but immaculate kitchen and great coffee. Cash only.

Cotogna   Italian $$

(☎415-775-8508; www.cotognasf.com; 490 Pacific Ave; mains $19-35; ⊙11:30am-10:30pm Mon-Thu, to 11pm Fri & Sat, 5-9:30pm Sun; ☞;

10, 12) Chef-owner Michael Tusk racks up James Beard Awards for a quintessentially Italian culinary balancing act: he strikes ideal proportions among a few pristine flavors in rustic pastas, woodfired pizzas and salt-crusted branzino. Reserve, especially for bargain $55 four-course Sunday suppers with $35 wine pairings – or plan a walk-in late lunch/early dinner.

In Situ   Californian, International $$

(415-941-6050; http://insitu.sfmoma.org; SF-MOMA, 151 3rd St; mains $14-34; 11am-3:30pm Mon & Tue, 11am-3:30pm & 5-9pm Thu-Sun; 5, 6, 7, 14, 19, 21, 31, 38, B Montgomery, M Montgomery) The landmark gallery of modern cuisine attached to SFMOMA also showcases avant-garde masterpieces –
but these ones you'll lick clean. Chef Corey Lee collaborates with star chefs worldwide, scrupulously recreating their signature dishes with California-grown ingredients so that you can enjoy Harald Wohlfahrt's impeccable anis-marinated salmon, Hiroshi Sasaki's decadent chicken thighs and Albert Adrià's gravity-defying cocoa-bubble cake in one unforgettable sitting.

Golden Gate Park & the Avenues

Dragon Beaux   Dim Sum $

(415-333-8899; www.dragonbeaux.com; 5700 Geary Blvd; dumplings $4-9; 11:30am-2:30pm & 5:30-10pm Mon-Thu, to 10:30pm Fri, 10am-3pm & 5:30-10pm Sat & Sun; ; 2, 38) Hong Kong meets Vegas at SF's most glamorous, decadent Cantonese restaurant. Say yes to cartloads of succulent roast meats – hello, roast duck and pork belly – and creative dumplings, especially XO dumplings with plump, brandy-laced shrimp in spinach wrappers. Expect premium teas, sharp service and impeccable Cantonese standards, like Chinese doughnuts, *har gow* (shrimp dumplings) and Chinese broccoli in oyster sauce.

Nob Hill, Russian Hill & Fillmore

Swan Oyster Depot   Seafood $$

(415-673-1101; 1517 Polk St; dishes $10-25; 10:30am-5:30pm Mon-Sat; 1, 19, 47, 49, California) Superior flavor without the superior attitude of typical seafood restaurants – Swan's downside is an inevitable wait for the few stools at its vintage lunch counter, but the upside of high turnover is incredibly fresh seafood.

State Bird Provisions
Californian $$$

(📞415-795-1272; http://statebirdsf.com; 1529 Fillmore St; dishes $9-30; ⏲5:30-10pm Sun-Thu, to 11pm Fri & Sat; 🚊22, 38) Even before winning back-to-back James Beard Awards, State Bird attracted lines for 5:30pm seatings not seen since the Dead played neighboring Fillmore Auditorium (p319). The draw is a thrilling play on dim sum, wildly inventive with seasonal-regional ingredients and esoteric flavors, like fennel pollen and garum. Plan to order multiple dishes. Book exactly 60 days ahead. The staff couldn't be lovelier.

Acquerello
Californian, Italian $$$

(📞415-567-5432; www.acquerello.com; 1722 Sacramento St; 3-/4-/5-course menu $95/120/140; ⏲5:30-9:30pm Tue-Sat; 🚊1, 19, 47, 49, 🚋California) A converted chapel is a fitting location for a meal that'll turn Italian culinary purists into true believers in Cal-Italian cuisine. Chef Suzette Gresham's generous pastas and ingenious seasonal meat dishes include heavenly quail salad, devilish lobster *panzerotti* (turnover) and venison loin chops. Suave *maître d'hôtel* Giancarlo Paterlini indulges every whim, even providing black-linen napkins if you're worried about lint.

✪ North Beach & Chinatown

Molinari
Deli $

(📞415-421-2337; www.molinarisalame.com; 373 Columbus Ave; sandwiches $10-13.50; ⏲9am-6pm Mon-Fri, to 5:30pm Sat; 🚊8, 10, 12, 30, 39, 41, 45, 🚋Powell-Mason) Observe quasi-religious North Beach noontime rituals: enter Molinari, and grab a number and a crusty roll. When your number's called, wisecracking staff pile your roll with heavenly fixings: milky buffalo mozzarella, tangy sun-dried tomatoes, translucent sheets of prosciutto di Parma, slabs of legendary house-cured salami, drizzles of olive oil and balsamic. Enjoy hot from the panini press at sidewalk tables.

Mister Jiu's
Chinese $$

(📞415-857-9688; http://misterjius.com; 28 Waverly Pl; mains $14-45; ⏲5:30-10:30pm Tue-Sat; 🚊30, 🚋California) Ever since the gold rush, San Francisco has craved Chinese food, powerful cocktails and hyperlocal specialties – and Mister Jiu's satisfies on all counts. Build your own banquet of Chinese classics with California twists: chanterelle chow mein, Dungeness-crab rice noodles, quail and Mission-fig sticky rice. Cocktail pairings are equally inspired – try jasmine-infused-gin Happiness ($13) with tea-smoked Sonoma-duck confit.

Tosca Cafe
Italian $$

(📞415-986-9651; www.toscacafesf.com; 242 Columbus Ave; mains $15-22; ⏲5pm-2am; 🚊8, 10, 12, 30, 41, 45, 🚋Powell-Mason) When this historic North Beach speakeasy was nearly evicted in 2012, devotees like Sean Penn, Robert De Niro and Johnny Depp rallied, and New York star chef April Bloomfield took over. Now the 1930s murals and red-leather banquettes are restored and the revived kitchen serves rustic Italian classics (get the meatballs). Jukebox opera and spiked house cappuccino here deserve SF-landmark status. Reservations essential.

✪ The Haight & Hayes Valley

Brenda's Meat & Three
Southern US $

(📞415-926-8657; http://brendasmeatandthree. com; 919 Divisadero St; mains $8-15; ⏲8am-10pm Wed-Mon; 🚊5, 21, 24, 38) The name means one meaty main course plus three sides – though only superheroes finish ham steak with Creole red-eye gravy and exemplary grits, let alone cream biscuits and eggs. Chef Brenda Buenviaje's portions are defiantly Southern, which explains brunch lines of marathoners and partiers who forgot to eat last night. Arrive early, share sweet-potato pancakes, and pray for crawfish specials.

Rich Table   Californian $$

(☏415-355-9085; http://richtablesf.com; 199
Gough St; mains $17-36; ⊙5:30-10pm Sun-Thu, to
10:30pm Fri & Sat; ☒5, 6, 7, 21, 47, 49, Ⓜ Van Ness)
⚑ Impossible cravings begin at Rich Table,
inventor of porcini doughnuts, miso-
marrow-stuffed pasta and fried-chicken
madeleines with caviar. Married cochefs
and owners Sarah and Evan Rich playfully
riff on seasonal California fare, freestyling
with whimsical off-menu amuse-bouches
like trippy beet marshmallows or the Dirty
Hippie: nutty hemp atop silky goat-
buttermilk *pannacotta*, as offbeat and
entrancing as Hippie Hill drum circles.

Cala   Mexican, Californian $$$

(☏415-660-7701; www.calarestaurant.com; 149
Fell St; ⊙5-10pm Mon-Wed, to 11pm Thu-Sat,
11am-3pm Sun, taco bar 11am-2pm Mon-Fri;
☒6, 7, 21, 47, 49, Ⓜ Van Ness) Like discover-
ing a long-lost twin, Cala's Mexico Norte
cuisine is a revelation. San Francisco's
Mexican-rancher roots are deeply honored
here: silky bone-marrow salsa and fragrant
heritage-corn tortillas grace a sweet potato
slow-cooked in ashes. Brace yourself
with mezcal margaritas for the ultimate
California surf and turf: sea urchin with
beef tongue. Original and unforgettable,
even before Mayan-chocolate gelato with
amaranth brittle.

🍷 DRINKING & NIGHTLIFE

🍸 Downtown, Civic Center & Soma

Pagan Idol   Lounge

(☏415-985-6375; www.paganidol.com; 375
Bush St; ⊙4pm-1am Mon-Fri, 6pm-1:30am Sat;
ⒷMontgomery, ⓂF, J, K, L, M) Volcanoes erupt
inside Pagan Idol every half hour, or until
there's a virgin sacrifice...what, no takers?
Then order your island cocktail and brace
for impact – these tiki drinks are no joke.
Flirt with disaster over a Hemingway Is
Dead: rum, bitters and grapefruit, served in
a skull. Book online to nab a hut for groups
of four to six.

🍽 Best Cheap Eats in the Mission

La Palma Mexicatessen (☏415-647-
1500; www.lapalmasf.com; 2884 24th St;
tamales, tacos & huarache $3-5; ⊙8am-6pm
Mon-Sat, to 5pm Sun; 🚶🍴; ☒12, 14, 27, 48,
Ⓑ24th St Mission) Follow the applause:
that's the sound of organic tortilla-
making in progress at La Palma. You've
found the Mission mother lode of handmade tamales, *pupusas* (tortilla pockets)
with potato and *chicharones* (pork crack-
ling), *carnitas* (slow-roasted pork), *cotija*
(Oaxacan cheese) and La Palma's own
tangy tomatillo sauce. Get takeout, or
bring a small army to finish that massive
meal at sunny sidewalk tables.

La Taqueria (☏415-285-7117; 2889 Mission
St; items $3-11; ⊙11am-9pm Mon-Sat, to 8pm
Sun; 🍴; ☒12, 14, 48, 49, Ⓑ24th St Mission)
SF's definitive burrito has no saffron
rice, spinach tortilla or mango salsa –
just perfectly grilled meats, slow-cooked
beans and tomatillo or mesquite salsa
wrapped in a flour tortilla. They're pur-
ists at James Beard Award–winning La
Taqueria. You'll pay extra to go without
beans, because they add more meat
– but spicy pickles and *crema* (sour
cream) bring burrito bliss. Worth the
wait, always.

Bar Agricole   Bar

(☏415-355-9400; www.baragricole.com; 355
11th St; ⊙5-11pm Mon-Thu, 5pm-midnight Fri
& Sat, 10am-2pm & 6-9pm Sun; ☒9, 12, 27, 47)
⚑ Drink your way to a history degree with

well-researched cocktails: Whiz Bang with house bitters, whiskey, vermouth and absinthe scores high, but El Presidente with white rum, farmhouse curaçao and California-pomegranate grenadine takes top honors. This overachiever wins James Beard Award nods for spirits and eco-savvy design, plus popular acclaim for $1 oysters and $5 aperitifs 5pm to 6pm Monday to Saturday.

Nob Hill, Russian Hill & Fillmore

Tonga Room   Lounge

(☎reservations 415-772-5278; www.tongaroom. com; Fairmont San Francisco, 950 Mason St; cover $5-7; ☉5-11:30pm Sun, Wed & Thu, to 12:30am Fri & Sat; 🚌1, 🚋California, Powell-Mason, Powell-Hyde) Tonight's San Francisco weather: 100% chance of tropical rainstorms every 20 minutes, but only on the top-40 band playing on the island in the middle of the indoor pool – you're safe in your grass hut. For a more powerful hurricane, order one in a plastic coconut. Who said tiki bars were dead? Come before 8pm to beat the cover charge.

Top of the Mark   Bar

(www.topofthemark.com; 999 California St; cover $10-15; ☉4:30-11:30pm Sun-Thu, to 12:30am Fri & Sat; 🚌1, 🚋California) So what if it's touristy? Nothing beats twirling in the clouds in a little cocktail dress on the city's highest dancefloor. Thursday to Saturday evenings are best, when a full jazz band plays; Wednesday there's piano music. Sunday to Tuesday it's quiet, but, oh, the views! Remarkably, it's often empty at sunset – and gorgeous on fog-free evenings. Expect $15 drinks.

North Beach & Chinatown

Specs   Bar

(Specs Twelve Adler Museum Cafe; ☎415-421-4112; 12 William Saroyan Pl; ☉5pm-2am; 🚌8, 10, 12, 30, 41, 45, 🚋Powell-Mason) The walls here are plastered with merchant-marine memorabilia, and you'll be plastered too if you try to keep up with the salty characters holding court in back. Surrounded by seafaring me-

mentos – including walrus genitalia over the bar – your order seems obvious: pitcher of Anchor Steam, coming right up. Cash only.

Comstock Saloon   Bar

(☎415-617-0071; www.comstocksaloon.com; 155 Columbus Ave; ☉4pm-midnight Sun-Mon, to 2am Tue-Thu & Sat, noon-2am Fri; 🚌8, 10, 12, 30, 45, 🚋Powell-Mason) Relieving yourself in the marble trough below the bar is no longer advisable – Emperor Norton is watching from above – but otherwise this 1907 Victorian saloon brings back the Barbary Coast's glory days with authentic pisco punch and martini-precursor Martinez (gin, vermouth, bitters, maraschino liqueur). Reserve booths or back-parlor seating to hear on nights when ragtime-jazz bands play.

Li Po   Bar

(☎415-982-0072; www.lipolounge.com; 916 Grant Ave; ☉2pm-2am; 🚌8, 30, 45, 🚋Powell-Mason, Powell-Hyde) Beat a hasty retreat to red-vinyl booths where Allen Ginsberg and Jack Kerouac debated the meaning of life under a golden Buddha. Enter the 1937 faux-grotto doorway and dodge red lanterns to place your order: Tsingtao beer or a sweet, sneaky-strong Chinese mai tai made with *baijiu* (rice liquor). Brusque bartenders, basement bathrooms, cash only – a world-class dive bar.

Caffe Trieste   Cafe

(☎415-392-6739; www.caffetrieste.com; 601 Vallejo St; ☉6:30am-10pm Sun-Thu, to 11pm Fri & Sat; 🎙; 🚌8, 10, 12, 30, 41, 45) Poetry on bathroom walls, opera on the jukebox, live accordion jams and sightings of Beat poet-laureate Lawrence Ferlinghetti: this is North Beach at its best, since the 1950s. Linger over legendary espresso and scribble your screenplay under the Sardinian fishing mural just as young Francis Ford Coppola did. Perhaps you've heard of the movie: *The Godfather*. Cash only.

The Haight & Hayes Valley

Smuggler's Cove   Bar

(☎415-869-1900; www.smugglerscovesf.com; 650 Gough St; ☉5pm-1:15am; 🚌5, 21, 47, 49,

M Civic Center, B Civic Center) Yo-ho-ho and a bottle of rum...wait, make that a Dead Reckoning (Nicaraguan rum, port, pineapple and bitters), unless you'll split the flaming Scorpion Bowl? Pirates are bedeviled by choice at this Barbary Coast–shipwreck tiki bar, hidden behind tinted-glass doors. With 550 rums and 70-plus cocktails gleaned from rum-running around the world – and $2 off 5pm to 6pm daily – you won't be dry-docked long.

Riddler — Wine Bar

(www.theriddlersf.com; 528 Laguna St; ⏱4-10pm Tue-Thu & Sun, to 11pm Fri & Sat; 🚌5, 6, 7, 21) Riddle me this: how can you ever thank the women in your life? As the Riddler's all-women sommelier-chef-investor team points out, champagne makes a fine start. Bubbles begin at $12 and include Veuve Cliquot, the brand named after the woman who invented riddling, the process that gives champagne its unclouded sparkle.

🌀 The Marina & Fisherman's Wharf

Buena Vista Cafe — Bar

(📞415-474-5044; www.thebuenavista.com; 2765 Hyde St; ⏱9am-2am Mon-Fri, 8am-2am Sat & Sun; 📶; 🚌19, 47, 🚋Powell-Hyde) Warm your cockles with a prim little goblet of bitter-creamy Irish coffee, introduced to America at this destination bar that once served sailors and cannery workers. That old Victorian floor manages to hold up carousers and families alike, served community-style at round tables overlooking the cable-car turnaround at Victoria Park.

Interval Bar & Cafe — Bar

(www.theinterval.org; 2 Marina Blvd, Fort Mason Center, Bldg A; ⏱10am-midnight; 🚌10, 22, 28, 30, 47, 49) Designed to stimulate discussion of philosophy and art, the Interval is a favorite spot in the Marina for cocktails and conversation. It's inside the Long Now Foundation, with floor-to-ceiling bookshelves, which contain the canon of Western lit, rising above a glorious 10,000-year clock – a fitting backdrop for a daiquiri, gimlet or

🍸 LGBTIQ San Francisco

In San Francisco, you don't need to trawl the urban underworld for a gay scene. The intersection of 18th and Castro is the historic center of the gay world, but dancing queens head to SoMa for thump-thump clubs. The Mission remains the preferred 'hood for many women and a diverse transgender community. Top picks for good times:

Aunt Charlie's Lounge (📞415-441-2922; www.auntcharlieslounge.com; 133 Turk St; free-$5; ⏱noon-2am Mon-Fri, from 10am Sat, 10am-midnight Sun; 🚌27, 31, M Powell, B Powell) Vintage pulp-fiction covers come to life when the Hot Boxxx Girls storm the battered stage at Aunt Charlie's on Friday and Saturday nights at 10pm ($5; call for reservations). Thursday is Tubesteak Connection ($5, free before 10pm), when bathhouse anthems and '80s disco draw throngs of art-school gays. Other nights bring guaranteed minor mayhem, seedy glamour and Tenderloin dive-bar shenanigans.

Twin Peaks Tavern (📞415-864-9470; www.twinpeakstavern.com; 401 Castro St; ⏱noon-2am Mon-Fri, from 8am Sat & Sun; M Castro St) Don't call it the glass coffin. Show some respect: Twin Peaks was the world's first gay bar with windows open to the street. The jovial crowd skews (way) over 40, but they're not chicken hawks (or they wouldn't hang here) and they love it when happy kids show up to join the party.

Active San Francisco

On sunny weekends, SF is out kite-flying, surfing or biking. Even on foggy days, don't neglect sunscreen: UV rays penetrate SF's thin cloud cover.

Coastal Trail (www.californiacoastaltrail. info; ☺sunrise-sunset; ☐1, 18, 38) Hit your stride on this 10.5-mile stretch, starting at Fort Funston, crossing 4 miles of sandy Ocean Beach and wrapping around the Presidio to the Golden Gate Bridge. Casual strollers can pick up the freshly restored trail near Sutro Baths and head around the Lands End bluffs for end-of-the-world views and glimpses of shipwrecks at low tide. At Lincoln Park, duck into the Legion of Honor or descend the gloriously tiled Lincoln Park Steps (near 32nd Ave).

Emperor Norton's Fantastic Time Machine (☑415-644-8513; www.emperor nortontour.com; $20; ☺11am & 2:30pm Thu & Sat, 11am Sun; ☐30, 38, ⒷPowell St, ⓂPowell St, ⌂Powell-Mason, Powell-Hyde) Huzzah, San Francisco invented time-travel contraptions! They're called shoes, and you wear them to follow the self-appointed Emperor Norton (aka historian Joseph Amster) across 2 miles of the most dastardly, scheming, uplifting and urban-legendary terrain on Earth... or at least west of Berkeley. Sunday waterfront tours depart from the Ferry Building; all others depart from Union Sq's Dewey Monument. Cash only.

aged Tom Collins, or single-origin coffee, tea and snacks.

🍸 The Mission, Dogpatch & Potrero Hill

%ABV   Cocktail Bar
(☑415-400-4748; www.abvsf.com; 3174 16th St; ☺2pm-2am; ☐14, 22, Ⓑ16th St Mission, ⓂJ) As kindred spirits will deduce from the name (the abbreviation for 'percent alcohol by

volume'), this bar is backed by cocktail crafters who know their Rittenhouse rye from their Japanese malt whiskey. Top-notch hooch is served promptly and without pretension, including excellent Cali wine and beer on tap and original historically inspired cocktails like the Sutro Swizzle (Armagnac, grapefruit shrub, maraschino liqueur).

20 Spot   Wine Bar
(☑415-624-3140; www.20spot.com; 3565 20th St; ☺5pm-midnight Mon-Thu, to 1am Fri & Sat; ☐14, 22, 33, Ⓑ16th St Mission) Find your California mellow at this neighborhood wine lounge in a 1895 Victorian building. After decades as Force of Habit punk-record shop – note the vintage sign – this corner joint has earned the right to unwind with a glass of Berkeley's Donkey and Goat sparkling wine and not get any guff. Caution: oysters with pickled persimmon could become a habit.

✪ ENTERTAINMENT

SFJAZZ Center   Jazz
(☑866-920-5299; www.sfjazz.org; 201 Franklin St; tickets $25-120; ☝; ☐5, 6, 7, 21, 47, 49, ⓂVan Ness) ✐ Jazz legends and singular talents from Argentina to Yemen are showcased at North America's newest, largest jazz center. Hear fresh takes on classic jazz albums and poets riffing with jazz combos in the downstairs Joe Henderson Lab, and witness extraordinary main-stage collaborations ranging from Afro-Cuban All Stars to roots legends Emmylou Harris, Rosanne Cash and Lucinda Williams.

Giants Stadium   Baseball
(AT&T Park; ☑415-972-2000, tours 415-972-2400; http://sanfrancisco.giants.mlb.com; 24 Willie Mays Plaza; tickets $14-349, stadium tour adult/child/senior $22/12/17; ☺tours 10:30am & 12:30pm; ☝; ⓂN, T) Baseball fans roar April to October at the Giants' 81 home games. As any orange-blooded San Franciscan will remind you, the Giants have won three World Series since 2010 – and you'll know the Giants are on another winning streak

when superstitious locals sport team colors (orange and black) and bushy beards (the Giants' rallying cry is 'Fear the Beard!').

Booksmith   Live Performance
(📞415-863-8688; www.booksmith.com; 1644 Haight St; ⏰10am-10pm Mon-Sat, to 8pm Sun; ♿; 🚌6, 7, 43, Ⓜ N) Throw a stone in SF and you'll probably hit a writer (ouch) or reader (ouch again) headed to/from Booksmith. Literary figures organize Booksmith book signings, mass giveaways of George Orwell's *1984*, boozy book swaps and politician-postcard-writing marathons. At monthly Shipwreck events, local writers wreck innocent classics by turning them into hastily written erotica, read with theatrical flourish – expect heaving below decks.

Fillmore Auditorium   Live Music
(📞415-346-6000; http://thefillmore.com; 1805 Geary Blvd; tickets from $20; ⏰box office 10am-3pm Sun, plus 30min before doors open to 10pm show nights) Jimi Hendrix, Janis Joplin, the Doors – they all played the Fillmore. Now you might catch the Indigo Girls, Willie Nelson or Tracy Chapman in the historic 1250-capacity, standing-room-only theater (if you're polite and lead with the hip, you might squeeze up to the stage). Don't miss the priceless collection of psychedelic posters in the upstairs gallery.

ⓘ INFORMATION

San Francisco Visitor Information Center
(www.sanfrancisco.travel/visitor-information-center) Muni passports, activities deals, culture and event calendars.

ⓘ GETTING THERE & AWAY

AIR

San Francisco International Airport (SFO; www.flysfo.com; S McDonnell Rd) is 14 miles south of downtown. BART provides a direct 30-minute ride to/from downtown. The SFO BART station is connected to the International Terminal; buy tickets ($8.95) from machines inside stations. Airport shuttles (one-way $17 to $20 plus tip) take 45 minutes to most SF locations. Taxis cost $40 to $55, plus tip.

Oakland International Airport (OAK; www.oaklandairport.com; 1 Airport Dr; 🚉; Ⓑ Oakland International Airport) is 15 miles east of downtown San Francisco. BART people-mover shuttles run every 10 to 20 minutes from Terminal 1 to the Coliseum station, where you connect with BART trains to downtown SF ($10.20, 25 minutes). Taxis cost $60 to $80 to SF.

TRAIN

Located outside Oakland, the Emeryville Amtrak station (EMY) serves West Coast and nationwide train routes; Amtrak runs free shuttles to/from San Francisco's Ferry Building, Caltrain, Civic Center and Fisherman's Wharf.

ⓘ GETTING AROUND

When San Franciscans aren't pressed for time, most walk, bike or ride **Muni** (Municipal Transit Agency; 📞511; www.sfmta.com) instead of taking a car or cab. Traffic is notoriously bad at rush hour, and parking is next to impossible in city-center neighborhoods.

○ **Cable cars** Frequent, slow and scenic, from 6am to 12:30am daily. Single rides cost $7; for frequent use, get a Muni Passport ($21 per day). Buy tickets at cable-car turnaround kiosks or on board from the conductor.

○ **Muni streetcar and bus** Reasonably fast, but schedules vary wildly by line; infrequent after 9pm. Fares are $2.50. Buy tickets from drivers (exact change required) or at underground Muni stations (where machines give change).

○ **BART** High-speed transit to East Bay, Mission St, SF airport and Millbrae, where it connects with Caltrain. Buy tickets at BART stations: you need a ticket to enter – and exit – the system.

○ **Taxi** Fares are about $2.75 per mile; meters start at $3.50.

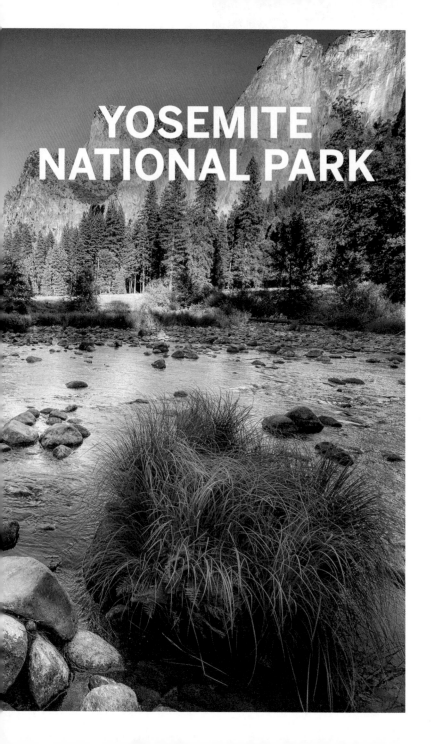

YOSEMITE
NATIONAL PARK

In this Chapter

Glacier Point 324
Half Dome 326
Yosemite Valley Waterfalls 328
Groveland 333
Mariposa 334

Yosemite National Park at a Glance...

The jaw-dropping head-turner of America's national parks, and a Unesco World Heritage Site, Yosemite (yo-sem-it-ee) garners the devotion of all who enter. From the waterfall-striped granite walls buttressing Yosemite Valley to the sky-high, wildflower-splashed meadows of Tuolumne, the place inspires a sense of awe. But lift your eyes above the crowds and you'll feel your heart instantly moved by unrivaled splendors: the haughty profile of Half Dome, the hulking presence of El Capitan, the drenching mists of Yosemite Fall and the gemstone lakes of the high country's subalpine wilderness.

Two Days in Yosemite National Park

With two days in Yosemite, you'll want to head straight to the valley, where you can stand agape at the twin marvels of **Half Dome** (p326) and El Capitan. Make the most of day two with a hike to see some of the valley's **waterfalls** (p328).

Four Days in Yosemite National Park

Get deeper into this incredible park by cruising the twisting two-lane blacktop of CA 120 to Yosemite's high country and **Tuolumne Meadows** (p333). If you're particularly ambitious, hike up to Glacier Point for a bird's-eye view of the valley's monuments or try a night or two in the backcountry.

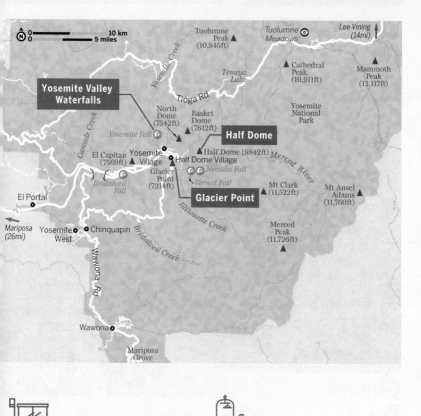

Arriving in Yosemite National Park

There are four main entrances to the park: South Entrance (Hwy 41), Arch Rock (Hwy 140), Big Oak Flat (Hwy 120 W) and Tioga Pass (Hwy 120 E). Visitor activity is concentrated in Yosemite Valley, which has the main visitor center and other services. Tuolumne (too-ahl-uh-mee) Meadows, toward the eastern end of Tioga Rd, primarily draws hikers, backpackers and climbers.

Where to Stay

All noncamping reservations within the park are handled by **Aramark/ Yosemite Hospitality** (☏888-413-8869; www.travelyosemite.com) and can be made up to 366 days in advance; reservations are critical from May to early September. There are a few quality hotels in Groveland proper, and accommodations east along Hwy 120 in the Stanislaus National Forest. For chain hotels, check out Mariposa. Competition for campsites is fierce; reserve at www.recreation.gov.

LUKAS BISCHOFF PHOTOGRAPH / SHUTTERSTOCK ©

Glacier Point

With granite peaks stretching out in the distance, Glacier Point offers one of the most commanding views in the state, including a bird's-eye view of El Capitan and Half Dome.

Great For...

☑ **Don't Miss**

At sunset, the granite faces of the Sierra are bathed in warm, golden light.

History

Almost from the park's inception, Glacier Point has been a popular destination. It used to be that getting up here was a major undertaking. That changed once the Four Mile Trail opened in 1872. A wagon road to the point was completed in 1882, and the current Glacier Point Rd was built in 1936. The cozy Glacier Point Trailside Museum was one of the park's first projects, a humble little stone hut that offers a great shelter from a passing storm.

The View

If you drove, the views from 7214ft Glacier Point might make you feel like you cheated – superstar sights present themselves to you with your having made hardly any physical effort. A quick mosey up the paved path from the parking lot and you'll find

ℹ Need to Know

The best time to visit is early spring or fall before the road closes for the season.

✕ Take a Break

Amble over to the Glacier Point amphitheater, an ideal picnic setting with incredible panoramas.

★ Top Tip

In the summer, a free shuttle leaves Badger Pass for Glacier Point every 20 minutes.

the entire eastern Yosemite Valley spread out before you, from Yosemite Fall to Half Dome, as well as the distant peaks that ring Tuolumne Meadows. Half Dome looms practically at eye level, and if you look closely you can spot hikers on its summit.

To the left of Half Dome lies the glacially carved Tenaya Canyon, and to its right are the wavy white ribbons of Nevada and Vernal Falls. On the valley floor, the Merced River snakes through green meadows and groves of trees. If you're not afraid of heights, sidle up to the railing, hold on tight and peer 3200ft straight down at Half Dome Village. Basket Dome and North Dome rise to the north of the valley, and Liberty Cap and the Clark Range can be seen to the right of Half Dome.

At the tip of the point is Overhanging Rock, a huge granite slab protruding from the cliff edge like an outstretched tongue, defying gravity and once providing a scenic stage for daredevil extroverts. Through the years, many famous photos have been taken of folks performing handstands, high kicks and other wacky stunts on the rock. The precipice is now off-limits.

Hiking Sentinel

Nearby, if you're still craving views, you can hike to Sentinel's summit (8122ft), the shortest and easiest trail up one of Yosemite's granite domes. For those unable to visit Half Dome's summit, Sentinel offers an equally outstanding 360-degree perspective of Yosemite's wonders, and the 2.2-mile round-trip hike only takes about an hour. A visit at sunrise or sunset or during a full moon is spectacular.

TAHA RAJA / 500PX ©

Half Dome

It's difficult not to feel a sense of wonder when your eyes first encounter this iconic, beautifully broken slab of granite, the most iconic physical feature of Yosemite.

Great For...

☑ **Don't Miss**

The reflection of Mt Watkins and Half Dome on Mirror Lake in spring and early summer.

Yosemite's most distinctive natural monument, Half Dome is 87 million years old and has a 93% vertical grade – the sheerest cliff in North America. Climbers come from around the world to grapple with its legendary north face, but good hikers can reach its summit via a 17-mile round-trip trail from Yosemite Valley. The trail gains 4900ft in elevation and has cable handrails for the last 200yd.

The hike can be done in a day but is more enjoyable if you break it up by camping along the way (Little Yosemite Valley is the most popular spot).

Legend

According to Native American legend, one of Yosemite Valley's early inhabitants went down from the mountains to Mono Lake, where he wed a Paiute named Tesaiyac. The

❶ Need to Know

Rangers check for valid permits at the base of the Half Dome cables.

✕ Take a Break

Settle in for a drink at the cozy **Majestic Bar** (www.travelyosemite.com; 1 Ahwahnee Dr, Yosemite Valley; ⊘11am-10pm), inside the Majestic Yosemite Hotel.

★ Top Tip

If you want to climb it, check www.nps. gov/yose/planyourvisit/hdpermits. htm for the latest information.

journey back to the valley was difficult, and by the time they reached what was to become Mirror Lake, Tesaiyac had decided that she wanted to go back down to live with her people at Mono Lake. However, her husband refused to live on such barren, arid land with no oak trees from which to get acorns.

With a heart full of despair, Tesaiyac began to run toward Mono Lake, and her husband followed her. When the powerful spirits heard quarreling in Yosemite, they became angry and turned the two into stone: he became North Dome and she became Half Dome. The tears she cried made marks as they ran down her face, thus forming Mirror Lake.

Half Dome Permits

To stem lengthy lines (and increasingly dangerous conditions) on the vertiginous

cables of Half Dome, the park now requires that all day hikers obtain an advance permit to climb the cables.

Preseason permit lottery (www.recreation. gov) Lottery applications ($10) for the 300 daily spots must be completed in March, with confirmation notification sent in mid-April; an additional fee of $10 per person confirms the permit. Applications can include up to six people and seven alternative dates.

Daily lottery Approximately 50 additional permits are distributed by lottery two days before each hiking date. Apply online or by phone (☏877-444-6777) between midnight and 1pm Pacific Time; notification is available late that same evening. It's easier to score weekday permits.

Backpackers Those with Yosemite-issued wilderness permits that *reasonably include* Half Dome can request Half Dome permits (from $12.50 per person) without going through the lottery process.

Yosemite Valley Waterfalls

Yosemite's waterfalls mesmerize even the most jaded traveler, especially when the spring runoff turns them into thunderous cataracts. In the spring melting snow makes these falls a spectacular demonstration of nature's power.

Great For...

ℹ Need to Know

Bring rain gear or expect to get soaked when the falls are heavy.

☑ **Don't Miss**

When the peak summer sun is hot, cool off in the refreshing mist of Vernal Fall.

Yosemite Fall

West of Yosemite Village, Yosemite Fall is considered among the tallest waterfalls in North America, dropping 2425ft (740m) in three tiers. Because it faces the open meadows, you'll be able to see this gorgeous cascade from vantage points throughout the valley. A slick trail leads to the bottom or, if you prefer solitude, you can clamber up the Yosemite Fall Trail, which puts you atop the falls after a grueling 3.4 miles. The falls are usually mesmerizing, especially when the spring runoff turns them into a thundering cacophony, but most are reduced to a trickle by late summer.

Bridalveil Fall

At the southwestern end of the valley, Bridalveil Fall tumbles 620ft (189m). The Ahwahneechee people call it Pohono (Spirit of the Puffing Wind), as gusts often blow the fall from side to side, even lifting water back up into the air. The waterfall usually runs year-round, though it's often reduced to a whisper by midsummer.

Park at the large lot where Wawona Rd (Hwy 41) meets Southside Dr. From the lot, it's a quarter-mile walk to the base of the fall. The path is paved but probably too rough for wheelchairs, and there's a somewhat steep climb at the very end. Avoid climbing on the slippery rocks at the fall's base – no one likes a broken bone.

Vernal & Nevada Falls

Vernal is one of Yosemite's iconic falls, where the thundering waters of the Merced River tumble 317ft (97m) down on the way to meet Yosemite Valley below. Mist Trail, the paved path to the falls, is one of the park's most popular. At the top of the falls, the view is jaw-dropping (and a little scary). Continue a short distance further on the trail and you'll come to Emerald Pool and Silver Apron. Both of these may be tempting on a sweltering summer day, but stay out; it is extremely dangerous to swim there. You can continue over a small bridge and take in a short stretch of the famed John Muir Trail, which leads back to the Yosemite Valley in about 4 miles. This return has big rewards with incredible views of Liberty Cap (look for climbers) and Nevada Fall.

There are spectacular views away from Nevada Fall, ricocheting 594ft (181m) as part of the 'Giant Staircase' that leads the Merced River down into Yosemite Valley. Either the Mist Trail or the John Muir Trail will get you to the top, but we recommend taking the Mist Trail up, passing Vernal Fall on the way, and the John Muir Trail down. Your knees will thank us.

Rafting in Yosemite

From around late May to July, floating along the Merced River from Stoneman Meadow, near Half Dome Village, to Sentinel Bridge is a leisurely way to soak up Yosemite Valley views. Four-person **raft rentals** (☏209-372-4386; per person $30; ◷late May-late Jul) for the 3-mile trip are available from the concessionaire in Half Dome Village and include equipment and a shuttle ride back to the rental kiosk. Children must be over 50lb. Or bring your own raft and pay $5 to shuttle back.

River rats are also attracted to the fierce Tuolumne River, a classic class-IV run that plunges and thunders through boulder gardens and cascades. Outfitters **OARS** (☏209-736-4677; www.oars.com) 🍃 and Groveland-based Sierra Mac (p333) offer guided trips.

✗ Take a Break

The Village Store (◷8am-8pm, to 10pm summer) in Yosemite Village has health-food items and organic produce for a picnic.

GNOHZ / SHUTTERSTOCK ©

★ Top Tip

Be cautious around wet footpaths and railings. People have been swept away in Yosemite's falls.

ℹ️ INFORMATION

DANGERS & ANNOYANCES

Yosemite is prime black-bear habitat. Follow park rules on proper food storage and utilize bear-proof food lockers when parked overnight. Mosquitoes can be pesky in summer, so bug spray's not a bad idea. And please don't feed those squirrels. They may look cute but they've got a nasty bite.

MEDICAL SERVICES

Yosemite Medical Clinic (☏209-372-4637; 9000 Ahwahnee Dr, Yosemite Village; ☺9am-7pm daily late May-late Sep, to 5pm Mon-Fri late Sep-late May) A 24-hour emergency service is available.

TOURIST INFORMATION

Yosemite Valley Visitor Center (☏209-372-0200; 9035 Village Dr, Yosemite Village; ☺9am-5pm; 🖥) The main tourist information center, with exhibits and free film screenings in the theater. Give yourself plenty of time, as lines are long in summer. Issues wilderness permits from November to April when the **Wilderness Center** (☏209-372-0745; Yosemite Village; ☺8am-5pm) is closed.

ℹ️ GETTING THERE & AWAY

CAR & MOTORCYCLE

Yosemite is accessible year-round from the west (via Hwys 120 W and 140) and south (Hwy 41), and in summer also from the east (via Hwy 120 E). Roads are plowed in winter, but snow chains may be required at any time. In 2006 a mammoth rockslide buried part of Hwy 140, 6 miles west of the park; traffic there is restricted to vehicles under 45ft. Big Oak Flat Rd was closed for several months after a 'slide,' really of an entire hillside, in February 2017.

Gas up year-round at Wawona inside the park (you'll pay dearly), at El Portal on Hwy 140 just outside its western boundary or Lee Vining at the junction of Hwys 120 and 395 outside the park in the east. In summer, gas is also sold at Crane Flat – the gas station in Tuolumne Meadows is now closed.

PUBLIC TRANSPORTATION

Yosemite is one of the few national parks that can easily be reached by public transportation. **Greyhound** (☏800-231-2222; www.greyhound.com) buses and **Amtrak** (☏800-872-7245; www.amtrak.com) trains serve Merced, west of the park, where they are met by buses operated by the **Yosemite Area Regional Transportation System** (YARTS; ☏877-989-2787; www.yarts.com), and you can buy Amtrak tickets that include the YARTS segment all the way into the park. Buses travel to Yosemite Valley along Hwy 140 several times daily year-round, stopping along the way.

In summer (roughly June through September), another YARTS route runs from Mammoth Lakes along Hwy 395 to Yosemite Valley via Hwy 120. One-way tickets to Yosemite Valley are $13 ($9 child and senior, three hours) from Merced and $18 ($15 child and senior, 3½ hours) from Mammoth Lakes, less if boarding in between.

YARTS fares include the park-entrance fee, making them a super bargain, and drivers accept credit cards.

ℹ️ GETTING AROUND

BICYCLE

Bicycling is an ideal way to take in Yosemite Valley. You can rent a wide-handled cruiser (per hour/day $11.50/32) or a bike with an attached child trailer (per hour/day $19/59) at the Yosemite Valley Lodge (p335) or **Half Dome Village** (per hr/day $12.50/30.50; ☺9am-6pm Mar-Oct). Strollers and wheelchairs are also rented here.

CAR & MOTORCYCLE

Roadside signs with red bears mark the many spots where bears have been hit by motorists, so think before you hit the accelerator, and follow the pokey posted speed limits. Valley visitors are advised to park and take advantage of the Yosemite Valley Shuttle Bus. Even so, traffic in the valley can feel like rush hour in LA. Note that Glacier Point and Tioga Rds are closed in winter.

Village Garage (☏209-372-8320; Tecoya Rd; ☺8am-5pm) Provides emergency repairs and even gasoline when you're in an absolute fix.

Groveland

From the Big Oak Flat entrance to Yosemite, it's 22 miles to Groveland, an adorable town with restored gold rush–era buildings and lots of visitor services.

◉ SIGHTS & ACTIVITIES

Rainbow Pool   Natural Pool
(www.fs.usda.gov/stanislaus) About 15 miles east of Groveland, in the Stanislaus National Forest, Rainbow Pool is a popular swimming hole with a small cascade; it's signed on the south side of Hwy 120.

ARTA River Trips   Rafting
(☑800-323-2782, 209-962-7873; www.arta.org; 24000 Casa Loma Rd) Nonprofit rafting outfitter runs one-day and multiday Tuolumne River trips, as well as day trips on the Merced River.

Sierra Mac   Rafting
(☑209-591-8027; www.sierramac.com; 27890 Hwy 120) One of two outfitters running the experts-only Cherry Creek; offers other Tuolumne and Merced River trips. Marty McDonnell, Sierra Mac's owner, has been river guiding since the 1960s. Sierra Mac's staging office is perched on a hill 13 miles east of town.

✖ EATING & DRINKING

Burgers, sandwiches and pizza aren't in short supply. Groveland also has a chef-driven contemporary American restaurant and a Mexican place – both are recommended. If heading to campgrounds or accommodations further east, you can stock up on groceries at the town supermarket.

Mar-Val   Supermarket $
(☑209-962-7452; 1900 Main St; ⊙7am-10pm, to 9pm winter) This large grocery store at the eastern end of town is a good place to stock up on food and supplies before heading into Yosemite.

⇨ Detour: Tuolumne Meadows

About 55 miles from Yosemite Valley via Tioga Rd (or Hwy 120 E), 8600ft Tuolumne Meadows is the largest subalpine meadow in the Sierra. It provides a dazzling contrast to the valley, with its lush open fields, clear blue lakes, ragged granite peaks and domes, and cooler temperatures. If you come during July or August, you'll find a painter's palette of wildflowers decorating the shaggy meadows.

The main meadow is about 2.5 miles long and lies on the northern side of Tioga Rd between Lembert Dome and Pothole Dome. The 200ft scramble to the top of the latter – preferably at sunset – gives you great views of the meadow. An interpretive trail leads from the stables to muddy Soda Springs, where carbonated water bubbles up in red-tinted pools. The nearby Parsons Memorial Lodge has a few displays.

Hikers and climbers will find a paradise of options around Tuolumne Meadows, which is also the gateway to the High Sierra camps.

PUNG / SHUTTERSTOCK©

**Fork & Love
Restaurant**   Modern American $$
(www.forkandlove.com; 18736 Main St; mains $17-28; ⊙6-9pm Thu-Sat, 9am-1pm Sun Mar-Nov) ✐ Scarce in these parts, 'local, organic and sustainable' is done right at this rustically refined restaurant in a historic saloon space in the **Hotel Charlotte** (☑209-962-6455; www.hotelcharlotte.com; ✳@🛜🐾).

The small plates, as well as the mains, like pork spatzle, carne masala (black Angus beef with homemade masala sauce) and artichoke fried rice, are innovative and best enjoyed by sharing.

Iron Door Grill & Saloon Bar
(☎209-962-6244; www.iron-door-saloon.com; 18761 Main St; ☺restaurant 7am-10pm, bar 11am-2am, shorter hours winter) Claiming to be the oldest bar in the state, the Iron Door is a dusty, atmospheric place, with swinging doors, a giant bar, high ceilings, mounted animal heads and hundreds of dollar bills tacked to the ceiling. There's live music summer-weekend nights, and the adjacent, more contemporary dining room serves good steaks, ribs and pasta dishes (mains $9.50 to $25).

❶ INFORMATION

There are two banks with ATMs and a gas station 1.5 miles west of town.

USFS Groveland Ranger Station (☎209-962-7825; www.fs.usda.gov/stanislaus; 24545 Hwy 120; ☺8am-4:30pm Mon-Sat Jun-Aug, reduced hours Sep-May) About 8 miles east of Groveland; offers recreation information for the surrounding Stanislaus National Forest and nearby Tuolumne Wild and Scenic River Area.

❶ GETTING THERE & AWAY

YARTS (☎209-388-9589; www.yarts.com) Buses run at least one morning trip daily between Sonora and Yosemite Valley via the Big Oak Flat entrance, with a stop in Groveland ($8 one way, 1¾ hours).

Mariposa

About halfway between Merced and Yosemite Valley, Mariposa (Spanish for 'butterfly') is the largest and most interesting town near Yosemite National Park. Established as a mining and railroad town during the gold rush, it has the oldest courthouse in continuous use (since 1854) west of the Mississippi, loads of Old West pioneer character and a couple of good museums dedicated to the area's history.

Mariposa

✕ EATING & DRINKING

Happy Burger
Diner $

(☎209-966-2719; www.happyburgerdiner.com;
Hwy 140, cnr 12th St; mains $8-14; ☯5:30am-
9pm; 🛜🅿🚻🐾) Burgers, fries and shakes
served with a heavy dose of nostalgic
Americana. Happy Burger, decorated with
old LP album covers, and boasting the
largest menu in the Sierra, offers one of the
cheaper meals in town. Besides burgers,
there are sandwiches, Mexican food, salads
and a ton of sinful ice-cream desserts. Free
computer terminal inside and a 'doggy
dining area' outdoors.

Savoury's
American $$

(☎209-966-7677; 5034 Hwy 140; mains $17-35;
☯5-9:30pm, closed Wed winter; 🅿) Upscale
yet casual Savoury's is the best restau-
rant in town. Black lacquered tables and
contemporary art create tranquil window
dressing for dishes like wild-mushroom
ravioli, Cajun-spiced New York steak with
pan-seared onions, and crab cakes with
cilantro-lime aioli.

Charles Street
Dinner House
Steak $$$

(☎209-966-2366; www.charlesstreetdinner
house.net; cnr Hwy 140 & 7th St; mains $19-32;
☯11am-2pm & 5-10pm Tue-Sat, 9am-1pm Sun)
As old school as it gets: expect wooden
booths, wagon wheels for decor and
hearty steaks on the menu. But it's classic
fare done well and the portions are large
enough to satisfy the heartiest appetite.

The Alley
Bar

(☎209-742-4848; www.thealleylounge.com;
5027 Hwy 140; ☯4-10pm Mon-Thu, to midnight
Fri & Sat) Californian wines and craft beers
are served up in a sophisticated, contemporary space inside this bar. But it's the
lovely backyard beer garden, open in warm
months, that puts the Alley over the top.

💬 Guided Tours of Yosemite

The nonprofit **Yosemite Conservancy**
(☎209-379-2317; www.yosemiteconservancy.
org) has scheduled tours of all kinds,
plus custom trips.

First-timers often appreciate the
year-round, two-hour **Valley Floor Tour**
(☎209-372-1240; www.travelyosemite.com;
adult/child $35/25; ☯year-round; 🚻), which
covers the valley's highlights.

For other options, stop at the tour
and activity desks at **Yosemite Valley
Lodge** (☎209-372-1240; 9006 Yosemite
Lodge Dr, Yosemite Valley; ☯7:30am-7pm),
Half Dome Village or Yosemite Village,
call ☎209-372-4386 or check www.
travelyosemite.com.

Nibble on Bavarian soft pretzels ($9) and
smoked salmon ($14) while enjoying the
laid-back atmosphere. Live music some
nights.

ℹ INFORMATION

John C Fremont Hospital (☎209-966-3631;
www.jcf-hospital.com; 5189 Hospital Rd; ☯24hr)
Emergency room.

Mariposa County Visitor Center (☎209-966-
7081; cnr Hwys 140 & 49; ☯8:30am-5:30pm;
🛜) Helpful staff and racks of brochures; public
restrooms.

ℹ GETTING THERE & AWAY

YARTS (☎209-388-9589; www.yarts.com) Buses
run year-round along Hwy 140 into Yosemite
Valley ($3 one way, 1¾ hours), stopping at the
Mariposa visitor center. Tickets include admission to Yosemite.

Washington, DC (p88)

In Focus

USA Today   p338
Find out how changing cityscapes, income inequality and gun violence are affecting the country.

History   p340
The American story, from struggling colony to world superpower.

Food & Drink   p350
Chow on the nation's diverse dishes, from gumbo to barbecue, oysters to pork tacos, along with locally made wine and beer.

Sports   p354
Beers, hot dogs and baseball, football and basketball: what could be more American?

Arts & Culture   p357
The USA's music, film, literature and visual arts have had a huge impact on the world's cultural scene.

USA Today

The controversial result of the 2016 election, which saw businessman Donald Trump lose the popular vote but win the presidency, thrust the US into an uncertain future, dividing the nation across hot-topic issues such as immigration and health care, and sparking waves of protests, with those on the left resisting the nation's sudden turn to the right. Meanwhile, cities blossom, and the divide between rich and poor grows ever wider.

Changing Cityscapes

Cities are booming in America, growing at a faster rate than the rest of the country. Far from being the burned-out hulls of decades past, American cities are safer, and have wide-ranging appeal (in the realms of culture, food, nightlife and livability). Yet with more people moving from the suburbs and the exurbs to city centers, this has brought many challenges – particularly in terms of housing and transportation. In many places, rent and housing prices have skyrocketed. Some mayors, such as Bill de Blasio of New York City and Ed Lee of San Francisco, have launched ambitious programs to create more affordable housing. De Blasio has stated that unless New York acts boldly, the city risks becoming a gated community of exclusivity rather than opportunity. The same could be said for many American cities.

belief systems
(% of population)

Protestant   Roman Catholic   Jewish   Mormon   Muslim   unaffiliated or other

if the USA were 100 people

65 would be white
15 would be Hispanic
13 would be African American
4 would be Asian American
3 would be other

population per sq mile

👤 ≈ 8 people

USA   Australia   Canada

A Divided Nation

Speaking of exclusivity, the income gap continues to widen in the US. The top 1% of the population earns more than 20% of the income (up from 9% in 1976). Meanwhile, the poor are getting poorer: the median wage-earner took home 2.5% less than in 1999. And privileged children are outpacing their peers by bigger margins (the gap in test scores between rich and poor is over 30% wider than it was two decades ago).

The challenge: how to fix the problems. The obvious solution – raising taxes on the rich – is considered political suicide, and both strengthening unions and creating universal pre-kindergarten programs have received little traction in the current political climate.

There is one silver lining: states from California and Washington across to New York plan to raise minimum wages to as high as $15 in the coming years in an attempt to lift their poorest citizens out of poverty.

Greener Futures

With more people moving to urban areas, cities have also grappled with transportation. Building more roads has never helped alleviate traffic congestion – as engineers have known since the 1960s. The answer has been greater investment in public transit. Cities, once deeply married to the automobile, have greatly expanded public transport options, with new light rail lines, express bus lanes and dedicated bus lanes.

Bike-sharing programs have also exploded across the country, with nearly 120 cities offering easy rental (usually by the day and week) for residents and visitors.

Gun Crazy

In the USA there have been scores of mass shootings over the past 30 years. On average, 32 Americans are murdered by people with firearms every day and another 216 wounded. Despite evidence (including a 2013 study published in the *American Journal of Medicine*) that more guns equals more murders, and the comparatively low rates of death by firearms in countries with strict gun laws, American legislators have been unwilling to enact even modest gun-control laws.

The reason in part: gun lobbies such as the National Rifle Association (NRA) wield incredible power, contributing over $35 million annually to state and national political campaigns. But Americans are also enamored of their guns: a recent Pew Research poll found that 52% of Americans said it was more important to protect the right of Americans to own guns versus 46% who said that it was more important to control gun ownership (ie have stricter hand-gun laws).

National Museum of Natural History (p94), Washington, DC

KAMIRA / SHUTTERSTOCK ©

History

From its early days as an English colony to its rise to number one on the world stage in the 20th century, America has been anything but dull. War against the British, westward expansion, slavery and its abolishment, Civil War and Reconstruction, the Great Depression, the postwar boom, and more recent conflicts in the 21st century – they've all played a part in shaping the nation's complicated identity.

8000 BC
Widespread extinction of ice-age mammals. Indigenous peoples begin hunting smaller game and gathering native plants.

7000 BC–AD 100
During the 'Archaic period,' corn, beans and squash (the agricultural 'three sisters') and permanent settlements are well established.

1492
Italian explorer Christopher Columbus 'discovers' America, making three voyages throughout the Caribbean.

Ford's Theatre (p101), Washington, DC

Enter the Europeans

In 1492 Italian explorer Christopher Columbus, backed by Spain, voyaged west – looking for the East Indies. He found the Bahamas. With visions of gold, Spanish explorers quickly followed: Cortés conquered much of today's Mexico; Pizarro conquered Peru; Ponce de León wandered through Florida looking for the fountain of youth. Not to be left out, the French explored Canada and the Midwest, while the Dutch and English cruised North America's eastern seaboard.

Of course, they weren't the first ones on the continent. When Europeans arrived, approximately two to 18 million Native American people occupied the lands north of present-day Mexico and spoke more than 300 languages. European explorers left in their wake diseases to which indigenous peoples had no immunity. More than any other factor – war, slavery or famine – disease epidemics devastated Native American populations by anywhere from 50% to 90%. By the 17th century, indigenous North Americans numbered only about a million, and many of the continent's once-thriving societies were in turmoil and transition.

1607	**1620**	**1773**
The English found the Jamestown settlement. The first few years are hard, with many dying from sickness and starvation.	The *Mayflower* lands at Plymouth with 102 English Pilgrims. The Wampanoag tribe saves them from starvation.	Bostonians protest British taxes by dumping tea into the harbor during what would be named the Boston Tea Party.

In 1607 English noblemen established North America's first permanent European settlement in Jamestown. By 1619 the colony had set up the House of Burgesses, a representative assembly of citizens to decide local laws, and it received its first boatload of 20 African slaves.

In 1620, a group of radically religious Puritans pulled ashore at what would become Plymouth, MA. The Pilgrims were escaping religious persecution under the 'corrupt' Church of England, and in the New World they saw a divine opportunity to create a new society that would be a religious and moral beacon. The Pilgrims signed a 'Mayflower Compact,' one of the seminal texts of American democracy, to govern themselves by consensus.

Capitalism & Colonialism

For the next two centuries, European powers competed for position and territory in the New World, extending European politics into the Americas. As Britain's Royal Navy came to rule Atlantic seas, England increasingly profited from its colonies and eagerly consumed the fruits of their labors – sweet tobacco from Virginia, sugar and coffee from the Caribbean.

Over the 17th and 18th centuries, slavery in America was slowly legalized into a formal institution to support this plantation economy. By 1800, one out of every five persons was a slave.

Meanwhile, Britain mostly left the American colonists to govern themselves. Town meetings and representative assemblies, in which local citizens (that is, white men with property) debated community problems and voted on laws and taxes, became common.

However, by the end of the Seven Years' War in 1763, Britain was feeling the strains of running an empire: it had been fighting France for a century and had colonies scattered all over the world. It was time to clean up bureaucracies and share financial burdens.

The colonies, however, resented English taxes and policies. Public outrage soon culminated in the 1776 Declaration of Independence. With this document, the American colonists took many of the Enlightenment ideas then circulating worldwide – of individualism, equality and freedom; of John Locke's 'natural rights' of life, liberty and property – and fashioned a new type of government to put them into practice.

Revolution & the Republic

In April 1775 British troops skirmished with armed colonists in Massachusetts, and the Revolutionary War began. George Washington, a wealthy Virginia farmer, was chosen to lead the American army. Trouble was, Washington lacked gunpowder and money (the colonists resisted taxes even for their own military), and his troops were a motley collection of poorly armed farmers, hunters and merchants, who regularly quit and returned to their farms due to lack of pay. On the other side, the British 'Redcoats' represented the world's most powerful military. The inexperienced General Washington had to improvise constantly, sometimes

1775
Paul Revere warns colonial 'Minutemen' that the British are coming. The next day the Revolutionary War begins.

1776
On July 4, the colonies sign the Declaration of Independence.

1787
The US Constitution is drawn up, balancing power between the presidency, Congress and judiciary.

wisely retreating, sometimes engaging in 'ungentlemanly' sneak attacks.

In 1778 Benjamin Franklin persuaded France (always eager to trouble England) to ally with the revolutionaries, and they provided the troops, material and sea power that helped win the war. The British surrendered at Yorktown, VA, in 1781, and two years later the Treaty of Paris formally recognized the 'United States of America.'

At first, the nation's loose confederation of fractious, squabbling states was hardly 'united.' So the founders gathered again in Philadelphia, and in 1787 drafted a new-and-improved Constitution: the US government was given a stronger federal center, with checks and balances between its three major branches; and to guard against the abuse of centralized power, a citizen's Bill of Rights was approved in 1791.

Slavery

From the early 17th century until the 19th century, an estimated 600,000 slaves were brought from Africa to America. Those who survived the horrific transport on crowded ships (which sometimes had 50% mortality rates) were sold in slave markets (African males cost $27 in 1638). The majority of slaves ended up in Southern plantations where conditions were usually brutal – whipping and branding were commonplace.

With the Constitution, the scope of the American Revolution solidified to a radical change in government, and the preservation of the economic and social status quos. Rich landholders kept their property, which included their slaves; Native Americans were excluded from the nation; and women were excluded from politics. These blatant discrepancies and injustices, which were widely noted, were the results of both pragmatic compromise (eg to get slave-dependent Southern states to agree) and also widespread beliefs in the essential rightness of things as they were.

Westward, Ho!

As the 19th century dawned on the young nation, optimism was the mood of the day. The 1803 Louisiana Purchase doubled US territory, and expansion west of the Appalachian Mountains began in earnest.

In the 1830s and 1840s, with growing nationalist fervor and dreams of continental expansion, many Americans came to believe it was 'Manifest Destiny' that all the land should be theirs. The 1830 Indian Removal Act aimed to clear one obstacle, while the building of the railroads cleared another hurdle, linking Midwestern farmers with East Coast markets.

In 1836 a group of Texans fomented a revolution against Mexico. (Remember the Alamo?) Ten years later, the US annexed the Texas Republic, and when Mexico resisted, the US waged war for it – and while it was at it, took California, too. In 1848 Mexico was soundly defeated and ceded this territory to the US. This completed the USA's continental expansion.

1803	1804–06	1849
France's Napoleon sells the Louisiana Territory to the US, extending the nation's boundaries westward.	President Jefferson sends Lewis and Clark west. They trailblaze from St Louis, MO, to the Pacific Ocean and back.	An epic cross-country gold rush sees 60,000 'forty-niners' flock to California's Mother Lode.

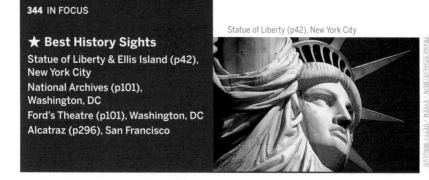

★ **Best History Sights**

Statue of Liberty & Ellis Island (p42), New York City

National Archives (p101), Washington, DC

Ford's Theatre (p101), Washington, DC

Alcatraz (p296), San Francisco

By a remarkable coincidence, only days after the 1848 treaty with Mexico was signed, gold was discovered in California. By 1849 surging rivers of wagon trains were creaking west filled with miners, pioneers, entrepreneurs, immigrants, outlaws and prostitutes, all seeking their fortunes. This made for exciting, legendary times, but throughout loomed a troubling question: as new states joined the USA, would they be slave states or free states? The nation's future depended on the answer.

The Civil War

The US Constitution hadn't ended slavery, but it had given Congress the power to approve (or not) slavery in new states. Public debates raged constantly over the expansion of slavery, particularly since this shaped the balance of power between the industrial North and the agrarian South.

Since the founding, Southern politicians had dominated government and defended slavery as 'natural and normal,' which an 1856 *New York Times* editorial called 'insanity.' The Southern proslavery lobby enraged Northern abolitionists. But even many Northern politicians feared that ending slavery would be ruinous. Limit slavery, they reasoned, and in the competition with industry and free labor, slavery would wither without inciting a violent slave revolt – a constantly feared possibility. Indeed, in 1859 radical abolitionist John Brown tried unsuccessfully to spark just that at Harpers Ferry.

The economics of slavery were undeniable. In 1860 there were more than four million slaves in the US, most held by Southern planters – who grew 75% of the world's cotton, accounting for more than half of US exports. Thus, the Southern economy supported the nation's economy, and it required slaves. The 1860 presidential election became a referendum on this issue, and the election was won by a young politician who favored limiting slavery: Abraham Lincoln.

In the South, even the threat of federal limits was too onerous to abide, and as President Lincoln took office, 11 states eventually seceded from the union and formed the Confederate States of America. Lincoln faced the nation's greatest moment of crisis. He had two

---

1861–65

American Civil War erupts between North and South. The war's end is marred by President Lincoln's assassination five days later.

1870

Freed black men are given the right to vote, but the South's segregationist 'Jim Crow' laws effectively disenfranchise blacks.

1880–1920

Millions of immigrants flood in from Europe and Asia, fueling the age of cities. New York, Chicago and Philadelphia swell in size.

choices: let the Southern states secede and dissolve the union or wage war to keep the union intact. He chose the latter, and war soon erupted.

It began in April 1861, when the Confederacy attacked Fort Sumter in Charleston, SC, and raged on for the next four years – in the most gruesome combat the world had ever known until that time. By the end, as many as 750,000 soldiers, nearly an entire generation of young men, were dead; Southern plantations and cities (most notably Atlanta) lay sacked and burned. The North's industrial might provided an advantage, but its victory was not preordained; it unfolded battle by bloody battle.

As fighting progressed, Lincoln recognized that if the war didn't end slavery outright, victory would be pointless. In 1863 his Emancipation Proclamation expanded the war's aims and freed all slaves. In April 1865, Confederate General Robert E Lee surrendered to Union General Ulysses S Grant in Appomattox, VA. The Union had been preserved, but at a staggering cost.

Great Depression, the New Deal & WWII

In October 1929, investors, worried about a gloomy global economy, started selling stocks, and seeing the selling, everyone panicked until they had sold everything. The stock market crashed, and the US economy collapsed like a house of cards.

Thus began the Great Depression. Frightened banks called in their dodgy loans, people couldn't pay, and the banks folded. Millions lost their homes, farms, businesses and savings, and as much as 25% of the American workforce became unemployed.

In 1932 Democrat Franklin D Roosevelt was elected president on the promise of a 'New Deal' to rescue the US from its crisis, which he did with resounding success. When war once again broke out in Europe in 1939, the isolationist mood in America was as strong as ever. However, the extremely popular President Roosevelt, elected to an unprecedented third term in 1940, understood that the US couldn't sit by and allow victory for fascist, totalitarian regimes. Roosevelt sent aid to Britain and persuaded a skittish Congress to go along with it.

Then, on December 7, 1941, Japan launched a surprise attack on Hawaii's Pearl Harbor, killing more than 2000 Americans and sinking several battleships. As US isolationism transformed overnight into outrage, Roosevelt suddenly had the support he needed. Germany also declared war on the US, and America joined the Allied fight against Hitler and the Axis powers. From that moment, the US put almost its entire will and industrial prowess into the war effort.

Initially, neither the Pacific nor European theaters went well for the US. In the Pacific, fighting didn't turn around until the US unexpectedly routed the Japanese navy at Midway Island in June 1942. Afterward, the US drove Japan back with a series of brutal battles recapturing Pacific islands.

In Europe, the US dealt the fatal blow to Germany with its massive D-Day invasion of France on June 6, 1944: unable to sustain a two-front war (the Soviet Union was savagely fighting on the eastern front), Germany surrendered in May 1945.

1908	1917	1920s
The first Model T car is built in Detroit, MI. Assembly-line innovator Henry Ford is soon selling one million automobiles annually.	President Woodrow Wilson enters US into WWI. The US mobilizes 4.7 million troops, and suffers 116,000 military deaths.	The Harlem Renaissance inspires a burst of African American literature, art, music and cultural pride.

The Haight (p311), San Francisco

★ **Best Historic Neighborhoods**

Georgetown, Washington, DC (p100)
Garden District, New Orleans (p212)
Greenwich Village, New York City (p66)
The Haight, San Francisco (p311)

Nevertheless, Japan continued fighting. Newly elected President Harry Truman – ostensibly worried that a US invasion of Japan would lead to unprecedented carnage – chose to drop experimental atomic bombs on Hiroshima and Nagasaki in August 1945. Created by the government's top-secret Manhattan Project, the bombs devastated both cities, killing over 200,000 people. Japan surrendered days later. The nuclear age was born.

The Red Scare, Civil Rights & the Wars in Asia

The US enjoyed unprecedented prosperity in the decades after WWII, but little peace.

Formerly wartime allies, the communist Soviet Union and the capitalist USA soon engaged in a running competition to dominate the globe. The superpowers engaged in proxy wars – notably the Korean War (1950–53) and Vietnam War (1954–75) – with only the mutual threat of nuclear annihilation preventing direct war. Founded in 1945, the UN couldn't overcome this worldwide ideological split and was largely ineffectual in preventing Cold War conflicts.

Meanwhile, with its continent unscarred and its industry bulked up by WWII, the American homeland entered an era of growing affluence. In the 1950s, a mass migration left the inner cities for the suburbs, where affordable single-family homes sprang up. Americans drove cheap cars using cheap gas over brand-new interstate highways. They relaxed with the comforts of modern technology, swooned over TV, and got busy, giving birth to a 'baby boom.'

Middle-class whites did, anyway. African Americans remained segregated, poor and generally unwelcome at the party. Echoing 19th-century abolitionist Frederick Douglass, the Southern Christian Leadership Conference (SCLC), led by African American preacher Martin Luther King Jr, aimed to end segregation and 'save America's soul': to realize color-blind justice, racial equality and fairness of economic opportunity for all.

Beginning in the 1950s, King preached and organized nonviolent resistance in the form of bus boycotts, marches and sit-ins, mainly in the South. White authorities often met these protests with water hoses and batons, and demonstrations sometimes dissolved

1941–45	**1963**	**1964**
WWII: America deploys 16 million troops and suffers 400,000 deaths.	President John F Kennedy is assassinated by Lee Harvey Oswald while riding in a motorcade in Dallas, TX.	Congress passes the Civil Rights Act, outlawing discrimination on basis of race, color, religion, sex or national origin.

into riots, but with the 1964 Civil Rights Act, African Americans spurred a wave of legislation that swept away racist laws and laid the groundwork for a more just and equal society.

Meanwhile, the 1960s saw further social upheavals: rock and roll spawned a youth rebellion, and the 1967 Summer of Love in San Francisco's Haight-Ashbury neighborhood catapulted hippie culture into mainstream America.

President John F Kennedy was assassinated in Dallas in 1963, followed by the assassinations in 1968 of his brother, Senator Robert Kennedy, and of Martin Luther King Jr. Americans' faith in their leaders and government was further shocked by the bombings and brutalities of the Vietnam War, as seen on TV, which led to widespread student protests.

Civil Rights Movement

Beginning in the 1950s, a movement was under way in African American communities to fight for equality. Rosa Parks, who refused to give up her seat to a white passenger, inspired the Montgomery bus boycott. There were sit-ins at lunch counters where blacks were excluded; massive demonstrations led by Martin Luther King Jr in Washington, DC; and harrowing journeys by 'freedom riders' that aimed to end bus segregation. The work of millions paid off: in 1964 President Johnson signed the Civil Rights Act, which banned discrimination and racial segregation.

Yet President Richard Nixon, elected in 1968 partly for promising an 'honorable end to the war,' instead escalated US involvement and secretly bombed Laos and Cambodia. Then, in 1972, the Watergate scandal broke: a burglary at Democratic Party offices was, through dogged journalism, tied to 'Tricky Dick,' who, in 1974, became the first US president to resign from office.

The tumultuous 1960s and '70s also witnessed the sexual revolution, women's liberation, struggles for gay rights, energy crises over the supply of crude oil from the Middle East and, with the 1962 publication of Rachel Carson's *Silent Spring,* the realization that the USA's industries had created a polluted, diseased environmental mess.

Reagan, Clinton & Bush eras

In 1980 Republican California governor and former actor Ronald Reagan campaigned for president by promising to make Americans feel good about America again. The affable Reagan won easily, and his election marked a pronounced shift to the right in US politics.

Reagan wanted to defeat communism, restore the economy, deregulate business and cut taxes. To tackle the first two, he launched the biggest peacetime military build-up in history, and dared the Soviets to keep up. They went broke trying, and the USSR collapsed.

Military spending and tax cuts created enormous federal deficits, which hampered the presidency of Reagan's successor, George HW Bush. Despite winning the Gulf War – liberating Kuwait in 1991 after an Iraqi invasion – Bush was soundly defeated in the 1992

1965–75	1989	1990s
The Vietnam War tears the nation apart; 58,000 Americans die, along with 5.5 million Vietnamese, Laotians and Cambodians.	The 1960s-era Berlin Wall is torn down, marking the end of the Cold War between the US and the USSR (now Russia).	The World Wide Web debuts in 1991. Silicon Valley, CA, leads a high-tech internet revolution, remaking communications and media.

National Museum of African American History & Culture

★ **Best History Museums**

National Museum of African American History & Culture (p95), Washington, DC

Lower East Side Tenement Museum (p63), New York City

Bob Bullock Texas State History Museum (p224), Austin

National Museum of American History (p95), Washington, DC

presidential election by Southern Democrat Bill Clinton. Clinton had the good fortune to catch the Silicon Valley–led high-tech internet boom of the 1990s, which seemed to augur a 'new economy' based on white-collar telecommunications. The US economy erased its deficits and ran a surplus, and Clinton presided over one of America's longest economic booms.

In 2000 and 2004, George W Bush, the eldest son of George HW Bush, won the presidential elections so narrowly that the divided results seemed to epitomize an increasingly divided nation. On September 11, 2001, Islamic terrorists flew hijacked planes into New York's World Trade Center and the Pentagon in Washington, DC. This catastrophic attack united Americans behind their president as he vowed revenge and declared a 'war on terror.' Bush soon attacked Afghanistan in an unsuccessful hunt for Al-Qaeda terrorist cells, then he attacked Iraq in 2003 and toppled its anti-US dictator, Saddam Hussein. Meanwhile, Iraq descended into civil war.

Obama Presidency

In 2008, hungry for change, Americans elected political newcomer, Barack Obama, America's first African American president. He certainly had his work cut out for him. These were, after all, unprecedented times economically, with the US in the largest financial crisis since the Great Depression. What started as a collapse of the US housing bubble in 2007, spread to the banking sector, with the meltdown of major financial institutions. The shock wave quickly spread across the globe, and by 2008 many industrialized nations were experiencing a recession in one form or another.

As Americans tried to look toward the future, many found it difficult to leave the past behind. This was not surprising since wars in Afghanistan and Iraq, launched a decade prior, continued to simmer on the back burner of the ever-changing news cycle. And the economy remained in bad shape.

With lost jobs, overvalued mortgages and little relief in sight, millions of Americans found themselves adrift, gathering in large numbers to voice their anger. This, in turn,

2001	2003	2005
The September 11 terrorist attacks destroy NYC's World Trade Center and kill nearly 3000 people.	After citing evidence that Iraq possesses weapons of mass destruction, President George W Bush launches a preemptive war.	Hurricane Katrina ruptures levees, flooding New Orleans. Over 1800 people die, and cost estimates exceed $110 billion.

gave birth to the Tea Party, a wing of politically conservative Republicans who believed that Obama was leaning too far to the left, and that government handouts would destroy the economy and, thus, America. High federal spending and government bailouts (of the banking and auto industries) roused their ire, as did Obama's landmark 2010 health-care reform (derisively named 'Obamacare').

When Obama returned to the White House in 2013 for his second term, he did so without the same hope and optimism that once surrounded him. Times had changed, and America, like much of the world, had struggled through tough years since the global economic crisis erupted in 2007.

Obama did manage to get unemployment rates back under 5% by 2016, but he had mixed success spurring the sluggish economy. As his presidency came to a close, he turned his focus to liberal and globally minded causes that stoked resentment on the populist right, including climate change, environmental protections, LGBT rights and the negotiation of rapprochements with Iran and Cuba. By the time Obama left office, America was a starkly divided nation of those who believed strongly in his progressive ideals, and others who felt increasingly left behind by the global economy.

President Trump

When Donald J Trump, real-estate magnate and former host of TV's reality game-show *The Apprentice,* announced he was running for President in June 2015, many around the world thought it was a publicity stunt. What ensued could only be described as a media circus: coverage of the protracted campaign, which eventually pitted Trump, with no prior political experience, against Hillary Clinton, former First Lady and then Secretary of State (2009–13), was relentless.

A contentious campaign followed. Trump refused to release his tax records, a common practice among presidential candidates. On October 7 *Access Hollywood* tapes leaked in which Trump admitted to assaulting women. On Clinton's side, opponents invoked the 2012 anti-US attacks in Benghazi, Libya, and her ties to Wall Street. A week before the election, FBI head James Comey stoked the conspiracy theories around Clinton by announcing in a letter to Congress that her emails, which she stored on a private server against security recommendations, were still under investigation. Still, polls gave Clinton a strong lead, and on election night, the country prepared to celebrate the election of the first female President of the United States. Clinton did win the popular vote, but the Electoral College math was not in her favor. She conceded to Donald Trump in the early hours of November 9 with an emotional speech that reminded 'all the little girls who are watching this, never doubt that you are valuable, and powerful, and deserving of every chance and opportunity in the world to pursue and achieve your own dreams.'

In his victory speech, Trump declared 'I will be president for all Americans,' though to many, Trump's definition of what it means to be an American remains unclear. Uncertainty, in fact, seems to be the defining quality of the Trump presidency.

2008–09	**2015**	**2016**
Barack Obama becomes the first African American president. The stock market crashes as the Global Financial Crisis hits.	In a historic decision, the US Supreme Court legalizes same-sex marriage. Gay couples can now wed in all 50 states.	Political outsider Donald Trump rides a populist wave into the White House in a surprise victory over opponent Hillary Clinton.

Barbecue ribs

Food & Drink

*The great variety found in American cuisine can be
traced to the local larder of each region, from the seafood
of the Atlantic to the fertile Midwestern farmlands and
the vast Western ranchlands. Texas barbecue, Louisiana
crawfish and California wines are but a few of the
regional specialties.*

Staples & Specialties

These days you can get almost every type of food nearly everywhere in the US, but regional
specialties are always best in the places they originated.

New York City: Foodie Capital

They say that you could eat at a different restaurant every night of your life in New York
City, and not exhaust the possibilities. Considering that there are an estimated 24,000
restaurants in the five boroughs, with scores of new ones opening each year, it's true.
Owing to its huge immigrant population and an influx of over 50 million tourists annually,
New York captures the title of America's greatest restaurant city, hands down. Its diverse

Mexican cantina, Los Angeles

neighborhoods serve up authentic Italian food and thin-crust pizza, all manner of Asian food, French haute cuisine and classic Jewish deli food, from bagels to piled-high pastrami on rye. More exotic cuisines are found here as well, from Ethiopian to Scandinavian.

Mid-Atlantic: Global Cooking & Blue Crabs

Washington, DC has a wide array of global fare – not surprising, given its ethnically diverse population. In particular, you'll find some of the country's best Ethiopian food.

DC also makes fine use of its unique geography, which puts it between two of the best food-production areas in America: Chesapeake Bay and the Virginia Piedmont. From the former come blue crabs, oysters and rockfish; the latter provides game, pork, wine and peanuts. Chefs take advantage of this delicious abundance.

The South: Barbecue, Biscuits & Gumbo

No region is prouder of its food culture than the South, which has a long history of mingling Anglo, French, African, Spanish and Native American foods in dishes such as slow-cooked barbecue, which has as many meaty and saucy variations as there are towns in the South. Southern fried chicken is crisp outside and moist inside. In Florida, dishes made with alligator, shrimp and conch incorporate hot chili peppers and tropical spices. Breakfasts are as big as can be, and treasured dessert recipes tend to produce big layer cakes or pies made with pecans, bananas and citrus. Light, fluffy hot biscuits are served well buttered, and grits (ground corn cooked to a porridge-like consistency) are a passion among Southerners, as are cool mint-julep cocktails.

★ **Best Local Breweries**

Right Proper Brewing Co (p115), Washington, DC

Revolution Brewing (p136), Chicago

ABGB (p235), Austin

NOLA Brewing (p216), New Orleans

Bluejacket Brewery (p113), Washington, DC

Right Proper Brewing Co

Louisiana's legendary cuisine is influenced by colonial French and Spanish cultures, Afro-Caribbean cooking and Choctaw traditions. Cajun food is found in the bayou country and marries native spices such as sassafras and chili peppers with provincial French cooking. Famous dishes include gumbo, a roux-based stew of chicken and shellfish, or sausage and often okra; jambalaya, a rice-based dish with tomatoes, sausage and shrimp; and blackened catfish. Creole food is more urban, and centered in New Orleans, where dishes such as shrimp rémoulade, crabmeat ravigote, crawfish étouffée, and beignets are ubiquitous.

Midwest: Burgers, Bacon & Beer

Residents of the Midwest eat big and with plenty of gusto. Portions are huge – this is farm country, where people need sustenance to get their day's work done. So you might start off the day with eggs, bacon and toast; have a double cheeseburger and potato salad for lunch; and fork into steak and baked potatoes for dinner – all washed down with a cold brew, often one of the growing numbers of microbrews. Chicago stands tall as the region's best place to pile a plate, with hole-in-the-wall ethnic eateries cooking alongside many of the country's most acclaimed restaurants.

The Southwest: Chili, Steak & Salsa

Two ethnic groups define Southwestern food culture: the Spanish and the Mexicans, who controlled territories from Texas to California until well into the 19th century. While there is little actual Spanish food today, the Spanish brought cattle to Mexico, which the Mexicans adapted to their own corn-and-chili-based gastronomy to make tacos, enchiladas, burritos, chimichangas and other dishes made of corn or flour pancakes filled with everything from chopped meat and poultry to beans. Steaks and barbecue are always favorites on Southwestern menus, and beer is the drink of choice for dinner and a night out.

California: Farm-to-Table Restaurants & Taquerias

Owing to its vastness and variety of microclimates, California is truly America's cornucopia for fruits and vegetables. The state's natural resources are overwhelming, with wild salmon, Dungeness crab and oysters from the ocean; robust produce year-round; and artisanal products such as cheese, bread, olive oil, wine and chocolate. Starting in the 1970s and '80s, star chefs such as Alice Waters and Wolfgang Puck pioneered 'California cuisine' by incorporating the best local ingredients into simple, yet delectable, preparations. The influx of Asian immigrants, especially after the Vietnam War, enriched the state's urban food cultures with Chinatowns, Koreatowns and Japantowns, along with huge enclaves of Mexican

Americans who maintain their own culinary traditions across the state. Global fusion restaurants are another hallmark of California's cuisine. Don't miss the forearm-sized burritos in San Francisco's Mission District, for example.

Beer & Wine

American beer is more popular than ever, and locals are uncorking plenty of wine, as well.

Craft & Local Beer

Today, beer aficionados (otherwise known as beer geeks) sip and savor beer as they would wine, and some urban restaurants even have beer 'programs,' 'sommeliers' and cellars. Many brewpubs and restaurants host beer dinners, a chance to experience just how beers pair with different foods.

Microbrewery and craft-beer production is rising meteorically, generating roughly $22 billion in retail sales in 2016. Today there are around 5000 craft breweries across the USA. In recent years, it's become possible to 'drink local' all over the country as microbreweries pop up in urban centers, small towns and unexpected places.

Wine

Almost 90% of US wine comes from California, while other regions are also producing wines that have achieved international status. In particular, the wines of New York's Finger Lakes, Hudson Valley and Long Island are well worth sampling.

So, what are the best American wines? Amazingly, though it's only been a few decades since many American restaurants served either 'red,' 'white' or sometimes 'pink' wine, there are many excellent 'New World' wines that have flourished in the rich American soil. The most popular white varietals made in the US are Chardonnay and Sauvignon Blanc; best-selling reds include Cabernet Sauvignon, Merlot, Pinot Noir and Zinfandel.

Wine isn't cheap in the US, as it's considered a luxury rather than a staple – go ahead and blame the Puritans for that. But it's possible to procure a perfectly drinkable bottle of American wine at a liquor or wine shop for under $12.

Vegetarian & Vegan

In many American cities, you'll find a wealth of restaurants that cater to vegetarians and vegans. Once you head out into rural areas and away from the coast, the options are slimmer. We note eateries that offer a good selection of vegetarian or vegan options by using the vegetarian (🖋) symbol. To find more vegetarian and vegan restaurants, browse the online directory at www.happycow.net.

Football

Sports

*What really draws Americans together, sometimes
slathered in blue body paint or with foam-rubber cheese
wedges on their heads, is sports. It provides a social
glue, so whether a person is conservative or liberal,
married or single, Mormon or pagan, chances are
come Monday at the office they'll be chatting about the
weekend performance of their favorite team.*

Seasons

The fun and games go on all year long. In spring and summer there's baseball nearly every day. In fall and winter a weekend or Monday night doesn't feel right without a football game on, and through the long days and nights of winter there's plenty of basketball to keep the adrenaline going.

Baseball

Despite high salaries and its biggest stars being dogged by steroid rumors, baseball remains America's pastime. It may not command the same TV viewership (and subsequent

Basketball, Los Angeles

advertising dollars) as football, but baseball has 162 games over a season versus 16 for football.

Besides, baseball isn't about seeing it on TV, it's all about the live version: being at the ballpark on a sunny day, sitting in the bleachers with a beer and hot dog, and indulging in the seventh-inning stretch, when the entire park erupts in a communal singalong of 'Take Me Out to the Ballgame.' The play-offs, held every October, still deliver excitement and unexpected champions. The New York Yankees, Boston Red Sox and Chicago Cubs continue to be America's favorite teams, even when they're abysmal.

Tickets are relatively inexpensive – the cheap seats average about $15 at most stadiums – and are easy to get for most games. Minor-league baseball games cost half as much, and can be even more fun, with lots of audience participation, stray chickens and dogs running across the field, and wild throws from the pitcher's mound. For info, click to www.milb.com.

Football

Football is big, physical and rolling in dough. With the shortest season and least number of games of any of the major sports, every match takes on the emotion of an epic battle, where the results matter and an unfortunate injury can deal a lethal blow to a team's play-off chances.

Football is also the toughest because it's played in fall and winter in all manner of rain, sleet and snow. Some of history's most memorable matches have occurred at below-freezing temperatures. Green Bay Packers fans are in a class by themselves when it comes to severe weather. Their stadium in Wisconsin, known as Lambeau Field, was the site of

Yankee Stadium

★ **Best Places to See a Baseball Game**

Wrigley Field (p126), Chicago
Yankee Stadium (p70), New York City
Giants Stadium (p319), San Francisco
Nationals Park (p116), Washington, DC

the infamous Ice Bowl, a 1967 championship game against the Dallas Cowboys where the temperature plummeted to −13°F – mind you, that was with a wind-chill factor of −48°F.

Different teams have dominated different decades: the Pittsburgh Steelers in the 1970s, the San Francisco 49ers in the 1980s, the Dallas Cowboys in the 1990s and the New England Patriots in the 2000s. The pro league's official website (www.nfl.com) is packed with information. Tickets are usually expensive and hard to get, which is why many fans congregate in bars to watch televised games.

Even college and high-school football games enjoy an intense amount of pomp and circumstance, with cheerleaders, marching bands, mascots, songs and mandatory pre- and post-game rituals, especially the tailgate – a full-blown beer-and-barbecue feast that takes place over portable grills in ball-ground parking lots.

The rabidly popular Super Bowl is pro football's championship match, held in late January or early February. The bowl games (such as Rose Bowl and Orange Bowl) are college football's title matches, held on and around New Year's Day.

Basketball

The teams bringing in the most fans these days include the Chicago Bulls (thanks to the lingering Michael Jordan effect), Detroit Pistons (a rowdy crowd in which riots have broken out), Cleveland Cavaliers, the San Antonio Spurs and, last but not least, the Los Angeles Lakers, which won five championships between 2000 and 2010. Small-market teams such as Sacramento and Portland have true-blue fans, and such cities can be great places to take in a game.

College-level basketball also draws millions of fans, especially every spring when March Madness rolls around. This series of college play-off games culminates in the Final Four, when the four remaining teams compete for a spot in the championship game. The Cinderella stories and unexpected outcomes rival the pro league for excitement. The games are widely televised – and bet on. This is when Las Vegas bookies earn their keep.

Other Sports

Car racing has revved up interest in recent years. Major League Soccer (MLS) is attracting an ever-increasing following. And ice hockey, once favored only in northern climes, is popular nationwide, with five Stanley Cup winners since 2000 hailing from either California or the South.

Mardi Gras (p202) jazz performance, New Orleans

Arts & Culture

The US has always been a chaotic, democratic jumble of high and low cultures: Frank Lloyd Wright and Frank Sinatra, Richard Wright and Lady Gaga, The Great Gatsby and Star Wars. America's arts are a pastiche, a crazy mix-and-match quilt of cultures and themes, of ideas borrowed and taken to create something new, often leaving dramatic new paradigms along the way.

Music

The South is the mother of American music. The blues developed there after the Civil War, out of the work songs, or 'shouts,' of black slaves and out of black spiritual songs and their 'call and response' pattern, both of which were adaptations of African music. Improvisational and intensely personal, the blues remain at heart an immediate expression of individual pain, suffering, hope, desire and pride. Nearly all subsequent American music has tapped this deep well. Famous musicians include Robert Johnson, Bessie Smith, Muddy Waters, BB King, John Lee Hooker and Buddy Guy.

Jazz was born in New Orleans. There ex-slaves adapted the reed, horn and string instruments used by the city's often French-speaking, multiracial Creoles – who themselves preferred formal European music – to play their own African-influenced music. This fertile

★ **Best Art Museums**

Museum of Modern Art (p46),
New York City

Metropolitan Museum of Art (p68),
New York City

Art Institute of Chicago (p124),
Chicago

National Gallery of Art (p95),
Washington, DC

National Gallery of Art

cross-pollination produced a steady stream of innovative sounds. Soon there was ragtime, Dixieland jazz, big-band swing, bebop and numerous fusions. Major players included Duke Ellington, Louis Armstrong, Billie Holiday, John Coltrane, Miles Davis and Charles Mingus.

Early Scottish, Irish and English immigrants brought their own instruments and folk music to America, and what emerged over time in the secluded Appalachian Mountains was fiddle-and-banjo hillbilly, or 'country,' music. In the Southwest, steel guitars and larger bands distinguished 'western' music. In the 1920s, these styles merged into 'country and western' music and became centered on Nashville, TN. For the originals, listen to Hank Williams, Johnny Cash, Patsy Cline and Dolly Parton.

Rock and roll, meanwhile, combined guitar-driven blues, black rhythm and blues (R&B), and white country-and-western music. Most say rock and roll was born when Elvis started singing. From the 1950s, it evolved into the anthem for nationwide social upheaval.

Finally, hip-hop emerged from 1970s New York, as young DJs from the Bronx began to spin and mix records together to drive dancefloors wild. Synonymous with urban street culture, hip-hop soon became the defining rebel sound of American pop culture.

Film & TV

Hollywood and American film are virtually inseparable. No less an American icon than the White House itself, Hollywood is increasingly the product of an internationalized cinema and film culture. This evolution is partly pure business: Hollywood studios are the show-pieces of multinational corporations, and funding flows to talent that brings the biggest grosses, regardless of nationality.

For many decades, critics sneered that TV was lowbrow, and movie stars wouldn't be caught dead on it. But times have changed. As cable TV has emerged as the frontier for daring and innovative programming, some of the TV shows of the past decade have proved as riveting and memorable as anything viewers have ever seen. Streaming services such as Netflix, Amazon and Hulu, and niche networks such as AMC and HBO, have created numerous lauded series. Recent favorites include *Transparent* (about a family coming to terms with having a transgender parent), *Atlanta* (a comedy-drama starring Donald Glover), *Stranger Things* (a supernatural saga set in the 1980s that recalls *The Goonies*) and *The Handmaid's Tale* (a near-future dystopia based on Margaret Atwood's 1986 novel).

Literature

With the dramas of world wars and a newly industrialized society for artistic fodder, American literature came into its own in the 20th century. Dubbed the 'Lost Generation,' many US writers, most famously Ernest Hemingway, became expats in Europe. Hemingway's novels exemplified the era, and his spare, stylized realism has often been imitated, yet never bettered. F Scott Fitzgerald eviscerated East Coast society life with his fiction, while

John Steinbeck became the voice of rural working poor in the West, especially during the Great Depression.

Between the world wars, the Harlem Renaissance also flourished, as African American intellectuals and artists took pride in their culture and undermined racist stereotypes. Among the most well-known writers were poet Langston Hughes and novelist Zora Neale Hurston.

After WWII, American writers delineated ever-sharper regional and ethnic divides, pursued stylistic experimentation and often caustically repudiated conservative middle-class American values. The South, always ripe with paradox, inspired masterful short-story writers and novelists Flannery O'Connor and Eudora Welty. The mythical romance and modern tragedies of the West have found their champions in Chicano writer Rudolfo Anaya, Larry McMurtry and Cormac McCarthy, whose characters poignantly tackle the rugged realities of Western life.

The Great American Novel

- *The Sound and the Fury* (William Faulkner)

- *The Great Gatsby* (F Scott Fitzgerald)

- *The Sun Also Rises* (Ernest Hemingway)

- *To Kill a Mockingbird* (Harper Lee)

- *Beloved* (Toni Morrison)

- *The Grapes of Wrath* (John Steinbeck)

- *The Goldfinch* (Donna Tartt)

- *The Underground Railroad* (Colson Whitehead)

- *Native Son* (Richard Wright)

In recent years, ethnic identity (especially that of immigrant cultures), regionalism and narratives of self-discovery remain at the forefront of American literature.

Visual Arts

Abstract expressionism is widely considered to be the first truly original school of American art. In the wake of WWII, painters such as Franz Kline, Jackson Pollock and Mark Rothko began exploring abstraction and its psychological potency through imposing scale and the gestural handling of paint. The movement's 'action painter' camp went extreme; Pollock, for example, made his drip paintings by pouring and splattering pigments over large canvases.

Once established in America, abstract expressionism reigned supreme. But it also inspired stylistic revolts, most notably pop art, for which artists drew inspiration from consumer images such as billboards, product packaging and media icons. Employing mundane mass-production techniques to silkscreen paintings of movie stars and Coke bottles, Andy Warhol helped topple the myth of the solitary artist laboring heroically in the studio. Roy Lichtenstein combined newsprint's humble Benday dots with the representational conventions of comics. Suddenly, so-called 'serious' art could be political, bizarre, ironic and fun – and all at once.

By the 1980s, civil rights, feminism and AIDS activism had made inroads in visual culture; artists not only voiced political dissent through their work, but embraced a range of once-marginalized media, from textiles and graffiti to video, sound and performance. Break-out artists Futura 2000, Keith Haring and Jean-Michel Basquiat moved from the subways and the streets to the galleries, and soon to the worlds of fashion and advertising.

To get the pulse of contemporary art in the US, check out works by artists such as Cindy Sherman, Kara Walker, Chuck Close, Kerry James Marshall, Eddie Martinez and Josh Smith.

Lombard Street (p307), San Francisco

Survival Guide

DIRECTORY A–Z   361

Accommodations 361
Climate............................ 362
Customs Regulations 362
Electricity........................ 362
Health.............................. 363
Insurance 363
Internet Access................ 363
Legal Matters 364

LGBTIQ Travelers 365
Money 365
Opening Hours................. 366
Public Holidays 366
Safe Travel...................... 366
Telephone 367
Time 368
Toilets............................. 368
Tourist Information.......... 368

Travelers with
Disabilities 368
Visas................................ 369
Women Travelers 370

TRANSPORTATION   371

Getting There & Away 371
Getting Around 372

Directory A–Z

Accommodations

For all but the cheapest places and the slowest seasons, reservations are advised. In tourist hot spots, book accommodations at least three months ahead in high season (June to August for summer resort areas, January to February for ski destinations), or up to a year ahead in popular national parks such as the Grand Canyon, Yosemite and Yellowstone.

Many hotels offer specials on their websites, while low-end chains sometimes give a slightly better rate over the phone. Chain hotels also offer frequent-flier mileage deals and other rewards programs; ask when booking.

Book Your Stay Online

For accommodations reviews by Lonely Planet authors, check out http://hotels.lonely planet.com/usa. You'll find independent reviews, as well as recommendations on the best places to stay. Best of all, you can book online.

Online travel booking, bidding and comparison websites are a good way to find discounted hotel rates – but are usually limited to chain hotels; check out Hotels.com, Hotwire (www.hotwire.com) and Booking.com. If you have a smartphone, each of these sites has a free app – which are often great for finding good last-minute deals. Hotel Tonight (www.hoteltonight.com) is another good app for booking rooms on the fly, and includes boutique hotels and historic properties.

Hotels

Hotels in all categories typically include in-room phones, cable TV, private bathrooms, wi-fi and a simple continental breakfast. Many midrange properties provide minibars, microwaves, hairdryers, internet access, air-conditioning and/or heating, swimming pools and writing desks, while top-end hotels add concierge services, fitness and business centers, spas, restaurants, bars and higher-end furnishings.

Motels

Motels – distinguishable from hotels by having rooms that open onto a parking lot – tend to cluster around interstate exits and on main routes into town. Some remain smaller, less-expensive 'mom-and-pop' operations; breakfast is rarely included, and amenities might be a phone and TV (maybe with cable); most also have free

Sleeping Price Ranges

The following price ranges refer to a double room in high season, excluding taxes (which can add 10% to 15%).

$ less than $100
$$ $100–250
$$$ more than $250

For New York City, San Francisco and Washington, DC, the following price ranges are used:
$ less than $150
$$ $150–350
$$$ more than $350

wi-fi. Motels often have a few rooms with simple kitchenettes.

House & Apartment Rentals

To rent a house or apartment from locals, visit Airbnb (www.airbnb.com), which has thousands of listings across the country. Budget travelers can also rent a room – a great way to connect with locals if you don't mind sharing facilities.

B&Bs

In the USA, many B&Bs are high-end romantic retreats in restored historic homes that are run by personable, independent innkeepers who serve gourmet breakfasts. Rates normally top $120, and the best run are $200 to $300. Some have minimum-stay requirements, and most exclude young children.

European-style B&Bs also exist: these may be rooms in someone's home, with plainer furnishings, simpler breakfasts, shared bathrooms and cheaper rates. These often welcome families.

B&Bs can close out of season, and reservations are essential, especially for top-end places. To avoid surprises, always ask about bathrooms (whether shared or private). Recommended B&B agencies:

Bed & Breakfast Inns Online (www.bbonline.com)

BedandBreakfast.com (www.bedandbreakfast.com)

BnB Finder (www.bnbfinder.com)

Select Registry (www.selectregistry.com)

Customs Regulations

For a complete list of US customs regulations, visit the official portal for US Customs and Border Protection (www.cbp.gov).

Duty-free allowance per person is as follows:

○ 1L of liquor (provided you are at least 21 years old)

○ 100 cigars and 200 cigarettes (if you are at least 18 years)

○ $200 worth of gifts and purchases ($800 if you're a returning US citizen)

○ If you arrive with $10,000 or more in US or foreign currency, it must be declared.

There are heavy penalties for attempting to import illegal drugs. Forbidden items include drug paraphernalia, lottery tickets, items with fake brand names, and most goods made in North Korea, Cuba, Iran, Syria and Sudan. Fruit, vegetables and other food or plant material must be declared or left in the arrival-area bins.

Climate

New York City

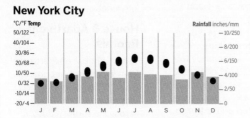

New Orleans

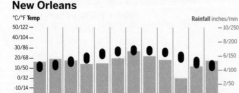

Los Angeles

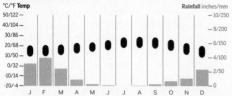

Electricity

**Type A
120V/60Hz**

Type B
120V/60Hz

Health

The USA offers excellent health care. The problem is that, unless you have good insurance, it can be prohibitively expensive. It's essential to purchase travel health insurance if your regular policy doesn't cover you when you're abroad.

Bring any medications you may need in their original containers, clearly labeled. A signed, dated letter from your physician that describes all medical conditions and medications, including generic names, is also a good idea.

Availability & Cost of Health Care

In general, if you have a medical emergency your best bet is to go to the nearest hospital's emergency room. If the problem isn't urgent, you can call a nearby hospital and ask for a referral to a local physician, which is usually much cheaper than a trip to the emergency room. Stand-alone, for-profit, urgent-care centers can be convenient, but may perform large numbers of expensive tests, even for minor illnesses.

Pharmacies are abundantly supplied, but you may find that some medications that are available over the counter in your home country (such as Ventolin, for asthma) require a prescription in the USA and, as always, if you don't have insurance to cover the cost of prescriptions, they can be shockingly expensive.

Insurance

No matter how long or short your trip, make sure you have adequate travel insurance, purchased before departure. At a minimum, you need coverage for medical emergencies and treatment, including hospital stays and an emergency flight home if necessary. Medical treatment in the USA is of the highest caliber, but the expense could bankrupt you.

You should also consider getting coverage for luggage theft or loss and trip cancellation. A comprehensive travel-insurance policy that covers all these things can cost up to 10% of the total outlay of your trip.

If you will be driving, it's essential that you have liability insurance. Car-rental agencies offer insurance that covers damage to the rental vehicle and separate liability insurance, which covers damage to people and other vehicles.

Worldwide travel insurance is available at www.lonelyplanet.com/travel-insurance. You can buy, extend and claim online anytime – even if you're already on the road.

Internet Access

Travelers will have few problems staying connected in tech-savvy USA. Most hotels, guesthouses, hostels and motels have wi-fi (usually free, though luxury hotels are more likely to charge for access); ask when reserving.

Across the US, most cafes offer free wi-fi. Some cities have wi-fi-connected parks and plazas. If you're not packing a laptop or other web-accessible device, try the public library – most have public terminals

Eating Price Ranges

The following price ranges refer to a main course. Tax (5% to 10%) and tip (generally 15% to 20%) is not included in price listings unless otherwise indicated.
$ less than $15
$$ $15–25
$$$ more than $25

(though they have time limits) in addition to wi-fi.

If you're not from the US, remember that you will need an AC adapter for your laptop, plus a plug adapter for US sockets; both are available at larger electronics shops, such as Best Buy.

Legal Matters

In everyday matters, if you are stopped by the police, bear in mind that there is no system of paying traffic or other fines on the spot. Attempting to pay a fine to an officer is frowned upon at best and may result in a charge of bribery. For traffic offenses, the police officer or highway patrol will explain the options to you. There is usually a 30-day period to pay a fine. Most matters can be handled by mail.

If you are arrested, you have a legal right to an attorney, and you are allowed to remain silent. There is no legal reason to speak to a police officer if you don't wish to, but never walk away from an officer until given permission to do so. Anyone who is arrested is legally allowed to make one phone call. If you can't afford a lawyer, a public defender will be appointed to you free of charge.

Foreign visitors who don't have a lawyer, friend or family member to help should call their embassy; the police can provide the number.

Drinking

Bars and stores often ask for photo ID to prove you're of legal drinking age (21 years or over). Being 'carded' is standard practice; don't take it personally. The sale of liquor is subject to local government regulations – some counties prohibit liquor sales on Sunday, after midnight or before breakfast. In 'dry' counties, liquor sales are banned altogether.

Driving

In all states, driving under the influence of alcohol or drugs is a serious offense, subject to stiff fines and even imprisonment. A blood alcohol level of 0.08% or higher is illegal in all jurisdictions.

Marijuana & Other Substances

The states have quite different laws regarding the use of marijuana, and what's legal in one state may be illegal in others. As of mid-2017, recreational use of small amounts of marijuana (generally up to 1oz/28g) was legal in Alaska, California, Colorado, Maine, Massachusetts, Nevada, Oregon, Washington and the District of Columbia. Another 13 states have decriminalized marijuana (treating recreational use as a civil violation similar to a minor traffic infraction). It's essential to know the local laws before lighting up – see http://norml.org/laws for a state-by-state breakdown.

Aside from marijuana, recreational drugs are prohibited by federal and state laws.

Practicalities

○ **Newspapers & Magazines** Leading national newspapers include the *New York Times, Wall Street Journal* and *USA Today*. *Time* and *Newsweek* are the mainstream news magazines.

○ **Radio & TV** National Public Radio (NPR) can be found at the lower end of the FM dial. The main TV broadcasting channels are ABC, CBS, NBC, FOX and PBS (public broadcasting); the major cable channels are CNN (news), ESPN (sports), HBO (movies) and Weather Channel.

○ **Smoking** As of 2017, 24 states, the District of Columbia and many municipalities across the US were entirely smoke-free in restaurants, bars and workplaces; an additional 11 states had enacted 100% public smoking bans in at least one of these venues. For more detailed state-by-state info on smoking laws, see www.cdc.gov and www.no-smoke.org.

○ **Weights & Measures** Weights are measured in ounces (oz), pounds (lb) and tons; liquids in fluid ounces (fl oz), pints (pt), quarts (qt) and gallons (gal); and distance in feet (ft), yards (yd) and miles (mi).

Possession of any illicit drug, including cocaine, ecstasy, LSD, heroin and hashish, is a felony potentially punishable by a lengthy jail sentence. For foreigners, conviction of any drug offense is grounds for deportation.

LGBTIQ Travelers

LGBTIQ travelers will find lots of places where they can be themselves without thinking twice. Beaches and big cities typically are the most gay-friendly destinations.

Hot Spots

Manhattan has loads of great gay bars and clubs, especially in Hells Kitchen, Chelsea and the West Village. A few hours away (by train and ferry) is Fire Island, the sandy gay mecca on Long Island. Other East Coast cities that flaunt it are Boston, Philadelphia, Washington, DC, Massachusetts' Provincetown on Cape Cod and Delaware's Rehoboth Beach.

In the South, Texas gets darn-right gay-friendly in Austin. In Florida, Miami and the 'Conch Republic' of Key West support thriving gay communities. New Orleans has a lively gay scene.

In the Great Lakes region, seek out Chicago. Further west, you'll find San Francisco, probably the happiest gay city in America. There's also Los Angeles and Las Vegas, where pretty much anything goes.

Attitudes

Most major US cities have a visible and open LGBTIQ community that is easy to connect with. Same-sex marriage was legalized nationwide by the US Supreme Court in 2015, and a 2016 Pew Research survey showed a majority of Americans (55%) supporting same-sex marriage, with millennials (71%) leading the way.

The level of acceptance varies nationwide. In some places, there is absolutely no tolerance whatsoever, and in others acceptance is predicated on LGBTIQ people not 'flaunting' their sexual preference or identity. Bigotry still exists. In rural areas and conservative enclaves, it's unwise to be openly out, as violence and verbal abuse can sometimes occur. When in doubt, assume locals follow a 'don't ask, don't tell' policy.

Resources

Advocate (www.advocate.com) Gay-oriented news website reports on business, politics, arts, entertainment and travel.

Gay & Lesbian National Help Center (www.glnh.org) Counseling, information and referrals.

Gay Travel (www.gaytravel.com) Online guides to dozens of US destinations.

Out Traveler (www.out traveler.com) Gay-oriented travel articles.

Purple Roofs (www.purpleroofs. com) Lists gay-owned and gay-friendly B&Bs and hotels.

Money

The currency is the US dollar. Smaller businesses may refuse to accept bills larger than $20.

ATMs

ATMs are available 24/7 at most banks, and in shopping centers, airports, grocery stores and convenience shops. Most ATMs charge a service fee of $2.50 or more per transaction and your home bank may impose additional charges. Withdrawing cash from an ATM using a credit card usually incurs a hefty fee; check with your credit-card company first.

For foreign visitors, ask your bank or credit-card company for exact information about using its cards in stateside ATMs. If you will be relying on ATMs (not a bad strategy), bring more than one card and carry them separately. The exchange rate on ATM transactions is usually as good as you'll get anywhere.

Credit Cards

Major credit cards are almost universally accepted. In fact, it's almost impossible to rent a car or make phone reservations without one (some airlines require your credit-card billing address to be in the USA – a hassle if you're booking domestic flights once in the country). It's highly recommended that you carry at least one credit card, if only for emergencies. Visa and MasterCard are the most widely accepted.

Money Changers

Banks are usually the best places to exchange foreign currencies. Most large city banks offer currency exchange, but banks in rural areas may not. Currency-exchange counters at the airport and in tourist centers typically have the worst rates; ask about fees and surcharges first. Travelex (www.travelex.com) is a major currency-exchange company, but American Express (www.american express.com) travel offices may offer better rates.

Taxes

Sales tax varies by state and county, and ranges from 5% to 10%. Hotel taxes vary by city from about 10% to more than 18% (in NYC).

Tipping

Tipping is not optional; only withhold tips in cases of outrageously bad service.

Airport & hotel porters $2 per bag, minimum per cart $5

Bartenders 15% to 20% per round, minimum per drink $1

Hotel maids $2 to $4 per night, left under the card provided

Restaurant servers 15% to 20%, unless a gratuity is already charged on the bill

Taxi drivers 10% to 15%, rounded up to the next dollar

Valet parking attendants At least $2 when handed back the keys

Opening Hours

Typical normal opening times are as follows:

Banks 8:30am to 4:30pm Monday to Thursday, to 5:30pm Friday (and possibly 9am to noon Saturday)

Bars 5pm to midnight Sunday to Thursday, to 2am Friday and Saturday

Nightclubs 10pm to 4am Thursday to Saturday

Post offices 9am to 5pm Monday to Friday

Shopping malls 9am to 9pm

Stores 9am to 6pm Monday to Saturday, noon to 5pm Sunday

Supermarkets 8am to 8pm, some open 24 hours

Public Holidays

On the following national public holidays, banks, schools and government offices (including post offices) are closed, and transportation, museums and other services operate on a Sunday schedule. Holidays falling on a weekend are usually observed the following Monday.

New Year's Day January 1

Martin Luther King Jr Day Third Monday in January

Presidents' Day Third Monday in February

Memorial Day Last Monday in May

Independence Day July 4

Labor Day First Monday in September

Columbus Day Second Monday in October

Veterans' Day November 11

Thanksgiving Fourth Thursday in November

Christmas Day December 25

During spring break (March and April), high school and college students get a week off from school so they can overrun beach towns and resorts. For students of all ages, summer vacation runs from June to August.

Safe Travel

Despite its seemingly apocalyptic list of dangers – violent crime, riots, earthquakes, tornadoes – the USA is a pretty safe country to visit. The greatest danger for travelers is posed by car accidents (buckle up – it's the law).

Crime

For the traveler it's not violent crime but petty theft that is the biggest concern. When possible, withdraw money from ATMs during the day, or in well-lit, busy areas at night. When driving, don't pick up hitchhikers, and lock valuables in your car trunk before arriving at your destination. In hotels, secure valuables in room or hotel safes.

Natural Disasters

Most areas with predictable natural disturbances – hurricanes in the South, earthquakes in California – have an emergency-siren system to alert communities to imminent danger. These sirens are tested periodically at noon, but if you hear one and suspect trouble, turn on a local TV or radio station, which will be broadcasting safety warnings and advice. Incidentally, hurricane season runs from June to November.

The US Department of Health and Human Services (www.phe.gov) has preparedness advice, news and information.

Scams

Pack your street smarts. In big cities, don't forget that three-card-monte card games are always rigged, and that expensive electronics, watches and designer items sold on the cheap from sidewalk tables are either fakes or stolen.

Government Travel Advice

○ **Australia** (www. smartraveller.gov.au)

○ **Canada** (www.travel. gc.ca)

○ **New Zealand** (www. safetravel.govt.nz)

○ **UK** (www.gov.uk/ foreign-travel-advice)

Telephone

Cell Phones

Tri- or quad-band phones brought from overseas will generally work in the USA. However, you should check with your service provider to see if roaming charges apply, as these will turn even local US calls into pricey international calls.

It's often cheaper to buy a compatible prepaid SIM card for the USA, such as those sold by AT&T, which you can insert into your international cell phone to get a local phone number and voicemail. Telestial (www.telestial.com) offers these services, as well as cell-phone rentals.

If you don't have a compatible phone, you can buy inexpensive, no-contract (prepaid) phones with a local number and a set number of minutes, which can be topped up at will. Virgin Mobile, T-Mobile, AT&T and other providers offer phones starting around $20, with a package of minutes starting around $20 for 400 minutes, or $30 monthly for unlimited minutes. Electronics stores such as Radio Shack and Best Buy sell these phones.

Huge swathes of rural America, including many national parks and recreation areas, don't pick up a signal. Check your provider's coverage map.

Phone Cards

If you're traveling without a cell phone or in a region with limited cell service, a prepaid phone card is an alternative solution. Phone cards typically come precharged with a fixed number of minutes that can be used on any phone, including land lines. You'll generally need to dial an 800 number and enter a PIN (personal identification number) before placing each call. Phone cards are available from online retailers such as amazon.com and at some convenience stores. Be sure to read the fine print, as many cards contain hidden charges such as 'activation fees' or per-call 'connection fees' in addition to the per-minute rates.

Phone Codes

All phone numbers within the USA consist of a three-digit area code followed by a seven-digit local number.

In some locations, local calls only require you to dial the seven-digit number; in others, you will need to dial the entire 10-digit number.

If you're calling long distance, dial 📞1 plus the area code plus the phone number.

If you're not sure whether the number is local or long distance (new area codes are added all the time, confusing even residents), try one way – if it's wrong, usually a recorded voice will correct you.

Toll-free numbers begin with 800, 888, 877, 866, 855 and 844, and when dialing are preceded by 1. Most can only be used within the USA, some only within the state, and some only from outside the state. You won't know until you try dialing. The 900 series of area codes, and a few other prefixes, are for calls charged at a premium per-minute rate – phone sex, horoscopes, jokes etc.

○ 1 is the international country code for the USA if calling from abroad (the same as Canada, but international rates apply between the two countries).

○ Dial 🕽011 to make an international call from the USA (followed by country code, area code and phone number).

○ Dial 🕽00 for assistance making international calls.

○ Dial 🕽411 for directory assistance nationwide.

○ 🕽800-555-1212 is directory assistance for toll-free numbers.

Time

The USA uses daylight saving time (DST). At 2am on the second Sunday in March, clocks are set one hour ahead ('spring forward'). Then on the first Sunday of November, clocks are turned back one hour ('fall back'). Just to keep you on your toes, Arizona (except the Navajo Nation) and Hawaii don't follow DST.

Time Zones

The continental USA has four time zones:

○ **EST Eastern** (GMT/UTC minus five hours): NYC, Washington, DC

○ **CST Central** (GMT/UTC minus six hours): Chicago, New Orleans, Austin

○ **MST Mountain** (GMT/UTC minus seven hours): Denver, Santa Fe, Phoenix

○ **PST Pacific** (GMT/UTC minus eight hours): San Francisco, Las Vegas

Most of Alaska is one hour behind Pacific time (GMT/UTC minus nine hours), while Hawaii is two hours behind Pacific time (GMT/UTC minus 10 hours).

So if it's 9pm in New York, it's 8pm in Chicago, 7pm in Denver, 6pm in Los Angeles, 5pm in Anchorage and 4pm (November to early March) or 3pm (rest of year) in Honolulu.

Toilets

Toilets in the USA are universally of the sit-down variety and generally of high standard. Most states have rest areas with free toilets along major highways; alternatively, you can seek out toilets at gas stations, coffee shops and chain restaurants – technically these are for the use of paying customers, but you may be able to use them free of charge by asking or discreetly entering. Public buildings such as airports, train and bus stations, libraries and museums usually have free toilet facilities for public use.

Tourist Information

For links to the official tourism websites of every US state and most major cities, see www.visit-usa.com. The similarly named www.visit theusa.com is jam-packed with itinerary planning ideas and other useful info.

Travelers with Disabilities

If you have a physical disability, the USA can be an accommodating place. The Americans with Disabilities Act (ADA) requires that all public buildings, private buildings built after 1993 (including hotels, restaurants, theaters and museums) and public transit be wheelchair accessible. However, call ahead to confirm what is available. Some local tourist offices publish detailed accessibility guides.

Telephone companies offer relay operators, available via teletypewriter (TTY) numbers, for the hearing impaired. Most banks provide ATM instructions in Braille and via earphone jacks for hearing-impaired customers. All major airlines, Greyhound buses and Amtrak trains will assist travelers with disabilities; just describe your needs when making reservations at least 48 hours in advance. Service animals (guide dogs) are allowed to accompany passengers, but bring documentation.

Some car-rental agencies, such as Budget and Hertz, offer hand-controlled vehicles and vans with wheelchair lifts at no extra charge, but you must reserve them well in advance. Wheelchair Getaways (www.wheelchair getaways.com) rents accessible vans throughout the USA. In many cities and towns, public buses are accessible to wheelchair riders and will 'kneel' if you are unable to use the steps; just let the driver know that you need the lift or ramp.

Most cities have taxi companies with at least one accessible van, though you'll have to call ahead. Cities with underground transport have varying levels of facilities such as elevators for passengers needing assistance – DC has the best network (every station has an elevator), while NYC has elevators in about a quarter of its stations.

Many national and some state parks and recreation areas have wheelchair-accessible paved, graded-dirt or boardwalk trails. US citizens and permanent residents with permanent disabilities are entitled to a free 'America the Beautiful' Access Pass. Go online

(www.nps.gov/findapark/passes.htm) for details.

For tips on travel and thoughtful insight on traveling with a disability, check out online posts by Lonely Planet's Accessible Travel Manager: twitter.com/martin_heng.

Some helpful resources for travelers with disabilities:

Disabled Sports USA (www.disabledsportsusa.org) Offers sport, adventure and recreation programs for those with disabilities. Also publishes *Challenge* magazine.

Flying Wheels Travel (www.flyingwheelstravel.com) A full-service travel agency, highly recommended for those with mobility issues or chronic illness.

Mobility International USA (www.miusa.org) Advises USA-bound disabled travelers on mobility issues, and promotes the global participation of people with disabilities in international exchange and travel programs.

Visas

Be warned that all visa information is highly subject to change. US entry requirements keep evolving as national security regulations change. All travelers should double-check current visa and passport regulations before coming to the USA.

The US State Department (www.travel.state.gov) maintains the most comprehensive visa information,

providing downloadable forms, lists of US consulates abroad and even visa wait times calculated by country.

Visa Applications

Apart from most Canadian citizens and those entering under the Visa Waiver Program (p370), all foreign visitors will need to obtain a visa from a US consulate or embassy abroad. Most applicants must schedule a personal interview, to which you must bring all your documentation and proof of fee payment. Wait times for interviews vary, but afterward, barring problems, visa issuance takes from a few days to a few weeks.

o Your passport must be valid for the entirety of your intended stay in the USA, and sometimes six months longer, depending on your country of citizenship. You'll need a recent photo (2in by 2in) and you must pay a nonrefundable $160 processing fee, plus in a few cases an additional visa-issuance reciprocity fee. You'll also need to fill out the online DS-160 non-immigrant visa electronic application.

o Visa applicants are required to show documents of financial stability (or evidence that a US resident will provide financial support), a round-trip or onward ticket and 'binding obligations' that will ensure their return home, such as family ties, a home or a job. Because of these requirements, those planning to travel

Visa Waiver Program

Currently under the Visa Waiver Program (VWP), citizens of the following countries may enter the USA without a visa for stays of 90 days or less: Andorra, Australia, Austria, Belgium, Brunei, Chile, Czech Republic, Denmark, Estonia, Finland, France, Germany, Greece, Hungary, Iceland, Ireland, Italy, Japan, Latvia, Liechtenstein, Lithuania, Luxembourg, Malta, Monaco, the Netherlands, New Zealand, Norway, Portugal, San Marino, Singapore, Slovakia, Slovenia, South Korea, Spain, Sweden, Switzerland, Taiwan and the UK.

If you are a citizen of a VWP country, you do not need a visa only if you have a passport that meets current US standards, and you have received approval from the Electronic System for Travel Authorization (ESTA) in advance. Register online with the Department of Homeland Security at https://esta.cbp.dhs.gov/esta at least 72 hours before arrival; once travel authorization is approved, your registration is valid for two years. The fee, payable online, is $14.

Visitors from VWP countries must still produce at the port of entry all the same evidence as for a non-immigrant visa application. They must demonstrate that their trip is for 90 days or less, and that they have a round-trip or onward ticket, adequate funds to cover the trip and binding obligations abroad.

In addition, the same 'grounds for exclusion and deportation' apply, except that you will have no opportunity to appeal or apply for an exemption. If you are denied under the VWP at a US point of entry, you will have to use your onward or return ticket on the next available flight.

through other countries before arriving in the USA are generally better off applying for a US visa while they're still in their home country, rather than while on the road.

○ The most common visa is a nonimmigrant visitor's visa: type B-1 for business purposes, B-2 for tourism or visiting friends and relatives. A visitor's visa is good for multiple entries over one or five years, and specifically prohibits the visitor from taking paid employment in the USA. The validity period depends on what country you are from. The actual length of time you'll be allowed to stay in the USA is determined by US immigration at the port of entry.

○ If you're coming to the USA to work or study, you will need a different type of visa, and the company or institution to which you are going should make the arrangements.

○ Other categories of nonimmigrant visas include an F-1 visa for students attending a course at a recognized institution; an H-1, H-2 or H-3 visa for temporary employment; and a J-1 visa for exchange visitors in approved programs.

Women Travelers

Women traveling alone or in groups should not expect to encounter any particular problems in the USA. The community website www.journeywoman.com facilitates women exchanging travel tips, and has links to other helpful resources.

If you're assaulted, consider calling a rape crisis hotline before calling the police, unless you are in immediate danger, in which case you should call ☎911. But be aware that not all police have as much sensitivity training or experience assisting sexual-assault survivors, whereas staff at rape crisis centers will tirelessly advocate on your behalf and act as a link to other community services, including hospitals and the police. Contact the 24-hour National Sexual Assault Hotline on ☎800-656-4673. Alternatively, go straight to a hospital emergency room.

Transpor-tation

Getting There & Away

Flights, cars and tours can be booked online at lonelyplanet.com/bookings.

Entering the USA

○ Everyone arriving in the US needs to fill out the US customs declaration. US and Canadian citizens, along with eligible foreign nationals participating in the Visa Waiver Program (VWP), can complete this procedure electronically at an APC (Automated Passport Control) kiosk upon disembarking. All others must fill out a paper customs declaration, which is usually handed out on the plane. Have it completed before you approach the immigration desk. For the question, 'US Street Address,' give the address where you will spend the first night (a hotel address is fine).

○ No matter what your visa says, US immigration officers have an absolute authority to refuse admission to the country, or to impose conditions on admission. They may ask about your plans and whether you have sufficient funds; it's a good idea to list an itinerary, produce an onward or round-trip ticket and have at least one major credit card.

○ The Department of Homeland Security's registration program, called Office of Biometric Identity Management, includes every port of entry and nearly every foreign visitor to the USA. For most visitors (excluding, for now, most Canadian and some Mexican citizens), registration consists of having a digital photo and electronic (inkless) fingerprints taken; the process takes less than a minute.

Passport

Every visitor entering the USA from abroad needs a passport. Visitors from most countries only require a passport valid for their intended period of stay in the USA. However, nationals of certain countries require a passport valid for at least six months longer than their intended stay. For a country-by-country list, see the latest 'Six-Month Club Update' from US Customs and Border Protection. If your passport does not meet current US standards, you'll be turned back at the border. All visitors wishing to enter the USA under the VWP must have an e-Passport with a digital photo and an integrated RFID chip containing biometric data.

Air

The USA has more than 375 domestic airports, but only a baker's dozen form the main international gateways. Many other airports are called 'international' but may have only a few flights from other countries – typically Mexico or Canada. Even travel to an international gateway sometimes requires a connection in another gateway city (eg London–Los Angeles flights may involve transferring in Houston).

The USA does not have a national air carrier. The largest USA-based airlines are American, Delta, United and Southwest.

Departure tax is included in the price of a ticket. International gateway airports:

Atlanta Hartsfield-Jackson International Airport (ATL; ☎800-897-1910; www.atl.com)

Boston Logan International Airport (BOS; ☎800-235-6426; www.massport.com/logan)

Chicago O'Hare International Airport (ORD; www.flychicago.com)

Dallas-Fort Worth International Airport (DFW; ☎972-973-3112; www.dfwairport.com; 2400 Aviation Dr)

Honolulu International Airport (HNL; ☎808-836-6411; http://hawaii.gov/hnl; 300 Rodgers Blvd)

Houston George Bush Intercontinental Airport (IAH; ☎281-230-3100; www.fly2houston.com/iah; 2800 N Terminal Rd, off I-59, Beltway 8 or I-45; 🛜)

Los Angeles International Airport (LAX; www.lawa.org/welcomeLAX.aspx; 1 World Way)

Miami International Airport (MIA; ☎305-876-7000; www.miami-airport.com; 2100 NW 42nd Ave)

New York JFK International Airport (JFK; ☏718-244-4444; www.kennedyairport.com; ⓢA to Howard Beach or E, J/Z to Sutphin Blvd-Archer Ave then ▣JFK Airtrain)

Newark Liberty International Airport (EWR; ☏973-961-6000; www.panynj.gov)

San Francisco International Airport (SFO; www.flysfo.com; ⓢ McDonnell Rd)

Seattle-Tacoma International Airport (SEA; ☏206-787-5388; www.portseattle.org/Sea-Tac; 17801 International Blvd; 🛜)

Washington Dulles International Airport (IAD; www.flydulles.com)

Getting Around

Air

When time is tight, book a flight. The domestic air system is extensive and reliable, with dozens of competing airlines, hundreds of airports and thousands of flights daily. Flying is usually more expensive than traveling by bus, train or car, but it's the way to go when you're in a hurry.

Main 'hub' airports in the USA include all international gateways plus many other large cities. Most cities and towns have a local or county airport, but you usually have to travel via a hub airport to reach them.

Airlines in the USA

Overall, air travel in the USA is very safe (much safer than driving out on the nation's highways); for comprehensive details by carrier, check out airsafe. com.

The main domestic carriers are:

American Airlines (www. aa.com) Nationwide service.

Delta Air Lines (www.delta. com) Nationwide service.

Frontier Airlines (www. flyfrontier.com) Denver-based airline with service across the continental USA.

JetBlue Airways (www.jetblue. com) New York City–based airline serving many East Coast cities, plus other destinations across the USA.

Southwest Airlines (www. southwest.com) Dallas-based budget airline with service across the continental USA.

Spirit Airlines (www.spirit.com) Florida-based budget airline; serves many US gateway cities.

United Airlines (www.united. com) Nationwide service.

Virgin America (www.virgin america.com) California-based airline serving over two dozen cities.

Bicycle

Cyclists must follow the same rules of the road as automobiles, but don't expect drivers to respect your right of way. Better World Club (www.betterworldclub. com) offers a bicycle roadside-assistance program.

For advice, route maps, guided tours and lists of local bike clubs and repair shops, browse the websites of Adventure Cycling (www. adventurecycling.org) and the League of American Bicyclists (www.bikeleague. org).

Bus

To save money, travel by bus, particularly between major towns and cities. Middle-class Americans prefer to fly or drive, but buses let you see the countryside and meet folks along the way. As a rule, buses are reliable, cleanish and comfortable, with air-con, barely reclining seats, lavatories and no smoking.

Greyhound (www.grey hound.com) is the major long-distance bus company, with routes throughout the USA and Canada. Other long-distance bus lines that offer decent fares and free wi-fi (that doesn't always work) include Megabus (www.megabus.com) and BoltBus (www.boltbus. com). Both operate routes along the East and West Coasts, with Megabus also offering service in Texas and the Great Lakes region.

Sample Greyhound standard one-way adult fares and trip times include: Boston–Philadelphia ($31 to $58; seven hours), Chicago–New Orleans ($89 to $164; 24 hours), Los Angeles–San Francisco ($24 to $48; eight hours), New York–Chicago ($56 to $102; 18 hours), New York–San Francisco ($139 to $318; 72 hours), Washington, DC–Miami ($72 to $145; 25 hours).

Reservations

Tickets for most trips on Greyhound, Trailways, Megabus and BoltBus can be bought online. You can print all tickets at home or, in the case of Megabus or BoltBus, simply show ticket receipts through an email on a smartphone. Greyhound also allows customers to pick up tickets at the terminal using a 'Will Call' service.

Seating is normally first-come, first-served. Greyhound recommends arriving an hour before departure to get a seat.

Car & Motorcycle

Automobile Associations

The American Automobile Association (AAA; www. aaa.com) has reciprocal membership agreements with several international auto clubs (check with AAA and bring your membership card from home). For its members, AAA offers travel insurance, tour books, diagnostic centers for used-car buyers and a wide-ranging network of regional offices. AAA advocates politically for the auto industry.

A more ecofriendly alternative, the Better World Club (www.betterworldclub. com), donates 1% of revenue to assist environmental cleanup, offers ecologically sensitive choices for every service it provides and advocates politically for environmental causes.

With these organizations, the primary member

Climate Change & Travel

Every form of transport that relies on carbon-based fuel generates CO_2, the main cause of human-induced climate change. Modern travel is dependent on aeroplanes, which might use less fuel per mile per person than most cars but travel much greater distances. The altitude at which aircraft emit gases (including CO_2) and particles also contributes to their climate change impact. Many websites offer 'carbon calculators' that allow people to estimate the carbon emissions generated by their journey and, for those who wish to do so, to offset the impact of the greenhouse gases emitted with contributions to portfolios of climate-friendly initiatives throughout the world. Lonely Planet offsets the carbon footprint of all staff and writer travel.

benefit is 24-hour emergency roadside assistance anywhere in the USA. Both also offer trip planning, free travel maps, travel-agency services, car insurance and a range of travel discounts (eg on hotels, car rentals, attractions).

Driver's License

Foreign visitors can legally drive a car in the USA for up to 12 months using their home driver's license. However, an International Driving Permit (IDP) will have more credibility with US traffic police, especially if your home license doesn't have a photo or isn't in English. Your automobile association at home can issue an IDP, valid for one year, for a small fee. Always carry your home license together with the IDP.

To ride a motorcycle in the USA, you will need either a valid US state motorcycle license or an IDP specially endorsed for motorcycles.

Insurance

Don't put the key into the ignition if you don't have insurance, which is legally required. You risk financial ruin and legal consequences if there's an accident. If you already have auto insurance, or if you buy travel insurance that covers car rentals, make sure your policy has adequate liability coverage for where you will be driving, as different states specify different minimum levels of coverage.

Car-rental companies will provide liability insurance, but most charge extra. Rental companies almost never include collision-damage insurance for the vehicle. Instead, they offer an optional Collision Damage Waiver (CDW) or Loss Damage Waiver (LDW), usually with an initial deductible cost of between $100 and $500. For an extra premium, you can usually get this deductible covered as well. Paying extra for some or all of this insurance increases the cost of a rental car by as much as $30 a day.

Many credit cards offer free collision damage coverage for rental cars if you rent for 15 days or less and charge the total rental to your card. This is a good way to avoid paying extra fees to the rental company, but note that if there's an accident, sometimes you must pay the car-rental company first and then seek reimbursement from the credit-card company. There may be exceptions that are not covered, such as 'exotic' rentals (eg 4WD Jeeps or convertibles). Check your credit-card policy.

Rental

Most rental companies require that you have a major credit card, be at least 25 years old and have a valid driver's license. Some major national companies may rent to drivers between the ages of 21 and 24 for an additional charge of around $25 per day. Those under 21 years are usually not permitted to rent at all. Car-rental prices vary wildly, so shop around. The average daily rate for a small car ranges from around $20 to $75, or $125 to $500 per week.

Road Conditions & Hazards

Road hazards include potholes, city commuter traffic, wandering wildlife and cell-phone-wielding, kid-distracted and enraged drivers. For nationwide traffic and road-closure information, click to www.fhwa.dot.gov/trafficinfo.

In places where winter driving is an issue, many cars are fitted with steel-studded snow tires, while snow chains can sometimes be required in mountain areas. Driving off-road, or on dirt roads, is often forbidden by car-rental companies, and it can be very dangerous in wet weather.

Road Rules

In the USA, cars drive on the right-hand side of the road. The use of seat belts is required in every state except New Hampshire, and child safety seats are required in every state. Most car-rental agencies rent child safety seats for $10 to $14 per day, but you must reserve them when booking. In some states, motorcyclists are required to wear helmets.

On interstate highways, the speed limit is sometimes raised to 75mph. Unless otherwise posted, the speed limit is generally 55mph or 65mph on highways, 25mph to 35mph in cities and towns, and as low as 15mph in school zones (strictly enforced during school hours). It's forbidden to pass a school bus when its lights are flashing.

Unless signs prohibit it, you may turn right at a red light after first coming to a full stop – note that turning right on red is illegal in NYC. At four-way stop signs, cars should proceed in order of arrival; when two cars arrive simultaneously, the one on the right has the right of way. When in doubt, politely wave the other driver ahead. When emergency vehicles (ie police, fire or ambulance) approach from either direction, pull over safely and get out of the way.

In many states, it's illegal to talk on a hand-held cell phone while driving; use a hands-free device instead.

The maximum legal blood-alcohol concentration for drivers is 0.08%. Penalties are very severe for 'DUI' – driving under the influence of alcohol and/or drugs. Police can give roadside sobriety checks to assess if you've been drinking or using drugs. If you fail, they'll require you to take a breath test, urine test or blood test to determine the level of alcohol or drugs in your body. Refusing to be tested is treated the same as if you'd taken the test and failed.

In some states it's illegal to carry 'open containers' of alcohol in a vehicle, even if they're empty.

Local Transportation

Except in large US cities, public transportation is rarely the most convenient option for travelers, and coverage can be sparse to outlying towns and suburbs. However, it is usually cheap, safe and reliable.

More than two thirds of the states in the nation have adopted ♪511 as an all-purpose local-transportation help line.

Subway

The largest systems are in New York City, Chicago, Boston, Washington, DC, the San Francisco Bay Area, Philadelphia, Los Angeles and Atlanta. Other cities have small, one- or two-line rail systems that mainly serve downtown areas.

Taxi & Ride-Share Service

Taxis are metered, with flag-fall charges of around $3 to start, plus $2 to $3 per mile. They charge extra for waiting and handling baggage, and drivers expect a 10% to 15% tip. Taxis cruise the busiest areas in large cities; otherwise, it's easiest to phone and order one.

Ride-sharing companies such as Uber (www.uber.com) and Lyft (www.lyft.com) have seen a recent surge in popularity as an alternative to taxis.

Tours

Group travel can be an enjoyable way to get to and tour the USA.

Reputable tour companies include:

American Holidays (www.americanholidays.com) Ireland-based company specializing in tours to North America.

Contiki (www.contiki.com) Party-hardy sightseeing tour-bus vacations for 18- to 35-year-olds.

North America Travel Service (www.northamericatravel service.co.uk) UK-based tour operator arranging luxury US trips.

Trek America (www.trekamerica.com) Active outdoor adventures for 18- to 38-year olds.

Train

Amtrak (www.amtrak.com) has an extensive rail system throughout the USA, with Amtrak's Thruway buses providing connections to and from the rail network to some smaller centers and national parks. Compared with other modes of travel, trains are rarely the quickest, cheapest, timeliest or most convenient option, but they turn the journey into a relaxing, social and scenic all-American experience, especially on western routes, where double-decker Super-liner trains boast spacious lounge cars with panoramic windows.

Commuter trains provide faster, more frequent services on shorter routes, especially the northeast corridor from Boston, MA, to Washington, DC. Amtrak's high-speed Acela Express trains are the most expensive, and rail passes are not valid on these trains. Other commuter rail lines include those serving the Lake Michigan shoreline near Chicago, IL, major cities on the West Coast and the Miami, FL area.

Classes & Costs

Amtrak fares vary according to the type of train and seating. On long-distance lines, you can travel in coach seats (reserved or unreserved), business class, or 1st class, which includes all sleeping compartments. Sleeping cars include simple bunks (called 'roomettes'), bedrooms with en-suite facilities and suites sleeping four with two bathrooms. Sleeping-car rates include meals in the dining car, which offers everyone sit-down meal service (pricey if not included). Food service on commuter lines, when it exists, consists of sandwich and snack bars. Bringing your own food and drink is recommended on all trains.

Generally the earlier you book, the lower the price.

Sample Amtrak standard, one-way, adult coach-class fares and trip times include: Chicago–New Orleans ($133; 20 hours), Los Angeles–San Antonio ($151; 29 hours), New York–Chicago ($108; 19 hours), New York–Los Angeles ($232; 63 hours), Seattle–Oakland ($109; 23 hours), Washington, DC–Miami ($147; 23 hours).

Reservations

Reservations can be made any time from 11 months in advance up to the day of departure. Space on most trains is limited, and certain routes can be crowded, especially during summer and holiday periods, so it's a good idea to book as far in advance as you can. This also gives you the best chance of fare discounts.

Behind the Scenes

Acknowledgements

Climate map data adapted from Peel MC, Finlayson BL & McMahon TA (2007) 'Updated World Map of the Köppen-Geiger Climate Classification', Hydrology and Earth System Sciences, 11, 163344.

Illustrations p96–7 by Javier Zarracina; p298–9 by Michael Weldon.

Photos pp273, 275 HOLLYWOOD™ & Design © Hollywood Chamber of Commerce. The Hollywood Sign and Walk of Fame are trademark and intellectual property of the Hollywood Chamber of Commerce. All Rights Reserved.

This Book

This guidebook was curated by Karla Zimmerman and researched and written by Karla, Kate Armstrong, Amy C Balfour, Robert Balkovich, Ray Bartlett, Andrew Bender, Alison Bing, Cristian Bonetto, Gregor Clark, Bridget Gleeson, Michael Grosberg, Mark Johanson, Adam Karlin, Ali Lemer, Hugh McNaughtan, Becky Ohlsen, Regis St Louis, John A Vlahides and Benedict Walker. The previous edition was written by Amy C Balfour, Sandra Bao, Sara Benson, Adam Karlin, Becky Ohlsen, Zora O'Neill, Kevin Raub, Brendan Sainsbury, Regis St Louis, Ryan Ver Berkmoes, Mara Vorhees, Greg Ward and Karla Zimmerman. This guidebook was produced by the following:

Destination Editors Evan Godt, Alexander Howard, Lauren Keith, Trisha Ping, Sarah Stocking, Clifton Wilkinson

Product Editors Amanda Williamson, Kate Mathews

Senior Cartographer Alison Lyall

Book Designer Wibowo Rusli

Assisting Editors Melanie Dankel, Victoria Harrison, Anne Mulvaney

Cartographer Julie Dodkins

Cover Researcher Naomi Parker

Thanks to Kate Chapman, Grace Dobell, James Hardy, Corey Hutchison, Elizabeth Jones, Anne Mason, Lauren O'Connell, Lyahna Spencer, Sam Trafford, Saralinda Turner, Diana Von Holdt, Tony Wheeler

Send Us Your Feedback

We love to hear from travelers – your comments keep us on our toes and help make our books better. Our well-traveled team reads every word on what you loved or loathed about this book. Although we cannot reply individually to postal submissions, we always guarantee that your feedback goes straight to the appropriate writers, in time for the next edition. Each person who sends us information is thanked in the next edition, the most useful submissions are rewarded with a selection of digital PDF chapters.

Visit lonelyplanet.com/contact to submit your updates and suggestions or to ask for help. Our award-winning website also features inspirational travel stories, news and discussions.

A – Z

A

accommodations 32, 361-2, *see also individual locations*

activities 19, 20, 22-4, *see also individual locations*

air travel 372

airlines 372

airports 371-2

Alcatraz 296-9, **298-9**

amusement parks, *see* theme parks

Animal Kingdom 183

aquariums

Aquarium of the Bay 312

New York Aquarium 82

Santa Monica Pier Aquarium 269

Shark Reef Aquarium 244

Shedd Aquarium 135

architecture 140, *see also* historic buildings

Chicago 128-9

Los Angeles 276-7

Miami 148-51

New York City 60-1

area codes 367-8

art 18

Art Basel 24, 158

Art Deco Historic District 148-51

art galleries 358, *see also* museums

Art Institute of Chicago 124-5

Asian Art Museum 306

Charles Hosmer Morse Museum of American Art 196

Children's Museum of the Arts 68

Fisher Landau Center for Art 63

Frick Collection 69

Gallery of Fine Art 245

Guggenheim Museum 69

Lowe Art Museum 158-9

Luggage Store Gallery 307

Margulies Collection at the Warehouse 158

Metropolitan Museum of Art 68

MoMA PS1 63

Museum of Contemporary Art 134

Museum of Modern Art 46-7

National Gallery of Art 95

New Museum of Contemporary Art 63, 66

New Orleans Museum of Art 209

Ogden Museum of Southern Art 211

Orlando Museum of Art 192

Phillips Collection 105

Renwick Gallery 100

Reynolds Center for American Art & Portraiture 101

Rubin Museum of Art 66

San Francisco Museum of Modern Art 306-7

SculptureCenter 63

SF Camerawork 306

Vizcaya Museum & Gardens 159

Whitney Museum of American Art 51

Wynwood Walls 158

Art Institute of Chicago 124-5

arts 357-9

arts centers

City Lights Books 310-11

Little Haiti Cultural Center 159-60

Lincoln Center 69-70

New World Center 154

Walt Disney Concert Hall 278

ATMs 365

Austin 15, 218-37, **221**, **230**

accommodations 221

activities 229

drinking & nightlife 235-6

entertainment 236-7

food 232-5

highlights 222-3

information 237

itineraries 220, 226-7, **226-7**

shopping 231-2

sights 228-9

tours 229, 231

travel to/from 221, 237

travel within 237

automobile associations 373

B

baseball 126-7, 318-9, 354-5, 356

basketball 356

bathrooms 368

bats 222-3

beaches

Baker Beach 311

El Matador State Beach 280

Los Angeles 281

North Avenue Beach 135

Original Muscle Beach 269

beer 353

bicycling 372

Bob Bullock Texas State History Museum 224-5

books 25, 358-9

botanicas 161

breweries 352

Broadway 52-5

Brooklyn Bridge 62

budget 17

bus travel 372-3

business hours 366

C

cable cars 294-5

Capitol Hill 98-9

car travel 373-4

casinos 244-5

cell phones 16, 367

Central Park 38-41

Chicago 12-13, 118-43, **121**, **132-3**
  accommodations 121
  activities 135-6
  children, travel with 131
  drinking & nightlife 139-41
  entertainment 141-2
  food 136, 137-9
  highlights 122-9
  information 143
  itineraries 120, 128-9, **128-9**
  shopping 136-7
  sights 130-1, 134-5
  tours 136
  travel to/from 121, 143
  travel within 143
Chicago Blues Festival 24
children, travel with 32-3
  Chicago 131
  New Orleans 209
  New York City 68
  Washington, DC 109
Chinatown, San Francisco 302
civil rights 346-7
civil war 344-5
climate 16, 22-4, 362, **16**
Coney Island 82
Congress Avenue Bridge Bat
  Colony 222-3
costs 17
credit cards 365-6
crime 366
cultural centers, see arts centers
culture 338-9, 357-9
currency 16
customs regulations 362

D

dangers, see safety
Declaration of Independence
  342-3
Delancy Street Preview Center
  191
disabilities, travelers with 368-9

drinking & nightlife 21, see
  also individual locations
drinks 353
driver's licenses 373
driving, see car travel
drugs 364-5

E

economy 338-9
electricity 362-3
Ellis Island 42-5
Empire State Building 58-9
entertainment 21, see also
  individual locations
environment 339
Epcot 182-3
events, see festivals & events

F

family travel, see
  children, travel with
FastPass+ 185
Ferry Building 300-1
festivals & events 22-4, see also
  individual locations
films 25, 358
Fisherman's Wharf 311-12
Flagstaff 262-3
food 18, 20, 32-3, 350-3, see
  also individual locations
  arepas 166
  barbecue 351
  Cuban sandwich 166
  food trailers 234
  pizza 138
  stone crabs 166
  Texas Barbecue Trail 236
  vegetarian & vegan 353
football 355-6
Fremont Street Experience 248

G

gambling terms 249

gay travelers 317, 365
Georgetown 114
Glacier Point 324-5
Golden Gate Bridge 292-3
Grand Canyon National Park 6,
  252-63, **255**
  accommodations 255
  geology 257
  highlights 256-7
  information 259, 261
  itineraries 254
  North Rim 260-2
  South Rim 256-7, 258-60
  travel around 260
  travel to/from 255, 259-60,
    262
Griffith Park 274-5
Groveland 333-4
gun ownership 339

H

Half Dome 326-7
health 363
High Line 48-51
historic buildings
  Alcatraz 296-9
  Biltmore Hotel 158
  Brill Building 52
  Capitol 98-9
  Capitol Records Tower 272
  Chicago Cultural Center 130
  Chrysler Building 68
  Empire State Building 58-9
  Ferry Building 300-1
  Flatiron Building 67
  Grand Central Terminal 68
  Grauman's Chinese Theatre
    273
  Library of Congress 99
  Louis Armstrong House 63
  National Archives 101
  One World Trade Center 62
  Radio City Music Hall 67

Robie House 142
Rockefeller Center 67
Rookery 130
Supreme Court 99
Texas State Capitol 228
Vizcaya Museum & Gardens 159
Watts Towers 281
White House 100
Willis Tower 130
historic sites 344
  Arlington National Cemetery 106
  cable cars 294-5
  Ellis Island 42-5
  Ford's Theatre 101
  Maritime National Historical Park 312
  National Mall 92-7
history 340-9
holidays 366
Hollywood 270-3

I

information 368, see also individual locations
insurance 363, 373-4
internet access 363-4
internet resources 17
  children, travel with 33
  disabilities, travelers with 369
  LGBTIQ travelers 365
Islands of Adventure 186-8
itineraries 26-31, **26**, **27**, **28**, **30**

K

Key Biscayne 152-3

L

language 16
Las Vegas 14, 19, 238-51, **241**
  accommodations 241
  activities 248-9
  casinos 244-5
  drinking & nightlife 250-1
  entertainment 251
  food 249-50
  gambling terms 249
  highlights 242-7
  information 251
  itineraries 240
  marriages 250
  sights 248-9
  travel to/from 241, 251
  travel within 251
legal matters 364-5
Legoland® Florida Resort 193
lesbian travelers 317, 365
LGBTIQ travelers 317, 365
literature 358-9, see also books
Little Italy, New York City 63
local life 20-1
Los Angeles 11, 264-87, **267**, **279**, **282**
  accommodations 267
  drinking & nightlife 285-6
  entertainment 286-7
  food 281, 283-5
  highlights 268-77
  information 287
  itineraries 266, 276-7, **276-7**
  shopping 286
  sights 278-81
  tours 273, 285
  travel to/from 267, 287
  travel within 287

M

magazines 364
Magic Kingdom 180-1
Mandalay Bay 244
Mardi Gras 22, 202-5
Mariposa 334-5
marriages 250
measures 364
medical services 363
Miami 12-13, 144-71, **147**, **156**
  accommodations 147
  activities 160
  drinking & nightlife 167-8
  entertainment 168-9
  food 162-7
  highlights 148-53
  information 169
  itineraries 146
  shopping 161-2
  sights 154-5, 157-60
  tours 160-1
  travel to/from 147, 169-70
  travel within 170-1
Millennium Park 122-3
mobile phones 16, 367
money 16, 365-6
money changers 366
motorcycle travel 373-4
Museum of Modern Art 46-7
museums 348, 358, see also art galleries
  Adler Planetarium 135
  Albin Polasek Museum & Sculpture Gardens 196
  American Museum of Natural History 70
  Art Deco Museum 151
  Backstreet Cultural Museum 208-9
  Beat Museum 311
  Blaine Kern's Mardi Gras World 211-12
  Bob Bullock Texas State History Museum 224-5
  Broad 278
  Cabildo 208
  Cable Car Museum 307
  California Academy of Sciences 307
  Chicago Children's Museum 131
  Chicago History Museum 134-5
  Chinese Historical Society of America 302

museums *continued*
de Young Museum 307
Dumbarton Oaks 100
Exploratorium 311
Field Museum of Natural History 135
Getty Center 278
Getty Villa 280-1
Grammy Museum 278
Historic New Orleans Collection 208
HistoryMiami 155
Hollywood Museum 272
International Spy Museum 109
Jewish Museum of Florida-FIU 154
La Brea Tar Pits & Museum 280
Los Angeles County Museum of Art 280
Lower East Side Tenement Museum 63
Mennello Museum of American Art 192
Mob Museum 248
Musée Mécanique 311
Museum of Science & Industry 142
Museum of Tolerance 279
National Air & Space Museum 94
National Museum of African American History & Culture 95
National Museum of American History 95
National Museum of Natural History 94
National Postal Museum 101
National September 11 Museum 56-7
Neon Museum – Neon Boneyard 248
New York City Fire Museum 68
Newseum 101
Patricia & Phillip Frost Museum

of Science 155
Pérez Art Museum Miami 155
Pinball Hall of Fame 248-9
Presbytère 208
Smithsonian Institution 94-5, 100
United States Holocaust Memorial Museum 101
White House Visitor Center 100
Wolfsonian-FIU 151
World Erotic Art Museum 154
Yavapai Geology Museum 258
music 21, 25, 357-8

N

National Mall 92-7, **96-7**
National September 11 Memorial & Museum 56-7
New Orleans 8-9, 198-217, **201**, **210**
accommodations 201
children, travel with 209
drinking & nightlife 216
entertainment 216-17
food 213-16
highlights 202-7
information 217
itineraries 200
shopping 212
sights 208-9, 211-12
tours 212
travel to/from 201, 217
travel within 217
New York City 4-5, 19, 34-87, **36-7**, **64-5**, **72-3**, **78**, **87**
accommodations 37, 87
activities 70
drinking & nightlife 81-4
entertainment 84-5
festivals & events 71
food 75-7, 79-81, 350-1
highlights 38-61
information 86
itineraries 36, 60-1, **60-1**

shopping 70, 74-5
sights 62-3, 66-70
tours 70-1
travel to/from 37, 86
travel within 86
newspapers 364
nightlife, *see* drinking & nightlife
North Rim 260-2

O

Obama, Barack 348-9
One World Trade Center 62
opening hours 366
Orlando 15, 192-6

P

painting 359
passports 371
phone cards 367
planning
calendar of events 22-4
itineraries 26-31, **26**, **27**, **28**, **30**
travel with children 32-3
USA basics 16-17
politics 338-9
population 339
public holidays 366

Q

Queens 63

R

radio 364
religion 339
ride-sharing services 375

S

safety 366-7
San Francisco 8, 288-319, **291**, **308-9**
accommodations 291
drinking & nightlife 315-18

entertainment 318-19
food 312-15
highlights 292-305
information 319
itineraries 290, 304-5, **304-5**
sights 306-7, 310-12
travel to/from 291, 319
travel within 319
Santa Monica Pier 268-9
scams 367
shopping 20, *see also individual
  locations*
slavery 343
Smithsonian Institution 94-5,
  100
smoking 364
South Rim 256-60
sports 354-6
St Charles Avenue Streetcar
  206-7
stadiums 356
  Giants Stadium 318-19
  Madison Square Garden 70
  MCU Park 82
  Nationals Park 116
  Wrigley Field 126-7
  Yankee Stadium 70
Statue of Liberty 42-5
Strip, the 242-5
subway 375

T

taxes 366
taxis 375
telephone services 16, 367-8
theme parks 33
  Animal Kingdom 183
  Epcot 182-3
  Islands of Adventure 186-8
  Legoland® Florida Resort 193
  Magic Kingdom 180-2
  Pacific Park 269
  Santa Monica Pier 268-9
  SkyJump 248

Stratosphere Thrill Rides 248
Universal Orlando Resort
  186-91
Universal Studios 188-9
Volcano Bay 190
Walt Disney World® Resort
  180-5
time 368
time zones 16, 368
tipping 366
toilets 368
tours 375, *see also individual
  locations*
train travel 375
transportation 371-5
travel seasons 16, 22-4
travel to/from USA 17, 371-2
travel within USA 17, 372-5
Trump, Donald 349
Tuolumne Meadows 333
TV 358, 364

U

Universal Orlando Resort 186-91
Universal Studios 188-9
urban design 338

V

visas 16, 369-70
vodou 161
Volcano Bay 190

W

walking tours
  Austin 226-7, **226-7**
  Chicago 128-9, **128-9**
  Los Angeles 276-7, **276-7**
  New York City 60-1, **60-1**
  San Francisco 304-5, **304-5**
Walt Disney World® Resort 15, 19,
  176-185, **179**
  accommodations 179
  highlights 180-5

itineraries 178
travel to/from 179
Washington, DC 7, 88-117, **91,
  102-3**
  accommodations 91
  children, travel with 109
  drinking & nightlife 112-15
  entertainment 116
  food 106-12, 351
  highlights 92-9
  information 116
  itineraries 90
  shopping 105-6
  sights 100-1, 104-5
  tours 105
  travel to/from 91, 117
  travel within 117
washrooms 368
weather 16, 22-4, 362
wedding chapels 250
weights 364
White House 100
wi-fi 363-4
wine 353
Winter Park 196-7
women travelers 370
Wrigley Field 126-7

Y

Yosemite National Park 10,
  320-335. **323**
  accommodations 323
  highlights 324-31
  information 332
  itineraries 322
  tours 335
  travel to/from 323, 332
  travel within 332
  waterfalls 328-31
Yosemite Valley waterfalls
  328-31

Z

zoos 33, 109, 209

Symbols & Map Key

Look for these symbols to quickly identify listings:

- ◉ Sights
- ☒ Eating
- ✛ Activities
- ⊖ Drinking
- ⊜ Courses
- ✪ Entertainment
- ⊙ Tours
- 🔒 Shopping
- ✪ Festivals & Events
- ℹ Information & Transport

These symbols and abbreviations give vital information for each listing:

🌿 Sustainable or green recommendation

FREE No payment required

- ☏ Telephone number
- ☺ Opening hours
- P Parking
- ⊖ Nonsmoking
- ❄ Air-conditioning
- @ Internet access
- 🔊 Wi-fi access
- 🏊 Swimming pool
- 🚍 Bus
- ⛴ Ferry
- 🚊 Tram
- 🚈 Train
- 📋 English-language menu
- 🍴 Vegetarian selection
- 👪 Family-friendly

Find your best experiences with these Great For... icons.

 Art & Culture

- 🖼 Art & Culture
- 📖 History
- 🏖 Beaches
- 💬 Local Life
- 💳 Budget
- 🐦 Nature & Wildlife
- ☕ Cafe/Coffee
- 📷 Photo Op
- 🚲 Cycling
- 🔭 Scenery
- Detour
- 🛍 Shopping
- Drinking
- Short Trip
- Entertainment
- 🌐 Sport
- Events
- Family Travel
- 🚶 Walking
- 🍽 Food & Drink
- ❄ Winter Travel

Sights

- 🏖 Beach
- 🦅 Bird Sanctuary
- 🛕 Buddhist
- 🏰 Castle/Palace
- ✝ Christian
- ☯ Confucian
- 🕉 Hindu
- ☪ Islamic
- 卍 Jain
- ✡ Jewish
- 🗽 Monument
- 🏛 Museum/Gallery/ Historic Building
- 🏚 Ruin
- ⛩ Shinto
- ☬ Sikh
- ☯ Taoist
- 🍷 Winery/Vineyard
- 🦁 Zoo/Wildlife Sanctuary
- ◎ Other Sight

Points of Interest

- 🏄 Bodysurfing
- 🏕 Camping
- ☕ Cafe
- 🛶 Canoeing/Kayaking
- ● Course/Tour
- 🤿 Diving
- 🍸 Drinking & Nightlife
- ☒ Eating
- 🎭 Entertainment
- ♨ Sento Hot Baths/ Onsen
- 🛍 Shopping
- 🎿 Skiing
- 🛏 Sleeping
- 🤿 Snorkelling
- 🏄 Surfing
- 🏊 Swimming/Pool
- 🚶 Walking
- 🏄 Windsurfing
- ✛ Other Activity

Information

- 💲 Bank
- 🛂 Embassy/Consulate
- ➕ Hospital/Medical
- @ Internet
- 👮 Police
- 📮 Post Office
- 📞 Telephone
- 🚻 Toilet
- ℹ Tourist Information
- ● Other Information

Geographic

- 🏖 Beach
- ⊢ Gate
- 🏠 Hut/Shelter
- 🚨 Lighthouse
- 🔭 Lookout
- ▲ Mountain/Volcano
- 🌴 Oasis
- 🌳 Park
-)(Pass
- ⛱ Picnic Area
- 💧 Waterfall

Transport

- ✈ Airport
- Ⓑ BART station
- ⊗ Border crossing
- ⊤ Boston T station
- 🚌 Bus
- ＋🚡＋ Cable car/Funicular
- －🚲－ Cycling
- ⊖ Ferry
- Ⓜ Metro/MRT station
- ⇒Ⓜ⇒ Monorail
- P Parking
- ⊕ Petrol station
- Ⓢ Subway/S-Bahn/ Skytrain station
- 🚕 Taxi
- ＋🚉＋ Train station/Railway
- ┈┈ Tram
- ⊖ Tube Station
- Ⓤ Underground/ U-Bahn station
- ● Other Transport

Taiwan and over a dozen titles about Japan), plus numerous articles for lonelyplanet.com.

Alison Bing

Over 10 guidebooks and 20 years in San Francisco, Alison has spent more time on Alcatraz than some inmates, become an aficionado of drag and burritos, and willfully ignored Muni signs warning that safety requires avoiding unnecessary conversation.

Cristian Bonetto

Cristian has contributed to over 30 Lonely Planet guides. His musings on travel, food, culture and design also appear in numerous publications around the world, including the *Telegraph* (UK) and *Corriere del Mezzogiorno* (Italy). When not on the road, you'll find the reformed playwright and TV scriptwriter slurping espresso in his beloved hometown, Melbourne. Instagram: rexcat75.

Gregor Clark

Gregor is a US-based writer whose love of foreign languages and curiosity about what's around the next bend have taken him to dozens of countries on five continents. Chronic wanderlust has also led him to visit all 50 states and most Canadian provinces on countless road trips through his native North America.

Michael Grosberg

Michael has worked on over 45 Lonely Planet guidebooks. Whether covering Myanmar or New Jersey, each project has added to his rich and complicated psyche and taken years from his (still?) relatively young life. Prior to his writing career, he has worked in development on the island of Rota in the western Pacific, in South Africa where he investigated and wrote about political violence and helped train newly elected government representatives, and in Quito, Ecuador, to teach.

Mark Johanson

Mark grew up in Virginia and has called five different countries home. His travel-writing career began as something of a quarter-life crisis, and he's happily spent the past eight years circling the globe reporting for travel magazines, newspapers and global media outlets. When not on the road, you'll find him gazing at the Andes from his home in Santiago, Chile. Follow him at www.markjohanson.com.

Adam Karlin

Adam has contributed to dozens of Lonely Planet guidebooks, covering an alphabetical spread ranging from the Andaman Islands to the Zimbabwe border. Adam is based out of New Orleans, which helps explain his love of wetlands, food and good music. Learn more at http://walkonfine.com or on Instagram @adamwalkonfine.

Ali Lemer

Ali has been a Lonely Planet writer and editor since 2007, and has authored guidebooks and travel articles on Russia, New York City, Los Angeles, Melbourne, Bali, Hawaii, Japan and Scotland. A native New Yorker and naturalized Melburnian, Ali has also lived in Chicago, Prague and the UK, and has traveled extensively around Europe and North America.

Hugh McNaughtan

A former English lecturer, Hugh swapped grant applications for visa applications, and turned his love of travel into a full-time thing. Having done a bit of restaurant-reviewing in his home town (Melbourne) he's now eaten his way across four continents. He's never happier than when on the road with his two daughters. Except perhaps on the cricket field.

Regis St Louis

Regis has contributed to more than 50 Lonely Planet titles, covering destinations across six continents. His travels have taken him from the mountains of Kamchatka to remote island villages in Melanesia and many grand urban landscapes. When not on the road, he lives in New Orleans. Follow him on www.instagram.com/regisstlouis.

John A Vlahides

John has been a cook in a bordello, hotel concierge, television host, safety monitor in a sex club and French-English interpreter. When not talking travel, he sings with the San Francisco Symphony, skis, hikes the Sierra Nevada and suns himself beneath the Golden Gate.

Benedict Walker

Benedict was born in Newcastle, Australia, and grew up in the 'burbs spending weekends and summers by the beach. Although he's drawn magnetically to the kinds of mountains he encountered in the Canadian Rockies and the Japan and Swiss Alps, beach life is in his blood. Currently based in Berlin, Benedict can be followed on Instagram: @wordsandjourneys.

Contributing Writers

Robert Balkovich, Bridget Gleeson, Becky Ohlsen

Our Story

A beat-up old car, a few dollars in the pocket and a sense of adventure. In 1972 that's all Tony and Maureen Wheeler needed for the trip of a lifetime – across Europe and Asia overland to Australia. It took several months, and at the end – broke but inspired – they sat at their kitchen table writing and stapling together their first travel guide, *Across Asia on the Cheap*. Within a week they'd sold 1500 copies. Lonely Planet was born.

Today, Lonely Planet has offices in Franklin, London, Melbourne, Oakland, Dublin, Beijing and Delhi, with more than 600 staff and writers. We share Tony's belief that 'a great guidebook should do three things: inform, educate and amuse'.

Our Writers

Karla Zimmerman

Karla lives in Chicago, where she eat doughnuts, yells at the Cubs and writes for books, magazines and websites when she's not doing the first two things. She has contributed to 40-plus guidebooks and anthologies covering destinations in Europe, Asia, Africa, North America and the Caribbean – a long way from her early days when she wrote about gravel for a construction magazine. To learn more, follow her on Instagram and Twitter: @karlazimmerman.

Kate Armstrong

Kate has spent much of her adult life traveling and living around the world. A full-time freelance travel journalist, she has contributed to over 50 Lonely Planet guides and trade publications. She is the author of several books and children's educational titles. Read more about her on www.katearmstrongtravelwriter.com and @nomaditis.

Amy C Balfour

Amy practiced law before moving to Los Angeles to try to break in as a screenwriter. If you listen carefully, you can still hear the screams of her horrified parents echoing. After a stint as a writer's assistant on *Law & Order*, she jumped into freelance writing, focusing on travel, food, and the outdoors.

Ray Bartlett

Ray is a travel writer specializing in Japan, Korea, Mexico and the United States. He has worked on many different Lonely Planet titles, starting with *Japan* in 2004 through to this current guide.

Andrew Bender

Award-winning travel and food writer Andrew has written three dozen Lonely Planet guidebooks (from *Amsterdam* to *Los Angeles*, *Germany* to

More Writers

STAY IN TOUCH LONELYPLANET.COM/CONTACT

AUSTRALIA The Malt Store, Level 3, 551 Swanston St, Carlton, Victoria 3053
☏03 8379 8000,
fax 03 8379 8111

IRELAND Digital Depot, Roe Lane (off Thomas St), Digital Hub, Dublin 8, D08 TCV4, Ireland

USA 124 Linden Street, Oakland, CA 94607
☏510 250 6400,
toll free 800 275 8555,
fax 510 893 8572

UK 240 Blackfriars Road, London SE1 8NW
☏020 3771 5100,
fax 020 3771 5101

 twitter.com/ lonelyplanet

facebook.com/ lonelyplanet

 instagram.com/ lonelyplanet

youtube.com/ lonelyplanet

 lonelyplanet.com/ newsletter